The Uralic Language Family

Facts, Myths and Statistics

Publications of the Philological Society, 35

The Uralic Language Family

Facts, Myths and Statistics

Angela Marcantonio

Publications of the Philological Society, 35

Oxford UK & Boston USA

Copyright © The Philological Society 2002

ISBN 0631–23170–6

First published 2002

Blackwell Publishers
108 Cowley Road, Oxford, OX4 1JF, UK

and
350 Main Street,
Malden, MA 02148, USA.

British Library Cataloguing in Publication Data
A catalogue record for this publication is available from the British Library

Library of Congress Cataloging-in-Publication Data
Applied for

Typeset by Joshua Associates Ltd., Oxford
Printed in Great Britain by
MPG Books Ltd, Bodmin, Cornwall

i.m. Giorgio Raimondo Cardona

CONTENTS

ACKNOWLEDGEMENTS

My sincere and grateful thanks go to all the colleagues and friends who have read previous versions of this work and provided valuable comments and criticisms: Juha Janhunen, Peter Michalove, Pirjo Nummenaho, Robert Orr, Péter Sárközy, Urmas Sutrop and the anonymous referees – without their crucial help, this book would not be here today.

I am also indebted to the many colleagues and friends who in various ways have helped me during this enterprise, whether by providing advice, discussion, or bibliographical information, and to those who gave me the support and encouragement to have faith in my unconventional views and pursue this project to publication. They include: Walter Belardi, Keith Brown, Amedeo Di Francesco, Roger Lass, Eeva-Kaarina and Heikki A. Salmi, Jonathan Shepard, Anna-Leena Talvio, Beatrice Töttössy and Nigel Vincent.

I would like too to acknowledge the support of my fellows and valued friends of the Rome 'School of Linguistics': Rosangela Ciani, Paolo Di Giovine, Mara Lepre, Marco Mancini and Paolo Martino.

I also wish to thank all the members of the 'Facoltà di Lettere e Filosofia' of the University of Rome 'La Sapienza' for allowing me to concentrate on this research by granting a sabbatical year.

This book is here today also because of the generous help of my husband, Dr. Robert Brady, who has closely assisted me in performing the statistical analysis and has helped with discussion on the methods and procedures of science. Finally, I am grateful to my children, Fiorenza and Graziano, who have always been very patient and understanding with the evenings and week-ends this work has entailed.

I am grateful to the following for granting me permission to reproduce copyright material: E. J. Brill, from which Figure 3.2 (Hajdú's diagram of isoglosses) and Figure 3.3 (Hajdú's circle diagram) have been reproduced; 'The Gallen-Kallela Museum & Authors & Artists' of Helsinki, from which the map of the Uralic languages and people has been reproduced.

LIST OF TABLES

LIST OF FIGURES

ABBREVIATIONS

Uralic languages and language groups

Most Uralic and several non-Uralic languages can be referred to with two names, one of which is the self-denomination (the one reported after the symbol '='; see also Chapter 9). Many of the Uralic and non-Uralic language names have several variants, the most frequent of which I have indicated in brackets (~ . . .). Throughout the book I will use the first of the two names or variants reported in the list below, to which the abbreviated form refers. This is also the case for all the diagrams reported in the book, including those from other works (unless they are reported within a quote). In this choice, for consistency of nomenclature, I have generally followed Rédei's (*Uralisches Etymologisches Wörterbuch*) way of referring to the Uralic and non-Uralic languages. Only in the Uralic family tree diagram (Figure 1.1) I have reported both the external and the self-denominations of the Uralic languages, according to the list below. Of course, if the language under discussion is mentioned within a quote, the original name and/or variant used by the author will be maintained.

B-F	Balto-Finnic[1]
Che.	Cheremis = Mari
Est.	Estonian = Viru ~ Viro[2]
Finn.	Finnish = Suomi
Finnic	Finnic (~ Fennic) languages (that is: 'non-Ugric'; see family tree in Figure 1.1
F-P	Finno-Permian
F-U	Finno-Ugric
F-V	Finno-Volgaic
Hun.	Hungarian = magyar
Lapp	Lapp = Saami
Mor.	Mordvin = Mordva
Mor. E.	Mordvin Erzya
Mor. M.	Mordvin Moksha
Ob-Ug.	Ob-Ugric (~ Ob-Ugrian)
Old Hun.	Old Hungarian
Ost.	Ostyak = Khanty
P	Proto
P-B-F	Proto-Balto-Finnic

Perm.	Permian (~ Permic)[3]
P-F-P	Proto-Finno-Permian
P-F-U	Proto-Finno-Ugric (Proto-Finno-Ugrian)
P-U	Proto-Uralic
P-S	Proto-Samoyed
P-Ug.	Proto-Ugric (~ Proto-Ugrian)
Sam.	Samoyed
Sam. Ka.	Samoyed Kamas = Kamassian
Sam. Ma.	Samoyed Mator = Motor
Sam. Se.	Samoyed Selkup = Ostyak-Samoyed
Sam. Ta.	Samoyed Tawgi = Nganasan
Sam. Ye.	Samoyed Yenisei = Enets
Sam. Yu.	Samoyed Yurak = (Tundra) Nenets
U	Uralic
Ug.	Ugric (~ Ugrian)
Vog.	Vogul = Mansi
Vot.	Votyak = Udmurt
Zyr.	Zyrian = Komi

Non-Uralic languages and language groups

A	Altaic
P-A	Proto-Altaic
Ave.	Avestan
Bas.	Bashkir
Bur.	Buryat (~ Buriat)
Cha.	Chagatay
Chu.	Chuvash
Dra	Dravidian
Ger.	German
Germ.	Germanic languages
Gold	Gold = Nanay (~ Nanai)
Got.	Gothic
Gre.	Greek
I-E	Indo-European
I-I	Indo-Iranian
Ira.	Iranian languages
Kir.	Kirgiz
Kor.	Koryak
Lat.	Latin
Latv.	Latvian = Lettish
Lit.	Lithuanian
Man.	Manchu

Mon.	Mongolian proper & Mongolian languages (~ Mongol)
OHG	Old High German
Old Ind.	Old Indian
Orok	Orok = U!ta (~ Oroki)
P-S	Palaeo-Siberian languages
San.	Sanskrit
Tat	Tatar (~ Tartar)
Tun.	Tungus =Evenki (~ Ewenki ~ Tunguz)
Tungusic	Tungusic languages = Manchu-Tungus (~ Manchu-Tunguz)[4]
Tur.	Turkish = Osmanli (Turkic language spoken in Turkey)
Turkic	Turkic languages
Ude.	Udeghe (~ Udehe)
Yak.	Yakut
Yuk.	Yukaghir (~Yukagir)

GRAMMATICAL ABBREVIATIONS

Abl.	Ablative
Acc.	Accusative
Asp.	Aspect
Com.	Comitative
CG	Consonant gradation
Dat.	Dative
Ela.	Elative
Ess.	Essive
Ep.Vow.	Ephentetic Vowel
Gen.	Genitive
Ger.	Gerundive
Ill.	Illative
Imp.	Imperfect
Ine.	Inessive
Inf.	Infinitive
Ins.	Instrumental
L-W	Loan-word
Lat.	Lative
Loc.	Locative
Nom.	Nominative
Obj.	Object
Part.	Participle
Partit.	Partitive
Past	Past (Tense)
Per.	Person
Perf.	Perfect
Plu.	Plural
Pre.	Present
Poss.	Possessive
Pro.	Prolative/Prosecutive
Sing.	Singular
Tran.	Translative
V	Vowel
VH	Vowel harmony

ABBREVIATIONS OF MAJOR JOURNALS AND DICTIONARIES

AEMAe   Archivum Eurasiae Medii Aevi (Lisse/Wiesbaden)
ALH   Acta Linguistica Academiae Scientiarum Hungaricae (Budapest)
AOH   Acta Orientalia Academiae Scientiarum Hungaricae (Budapest)
BOH   Bibliotheca Orientalis Hungarica (Budapest)
C2IFU   Congressus Secundus Internationalis Fenno-Ugristarum (eds: P. Ravila et al.; Helsinki 1965)
C4IFU   Congressus Quartus Internationalis Fenno-Ugristarum (ed.: Gy. Ortutay; Budapest 1975)
C5IFU   Congressus Quintus Internationalis Fenno-Ugristarum (ed.: O. Ikola; Turku 1980)
C7IFU   Congressus Septimus Internationalis Fenno-Ugristarum (eds: L. Keresztes et al.; Debrecen 1990)
C8IFU   Congressus Octavus Internationalis Fenno-Ugristarum (eds: H. Leskinen et al.; Jyväskylä 1995)
C9IFU   Congressus Nonus Internationalis Fenno-Ugristarum (eds: A. Nurk et al.; Tartu 2000)
ÉFOu   Études Finno-Ougriennes (Paris)
EWUng   Etymologisches Wörterbuch des Ungarischen, I–III (ed.: L. Benkő; Budapest: Akadémiai Kiadó 1993–5)
F-U   Fenno-Ugristica (Tartu)
FUF   Finnisch-Ugrische Forschungen (Helsinki)
JSFOu   Journal de la Société Finno-Ougrienne (= Suomalais-Ugrilaisen Seuran Aikakauskirja; (Helsinki))
LU   Linguistica Uralica (= Sovetskoe Finno-Ugrovedenie (Tallinn))
KSz   Keleti Szemle (= Revue Orientale pour les Études Ouralo-altaïques; (Budapest))
IEW   Indogermanisches Etymologisches Wörterbuch, I–II (ed.: J. Pokorny; Bern – Stuttgart: Francke Verlag 1959–69)
MNy   Magyar Nyelv (Budapest)
MSFOu   Mémoires de la Société Finno-Ougrienne (= Suomalais-Ugrilaisen Seuran Toimituksia; (Helsinki))
MUSz   Magyar-ugor összehasonlító szótár (by J. Budenz; Budapest: Akadémiai Kiadó 1873–81. Reprinted as: *A Comparative Dictionary of the Finno-Ugric Elements in the Hungarian Vocabulary*. Bloomington: Indiana University 1966).
NyÉrt   Nyelvtudományi Értekezések (Budapest)

NyK	Nyelvtudományi Közlemények (Budapest)
Nyr	Magyar Nyelvőr (Budapest)
SKES	Suomen Kielen Etymologinen Sanakirja, I–VII (eds: Y. H. Toivonen, E. Itkonen, A. J. Joki & R. Peltola; Lexica Societatis Fenno-Ugricae. Helsinki: SKS 1955–81)
SKS	Suomalaisen Kirjallisuuden Seuran Toimituksia[5]
SO	Studia Orientalia (Helsinki)
SSA	Suomen Sanojen Alkuperä: Etymologinen Sanakirja, I–II (eds: U. M. Kulonen and E. Itkonen; Helsinki: SKS 1992–5)
SpS	Specimina Sibirica (Pécs)
SUA	Studia Uralo-Altaica (Szeged)
TESz	A magyar nyelv történeti-etimológiai szótára, I–III (ed.: L. Benkő; Budapest: Akadémiai Kiadó 1967–84)
UAJb	Ural-altaische Jahrbücher. Internationale Zeitschrift für uralische und altaische Forschung (Wiesbaden)
UEW	Uralisches Etymologisches Wörterbuch, I–VIII (ed.: K. Rédei; Budapest: Akadémiai Kiadó 1986–91. German edition by O. Harrassowitz)
UngJb	Ungarische Jahrbücher (Berlin)
Vir	Virittäjä (Helsinki)
WSOY	Werner Söderström Osakeyhtiö

TRANSCRIPTION AND REFERENCES

It is acknowledged that the most comprehensive source for the Uralic languages is Rédei's *Uralisches Etymologisches Wörterbuch* (UEW). Therefore, unless otherwise stated, the examples in this book adopt the transcription of UEW. For consistency, examples from other sources are also made to be consistent with this convention if they are also listed in UEW, otherwise the transcription of the original source is used, as indicated in the reference. Direct quotations are not converted. The same policy applies also to the quoted examples from non-Uralic languages.

I believe this is the only way, at the moment, to face and sort out the problems associated with the transcription of several Uralic languages (including the varieties of transcriptions encountered), although better transcriptions than UEW are available in the literature for some languages and dialects (see, for example, Salminen (1997a) and Janhunen (1986) for Samoyed Yurak (Tundra Nenets), and Nielsen (1932–62) for some Lappic languages).

Since UEW is indexed by its reconstructed forms, I generally report UEW's reconstruction and page reference for each etymological set examined or mentioned. The purpose of this is for the reader to retrieve the reference and compare the original languages, and it does not necessarily denote general acceptance of the reconstruction in the literature or by the author of this book. For a review of the general acceptance or otherwise of UEW's reconstructions, see Kulonen (1996).

At this point, it is worth informing the reader on how to interpret the UEW's reconstructed forms, even before the actual discussion of the reconstructed sound-structure of Proto-Uralic. UEW (I: X–XXI) basically adopts the reconstructed consonantism as outlined in Chapter 4, but with a few, major divergences which will be pointed out in the course of the discussion.

Regarding vocalism, UEW acknowledges that there is not much consensus in the literature about its reconstruction, due to the high level of variation encountered. Therefore, UEW takes into account two possible, alternative vowel systems: one containing only short vowels, and one containing also long vowels, as in the term for 'language/tongue': *kele* (*kēle*) (UEW 144), whereby the first reconstructed form is considered to be the most likely one. If instead a 'tilde' is present between the two given alternative forms (independently of whether the variation regards vocalism or consonantism), it means that these forms are variants, as in the case of the term for 'urine': *kunce* ~ *kuce* (UEW 210).

UEW does not generally highlight other kinds of variation as clearly as in the two examples above. If an etymological set presents irregularity/ irregularities or difficulties in the sound and/or semantic match which are considered to be justifiable, the etymology which contains it/them is accepted and the single irregularities/difficulties are highlighted. If the irregularity/irregularities are not considered to be justifiable, the etymology in question is marked with one or two '?', according to how serious the difficulties are supposed to be. When within an etymological set too many parallels are considered irregular, the overall reconstruction is classified as uncertain, and it is reported not in bold characters, as it would be normally, but in italics. The symbol 'V_1' indicates a non-identifiable velar vowel of first syllable; the symbol '3' indicates a non-identifiable vowel of first and non-first syllable. UEW (I : XXI) leaves open the question of whether the non-U etymologies it reports are to be considered cognates or loan-words.

Apart from these basic points, the dictionary does not talk much about sound-structure and sound-laws, as also pointed out by Kulonen (1996: 44–5, 60), so that, to an external reader, it may not always appear clear what criteria are being utilised to establish a given etymology and to assess its degree of certainty or otherwise.

1

INTRODUCTION

Though it turned out wrong, the steady-state theory was a 'good' theory in that it made very clear-cut and testable predictions; . . . A 'bad' theory, in this sense, is one that is so flexible that it can be adjusted to account for any data. The eminent . . . physicist Wolfgang Pauli would deride such vague ideas as 'not even wrong'[1]

Martin Rees

1.1. AIMS OF THIS BOOK

It is often claimed (see, for example, Dixon 1997: 28) that the family-tree model of historical linguistics is realistically only applicable to a small number of language families, namely Indo-European, Semitic, Polynesian and Uralic. The purpose of this book is to examine closely the foundation of this claim for Uralic, by bringing together the main linguistic and non-linguistic evidence in one volume.

My conclusions on the origin and nature of the Uralic languages will differ in several important respects from the conventional view. The detailed analysis which is carried out in this book has uncovered a total absence of scientific evidence in favour of the notion that the Uralic languages form a language family, that is, a genetically coherent group of related languages. Therefore, in short, I shall conclude that Uralic is not a valid node.

1.2. THE STANDARD URALIC THEORY

The languages forming the Uralic family are spoken in north-eastern Europe and parts of Siberia. They comprise Finnish, Hungarian, Estonian, Samoyed, Vogul, Ostyak, Lapp, and many other languages. A typical family tree[2] is shown in Figure 1.1, which is adapted from Austerlitz (1987: 178), and a map showing the distribution of the Uralic people and languages is given at the end of the book (from 'The Gallen-Kallela Museum & Authors & Artists' (eds) (2000)).

In addition to this conventional family tree, many alternative models have been published to account for the development of the Uralic languages and their closest relatives. Broadly, these range from models which question the

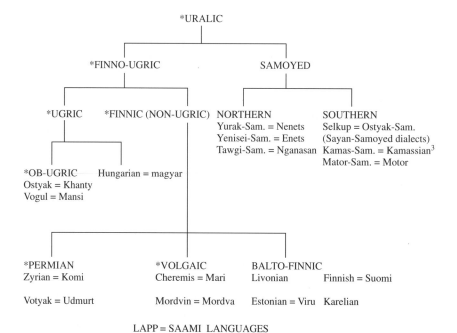

Figure 1.1 The Uralic language family tree as usually reported in textbooks

genetic affinity of the Uralic languages – some of which reject the proposition that they have any genetic relationship at all – to interpretations that go the other way and include other languages, such as Altaic or Yukaghir, in the genetic unity. These various interpretations are reviewed in Chapter 3.

Amongst those scholars who support the mainstream model, and who believe that the Uralic languages form a unique genetic family that is unrelated to any of its neighbours, one finds a range of interpretations regarding the evidence on which this model is founded. For example, some researchers acknowledge that the Uralic corpus is significantly irregular, such as Janhunen (2000: 64):

> the irregularities present in the Uralic etymological corpus are a natural consequence of the early dating. . . . It is therefore no wonder that there is hardly a single Proto-Uralic etymon that would have a perfectly regular representation in every single Uralic idiom. This is, however, not a reason to dismiss the family as a whole.

However, other researchers, in common with textbooks, normally report that the Uralic corpus is essentially regular. For example, Abondolo ((ed.) 1998: 8) says

The historical development of these families has been established, by means of the comparative method, to a degree of precision which is both predictive and productive. 'Predictive' means that given form X in language Y we can predict . . . what the form of its cognate, form Z in related language W, will be. 'Productive' means that such predictions will either prove to be correct, buttressing and fleshing out the detail of the family's genetic integrity, or they will fail, forcing the investigator to re-hone his or her tools and to ask different, perhaps more penetrating questions about the family's internal relations.

Whatever the interpretation, the dominant model remains a simple, clear-cut picture where the Uralic languages form an 'ideal' language family. The following are the basic (sometimes implied or hidden) assumptions, or 'tenets', that are believed by most of the scholars who accept this main-stream approach. For clarity in this book I shall describe the following as forming the 'standard Uralic theory' or the 'textbook interpretation':

Tenet 1: The modern Uralic languages derive from a single genetic parent called Proto-Uralic, and they have no genetic relationship with the surrounding languages. Although it is recognised that there are correlations with languages outside the Uralic group, these are considered to be the result of borrowing or chance resemblance. In particular, the words of Turkic origin present in Hungarian are all classified as borrowed and, for most of them, the exact chronology and donor language has been clearly identified.

Tenet 2: Most of the Proto-Language, and the lower nodes of the family tree, have been reliably reconstructed. The reconstruction extends to all the expected features, including phonological and morpho-logical structure, and is generally regarded to be consistent with the available data.

Tenet 3: Proto-Uralic was spoken in the area of the Ural mountains, at least 6,000–8,000 years ago. The location and antiquity are evidenced by the reconstruction in Proto-Uralic of the names of plants which were present in the area at that time. The antiquity is also supported by the very poor quality of the Uralic corpus and by the fact that Proto-Uralic contains loan-words of Indo-European origin which are very old.

Tenet 4: The reconstructed family tree is consistent with the correlations that are observed in the modern languages. For example, the first binary splitting of Proto-Uralic was very ancient, and it produced Proto-Finno-Ugric and Proto-Samoyed. This splitting can be confirmed by reconstructing shared archaic features. The modern languages under the Finno-Ugric node are comparatively close to one another, and there is a measurably greater distance from the languages under the Samoyed node.

Tenet 5: The daughter languages which have been formed as a result of subsequent, ordered, binary splits from the mother language contain appropriate shared innovations and retained archaic features consistent with the model.

Tenet 6: The current sound-system of the daughter languages is the result of sound-changes that are essentially regular and systematic.

Tenet 7: The ancient Proto-Language was rich in morphology.

In this book, I intend to demonstrate that these tenets are not supported by the evidence. Whilst there are undeniable correlations between the Uralic languages that can be understood using a genetic model – or using alternative models – these correlations are also present, and just as strong, in some of the surrounding languages. I believe that the above tenets have now become myths that have the effect of holding back research in the field, and that a revision of the entire paradigm is in order.

1.3. METHOD

1.3.1. *Evidence vs opinion*

My central point of departure from the conventional approach to Uralic studies stems from the fact that the literature frequently fails to differentiate between scientific evidence, which by definition must be falsifiable, and opinions or interpretations, which are usually not falsifiable. As a result, a reader may be forgiven for becoming confused as to exactly what is opinion and what constitutes scientific evidence in the field.

It is important to be clear at this point what is meant by 'scientific evidence'. Much of the literature on the Uralic language family is founded on a network of self-consistent assumptions and reconstructions, and a significant part of this book is dedicated to quantifying and examining them. I do not claim that these reconstructions and assumptions are wrong. They may indeed represent valid opinions or interpretations on the origin of these languages. However, it will be a recurring theme throughout this book that many of them can be demonstrated to be 'not even wrong', that is, there is no objective way to test whether the assertion is true or false. These items must properly be labelled opinions or speculations, since they do not constitute scientific evidence on the criteria normally adopted in scientific research.

For example, in Chapter 4 we observe that the accepted reconstruction of the P-Uralic node contains more sound-rules than regular etymologies. If one regards the reconstruction as a 'scientific model', its significance would be discounted because it contains more 'adjustable parameters' (that is, sound-rules) than items of evidence. The reconstruction is therefore very flexible in fitting the data. In rejecting theories based on models of this sort, Rees (1999/2000: 76) says:

> A 'bad' theory . . . is one that is so flexible that it can be adjusted to account for any data. The eminent, and arrogant, physicist Wolfgang Pauli would deride such vague ideas as 'not even wrong'

These observations mean that the reconstruction must be viewed as an exercise in stating the sound-laws of the P-Uralic node, if the node exists. The reconstruction is a consequence of, and not evidence for, the existence and validity of the P-Uralic node. This appears to accord with the method and purpose of the original author. Rather than attempting to collate evidence in support of the P-Uralic node, its existence and validity are assumed throughout. The purpose (Janhunen (1981a: 246), my translation) is to give 'at least a general picture of the sound-structure of the Proto-Language', whilst stressing that important elements of the reconstruction are 'totally tentative' and that there is 'the possibility of alternative interpretations' (see Chapter 4 for details).

The question of the status of this P-Uralic corpus merits a 'second opinion' in the form of an alternative test. In Chapter 5 we compare the same corpus with a 'control case', equivalent to random words that are matched using statistically equivalent criteria. We report that these two samples – the true Lexicon and the random words – are statistically almost identical. In other words, the test fails to distinguish whether the corpus is the result of a true linguistic connection or chance resemblances. To take an analogy, if the Uralic corpus were a medical drug, it would be rejected on the grounds that its performance is not discernibly different from a control-case placebo.

These observations do not demonstrate that the reconstructions are wrong. It is certainly a valid opinion that at least some of them represent a true linguistic correlation. I hold this opinion, at least for a small number of these lexical items. But they do not constitute scientific evidence because, both according to conventional methods and according to more detailed statistical methods, they cannot be distinguished from accidental look-alikes.

To take another example, the P-Uralic corpus is (often) recognised to be small and to contain many irregularities, contrary to what would be expected for a language family of this sort. One possible explanation is that the Uralic languages are not related in the way that is usually stated. However, the accepted explanation is that the languages are genetically related but the language family is very old, so that the lack of quality and quantity is a consequence of the great time depth. In order to distinguish between these alternative explanations, independent evidence is required. As we shall see in Chapter 7, there is in fact no independent evidence that the family is very old. The only evidence is – in a circular argument – the very lack of quality and quantity in the Uralic corpus itself. In fact, the antiquity of the P-Uralic node is a consequence of, and not evidence for, the assumption that the U languages are genetically related.

A third example is the way in which proper names are interpreted in Uralic studies. As we shall see in Chapter 2, the concept of the Uralic theory originated in an apparent similarity of proper names (*hungarus-Yugria* and *magyar-Mansi*). This latter ethnonym is discussed at length in modern textbooks, where it is cited as evidence in favour of the Uralic theory. This approach is perfectly respectable in principle, since proper names are sometimes regarded outside Uralic studies as particularly stable forms of language. For example, Renfrew (1987: 21) says

> place names . . . do continue to be used in a given area long after their original meaning has been forgotten, so that words belonging to a much earlier and pre-literate form of language can be preserved by spoken tradition, and first set down in writing long after the original language form has disappeared.

However, as we shall see in Chapter 9, the connection *hungarus-Yugria* is no longer regarded as valid in most modern textbooks, and the connection *magyar-Mansi* is made through a reconstruction that differs from the historically attested form and is linguistically ad hoc. Further, there is a significant number of other connections between proper names in the same geographical region, which span the supposed boundary of the Uralic area, and which therefore are inconsistent with the Uralic theory. Some of these parallels have clear characteristics that mean they cannot be the result of chance resemblances. This evidence is well known in Uralic studies, and it has become common practice to 'explain it away' by assuming that one can deduce nothing from proper names, because they are highly susceptible to change (with the exception, of course, of *magyar-Mansi*).

The etymology *magyar-Mansi*, its assumed significance, and the practice of disregarding other proper names so as to avoid their contradiction with the Uralic theory, might, for all we know, all be correct; but they are ad hoc: they are not even wrong, because there is no objective way to tell if they are true or false.

Textbook writers and my colleagues in Uralic studies are certainly aware of the distinction between evidence and opinion, and it is not due to sloppiness that this distinction is so often blurred. There is a much deeper assumption at work here. It is believed that the question of the origin of the Uralic languages was settled over 100 years ago by the founder of the field, a German researcher working in Hungary named Budenz. If you assume that the Uralic language family was scientifically established beyond doubt over 100 years ago, then the assumptions referred to above cease to be ad hoc: they are motivated by the established model or paradigm.

This is why my treatise must begin by describing the historical foundation of the Uralic paradigm, and in particular the chief question posed by Budenz, namely the relationship between Hungarian, Turkic and the languages of north-eastern Europe. As will become evident, the claim that the Uralic language family was scientifically established beyond doubt (over 100 years ago) is, in fact, not correct.

1.3.2. *The history of the Uralic theory*

As we shall see in Chapter 2, the concept of the Uralic language family originated, between the sixteenth and eighteenth centuries, in an apparent similarity between the Latin ethnonym for the Hungarians, *hungarus*, and the Russian toponym for a location near the Ural mountains, *Yugria* – hence the terms 'Uralic' and 'Ugric'.

In the late 1800s, a German linguist working in Hungary, J. Budenz, tried to apply the 'Comparative Method' in order to prove the relationship between Hungarian and the other Ugric languages (which he extended to include other languages of north-eastern Europe, such as Finnish). One can observe today that Budenz did not apply the Comparative Method properly in this corpus; for example, he did not state the sound-rules on which his 'correspondences' were supposed to be based, and arbitrary stretches of meaning were often used. In fact, in examining a sample of Budenz' 'correspondences', 81% are no longer considered valid in the modern literature. Further, as we shall see in Chapter 4, it is now widely accepted that Hungarian is radically different in Morphology, Phonology, Lexicon and Syntax from the other Ugric languages, so that it has proven impossible to reconstruct the Ugric node from the primary linguistic evidence. It should not be surprising to find such a large variance between Budenz' comparative corpus and the modern literature on the same topic, since the Comparative Method was in its infancy at the time; and, indeed, a similar situation is found in the Indo-European context, where, as Fox (1995: 11) says:

the forms of reconstructed Proto-Indo-European have changed out of all recognition as successive generations of scholars have refined and amended their predecessors' work

More seriously, it usually goes unmentioned in the literature that Budenz' conception of the Uralic family differs significantly from the modern theory he is supposed to have 'scientifically established'. In the modern theory, the Uralic languages are held to be completely unrelated to the Altaic languages. One consequence of this is that all the words of Turkic origin present in Hungarian are now classified as loan-words, and, as we shall see in Chapter 2, much of the study of Hungarian prehistory is based, in the sense described above, on this cornerstone. Yet Budenz made no such claim. Quite the contrary. He classified Hungarian as belonging to the extended

Ugric branch (including the languages of north-eastern Europe) and, in his model, the Ugric branch, the Turkic branch and other Asiatic branches all belonged to the 'wide Altaic family'. He supported this model by identifying specific correspondences that he claimed were indicative of a genetic relationship (from a higher level) between Turkic and Hungarian.

At some point in the development of the paradigm, the Uralic languages came to be 'split off' from the languages left behind in the Altaic family. It is an astounding omission that I can find no original work to substantiate this assumed splitting-off. Nonetheless, in spite of the lack of any original reference, it is generally believed that the uniqueness of these language groups has been scientifically established beyond doubt, yet again through the method of comparative linguistics.

1.3.3. *The Comparative Method*

In the method of comparative linguistics the concept of 'regular' sound-laws is central. It is assumed that one can distinguish genetic relations by the regularity of their associated sound-correspondences and sound-changes, whilst words that do not obey regular sound-laws are classified as merely borrowed or accidental look-alikes. The cumulative effect of many words, all obeying the same sound-laws regularly, is supposed to establish the correlations to a high degree of probability.

Unfortunately, all of these elements are untestable or completely missing in the Uralic context. We have already identified above that the accepted reconstruction of P-Uralic contains more sound-rules than regular etymologies, so that there is no 'cumulative effect' in this corpus. Most other research on the Uralic family is silent on what the sound-rules are actually supposed to be, or at best only a handful of them are identified. For example, the main Uralic dictionary, *Uralisches Etymologisches Wörterbuch* (UEW), does not state the phonological criteria on the basis of which its 472 P-Uralic etymologies have been established, and it is not easy to infer them from the etymologies that are listed because of inconsistencies in sound and meaning. This means it is impossible to apply the Comparative Method to any testable degree using this evidence.

Turning to the way in which linguistic items are classified, there is an important bias in the way the Comparative Method is usually applied in the Uralic context. This bias is most evident when one examines the relationships between the Uralic languages and the apparently similar nearby languages to the East.

The method proceeds as follows. One first identifies the languages that are supposed to be genetically related. From these languages, one then reconstructs the relevant Proto-Forms, Proto-Phonemes and sound-changes (as we have noted, these are in fact usually only partially stated in publications). Words that match the predictions of the model can now be cited as 'evidence' in favour of the original assumptions, whilst words that do not match the predictions are dismissed as, variously, in error, irrelevant, chance similarities, *Wanderwörter*, borrowed or (for particularly good matches that cross the Uralic boundary) due to 'convergent development' or 'regular direct borrowing'. Alternatively, as Abondolo ((ed.) 1998: 8) suggests, words that do not match the predictions force the researcher to 're-hone his or her tools and to ask different, perhaps more penetrating questions about the family's internal relations', presumably as an alternative to acknowledging them, more simply, as items of evidence that do not fit the model.

Even with the die biased in favour of the Uralic language family in this way, we shall see in Chapter 6 that many words match better with languages outside the Uralic family than within the family. For example, Sinor (1975: 251) says:

> I find it hard to believe that a correspondence as **flawless** in form and meaning as that existing between the Uralic and Tunguz forms could be coincidental . . . I would not like to exclude the possibility that the . . . words . . . are **direct borrowings** from Tunguz (bold is mine)

In a situation where several researchers recognise within the field that the Uralic corpus is very small and contains many irregularities, why are these 'flawless' correspondences not interpreted as evidence of a genetic relationship? What distinguishes a 'borrowing', which can be identified because it is 'irregular', from a 'direct borrowing' which is the opposite? The only justification for these classifications seems to be that there is an a priori assumption – which is held to have been settled historically – about which languages are genetically related and which are not. At this point one may feel entitled to ask how the literature would have reported this evidence if, by an accident of history, the Uralic paradigm had developed in a different way. It is hard to believe that the 'flawless' correspondences reported above would not have been cited as strong evidence for a genetic relationship between Tungus and some of the northern Uralic languages. Conversely, it is hard to believe that the acknowledged very poor correspondences between (say) Hungarian and the other Ugric languages could have failed to be dismissed as in error or not significant.

A similar bias has also been noted outside the Uralic sphere. For example, as Fox (1995: 63) says, the fundamental problem lies in:

> assuming that forms are cognate because they can be reconstructed with the same proto-phoneme, where the proto-phoneme is itself the result of assuming that they *are* cognate.

In addition to the problems in the way the Comparative Method is usually applied, there are now acknowledged to be inconsistencies between the evidence from other language groups and the founding principles of the method itself. The fundamental assumption of the Comparative Method is the 'regularity principle', according to which inherited words obey regular sound-laws whilst borrowed words are irregular. Recent studies in linguistics have demonstrated that these foundations are not supported by the evidence.

As we shall see in Chapter 6, borrowed words tend to become assimilated into the sound-structure of the recipient language rather rapidly, so that they become indistinguishable from inherited words after only a few generations, if not at the very time of borrowing. This means that, in the absence of historical records or other types of information, it is difficult, if not impossible, to distinguish borrowed words from inherited words linguistically.

Secondly, there is evidence that the majority of sound-changes do not in fact proceed regularly after all, because of the disturbing interference of several factors, which include social, geographical and generational variation; mixture of languages and dialects due to contact; and the intricate, often arbitrary processes by which changes diffuse, complete or abort. As Lass (1993: 179) says:

> It is really only within the past two decades or so that Neogrammarian *regelrecht* correspondences have come to be naturally interpretable as the end results of long-term processes of much messier change, involving variation, and often lexeme-specific mutation

This counter-evidence has arisen from several areas of linguistic studies: 'languages in contact' (since Weinreich 1953), Dialectology (see, for example, Chambers & Trudgill 1980: 37–38), Sociolinguistics (see, for example, Labov 1963, 1972, 1980, 1994; Weinreich, Labov & Herzog 1968) and from the field of 'lexical diffusion' (see, for example, Wang 1969, 1979; Chen 1972). For the question of the 'regularity' vs 'non-regularity' of sound-changes see Schuchardt (1885), Labov (1981) and Campbell (1996). For a general review of the strengths and weaknesses of the Comparative Method see Fox (1995) and Lass (1997).

1.3.4. *The programme followed in this book*

In this book I shall try to describe, as clearly as I am able, the evidence, the assumptions and the models that are used to account for the Uralic language family. I shall review both the mainstream 'textbook' interpretation and the many alternatives that appear in the literature. I shall refer to primary evidence wherever possible in order to place these interpretations into the appropriate context. I shall always try to separate out the scientific evidence from the assumptions, the interpretations and the speculations.

To help in this separation, I shall use statistical methods as well as conventional linguistic methods of analysis. I shall report data from the fields of history, Phonology, Lexicon, Morphology, Morpho-syntax, Typology, Onomastics and, briefly, other non-linguistic areas such as archaeology and genetics.

Although I believe the use of the Comparative Method can be misleading in this context, for the reasons outlined above, I shall, where appropriate, review the interpretations that use this method, as dispassionately and as positively as possible, in their own terms – that is, assuming that the Comparative Method is applicable and genuinely applying it together with its known advantages and limitations.

At this point I must ask for the indulgence of my colleagues and readers. As identified above, the current approach to Uralic studies is based on an interlocking network of self-consistent assumptions, interpretations and reconstructions. As we shall see in Chapter 2, re-interpretations of historical evidence, so that it appears to be more consistent with the mainstream model, are also involved. Each of these assumptions, reconstructions and interpretations reinforces another, in a kind of 'Gordian knot'. In my attempt to disentangle some of the more 'Gordian' aspects, it is inevitable that I shall use evidence from sources in support of an interpretation with which the original authors might not agree. Therefore, despite my best intentions, there is always the danger that I might misrepresent the views and interpretations of the scholars who deal with these topics. If this is the case then I proffer my apologies in advance.

In particular, I shall use many examples from Rédei's UEW (1986–91), because this goes back systematically and comprehensively to the original sources, reporting the actual languages and dialects both within the Uralic area and to some extent outside it. I shall refer extensively to Abondolo ((ed.) 1998), which is the most recent English-language publication with a detailed description of all the Uralic languages, and which also largely mirrors the conventional interpretation. I shall examine in detail the reconstructions of P-Uralic and of the rest of the family tree, by Janhunen (1981a) and Sammallahti (1979, 1988) because these represent closely researched scientific models with clear criteria that are amenable to quantitative scrutiny. Regarding the specific subject of the parallels with languages outside the Uralic area, I shall pay particular attention to the comprehensive works of Sinor (1975, 1988, 1990), Ligeti (1986) and Johanson & Csató ((ed.) 1998).

Although my interpretation of the evidence reported in these sources will differ in many respects from those of the original authors, these sources stand by themselves as sources of original data and they are at the foundation of the field, whatever interpretation is chosen by the reader.

No review of this nature would be complete without my personal interpretation of the relationships between the languages involved and the processes that led to them. This is given at the appropriate places. Here, I want to clarify that I am not a proponent of any specific linguistic 'school'. My personal view is that there are several processes that can equally well explain the correlations that are observed today amongst these languages; these include genetic inheritance, areal convergence, and Renfrew's (1987) model of the cumulative effect of small random movements of individuals. All of these processes have their place, and it is my central claim that it is usually not possible to tell them apart. Sometimes, in explaining my personal interpretations, I shall select one or other of these processes for the sake of concreteness; this is not intended to exclude the other processes unless specifically stated.

It is possible that Uralic studies are not alone in being susceptible to re-examination; however, the purpose of this book is to examine the Uralic languages and I shall remain true to this focus. I speculate on any applicability outside the Uralic sphere in the final chapter.

1.4. SYSTEMATIC RE-INTERPRETATION OF EVIDENCE COUNTER TO THE STANDARD THEORY

In this book I hope to show, by careful examination of the evidence and the literature, that the tenets of the Uralic theory are not supported by the evidence, and indeed there is a large body of evidence counter to them. However, it is striking to observe in the literature how the counter-evidence becomes consistently diluted as it makes its way in turn from reported data, to authors' conclusions, to the general literature and to English-language textbooks. In original papers, the individual items of counter-evidence are usually recognised explicitly. However, when drawing conclusions, authors usually say that they neglect them, or that they consider them not relevant, or in other ways minimise their importance. This process appears to be repeated at each step in the chain, so that, in the final step, textbooks usually present a highly idealised picture. The result for the field is that the counter-evidence is systematically minimised or re-interpreted, and the evidence, as propagated into the general literature, seems to be consistent with the conventional paradigm.

As was observed by Kuhn (1970), it is quite normal in science for evidence that is counter to an established paradigm to be consistently minimised or re-interpreted. Typically the individual items of counter-evidence are not strong enough on their own to mount a challenge to the established paradigm. After all, any individual items of evidence may be subject to misinterpretation or statistical error or other problems. The result is that authors will often willingly choose a presentation and interpretation that makes the work appear as consistent as possible with the established theory. This phenomenon is sometimes extended into the peer-review process, so that if a paper submitted for publication describes such evidence and reaches a conclusion that is inconsistent with the accepted paradigm, it will probably (and arguably correctly) be rejected for publication unless the mismatch with the paradigm is minimised.

Here are some examples of this process at work in the Uralic context.

A linguistic model that is established in other language families may be 'adjusted' in so far as it applies to Uralic studies if it is inconsistent with the Uralic evidence. In this way the evidence is made to appear consistent with the Uralic theory. For example, some of the basic words at the heart of the Comparative Method are kinship terms and number terms. According to the comparative model, these are particularly stable forms of language (see, for example, Comrie ((ed.) 1987b: 24–5) in the Indo-European context). However, most of these words are irregular in Uralic. Rather than acknowledging this as evidence that does not match the established model, it is the model itself which is adjusted specifically for the Uralic context. This irregularity is classified in Uralic as if it were a systematic phenomenon. It is called, in the jargon of the field, the 'typical lability' (Janhunen[4] 1981a) of the 'affective words' (UEW[5]). It is now seemingly part of the model in Uralic studies that these words, which are usually considered at the heart of the Comparative Method, are irregular because of their 'affective character' and 'high frequency of use' – but I can discover no explanation as to why affective character and frequency of use should produce this effect in the Uralic languages but the opposite effect in, for example, Indo-European languages.

It is sometimes the evidence that is 'corrected' (or 're-interpreted') if it is inconsistent with the theory. For example, as we shall see in Chapter 2, the earliest records, from the 9th/10th century, consistently refer to the Hungarians as 'Turks'. This is directly counter to the thesis of a Uralic origin. It is therefore assumed that the contemporary sources had become 'confused': the Hungarians were not Turks, but had become similar in appearance and behaviour to the Turks through a long period of co-habitation. This long co-habitation is supposedly supported by the writings of the Byzantine emperor Constantine Porphyrogenitus, who is usually quoted as stating that the Hungarians were in contact with the Turks for about three hundred years. His actual record states that a group of seven Turkic clans [re-interpreted as the Hungarians] were in contact with the [Turkic] Khazars for three [re-interpreted as three hundred] years, but historians simply assume that the emperor, too, was in error, so that in modern accounts he is usually held to refer to different populations and to a different length of time than is actually stated in the original text. The emperor's 'errors' and the re-interpretations to make the text consistent with the Uralic paradigm may go unmentioned in textbooks or even in specialist literature (see as a recent example Rédei[6] 1998: 57).

In another process of minimisation, counter-evidence may be reported, but its significance may be diluted in conclusions. For example, in numerous publications on various Uralic and Altaic correlations, Sinor reports striking shared lexical and morphological features. We have already noted above the 'flawless' correspondences that the author has identified between Tungusic and Uralic, and these are reaffirmed in a later paper (Sinor 1988: 738–9; see discussion in Chapter 6)

> I am quite certain that if from all the Uralic and Altaic languages only the [Altaic] Northern Tunguz and [Uralic] Ob-Ugric were known, no one would deny their genetic relationship.

This is directly counter to the predictions of the accepted models, and perhaps in other scientific spheres the reader would expect an explicit statement to this effect. However this is not the case. Instead, the paper appears to reject the concept that the accepted models might be falsifiable at all:

> Uralic, Altaic, and Uralo-Altaic comparative linguistics should shake themselves free from simplistic – black and white, yes and no – solutions

Finally, this paper, which contains strong counter-evidence to the accepted models, concludes with merely a diluted call for further research leading to a possible 'revision of the traditional approach to Uralic-Altaic comparative studies'. Its final words are:

> I can but conclude with a suggestion I made years ago, that Uralic and Altaic comparative linguistics should not ignore each other, and that the truth should not be proclaimed but searched for.

Finally, where conclusions that do not fully support the conventional paradigm are clearly stated in original papers, these conclusions may be diluted in works that quote them or are based on them. For example, as we shall see in Chapter 4, Sammallahti (1988) reconstructs the full conventional Uralic family tree, starting from Janhunen's (1981a) reconstruction of the P-Uralic node. About 50% of the examples that are quoted in support of the reconstructed family tree are in fact identified as 'irregular', 'problematic' or 'troublesome' in the original work of Janhunen. This is not mentioned. On the contrary; for example, it is asserted (1988: 479) that Janhunen's corpus contains '140 regular cases' when the original paper classifies only 94 cases as acceptable parallels, some of which are identified to have irregularities that the author believes can plausibly be explained. A reader who has not read this original work of Janhunen (in Finnish) may be led to the false conclusion that there is a great deal of regularity and consistency in both corpuses. This picture becomes even further idealised in textbooks; for example, Csepregi (1998) gives selected examples showing the apparent complete regularity of a few reflexes, omitting mention of any recognised irregularities at all. We shall see further details in Chapter 4.

These are not isolated examples. I believe that a careful examination of the counter-evidence reveals a wide scope and a clear pattern: the counter-evidence has now reached the point of critical mass. A revision of the paradigm is now in order. The time has come for all the evidence and counter-evidence relating to the Uralic languages to be brought together in a systematic and comprehensive way.

1.5. KEY PATTERNS IN THE EVIDENCE

My personal interpretations regarding the methods that are conventionally used to classify correlations between languages, and specifically regarding the nature of the correlations between the Uralic languages, is given at the end of the book. Here, I limit myself to outlining the key patterns to which I believe the reader will objectively be drawn, after examining the evidence set forth in this book.

The first conclusion is that there are a great many structural (morpho-syntactic and typological) elements, and a handful of non-structural elements, that span most of the Uralic languages and which are unlikely to be the result of chance resemblances. Almost all of these common elements are also shared with the other languages that are conventionally classified as Altaic and Yukaghir. The small number of non-structural elements include: some phonological features (such as richness of vowels, paucity of consonants, and some shared sounds and sound-changes), a handful of basic words, and a few basic formants consisting of the most natural, common phonemes.

Secondly, clusters of isoglosses can be identified at several levels of language (Morphology, Phonology, Lexicon, Onomastics etc.) that are broadly consistent with one another. A number of these clusters run right across the conventional boundary of the Uralic area.

Thirdly, with regard to Morphology, the modern Uralic languages have varying degrees of complexity, ranging from the simplest, such as Vogul and Ostyak, to the most complex, such as Finnish, Hungarian and Mordvin. In the morphologically rich languages, the basic processes through which Morphology is formed (Exaptation and Grammaticalisation) are clearly observable, and one is drawn to the conclusion that the complexity in this area is a recent innovation. Whatever the nature of the ancestor or ancestors, the evidence suggests they were morphologically simple.

Fourthly, whilst researchers in the past have relied mainly on the family tree model to interpret and explain the relationships among the Uralic languages, this model is simply not supported by the evidence. If one is to adopt standard scientific principles, one must conclude that there is no evidence that the Uralic languages form a coherent family in the sense conventionally understood by the term, so that Uralic must not only be removed from the list of 'well-behaved' language families, it must also be removed from the list of language families altogether. Instead, the linguistic relations among the languages are best described in terms of intersecting isoglosses.

Finally, the U languages and the nearby languages to the East form a dialectal continuum whose formation may be the effect of several processes, including genetic inheritance and areal convergence, but, on the basis of current evidence it is, in the main, not possible to tell these processes apart.

1.6. INTRODUCTION TO THE LITERATURE SUPPORTING AND OPPOSING THE URALIC THEORY

The U paradigm/theory has been successfully passed on, to this day, through a vast body of articles and books. Amongst the most recent of the publications that propagate the textbook U theory one can include the volume *The Uralic Languages*, edited by D. Abondolo (1998); the paper by L. Campbell (1997): *On the linguistic prehistory of Finno-Ugric*; the book *Finnugor kalauz*, the 'Finno-Ugric guide', edited by M. Csepregi (1998); the book by G. Bereczki: *Fondamenti di Linguistica Ugro Finnica* (1998); the book by K. Rédei (1998): *Ōstörténetünk kérdései* 'The questions of our pre-history'; the book by J. Laakso (1999b) *Karhunkieli*, literally 'the language of the bear'.[7] Compare also Esa Itkonen (1998 and 1999), supporting the validity of the family tree model in general and within U studies.

Despite its popularity among linguists and the general public, and despite the fact that it is generally presented as proven beyond doubt, the standard Uralic theory is far from unquestioned. As we shall see in detail in Chapter 3, one can find several different analyses and points of view about the origin and classification of the Uralic language family, which seldom get the chance to be brought to the attention of the broader circles of readers, and therefore to be seriously considered.

Such a contrast between the simple textbook picture, and the, sometimes, contradictory interpretations found in the specialist literature might seem at first surprising. However, as pointed out by Lass (1997: 5–6) with regard to the histories of languages in general:

The histories of languages (as objects available to or made by linguists) are, like all histories, myths. We do have documents for portions of many of our histories; but even these are subject, like scripture, to exegesis: we don't *know* what they mean (the less, the older they are). We do however tell (and believe) stories about them, not just the documents but the languages they supposedly reflect, the reality (phonic, grammatical, semantic etc.) . . . But a venerable rational mythology, apparently grounded in argument and extrapolation from putative evidence, can pose a major problem: the longer it exists, the less succeeding generations or practitioners tend to know, or remember (if they ever knew) or even care about how it came into being, or what supports its main tenets. . . . in many important cases, we may be passing on, as precious and firmly held beliefs, replicas of assertions that someone somewhere once made, transformed into Articles of Faith

In more detail, within U studies one finds, for example, that documents, archaeological and ethnographic records are scanty in relation to the U languages and people. Publications often refer to the 'mystery' surrounding these languages and the archaeology and ethno-history associated with them. There is clearly a requirement to interpolate heavily between the available data, and this might well increase the potential for a 'mythological' component in putting together the pieces of the puzzle.

There is a body of research recognising the inadequacy of the conventional family tree in accounting for the history and nature of the U languages, which has been often ignored in both the specialist and the general literature. The criticisms raised against (at least some of) the tenets of the standard U theory have recently intensified, particularly by some Finnish, Estonian and Hungarian scholars. These scholars also recognise that the field has to renew itself by taking into consideration, in addition to the conventional concepts, new ideas and methods, including the results of disciplines outside linguistics, mainly human genetics and archaeology. Compare, for example, some of the papers contained in the volumes edited by Julku & Äärelä (1997), by Fogelberg (1999) and by Künnap (2000). Compare also some recent books (such as Kiszely[8] 1992), which challenge the U origin of the Hungarian language and people. In some cases, new models have also been proposed. For example, in one proposal, P-U can been regarded as the lingua franca of the hunters and gatherers of north-eastern Europe. The Balto-Finnic languages are considered as 'mixed' languages, intermingled with Indo-European languages. For Hungarian, the once popular thesis of their Turkic origin has been recently reconsidered.

As pointed out in Section 1.3.3 above, modern linguistic theories have to some extent overtaken the family tree model in general. The academic acceptance of the Uralic theory into the establishment dates back to the end of the 19th century. At that time, the family tree model was practically the only one fashionable and used (the alternative 'wave model', proposed by Schmidt in 1872, was not considered a mainstream model). Since that time, the Uralic theory has been 'passed on' from one generation of practitioners to the next practically as an 'Article of Faith' (as also remarked by Häkkinen[9] 1996: 52). As a result, there has been a very surprising lack of modification of the paradigm, in the face of the deeper linguistic knowledge available today.

Other researchers have independently come to the conclusion that there are a number of myths connected with the U theory, although their views about the nature and classification of the U languages may differ from mine. For example, in a recent review article, *Facts and myths about Uralic studies*,

Salminen (1997b: 86f.) describes what he calls 'the most persistent myths in the field':

> In practically all textbooks, the standard claim is that the Uralic family is a union of two very distantly related groups of languages, called Finno-Ugrian and Samoyed. This claim is false. While it is true that the Samoyed branch is very independent, there is little or no evidence for the rest of Uralic as a unit in its own right

He goes on to say:

> The standard classification continues to split the 'main' branch, i.e. Finno-Ugrian, into Finno-Permian and Ugrian, Finno-Permian further into Finno-Volgaic and Permian, . . . This practice is also unfounded, and originally based on a nationalistic Finnish view which wanted to see the Finnish language literally as the highest spring of the sacred family-tree

Künnap (1997a: 65–6) states that:

> The wish of the majority of Uralists is to take the origin of possibly numerous features of modern Uralic languages back to a single and unitary source – to Proto-Uralic – ; it is psychologically understandable: a simple starting position emerges. Unfortunately it has become clear to date that alongside of this an inadmissible simplification takes place. The simplification which casts aside the abundance and variety of languages, their irregularities and internal contacts. . . . In most cases the reconstruction of Proto-Uralic is declared to be an indispensable methodological mean in the research of historical linguistics. Is it really so if we bear in mind the number of misinterpretations it can create about modern Uralic languages? I am firmly convinced that the methodological mean does more harm than good. A linguistic game with combined rules has been created but its incompatibility with the evidence of modern Uralic languages . . . today becomes more and more evident by the day. Why should Uralists keep playing this game?

Finally, Nuñez (2000: 60) states that:

> There are a number of biases affecting our perception of Finnish origins . . . Among these is a legacy of strong migrationistic and nationalistic orientations and of old linguistic concepts such as family trees and ancestral homelands. Since the beginning of the century, a series of circular arguments have been incorporated in order to create a self-sustaining closed theoretical model that fed and legitimized itself

In the following chapters I shall go into the details of what I believe to be the facts and the myths relating to the U language family, according to the stated aim of this book.

2

THE HISTORICAL FOUNDATION OF THE URALIC PARADIGM

This . . . belief in the Hungarians' close relationship with the Ob-Ugrians is based not so much on scientific arguments as on the fact of the Latin names Hungarus *and* Hungaria. *. . . the land of the Voguls . . . and Ostyaks . . . was referred to in Russian and West European sources as* Ugra, Yugra, *or* Yugria *. . . it was taken almost for granted that Yugria in the Ural region was the Hungarians' ancestral home*[1]

Béla Kálmán

It is usually taken for granted that the uniqueness of the U node, and therefore the existence of a unique U family, was scientifically established in the final decades of the 19th century. This is supposed to be based on clear historical evidence, mainly from the Greek emperor Constantine Porphyrogenitus, as well as compelling linguistic evidence, mainly from two key linguists, J. Budenz and O. Donner. The purpose of this chapter is to review the historical evidence, and to see how the U theory was founded and evolved into the version that we observe today. As we shall see, the claim that the 'U theory was founded scientifically and beyond doubt in the final decades of the 19th century' is not, in fact, correct, since the evidence put forward by the founders of the field to 'prove' the existence of the U family would not nowadays be accepted as 'scientific'.

We examine first the historical records, of which there are in fact very few. As we shall see, none of them point to a Uralic origin. Several sources appear to contradict the theory (such as the records of Constantine Porphyrogenitus) but these have been massively 're-interpreted', and are usually reported today as if they instead support the theory.

Next we examine the early origins of the Uralic theory. It was known that the Chronicles had indicated an unspecified Eastern homeland for the Hungarians. Between the 15th and 17th centuries it came to be taken for granted that this homeland could be identified with an area near the Ural mountains called *Yugria* (hence the terms 'Uralic' and 'Ugric'). This belief was based on the apparent similarity between the toponym *Yugria* and the ethnonym *hungarus*. It is unclear whether this connection is still accepted in modern literature, since *hungarus* is now usually reported as connected with the *On-ogur* Turkic tribe. This connection was supported by the later discovery that one of the populations in the area (the Voguls) called themselves *Mansi*, which, according to Kálmán (1988: 395) 'to the lay ear slightly resembles the name *magyar*'. Today, the connection *magyar/Mansi* is regarded as strong evidence for the Uralic theory, having been justified using an etymology which – as we shall see in Chapter 9 – is ad hoc and does not in fact accord with the historically attested forms. It is assumed to this day that Hungarian shares a privileged relationship with the languages in the *Yugria* area (Vogul and Ostyak), and that together they form the so-called 'Ugric' node. However, as we shall see in Chapter 4, it is generally recognised that Hungarian is radically different in Phonology, Morphology, Lexicon and Syntax from the other Ugric languages, so the principal evidence to support the Ugric node appears to remain these historical etymologies.

In a period of about thirty years to the end of the 19th century, researchers began to apply Darwinian models to language and to use the Comparative Method, which was in its infancy at the time. As a result of this, the Ugric theory was extended, and put on a supposedly scientific footing. At the end of this period the theory had evolved into a curious mixture that combined the historical Ugric theory with the new and conflicting methods of two main researchers, Budenz and Donner.

Starting in the 1870s, Budenz argued that Hungarian was 'more closely related' to the languages of north-eastern Europe (the Ugric languages plus others such as Finnish) than it was to Turkic. Therefore, it was to be classified as a 'Ugric' and not as a Turkic language. He supported this conclusion with a corpus of lexical 'Ugric correspondences'. As we shall see, in this original work the sound-rules are not specified by which the correspondences are supposed to be established, so that the Comparative Method was not actually applied as claimed. In addition, arbitrary stretches of meaning are often accepted in order to establish the desired correspondence (such as navel/tongue/rope etc.). We observe that this corpus is of poor quality, and indeed, in a sample of these correspondences, 81% are no longer considered valid in the modern literature. We also observe that the evidence put forward by Budenz in support of the 'closer' relations between Hungarian and the north-eastern European languages is rather inconclusive.

Later in the 19th century, Donner rejected the lexical approach of Budenz and attempted to use a small number of morphological features, together with the distribution of vowel harmony and consonant gradation, to establish the genetic affinities of the Samoyed languages. He concluded that these features are widely spread in all the languages of Eurasia, but he expressed a personal opinion that on balance Samoyed is 'closer' to the north-eastern European languages than to Turkic or Mongolian. Donner's opinions were adopted by the linguistic community and grafted on to Budenz' linguistic family so that, by the end of the 19th century/beginning of the 20th century, it came to be believed that all these languages (north-eastern European languages, Hungarian and Samoyed) formed a genetic family and that the family was scientifically established through a proper application of the Comparative Method.

Finally, a further shift in the U theory took place during the 20th century. At the end of the 19th century it was widely accepted that there was an overarching genetic relationship spanning all the languages that are now classified as U and Altaic. For example, Budenz cited several correspondences between Hungarian and Turkic as evidence of a genetic relationship. Some time during the 20th century, it came to be believed that the U and Altaic families were genetically unrelated. There is no original reference to substantiate this 'splitting off'.

Table 2.1 summarises the formation and evolution of the Uralic paradigm from the mid 1800s to this day.

2.1. THE FIRST HISTORICAL SOURCES

There are no historical sources relating to U or F-U peoples, or to U and F-U languages, although there are historical sources relating to one or the other of the people/languages which are now classified as U/F-U. These sources are quite late, and generally exhibit a great deal of confusion in naming and referring to peoples, tribes, nations, places, dates, etc., so that they are not always reliable as to the details they provide, and a lot of interpretation is needed to fill in the gaps in the flow of information, and to build up a plausible story. Much of the early history of the region, until the end of the first millennium of our era, has to be based on surmise.

2.1.1. *The Finnic people*

The word '*Finn*' is first mentioned in the first century AD by the Roman historian Tacitus (*Germania*, Chapter 45), in the form *fenni*. However, it is possible that he was simply referring in general to the people of northern Europe, particularly to the Lappic people. After that, the name *finni ~ fenni* is used by the Alexandrine historian Claudios Ptolemaios (about 170 AD), and the Gothic writer Jordanes, in his *Getica* (about 551 AD), where we find the designation *Skrerefennit*, whereby the first part, *skrere-*, is believed to be a Swedish word meaning 'to ski, slide'. The first sure mention of this name in the western sources as referring to the nowadays Finns is considered to be in the Anglo-Saxon epic *Beowulf*, compiled probably around 800 AD. Here we find the phrase 'on finna land' (Beowulf, after having battled with sea monsters, swims many days to the land of the Finns), even if no other indications or pieces of information are provided in connection with this name (Gallén 1984: 250). Information about the *Finnit* and other Finnic tribes, become then much more numerous starting from the Viking era (800–1050). It was not until about 1171 that the word *Finni* was employed to mean the Finns.

The term *Eesti*, now the self- and external denomination of the Estonians,

Table 2.1 The formation and development of the Uralic paradigm

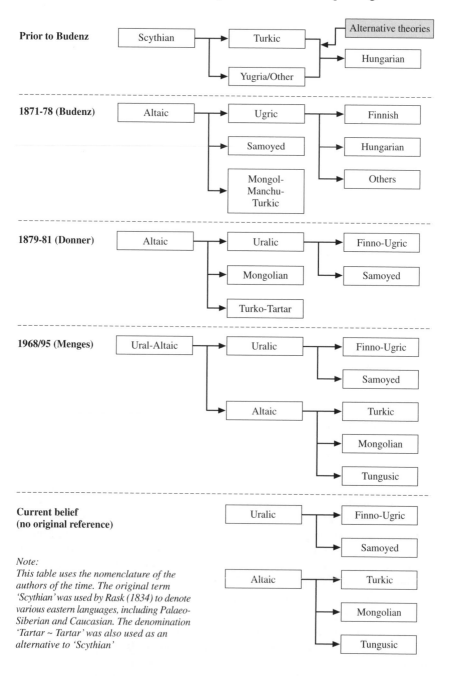

Note:
This table uses the nomenclature of the
authors of the time. The original term
'Scythian' was used by Rask (1834) to denote
various eastern languages, including Palaeo-
Siberian and Caucasian. The denomination
'Tartar ~ Tartar' was also used as an
alternative to 'Scythian'

occurs first again in Tacitus, in the form *aesti,* but it is believed to indicate Baltic tribes. Then, in the *Northern Sagas* (since the 9th century) and in documents of the 13th century, the term started to be used to indicate the Estonians (SSA I, 99–100). Hydronyms such as *Aista,* in Lithuania, seem to confirm that the population referred to by Tacitus are indeed to be identified with the old Prussians or some other Baltic tribes. However, the name itself is of unknown origin.

In an anonymous Norwegian text, probably dated between the 11th and 12th centuries, we find the first mention of the name '*kiriali*', referring to the Karelians, as well as the term '*cornuti Finni*', interpreted as referring to the Lapps. The term '*lapper*' on the other hand, used to indicate the modern Lapps, is found in an Icelandic text of the 12th century.

The name '*sum*', that is *Suomi* (for whose etymology see Chapter 9), and the name of other Finnic tribes, is found in the oldest Russian chronicles, starting from the 11th century. In the introduction of the oldest Russian chronicle, *Nestor's Chronicle* (1000–1100),[2] the names of other Finnic tribes are also listed, including: Veps, Cheremis, Mordvin, Permian. The text also mentions that these tribes speak their own language, even if they pay tributes to the Russians (see for more details Häkkinen 1996: 23–31; Gallén 1984; Pekkanen 1984).

The Cheremis people too are believed to be mentioned by Jordanes, by the name '*Sremnisc*', together with their close relatives, the Merens. This last name seems to be a Latinised form identical with the present-day self-designation of the Cheremis, that is, *Mari* (Kangasmaa-Minn 1998: 219).

2.1.2. *The Hungarians*

The historical sources relating to the Hungarians are much more numerous than those relating to the other U peoples, although these too are quite late. In examining them, one is immediately struck by the apparent contradiction between the historical evidence, which consistently points to a Turkic origin for the Hungarians, and the modern interpretations of that same data, which flatly deny that conclusion and maintain their F-U origin. Scholars recognise that this gives rise to many inconsistencies, which are described as 'para-doxes', 'questions' or 'problems', but they fail to mention that they would all be resolved by taking the most straightforward conclusion, that is, the Hungarian language and people are not of U origin. This conclusion, in turn, could not be contradicted by the linguistic data, as will emerge from the analysis carried out below.

2.1.2.1. *Summary of the historical sources*

Table 2.2 presents a summary of the main historical sources relating to the origin of the Hungarians, disentangled from the many, at times contradictory, interpretations they have been given in the extended literature which deals with them.[3] This will help the reader to form his own opinion on the complex, fascinating, and still unsettled question of the origin and prehistory of the Hungarians (see Di Cave 1995 for a good summary of the historical sources and the intense debate on their interpretation).

Table 2.2 The main historical sources relating to the origin of the Hungarians

Date AD	Source	Data (see text for details and interpretation)
Fifth century 463	Priscus Rhetor, Greek historian	Mentions the *On-ogur* Turkic tribe and other Turkic tribes including the Avars. (The textbook interpretation is that there is a linguistic connection between the terms *hungarus* and *On-ogur*.)
Ninth century	*Annales* of the Monastery of Fulda (Germany)	Report the presence of the Hungarians in the area of the Danube river in the years 894, 896, 900. The Hungarians are identified with the Avar population: 'Avari, qui dicuntur Ungari'. (This contradicts the textbook view that this area was basically unoccupied until the Hungarians arrived in 896.)
Tenth century	Latin, Greek, Slavic sources	Several mentions of names such as *Hun*, *[h]ung[r]*, *Ungr*, *Turk*, *Avar*, etc., all consistently referred to as Turkic people.
	Arabic sources	Mention 'a race of Turks' with the names *majǧir* and *bajǧir* as variants. (The modern terms *magyar* and *Bashkir* are derived from *majǧir* and *bajǧir* respectively.[4])
	Constantine Porphyrogenitus, Byzantine emperor (Greek)	Lists the names of seven Turkic clans. The third clan in the list is named Μεγέρη. The original text states that the 'nation of the Turks lived next to the Khazars for three years'. (Caution, most interpretations re-interpret this as 'the Hungarians were in close contact with the Turkic Khazars for about three hundred years'.)
Twelfth/Thirteenth centuries	First Hungarian text	Morphological and phonological structure indicate that the Hungarian language is in the process of formation.
	Medieval Chronicles (Latin)	Link the Hungarians to the Scythians[5] and the Huns.[6] One of these texts refers to the *Hungarii Mogerii* (~ *Mogerij*).
Thirteenth century 1235	Writings of the Dominican monk, Riccardus (Latin)	Riccardus reports the explorations of Friar Julianus. He explored the area traditionally called *Magna Hungaria*, located nearby modern Bashkiria. He found a nomadic population that lived by arms and horses and did not cultivate land, with whom he could communicate in Hungarian. They told him that, according to their oral tradition, the Hungarians of the Carpathians were their descendants.

Basically, there is a body of sources, starting from the 9th/10th century AD, written in different languages. In Arabic sources we find the designations: *majǧir* and *baǧǧir ~ baǰγir* used as variants, as well as *turk*. In Greek sources we find the designations: *hun, ungr, turk, savard*. In Latin sources we find the designations: *[h]ung[r], pannon, avar, hun, turk, agaren*. In Slavic sources we find: *ug(o)r, peon* (Kristó 1996: 57; Imre 1972: 328–9). Although it is unclear whether these many different designations refer to the same population, the mainstream interpretation is that most or all of them refer to the Hungarians. All of these populations are considered as Turkic in the original texts (Gy. Moravcsik 1958; Kristó 1996; Macartney 1930/68). In modern times, it has been identified that the Turkic Bashkir language shares several lexical items, including ethnonyms and toponyms, with Hungarian, most notably the above mentioned self-designations *magyar* (< *majǧir*) and *Bashkir* (< *bajǧir ~ baǰγir*).

2.1.2.2. *Fifth-century sources and their interpretation*

According to textbooks and mainstream interpretations, the first possible mention of the Hungarians in history is in the 5th century, when the Greek historian Priscus Rhetor reports migrations of *On-ogur* tribes in year 463 AD. Hungarian scholars (Hajdú 1972: 29–30; Györffy 1959: 78–9), speculate that this migrating confederation of Turkic tribes included a significant proportion of Hungarian people, because of a possible linguistic connection between the ethnonyms *On-ogur* 'seven tribes' and *Hungarian*, whereby *hungar-* is assumed to be a derivation from *On-ogur*.

The Onogurs ~ Onoγurs were Bulgar (or 'Oghur/Oghuz') Turkic tribes (Golden 1998: 18 and 1990a: 257–8; Johanson 1998: 81). These tribes built a short-lived empire in the north Caucasian region, which was conquered by the Turkic Khazars about the year 650 AD. The Bulgar tribal union was a fusion of several elements, including Hunnic elements. After the disintegration of their empire, the Bulgar Turkic people split into three parts, and, eventually, became extinct together with their language. One group migrated westward, towards modern Bulgaria, where they were completely assimilated by the Slavs, today's Bulgarians. A second group remained in the north Caucasian region, between the river Don and the Sea of Azov, basically in the same areas where Hungarian tribes are supposed to have been. Both this second group of Bulgar Turkic tribes, and the Hungarian tribes (supposedly) came under the supremacy of the Khazars. A third, major group of Bulgar Turkic people migrated north, in the region of the middle Volga, where they founded the Volga Bulgar empire (see below), which was defeated by the Mongols in the 13th century (Golden 1998: 23; Zimonyi 1990).

As we shall see, it is one of the cornerstones of the U paradigm and of Hungarian prehistory that the Hungarians lived in close symbiosis for a long time with On-ogur tribes, starting (at least) from the 5th century. This fundamental assumption is based on the linguistic connection established between the two ethnonyms, as described above. However, there is no way to verify the correctness of such a connection, and, in fact, several other names can and have been associated to *hungar-* in the literature. Compare for example the Bashkir and Russian name *Ungar*, the name *Hunnor* mentioned in the Chronicles as referring to Attila's family tree and the name of the Turkic people *Ujgur*, to mention just a few names (see a complete list of competing associations in Czeglédi 2000). Furthermore, *hungar-* was associated in the past with the toponym *Yugria*, that is 'Ugric ~ Ugrian', as discussed below.

Note that Priscus Rhetor mentions also the names of other tribes who were migrating together with the On-ogurs, and he explains that these tribes were pushed away by the *Savirs*, in turn pushed away by the *Avars* (this is also the first mention of the Avars in the west (Czeglédy 1983: 97). This means that, even supposing that the linguistic connection *On-ogur/hungar-* is correct, there is no evidence that the Hungarians were already entertaining privileged contacts with the On-ogur tribes, rather than with other Turkic tribes.

2.1.2.3. *Ninth/Tenth-century sources and their interpretation*

Latin sources

One of the Latin sources, the *Annales Fuldenses* (in Gombos (ed.) 1937–43: I, 132–3), that is, the Annales of the Monastery of Fulda (Germany), in describing the events of the year 894, 896, 900 AD, talk about the Hungarians and report their presence in the area of the Danube river. The *Annales* consistently identify the Hungarians with the Avars, a nomadic population of Hunnic-Tataric type, originating from Mongolia: 'Avari, qui dicuntur Ungari, in his temporibus ultra Danubium peragrantes multa miserabilia perpetravere'[7] (for more details see, for example, Kristó 1996: 176–7). Note that according to textbooks, the Hungarians occupied the present-day territory in 896 AD (see below).

Arabic sources

The Hungarians' self-appellation *magyar* is reported to appear first in the book by the Arabic geographer Ibn Rusta: *The Book of the Precious Stones*, written around 930 AD, where the form *majγerija* (to use Imre's 1972: 328 transcription) occurs several times. For details of this and other Arabic sources see Macartney (1930/68: 2–19). Ibn Rusta, who is credited as the most reliable of the Arabic sources, explicitly states that: 'The Magyars are a race of Turks . . .' (Macartney 1930/68: 30). His text has also preserved two other famous 'Hungarian' words, which are actually of Turkic (and/or Altaic) origin: *gyula* 'vice-king, a sort of civilian king' (this has become a proper name in Modern Hungarian, *Gyula*), and *kündü* (~ *kende*) 'chief-king', a sort of military king'. According to TESz (II, 441), the precise origin of *kündü* could be from Turkic Khazar. In turn, the Turkic languages are supposed to have received this word from Mongolian: compare Mon. *kündü*, but also Man. *kundule-*, with the same nobility meaning (see also Ligeti 1986:

482; EWUng I, 727). These data are then found again in later Muslim sources.

Although there is the difficulty of the vowels, which are not well specified in Arabic script and therefore have to be reconstructed, the transcription *majɣeríja* of the actual spelling *m.ǧ.ɣ.r-īya* ~ ? *m.ḥ.f.r-īya* (TESz II, 816) is generally accepted. In turn, *majɣeríja* is assumed to correspond to Modern Hun. *magyar*, reconstructed as Old Hun. **mogyër(i)* (UEW 84; Gheno & Hajdú 1992: 15), or **majǧër(i)* (Ligeti 1986: 376). The internal consonant is /d'/, written *gy* in Modern Hungarian.

Ligeti (1986: 376) observes that transcriptions of the type *majɣeríja* are not accurate with regard to the vowel of second syllable -*e*-. In fact, in order for the Arabic forms to correspond to the reconstructed Old Hungarian form with a 'closed -*ë*-', one should adopt the transcription *majǧir* (or *majǧiri*[8]). This transcription is in better agreement with the other variants of this name found in the Arabic sources. According to Ligeti's transcription (1986: 376–7, 396, 400), these variants are as follows:

(a) *majǧir(i)*; **(a1)** *bajǧir(d)* $\longrightarrow$ *bašǧir(d)* *bašǰir(t)* ~ *bašɣir* etc.

In other words, some Arabic sources use the forms in (a1), that is, the name 'Bashkir', as variants of *majǧir*. The initial *m* ~ *b* alternation is a regular one within Turkic (common Turkic *m*- vs Bulgar Turkic, Khazar *b*-), and so is the correspondence of the first consonant of the internal consonant cluster, that is /d'/ vs /š/. This in turn means that the Arabic sources clearly link the *magyars* directly with the Turkic Bashkir[9] population. This link between Hungarian and Bashkir extends to other areas beyond the self-denomination, including proper/ethnic names and toponyms/hydromyms, recurring both in the present-day Hungarian territory and in the Russian/Bashkir territory (see Chapter 9).

Greek sources

The most extensive of the 10th century texts which is reported to deal with the Hungarians is the famous *De Administrando Imperio*, written in Greek, approximately between 947 and 952 AD, by the Byzantine emperor Constantine Porphyrogenitus. More precisely, it is widely reported that Constantine mentions the name *magyar*, by this referring to what has now become the nation of the Hungarians/*magyars*. However, this is not quite the true story, since the emperor never actually mentions the name *magyar*; he mentions instead the name Μεγέρη. The structure of the text suggests that he is referring to the name of a clan leader, but it is widely interpreted that he was referring to the ancestors of the *magyars*. This is because a linguistic connection has been made between the term Μεγέρη and the modern term *magyar*, even though these names are not regular correspondences.[10] The details of this linguistic connection, as well as the chain of interlocking (historical and linguistic) assumptions associated with it, will be discussed in Chapter 9.

In describing the events and the way of life of the 'nation of the Turks' ('*Τούρχων ἔθνος*'; Chapters 38–40), Constantine mentions, for example, that they consist of seven (subsequently eight) clans, and that they do not have a clear overall political authority. He also documents language contact between these clans: in Chapter 39 he says that the Turks learnt the language of the Khazar clan from the Kabar clan who had moved into their area.

At the beginning of Chapter 40, entitled 'Of the clans of the Kabaroi and the Turks', the emperor makes a list of Turkic clans, and the third clan in his list is named '*Μεγέρη*'. As mentioned, this name is interpreted as referring to the ancestors of the Hungarians; its regular Hungarian reading is assumed to be *Megyeri* (Németh 1930/91: 245), or *Med'eri* (Gy. Moravcsik 1958: 186). Here is the relevant text using Jenkins' translation (Moravcsik & Jenkins 1949: 175): 'The first is this aforesaid clan of the *Kabaroi* which split off from the Chazars; the second, of *Nekis*; the third of *Megeris*, the fourth, of *Kourtou-germatos*;[11] the fifth, of *Tarianos*; the sixth, *Genach*; the seventh, *Kari*, the eighth, *Kasi*'. As is evident, the name *Μεγέρη* (like most clan names) appears in the genitive construction: '*τρίτη τοῦ Μεγέρη*'. Regarding this passage, Gy. Moravcsik (in Jenkins (ed.), 1962: 150) comments as follows:

> The text gives the impression that these names appearing in the genitive case (. . .) are forms of personal names (. . .); but there is no doubt that it is the Hungarian tribal names that are given. The construction in all probability corresponds to the Old Hungarian mode of expression

Moravcsik does not explain why 'there is no doubt' about the fact that the 'Hungarian tribal names' would be indicated here, neither, to the best of my knowledge, is there any evidence of that particular construction being an 'Old Hungarian mode of expression'. Soon after, Moravcsik remarks that two of these clan names are of F-U origin, *Νέκη*/*Nekis*, to be identified with the Hungarian proper name *Nyék* (Németh 1930/91: 24), and *Μεγέρη*/ *Megyeri*, to be identified with the Hungarians' self-denomination *magyar*, whilst all the other clan names are of Turkic origin. The author does not justify his statement about the F-U origin of *Νέκη* and *Μεγέρη* either here, or in his *Byzantinoturcica* (1958), but he refers to other authors' explanations and etymologies, including Gy. Németh's[12] etymologies (1930/91: 233–1).

Indeed, Moravcsik' analysis and statement reflect the widely accepted claim that all the Old Hungarian clan names (as listed by Constantine) are of Turkic origin, with the notable exception of *Μεγέρη*/*Megyeri*/*magyar* (and, possibly, *Νέκη*/*Nyék*), which is instead of U origin. In turn, the U (specific- ally Ugric) origin of at least *Μεγέρη*/*Megyeri*/*magyar* is widely cited as constituting evidence in support of the U origin of the Hungarians, even though this appears to be contradicted by the Turkic origin of all the other Hungarian clan names. This conventional analysis has been re-affirmed in a recent paper by Berta (1989/91), although the author (1989/91: 26–7), following Ligeti (1986), remarks that the 'standard' U etymology of Μεγέρη/ *magyar* presents serious difficulties.

The issue of the presumed U origin of *magyar* and of the Turkic origin of the other Hungarian clan names will be dealt with in detail in Chapter 9.

2.1.2.4. *Medieval sources and their interpretation*

The first Hungarian text
The first Hungarian text, a translation from Latin of a funeral oration, appears in the 12th century. This shows several elements of language in formation, including Case endings and postpositions (see Chapter 8).

The Latin sources
The next mention of the Hungarian people is found in medieval Chronicles and other texts. These consistently point to an 'eastern' origin for the Hungarians, by linking them to the Scythians, who supposedly used to occupy a wide Eurasiatic area, and to the Huns (K. László 1998; Sherwood 1996). The most important texts are reported below.

The Chronicle *Anonymus Gesta Hungarorum*
This Chronicle, generally known as *Anonymus*,[13] was written circa 1200 (Szentpétery et al. (eds) 1937–8: I, 33–119). It reports the denomination *Mogerii*, interpreted as Hun. *magyeri* (Ligeti 1986: 400). The anonymous author states that the Hungarians, of Scythian origin, call themselves, in their own language, *Mogerii* (~ *Mogerij*): '. . . populus de terra Scithica[14] egressus per ydioma alienigenarum *Hungarii* et in sua lingua propria *Mogerii* vocantur' (Szentpétery et al. (eds) 1937–8: I, 33). This seems to be the first explicit, clear association of the two designations *hungar-* and *magyar*. The text also talks about seven peoples/tribes: 'VII principales persone, que *Hetumoger*[15] vocantur', and of their previous home land, *Ungaria maior*, generally referred to in the literature as *Magna Hungaria* (see also TESz II, 816 and discussion below).

The Chronicle *Gesta Hungarorum*
This Chronicle was written by Simon Kézai between 1282 and 1285 (Szentpétery et al. (eds) 1937–8: I, 129–4; see also Györffy (ed.) 1986: 183–4). It establishes a complete identity between the Hungarians and the Huns: '*Huni sive Hungari*'.[16] The author of the Chronicle, before giving the history of the Hungarians, provides that of the Huns. The idea of a Hungarian/Hun connection is found already in *Anonymus* (Imre 1972: 332; Fodor 1975c: 30) and in other western, Latin texts (Györffy 1948: 130).

The other intriguing bit of information provided by Kézai is the following: the 'Scythian homeland' of the Hungarians/Huns is divided into three smaller kingdoms, one of which is called *Barsatiam* (Szentpétery et al. (eds) 1937–8: I,146). This term has been identified by some scholars with the term 'Bashkiria'. For example Vásáry (1985/7: 206) states that *Barsatiam* 'evidently refers to Bashkiria'. Vásáry also points out that the emergence of Bashkiria as the 'primordial' homeland of the Hungarians is found in other 13th century western sources (in addition to some Hungarian Chronicles and the 10th century Arabic sources), such as the reports by Franciscan travellers. For example, one of these travellers, Rubruck, says: '*Pascatur*, que est *maior Hungaria*; De illa regione *Pascatur* exierunt *Huni* qui postea *Hungari*, unde est ipsa *maior Hungaria*' (Van den Wyngaert (ed.) 1929: 181, 219; see also Ligeti 1986: 396).

Report by Friar Riccardus

In 1235 Friar Julianus, together with other colleagues, embarked on a journey to the east, in search of those Hungarians who, according to Chronicles' tradition, had remained behind in their earlier homeland *Magna Hungaria*. The expedition was financed by Prince Béla (1235–70, the future King Béla IV), and the purpose was to convert them to Christianity.

Hungarian-speaking people were actually found by the travellers, and found in a district of the Volga Bulgar territory, along the Volga river, in an area nearby modern Bashkiria (both the Bashkirs and the Hungarians were under the supremacy of the Volga Bulgars at the time). The report about this expedition was written by Julianus' superior, Friar Riccardus (Szentpétery et al. (eds) 1937–8: II, 536–9; Bendefy (ed.) 1937: 24f.). Here is the part of the text where the 'eastern' ('keleti') Hungarians, to use Fodor's terminology (1975c: 60), are shown to understand the language of the 'western' Hungarians, and talk about their connections (Szentpétery et al. (eds) 1937–8: II, 539):

[The eastern Hungarians] diligentissime audiebant, quia omnino habent Ungaricum ydioma, et intelligebant eum, et ipse [Friar Julianus] eos . . . Sciunt enim per relationes antiquorum, quod isti Ungari [the western ones] ab ipsis descenderant; sed ubi essent, ignorabant.

It is generally stated that this report is genuine; in other words, there does not seem to be any evidence that the text was manipulated at the time.

The information provided by these Chronicles and reports again suggests an eastern origin for the Hungarians. In particular, the report of Friar Riccardus, which has become one of the most debated issues of Hungarian prehistory, lends further support to the close relationship between the magyars and the Bashkirs, a relationship that had already been identified through the common origin of their respective self-denominations. The other major problem is that of the easy communicability between the 'eastern' and the 'western' Hungarians. In fact, although it is not possible to establish exactly when the Hungarians moved in and out of *Magna Hungaria*, it is generally assumed that they had been living in the north Caucasian region since about the 5th/7th centuries, if not earlier (see below), before moving westward. How then could they have been able to communicate with the small group of magyars left behind in *Magna Hungaria* in the year 1235, after centuries of separation, and at a distance of about 2,000 kilometres? This issue has given rise to many interpretations and speculations, such as those by Fodor (1975a, 1975b, 1982), Györffy (1948) and Gy. László (1970, 1978, 1988, 1990). Some of these interpretations and speculations will be reported below, as part of the summary of the Hungarian prehistory.

2.1.2.5. *Interpretations between the 15th and early 19th centuries*

Between the 15th and 17th centuries, a belief arose that Hungarian is closely related to Vogul and Ostyak, that is, the 'Ugric' people. According to Kálmán (1988: 395), this belief was based on a coincidence rather than on scientific evidence. The words *Ugra*, *Yugra* or *Yugria* (hence 'Ugric ~ Ugrian') were first mentioned in Russian sources from the 15th century; by this name the sources referred to the Vogul and Ostyak area in the Ural mountains. Apparently because of the similarity of the Latin word *hungar-us* with the Russian word *Yugria* etc., the presumption was that the eastern ancestral home of the Hungarians (as indicated by the Chronicles) could be identified with the *Yugria* area (see also Zsirai 1937: 484). In other words, the belief arose that those Hungarians who had remained behind in their eastern homeland were the *Ugrians ~ Yugrians*, whilst those who migrated came to be known as the *Hungari ~ Ungarn* etc. This belief took strong hold, and was reinforced by the discovery, in the 19th century, that some of the people living in the Yugrian area called themselves *Mansi*, a name which, to the lay ear, resembles *magyar* (see Chapter 9 for the etymological connection).

Notice that according Hajdú (1972: 29–30), the separation of the Hungarians from the Vogul and Ostyak people can be dated about the 5th century BC. This being the case, and supposing that the derivation *On-ogur* > *Hungarian* is correct, about 1,000 years (and even more, according to other estimates) would have elapsed before the Hungarians made their first appearance in history. Hajdú refers to this long period as an 'obscure' one, because there are absolutely no traces of the Hungarians and their presumed migration from their 'Ugric homeland' (wherever it might have been) towards the west.

Between the 17th and the beginning of the 19th centuries, there were several attempts to identify correlations between Hungarian and other languages of northern Europe, including the one by the German philosopher G. W. Leibniz, the Swedish army officer P. J. von Strahlenberg, and the German historian A. L. von Schlözer (Zsirai 1951: 6–14). Among the relevant works, one may quote: the manuscript by M. Fögel: *De Fennicae linguae indole observationes* (Hamburg 1669), where the author tried to demonstrate the affinity of the Finnish language with Hungarian and Lapp; the publication in 1770 by the Hungarian Jesuit J. Sajnovics, who attempted to show that Hungarian is related to Lapp (*Demonstratio idioma Ungarorum et Lapponum idem esse*; Copenhagen; reprinted in 1967 by Indiana University, Uralic and Altaic Series 91); the publication in 1799 of the work by

S. Gyarmathi, identifying much wider correlations with what is now called the U area (*Affinitas linguae Hungaricae cum linguis Fennicae originis grammatice demonstrata*; Göttingen; reprinted in 1968 by Indiana University, Uralic and Altaic Series 95 ; see also Hanzeli 1983); and the works by Castrén, who also studied at length the Samoyed languages (Castrén 1854) and first proposed the traditional division of the U languages into the two major sub-branches: the Samoyed languages and all the rest of them (see below).

By the beginning of the 19th century, there was thus already a body of research which considered the languages of north-eastern Europe, Hungarian, and, occasionally, Samoyed, as forming a family, even before the emerging of the Comparative Method and its application to the Indo-European languages in 1816 (Pedersen 1931). Notice however, that Sajnovics, Gyarmathi, Castrén, and the like also believed that these languages were in turn part of a wider Asiatic family. On the other hand, the Turkic/Hungarian connection was kept alive, as demonstrated by the following work by J. Deguignes: *Histoire générale des Huns, des Turcs, des Mogols et des autres Tartares occidentaux* (Paris 1756–8). The author, basing his analysis on the testimony of Arabic and Chinese sources, connects the name *hungarus* with the Turkic tribe name *Igur ~ Ujgur*, and considers the Hungarians for sure as western Turks.[17]

2.1.2.6. The textbook interpretation of the prehistory of the Hungarians

Between the end of the 19th century and the beginning of the 20th century, following the trend of research of the previous two centuries, several influential scholars argued that there was indeed enough evidence to establish the F-U and the U nodes, that is, the U language family. In this context, Hungarian was believed to belong to this newly established group, and the Hungarian people to be of U origin. As a consequence, basically all the Turkic elements contained in the language had to be re-interpreted as borrowed.

The emergence of the F-U/U paradigm will be dealt with in detail in the following sections. In this section, I shall report how the information provided by the historical sources about the 'Turkic' origin of the Hungarians has been re-interpreted in the light of this new paradigm. In other words, I shall outline the generally accepted reconstruction of the origin and prehistory of the Hungarian nation (see among the many publications on this topic, for example: Ligeti (ed.) 1943; Sinor 1958; Németh 1966b; Bartha 1988; Rédei 1998: 28–9, 57; Fodor 1977: 81; Dienes 1972: 7; Székely (ed.) 1984; Bartha, Czeglédy & Róna-Tas (eds) 1977; Benkő 1984; Hajdú 1976; Golden 1990b: 242–8). There are several, competing variants of this reconstruction, some of them contradictory, and the following is an attempt to make sense, in few lines, of a story (and its interpretations) that is rather unclear.[18]

At some time in unrecorded history, the ancestors of the Hungarians, after separating from the P-Ugric community, moved further south from the original Ugric homeland, which was located in the Volga-Kama region, on the western side of the Ural mountains. The Hungarians' first homeland was located in the territory traditionally called *Magna Hungaria* (their 'eastern' homeland), along the middle Volga river, in an area believed to be somewhere near present-day Bashkiria. The Hungarians are assumed to have lived, from the 5th century or earlier, together with the *On-ogur* confederation of Bulgar Turkic tribes, who were present in the area at the time. The name *Hungarian* is assumed to be derived from the Turkic term *On-ogur* (although there are other possible parallels), but the populations and languages are supposed to have remained separate.

At some time between the middle of the 5th century and about 800, the Hungarians moved to a region north of the Black Sea, between the Don, Dnepr and Kuban rivers. This region was close to the area occupied by the Turkic Khazars, and was also inhabited by the Bulgar Turkic tribes (those tribes that had not migrated westwards or northwards). Two particular areas within this region are mentioned: the one called *Levedia* (~ *Lebedia*), and the one called *Etelköz* (*De Administrando Imperio*, Chapter 38). From about this time, the Hungarians (as well the Bulgar Turkic tribes living in the region), came under the influence and power of the Western Turkic Khazars, whose empire, built around 570 AD, covered a vast north Caucasian area, up to the lower Volga.

The Hungarians remained in the north Caucasian area until the 9th century (traditionally until 889), when they were pushed out by other Turkic tribes. They began a migration which eventually brought them many kilometres westward to what is now Hungary. The conquest of the present-day Hungarian territory (called *honfoglalás* 'home conquest/occupation') is traditionally dated in the year 896 AD, and was accomplished under the leadership of the chief Árpád.

At around this time, a Turkic tribe (of Kipchak type) moved into the area vacated by the Hungarians. Presumably because of the confusion that arose, this Turkic tribe came to be called by the same name as the Hungarians, but in the Turkic variant *bajǧir(d)* ⟶ *bašɣir*, that is 'Bashkir'. It is not clear, however, how this Turkic tribe also adopted a significant number of Hungarian proper names (as discussed in Chapter 9). This tribe subsequently migrated to the area of the middle Volga river (nearby the *Magna Hungaria* homeland), and is now identified with the Bashkir population.

All in all, according to this reconstruction, contacts between the Hungarian and (mainly) Bulgar Turkic tribes are traditionally estimated to have lasted about 300–400 years – this assumption is claimed to be confirmed by the text *De Administrando Imperio*, as discussed below (Section 2.4.1). During this long period of co-habitation, the Hungarians and the Turks are held to have shared the same way of life, including economic, social and military organisation. Nevertheless, the Hungarians are supposed to have maintained intact their original U language and identity (Hajdú 1972; Györffy 1975a, 1975b, 1990; Di Cave 1995; Macartney 1930/68; Imre 1972: 328). As is perhaps obvious (and confirmed by modern studies of languages in contact), it is highly unlikely that a minority group like this with no specific differentiator (such as religious, military or political) would be able to maintain its language and identity in these circumstances. However, this fact goes generally unremarked in the Uralic literature, so that a reader may be left with a false impression that this is an uncontroversial process.

Gy. László, through a number of works (see for example 1970, 1988, 1990) has proposed a major modification to the above-outlined reconstruction, which would account for some of the unsolved problems and contradictions of Hungarian prehistory (a modification supported also by several, relevant archaeological findings (László 1978)). According to the author, a significant portion of Hungarians reached the present-day territory about two centuries earlier than the 'official' conquest on behalf of the 'Árpád people'. It is the so-called thesis of the '*kettős honfoglalás*', 'double home conquest' (1970: 161f.). Still according to the author, this thesis explains why in the Latin sources the Hungarians are clearly identified with the Avars and the Huns (see Sections 2.1.2.3, 2.1.2.4 above), as well as why there are shared Avar/Hungarian toponyms. The explanation goes as follows (greatly simplified): (a) it is known from contemporary sources that the Avars[19] were present in the Carpathian Basin, terrifying the locals with their raids, round about the 670s (Czeglédy 1983: 34f.); (b) a massive group of Hungarians left their original home *Magna Hungaria* to follow the Avar people who migrated westwards and eventually reached the Carpathian Basin; these Hungarians can be considered as 'Proto-Hungarians'; (c) these Hungarians survived the (partial ?) destruction of the Avars and were joined later on by the Árpád people. It is this first Hungarian group, whose language had not been under such a heavy Turkic influence (like that of the Hungarians who migrated later on), who ensured the linguistic and ethnic continuity with the Hungarians left behind in their eastern homeland, even beyond the conquest of the Árpád people.

László's thesis has been often criticised (see, for example, Rédei 1998: 31), although the following is generally recognised: (a) the Hungarians reached their present-day territory through more than one single migratory wave (as also testified by the *Annales Fuldenses*); (b) they settled in this territory together with other nomadic tribes (Turkic, Mongolian, Iranian and others); (c) the Avars had already occupied the present-day Hungarian territory, together with some of their subject tribes, before the arrival of the Árpád people (Czeglédy 1983; Kiszely 1979; Golden 1998: 18; Niskanen 2000: 44). Before the Avars, the Huns had settled in Pannonia (see Note 6). These facts are indeed consistently supported by the historical, archaeological and even anthropological records (Lipták[20] 1975b and 1977: 39), and by the presence of Avar toponyms in the northern and north-eastern part of the Carpathian Basin (Kristó 1996: 180). The situation has been summarised by Halasi-Kun (1986/8: 31) and Róna-Tas (1988b: 134) respectively, as follows:

> As established by linguists of the nineteenth century, Hungarian is without doubt a Finno-Ugric language. Nevertheless, from the point of view of character, social structure, culture and tradition, Conquest-time Hungarians had shown all the features of a Turkic people

> Tenth-century Hungarians were a conglomerate of people speaking a Finno-Ugric language while following Turkic traditions (my translation)

2.2. THE ORIGIN OF THE FINNO-UGRIC NODE: THE 'UGRIC-TURKIC BATTLE'

2.2.1. *History*

In the late 19th century there were two competing interpretations of the origin of the Hungarians. On the one hand, there was the belief in a Turkic origin, as suggested by the historical sources and the tradition of the Chronicles. On the other hand, there were the various publications that identified linguistic correlations between Hungarian and the languages of north-eastern Europe. The scene was now set for an important linguistic battle: the debate centred on whether the Hungarians hailed from the Turkic area or from elsewhere, the Ugric and possibly the Finnic areas. This debate was called the 'Ugric-Turkic battle' (*'ugor-török háború'*). The leading figures in the Battle were Á. Vámbéry and J. Budenz.[21] Vámbéry at first published linguistic evidence in support of the 'mixed' character, Turkic and Ugric, of Hungarian. He argued that the Hungarian/Turkic relationship is of 'secondary nature', basically the result of *'összeolvadás'* ('fusion'), whilst the Ugric/Hungarian relationship is of 'primary nature'. Later on, in response to heavy criticism, the author strongly argued in favour of the pure Turkic origin of the Hungarian language and people.[22] In contrast, J. Budenz believed that languages can only have one single parent, in line with the dominant belief of the time. Therefore, he argued that Hungarian had to be classified purely and simply as 'Ugric'.

Leaving to the next sections the discussion of the evidence put forward by Budenz to prove the Ugric origin of Hungarian, it suffices here to highlight the following points, which will help to place this 'battle' into the appropriate context.

In 1869 Vámbéry published an alphabetical list of words similar in Hungarian and Turkic; this list includes basic vocabulary (123 items). The work identified similarities between the words in the two languages, but did not examine whether consistent sound-rules were involved. Furthermore, associations of meanings were often rather elastic. For example, the author associated the Hungarian term for 'seed of (any) fruit' with the Turkic term for 'verruca, mole' (1869: 131). These facts were and still are regarded, correctly, as major weak points of his work, and led to universal criticism and rejection of his data. Budenz (1871–3) too rejected Vámbéry's analysis. In order to prove that Hungarian belonged to the Ugric (read Finno-Ugric) language group, he closely analysed Vámbéry's Hungarian/Turkic 'correspondences'. He argued that the great majority of them – but not all – were wrong, mainly because the Comparative Method was not applied.

Budenz was recognised as the victor of the Ugric-Turkic battle, and the F-U family was held to be scientifically and definitively established. Budenz was the victor mainly because he laid greater claim to scientific credibility. He argued that the only way to sort out the complex matter of the genetic relationship of the 'Altaic' languages was to apply the then recently introduced Comparative Method. He himself attempted to do so in his works, as systematically and accurately as he possibly could at the time. It is generally believed that Budenz' etymological corpus is of very good quality. For example, Gy. Décsy, in his introduction to Budenz' reprinted MUSz dictionary (1966: 2–3) states the following:

> By finally proving the Finno-Ugric origin of Hungarian, Budenz established the specific number of languages in the Finno-Ugric group. He did this in a form that required no alteration thereafter. This is why he must be regarded as the founder of modern Finno-Ugric comparative linguistics. . . . A large percentage of the materials of the dictionary and the etymological explanations given by Budenz therein are not yet outdated

However, this statement does not correspond to reality, as indeed observed by a few researchers (such as Pusztay[23] 1977: 107). Despite his programmatic intentions and his best efforts, Budenz' comparative corpus (that is, his Hungarian/Ugric correspondences) is of very poor quality, and his word associations often suffer from the same stretching of meaning of which Vámbéry was guilty, as will be shown below.

Budenz' views are often misreported in modern literature. In his works Budenz is very clear that there are a certain number of correct Hungarian/ Turkic correspondences in Vámbéry's list, most of which are to be interpreted as indicative of genetic relations. Budenz is often misquoted, either as if he claimed there are no correct correspondences at all, or as if he claimed that all the correct correspondences are due only to borrowing. For example, Róna-Tas (1978a: 263–4) states that:

> J. Budenz and other scholars offered scientific arguments in favour of the Finno-Ugrian origin of the Hungarian language. They insisted that the Turkish[24] elements in the Hungarian language are loan-words from several periods.

For the correct interpretation see however Räsänen[25] (1963/4: 184).

Budenz did not even attempt to reconstruct the F-U node and those other intermediate nodes which represent a cornerstone of the modern family tree, and whose validity will be questioned in Chapter 4 (although occasionally he also mentions a 'Finno-Ugric' node, for example in his article of 1869 and 1870). In fact, Budenz (1871–3, 1878/9) generally referred to a 'Ugric' branch. By this he meant that the Ugric branch (of the Altaic family) was not divided into sub-groups or sub-nodes, but directly into main languages ('Hauptsprachen'). More precisely, in Budenz (1878/9: 196) the Ugric languages were divided into two major groups: (a) 'North-Ugric', which includes: Lapp, Permian (Zyrian and Votyak), Ob-Ugric (Vogul and Ostyak) and Hungarian; (b) 'South-Ugric', which includes Balto-Finnic, Mordvin and Cheremis. This division is motivated by the distribution of initial ń- (North-Ugric) vs n- (South-Ugric).

2.2.2. Linguistic analysis of Budenz' original data

2.2.2.1. Introduction

Before entering into the details of Budenz' data, it is worth reporting a few original quotes in support of the remark made above, that Budenz' views have been generally misreported in the literature. These quotes are from his article of 1869 and 1870 (an article split into two parts): *A magyar és finn-ugor nyelvekbeli szóegyezések* 'Hungarian and Finno-Ugric lexical correspondences'. In this article, Budenz argues strongly in favour of the necessity of applying the Comparative Method both within the Altaic and the Ugric (F-U) language groups.

The first relevant quote is as follows (translations are mine):

A nagy altaji nyelvcsaládot egyes nyelvcsoportok teszik : 1) mongol-mandsu-török ; 2) finn-ugor ; 3) szamojed, melyek a szóalakulás jelle-mére, a származott szók és viszonyított nyelvalakok miképen való képzésére, s a szók összeszerkesztésének néhány fővonásaira nézve egymással egyezőknek mutatkoznak (1869: 375)
The wide Altaic language group is formed by various individual groups: 1) Mongol-Manchu-Turkic; 2) Finno-Ugric; 3) Samoyed. These groups, judging from the nature of the development of the words, the formation of the derived words and the compared language forms, as well as some general tendencies of assembling the words, show similarities with each other.

Here is the second quote:

Azonban tény az is, hogy az egyes altaji nyelvcsoportok között mégis több-kevesebb és többé-kevésbé föltünő [sic] szóegyezések mutatkoznak. De ezek nem mind az őseredeti rokonság nyomainak tekinthetők.

Ellenkezőleg közülök épen a hangalakìlag [sic] legtökéletesebb szóegyezések többnyire olyanok, melyek nem őseredeti rokonságnál fogva, hanem későbbi kölcsönvétel folytán keletkeztek (1869: 376)
However, it is also a fact that even within the individual Altaic language groups there are more or less remarkable word correspondences. But these are not all to be regarded as remnants of the old, original genetic relationship. On the contrary, among them, especially those showing the most complete sound-correspondences, in the majority of the cases, there are such words that arose not as a result of genetic relationship, but as a result of later borrowings

Nevertheless, Budenz admits, there are striking correspondences shared by the Altaic (but not other) language groups, some of which can hardly be explained through chance, ('véletlen történetességből' (1869: 375)), or through borrowing, ('bajosan kölcsönvételnek' (ibid.)). Therefore, the author concludes, one can only assume that 'also the individual Altaic language groups did form at some point in time a unitary language' ('az egyes altaji nyelvcsoportok is valamikor egy egységes nyelvet képeztek' (ibid.)).

Budenz carries on claiming that Altaic linguistics has the important task first of discriminating the possible loan-words from the real cognates, and, second, of establishing the various sub-groups. One might wonder at this point which criteria could form the basis of this discrimination, especially in those cases where 'the most complete sound-correspondences' are encountered. I shall come back to this issue in Chapter 6.

Finally, Budenz also admits that, despite the effort to apply rigorous, objective criteria, a great deal of subjectivity is quite often involved in the process of word comparison (1869: 381).

To conclude this excursus, notice that, despite the title and the programmatic commitment to the methods of comparative linguistics, no description, no mention is made in this paper of sound-laws and sound-changes.

2.2.2.2. The original data

In 1871–3 Budenz wrote the article titled: *Jelentés Vámbéry Á. magyar-török szóegyezéseiről*, 'Report on the Hungarian-Turkic word correspondences by Á Vámbéry', in response to the article by Vámbéry of 1869: *Magyar és török-tatár szóegyezések* 'The Hungarian and Turkic-Tatar word correspondences'. As mentioned, Budenz argued that the great majority, but not all, of Vámbéry's Hungarian/Turkic correspondences were wrong. He divided them into four classes (1871–3: 75):

- **Class I** contains 'correct correspondences'. They can be considered testimony either of 'original, genetic relationship', or of 'borrowing' from Turkic.[26]
- **Class II** contains correspondences which look good at first, but are incorrect ('látszatos egyezések', 'apparent correspondences').

- **Class III** contains correspondences which are clearly wrong ('helytelen egyezések', 'incorrect correspondences').
- **Class IV** contains irrelevant correspondences (clear recent borrowing, or onomatopoeic, or irrelevant for other reasons).

For each of the incorrect Hungarian/Turkic parallels as listed in Classes II and III, Budenz proposed an alternative parallel from one or the other Finnic and/or Ugric languages, intending to prove, on the basis of phonological and semantic criteria, that the Hungarian/Ugric parallels, and not the Hungarian/Turkic parallels, were correct. This list of etymologies also formed the basis of his future dictionary: *Magyar-ugor összehasonlító szótár* (MUSz).

If one examines all the core-Lexicon parallels listed in the Classes I–III, totalling 123 items, the following picture emerges (from Marcantonio, Nummenaho and Salvagni 2001;[27] see also Salvagni 1999):

(**a**) the 'correct' parallels (Class I) amount to 42 items. Of these 42 parallels, the majority (34) are considered by Budenz as indicative of old, genetic relationship ('ősrokonság') between Hungarian and Turkic, whilst only 8 are considered as the result of borrowing. This is of course a significant result, and one hardly ever reported in the literature. The other interesting element here is that there do not seem to be any clear criteria (or at least, they are not always specified) on the basis of which Budenz makes his judgement as to whether these 'correct correspondences' are to be interpreted as cognates or loan-words. Budenz himself seems to recognise this fact by marking with a question mark one or the other sub-classification.

(**b**) the 'incorrect' parallels (Class II and III) form the remaining 81 items, for which a 'correct' Hungarian/Ugric alternative is proposed by Budenz. However, as already mentioned, this Hungarian/Ugric comparative corpus is of very poor quality, as illustrated by the graphs reported in Figure 2.1 below. These graphs, obtained by comparing Budenz' corpus with the modern U dictionary UEW, show the rate of agreement between Budenz' vs UEW classification of the 123 parallels under discussion (actually 119 parallels, because of the existence of a few duplets). In particular, the first graph represents Budenz' own classification of the 119 parallels; the second graph represents the UEW classification of Budenz' parallels; the third graph reports the level of 'agreement' between UEW and Budenz' classification of these parallels. The classification 'Uralic+' means that the parallels in question, according to UEW, are also found beyond the U area (from Marcantonio, Nummenaho & Salvagni 2001: 92–3):

In summary, the percentage of the 'pure U' etymologies for which there is agreement between the two sources is 19% only. This is the case despite the

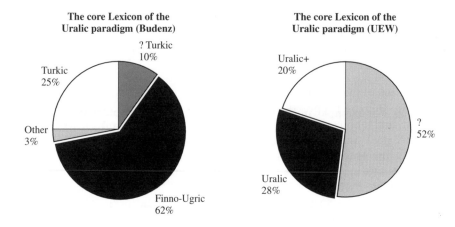

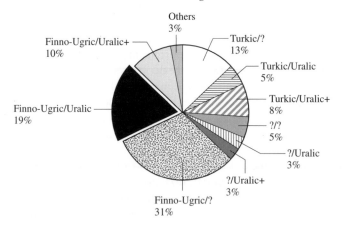

Figure 2.1 Analysis of Budenz' core Lexicon

fact that the phonological and semantic criteria adopted by UEW to establish its etymologies are, in turn, rather lax, as shown in Chapter 5.

In addition to this, there are other weaknesses in Budenz' corpus. Firstly, Budenz' choice of the single Finnic and/or Ugric parallel may be wrong, even if the overall proposed etymology appears to be correct. For example, Budenz connects Hun. *boka* 'ankle' to Finn. *pahka* 'gnarl, protuberance, node', and Mor. E. *pov, povka* 'button, knob' (MUSz 460). However, Hun. *boka* is not listed in UEW and is considered of old Turkic origin in TESz I, 327. On the other hand, Finn. *pahka,* according to UEW 350, is connected to Mor. M. *pakš* (< P-U *paFkša*). Hun. *orr* 'nose' is connected by Budenz to Finn. *turpa* 'muzzle'/Mor. *turva* 'lip'/Zyr. *tȋrp*/Ost. *torȋp* (MUSz 842).

According to UEW 801, the Finnish, Mordvin and Zyrian etymologies are sound, but the presumed Hungarian and Ostyak correspondences are wrong, the etymology being classified only as Finno-Permian.

Secondly, the meaning of a given etymology may often be stretched beyond any common sense in order to establish a connection between Hungarian and another Ugric language, or, conversely, to reject a Hungarian/Turkic parallel. For example, in (2.1) below, Budenz rejects the connection between similar words in Hungarian and Turkic for 'navel', also on the grounds that the semantic match is not present in all the Turkic dialects. Instead he makes an improbable semantic connection between the Hungarian term for 'navel' with the U term for 'tongue', 'dumb' or 'rope':

(2.1) a. according to Vámbéry (1869: 161), Hun. *köldök, kŏdök*[28] 'navel' correspond to Cha. *köndük*/Tur. *köbek, göbek* 'navel'

b. according to Budenz (1871–3: 104), *köldök* belongs to Class II, that is, the Hungarian/Turkic connection is wrong. This is because Tur. *göbek* does not agree with the Hungarian form. The form in -*l* is Ugric. Notice however that no explanation is given as to why the form in -*l* should be Ugric

c. according to Budenz (MUSz 41–2), *köldök* is to be connected with Lapp *kiäldak* '*chorda, fides, nervus*'/Finn. *kieli* 'tongue, language'/ Mor. *käl* 'tongue, language'/Vog. *kaĺ* 'dumb, mute, speechless' etc. This is because the real meaning of the Finnish word is held to be 'thin dangling body' ('fityegő vékony test'), as testified by the Finnish phrase *kello-n kieli* 'bell-of tongue, tongue of bell'. Similarly, the Hungarian word would not really mean 'navel', but 'navel cord' ('nabels schnur')

d. *köldök* is not listed in UEW

However, Finn. *kieli* 'tongue'[29] derives from a totally different root, reconstructed as U *kele (*kēle) by UEW 144, whilst Hun. *köldök* is today considered to have been borrowed from Turkic *kin-dik* (Róna-Tas (1988a: 744); see below Section 6.2.2 and example (6.3)). The other interesting aspect to note here is that Budenz is aware of the existence of similar words in meaning and sound between Tatar (*kündük, kindik*) and Hungarian, nevertheless he simply states that one cannot 'call into question the Ugric nature of the word' just because of this similarity.

In example (2.2), Budenz rejects the connection between the Hungarian and Turkic words for 'hair', on the grounds that the former relates to the hair of the head and the latter to the hair of the body. Instead, he connects the Hungarian term for 'hair of the head' with Ugric words meaning variously 'hair', 'fibre' or 'horsehair'.

(2.2) a. according to Vámbéry (1869: 149) Hun. *haj* 'hair (of head)' is to be connected to Cha. *kil*/Tur. *kịl*, with the same meaning.

b. according to Budenz (1871–3: 118), *haj* belongs to Class III; it cannot be connected to the Turkic forms, because their meaning is 'hair of body'
c. according to Budenz (MUSz 129), *haj* is to be connected to Vot. and Zyr. *si* 'hair (of head), fibre'/Finn. *hiukset* 'hair (of head)'
d. according to UEW 854, the Hungarian term derives from the Ugric form **kajɜ*, to be connected to Vog. χōj, kōj

It is now recognised that Finn. *hiukset* is not connected to Hun. *haj*; actually, the Finnish word does not seem to be connected to any other word within U (apart from Balto-Finnic). Furthermore, Vot. and Zyr. *si* derive from a totally different root, reconstructed as U **sije* (**süje*), which means 'annual ring of a tree, fibre', and which is connected to Finn. *syy*, of the same meaning (UEW 443).

To conclude this analysis of Budenz' data, it is worth reporting his original words regarding how to interpret the question of the 'ősrokonság', that is, 'the original genetic relationship'. Budenz (1871–3: 69) states the following:

> Ilyen magyar szók, melyek nem tekinthetők kölcsönvetteknek, hanem 'közös altaji (ugor-török) rokonságra' mutatnak, nem képezhetik ennélfogva egy különösebb magyar-török valódi rokonság bizonyítékait . . . Ehhez képest pedig az ilyen magyar-török szóegyezések szorosan véve csak az ugor (finn-ugor) és a török nyelvcsoportok közt fennálló ős-rokonsági viszony tárgyalásának szolgálnak anyagúl
>
> The Hungarian words [classified in Class I], which are not to be regarded as the result of borrowing, but which indicate a 'common Altaic (Ugric-Turkic) relationship', cannot be taken as proof of a privileged, closer, direct relationship between Hungarian and Turkic . . . Instead, these Hungarian-Turkic correspondences are to be considered as the basic material for dealing with the topic of the original genetic relationship existing between the two linguistic groups, the Ugric (Finno-Ugric) one and the Turkic one

2.3. THE ORIGIN OF THE URALIC NODE

2.3.1. *History*

In 1879/80 O. Donner criticised Budenz' method and resulting tree, particularly because it seemed inappropriate to build an entire family tree on the basis of one sound-change only (palatal vs non-palatal *n*-). Donner proposed a family tree which, unlike Budenz' tree, exhibits the F-U node, although no reconstruction of its sound-structure is provided (see also Donner 1874–88). This node split into: Ugric (Vogul, Ostyak and Hungarian) and Finnic. The Finnic node in turn consisted of Finno-Lappic ('finnisch-lappisch'), Mordvin and Cheremis ('Wolga Sprachen') and the

Permian languages ('permisch'). This is, basically, the conventional family tree.

In support of the more complex stratification of his tree Donner (1879/80: 49) used essentially morphological features, rather than phonological features. This is because, in his opinion, sound-changes may take place in similar ways in totally unrelated languages, evolving according to common, physiological laws; therefore, they may be unreliable for the purpose of assessing genetic relations. However, as we shall see in Chapter 8, the U languages lack a common, complex morphological system, so that no significant reconstruction can be achieved at this level of language through the Comparative Method. This means that Donner did not provide any reconstruction whatsoever for his proposed family tree, either at the phonological level or at the morphological level.

In 1881 Donner argued in favour of what has since become known as the 'Uralic family', that is in favour of a close relationship between the Samoyed languages and the F-U node – an idea that had already been put forward before him by researchers such as Rask and Catrén. Donner claimed that the Samoyed and the F-U languages shared a period of common development after they had separated from the Turko-Tartars and the Mongols. In the main body of his work, Donner examined a few (irrelevant for the task) phonological features, several grammatical and functional endings, and some other syntactic and typological features. Donner observed that the features he examined were also present in most of the Altaic languages. However, he argued that, on balance, these common features suggested that Samoyed was 'closer' to F-U than to the other Altaic languages. It is unclear from his (1881) paper what precisely is the basis of this conclusion, as shown below.

Donner's model and family tree were accepted and propagated by E. N. Setälä through several works (1912/14, 1913–18, 1926), including an encyclopaedia (*Tietosanakirja*, 1917) meant for the general public. In his paper of 1912/14 he proposed minor modifications regarding the U sub-branching and traced a few sound-changes details. In his work of 1913–18 he made a long list of words which are 'similar' in the Finnic, Ugric and Samoyed languages, many of which however are also present in other language families, such as the term for 'tongue, language', 'tree', 'fish' etc. In his conclusion (1913–18: 98) the author recognised that, after all, a P-U language cannot be really reconstructed. And, in fact, as Janhunen (1984a: 203) puts it, Donner's/Setälä's tree diagram became widely accepted by the scientific community, even if, at that stage, the genetic relationship of the U languages was still 'an unproven hypothesis' ('todistamattomana hypotee-sina'). It was then Paasonen (1912/13–1916/1917) who attempted to give a somewhat more systematic account of the sound-correlations among the U languages. However, the author provides no reconstructions of the F-U node (whose existence is merely assumed without proof), or of any other intermediate nodes, and no sound-laws between the assumed F-U node and

Samoyed. In other words, since those times, until recently, the U paradigm and related tree diagram have been accepted basically as self evident, without any further scrutiny of its foundations and its sound structure.

At this point, the reader should beware that Donner's work too, like Budenz', is often misquoted in modern literature. Donner sought to establish a distinct U node, but still within the wider Altaic family, this being in line with the views of other contemporary researchers (Rask, Castrén, etc.). Indeed, the correlations that he reports can only be explained through the wider Altaic relationship. However he is often quoted as if he had established a separate U node, totally independent of the rest of the Altaic family (see below).

2.3.2. *Linguistic analysis of Donner's original data*

As already mentioned above (see Table 2.1), until the end of the 19th century, the Samoyed branch was widely considered to be an 'independent' branch of the Altaic node. The researcher who, supposedly, changed the situation by providing the 'compelling' evidence for a privileged relationship between F-U and Samoyed, to the exclusion of the other Altaic languages, is O. Donner (1881). The following list includes the features put forward by Donner as evidence in favour of his claim:

(a) Vowel harmony and consonant gradation (1881: 233–5). However, these are not relevant features for the purpose of assessing genetic relationship. Furthermore, they are present, in various degrees of completeness and consistency, also in one or the other of the Altaic and Palaeo-Siberian languages, as noted by Donner himself;

(b) The terms indicating the numbers '1' to '7' (1881: 239–1). However, in the light of modern knowledge, only the terms for '2', '3', '4', '5' and '6' are of common U or F-U origin (Honti 1987; Vértes 1994). The term for '1' is different in the various branches, whilst the term for '7' is of Iranian origin. Furthermore, all these number terms present sound irregularities, either in the vocalism or in the consonantism, or both (see UEW at the respective items, and Janhunen (1981a); see also discussion in Chapter 4). Some of these terms may have parallels in non-U languages: the term for '2' appears to have a parallel in Yuk. *kiji* (at least according to UEW 118); the terms for '4' and '1' are claimed by Tyler (1968) to have parallels in the Dravidian languages (item (66) and (105) respectively).

(c) Personal, demonstrative, possessive and interrogative pronouns (1881: 241–3; 244–5). However, according to modern sources, these items too are shared with other, non-U languages, including Indo-European, Altaic and the Palaeo-Siberian languages, unless one considers them as the result of mere chance resemblance.

(d) Structural and typological similarities, such as the formation of nominal constructions of the verb, or the fact that the same personal suffix can be used both with the noun and the verb (1881: 243–5). However, these features are equally present in the Altaic languages.

(e) The plural suffix *-t* (1881: 237). This suffix is not present in Lapp and Hungarian, but it is present in Mongolian, as the author himself points out.

(f) The Case endings: Gen. *-n*, Acc. *-m*, Loc. *-na*, Lat.-Dat. *-ne*, Abl. *-ta* (according to Donner's reconstruction (1881: 238)). However, here too, the author himself acknowledges the presence of these endings in the Altaic languages. Indeed, the distribution of most of them covers a vast area, which includes also Yukaghir.

(g) The causative suffix in *-t* ~ *-d*, which is present in Samoyed and in Finnic, but also in Turkic, as Donner himself points out (1881: 245).This is in fact another widespread Eurasiatic morpheme.

(h) The imperative/optative endings *-ka* ~ *-ke* ~ *-kä*, *-ga* ~ *-ge*, and *-ko* ~ *-kö* ~ *-ku* (as reconstructed by Donner (1881: 246–7)). They are present in some F-U languages and in Samoyed Yurak and Kamass. However, Donner himself points out the Buryat imperative *-hu* (1st Person) and *-k*, *-gi* (3rd Person).

(i) The U postposition **ala-* '[space] under', and the Finnish postposition *taka-* '[space] behind' (1881: 248–9). However, both these postpositions have parallels in non-U languages (see UEW 6 and 506–7 respectively). It is now well known that several other 'spatial' nouns of this kind have equivalent forms in the Altaic languages as well as in Yukaghir. In addition, these nouns have often undergone the process of grammaticalisation to become postpositions and/or Case endings, more or less in parallel, in all these language (see, in this regard, Fokos-Fuchs 1962: 81–2). All these features, their distribution and relevance will be discussed in Chapter 8.

The above-listed features cannot constitute any compelling evidence in favour of a 'closer' relationship between the Samoyed and the F-U branch, as Donner claims – a picture which will be reaffirmed through the analysis carried out in this book. Furthermore, one can observe that Donner does not provide any lexical or phonological evidence in favour of his thesis, apart from the two quoted postpositions. As already mentioned, Donner does not trust sound-laws.

The etymological and phonological connection between the two key branches of the conventional U tree (F-U and Samoyed) had to wait a long time, until 1981, before being systematically and rigorously dealt with. But, even if Donner had been able to prove his point, the fact remains that he did not at all deny a genetic relationship between the F-U, the Samoyed and the Altaic languages, as clearly shown by the following quote (1881: 249):

Die oben angegebenen Übereinstimmungen in grammatikalischen Baue der Samojedischen und Finnisch-ugrischen Sprachen . . . scheinen uns zur

Annahme einer gemeinschaftlichen Entwickelungs Periode der betreffen-
den Völker zu berechtigen, nachdem sie sich bereits von den Turko-
tatarischen und Mongolischen Völkerschaften geschieden hatten

See also Donner (1872 and 1901) for similar ideas.

2.4. LINGUISTIC MODELS FROM THE EARLY 20TH CENTURY

2.4.1. *Models*

After the introduction of the F-U and U nodes towards the end of the 19th
century, the work of several researchers was characterised by ambiguity. The
basic confusion arose as the term 'Altaic' slowly changed its meaning so as
to exclude the U (and F-U) node, but there appears to be no work explicitly
establishing this. As Georg et al. (1999: 75f.) put it:

> Undoubtedly, it was the discovery of compelling evidence that Finno-
> Ugric and Samoyedic form a unit which came to be called Uralic (see
> Donner 1881 . . .), which led to the fairly general acceptance of the idea
> that Turkic, Mongolian and Tungusic formed another unit. In any case,
> for a generation or so, the term 'Altaic' was itself ambiguous . . . thus
> helping to make the point that the relatedness of Turkic, Mongolian and
> Tungusic languages was first postulated merely as part of a larger scheme,
> encompassing Finno-Ugric and Samoyed as well, and that the idea of
> Altaic in the modern sense took shape only gradually[30]

As the idea of a complete unrelatedness between the newly established U
node and the rest of Altaic took place, basically all the similarities shared by
Hungarian and Turkic, particularly extended at the lexical and phonological
level, started to be characterised as 'borrowings' and 'convergent sound
developments', and they still are today. The extent of the borrowing is
accounted for through the (assumed) prolonged period of symbiosis between
the Hungarians and the Turkic clans, as mentioned in Section 2.1.2.6.
Similarly, the lexical correlations between the other U languages and the
other Altaic languages were basically all considered to be the result of
'borrowings', or just 'similarities' (this topic will be discussed in Chapter 6).

However, the claim of a prolonged period of symbiosis between the
Hungarians and the Turks is based essentially on linguistic evidence,
rather than historical evidence, given that the historical sources do not
provide any specific information in this regard. For example, the reader may
recall that the contacts with the Bulgar Turkic *Onogurs* in the 5th century are
only 'assumed' on the basis of a linguistic connection between two
ethnonyms. In 1235, Friar Julianus found the eastern Hungarians in an
area located nearby modern Bashkiria, under the supremacy of the Volga

Bulgars, but there is no way to assess for how long the Hungarians had been living in that region.

The one exception to this absence of specific data is in contradiction with the conventional paradigm: the text of Constantine Porphyrogenitus. At one point (Chapter 38, line 13–14) the author says that the Turks [interpreted in modern texts as 'Turkic magyars'] 'lived together with the Chazars[31] for three ($\tau\rho\epsilon\hat{\iota}\varsigma$) years, and fought in alliance with the Chazars in all their wars' (Moravcsik and Jenkins 1949: 170–1). This is a relevant datum, because the Khazars are considered to be a Bulgar Turkic type of population (at least by some scholars), and the Bulgar Turkic are that very population from whom the Hungarians are supposed to have got the majority of their Turkic loan-words (see Chapter 6). Therefore, three years is not a long enough period to justify such an extensive, deep influence of Turkic on Hungarian, if it is assumed that Hungarian is purely and simply a F-U language. Given that the text by Constantine has been recognised as containing inaccurate information in other areas of the narration, this particular bit of information has generally been regarded as wrong (Grégoire[32] 1937: 636, 1952: 280). Some authors explain this contradiction by referring to the narration of the emperor as having a 'mythical character' (Deér 1952: 108). A correction therefore is required: instead of the word for 'three' ($\tau\rho\epsilon\hat{\iota}\varsigma$), one should read only the initial letter τ', which is the standard way of writing 'three hundred' in Byzantine Greek, whilst the number 'three' is generally written as 'γ' (see for example Deér 1952; Gy. Moravcsik[33] 1930: 107, 1984/8: 42–3; but see Shepard[34] 1998: 25 for a different interpretation). As a result of this re-interpretation by historians in order to make the text consistent with the linguistic model, textbooks generally report that there were 'several centuries' of long co-habitation between the Turks and Hungarians. This is usually reported as historical 'evidence', rather than what it actually is, that is, an interpretation or re-interpretation.

2.4.2. *Linguistic analysis*

There appears to be no discussion of the fact that the 'borrowing' model, apart from being in contradiction with at least one of the historical data, is inconsistent with the thesis of the genetic relationship between Hungarian and Turkic (however much remote and indirect), as it was argued in the original works of Budenz, Donner, and other scholars. As the reader may recall, Budenz too was in favour of the 'borrowing' interpretation, but he had to admit that this interpretation could not apply to **all** the shared Hungarian/Turkic lexical correlations. One can only speculate on how this omission occurred: perhaps researchers concentrated on one or the other aspect of the U languages and U paradigm, and did not consider these wider questions, assuming that the matter had been settled in some way.

This model of borrowing has serious linguistic weaknesses. According to modern studies of languages in contact (see, for example, Trudgill 1996; Thomason & Kaufman 1988; Sammallahti 1995), when two languages come into close symbiosis, the minority and/or less prestigious language tends to disappear (often without leaving any trace in the target language), or creolisation tends to occur. These processes are also rather rapid. Heavy borrowing, instead of assimilation, can also occur, but this is more likely to happen if there is a strong sense of national identity, and therefore a strong, conscious resistance to assimilation (Thomason & Kaufman 1988: 94). This is indeed the case of the Finns, for example, whose language has survived a rather long Swedish supremacy. However, this does not appear at all to be the assumption with regard to the Hungarians. If the Hungarian language had indeed survived about three or more centuries of such a close symbiosis with the Turks, to the point where none of the contemporary sources (supposedly) could distinguish between them, or to the point where most (if not all) of the Hungarian clan names were of Turkic origin, then one would have expected the Hungarian language to have become at least a 'mixed language'. There have been in fact scholars who have argued for the mixed, bilingual nature of the old Hungarians. For example, Györffy (1975a, 1975b) claims that the Hungarian upper, military class spoke a Turkic language, whilst the ordinary population spoke a F-U one. There have also been attempts to account for the situation through the thesis of the language switch: the Hungarians were racially Turks, but, after conquering F-U ethnic groups, they switched their original language for a F-U one, from which Hungarian later on developed, probably before the 5th century AD (Zichy 1939; Halasi-Kun 1986/8, 1990: 8–10).

To conclude, it is worth noticing that some Hungarian scholars have been well aware of the major weakness pointed out here, that is the 'paradox problem' (to use Róna-Tas' (1978a: 213) definition) of a language of F-U origin which survives within a Turkic tribal system, and with essential Turkic participation.

2.5. THE URAL-ALTAIC THEORY

The question of whether the U family is genetically related to the similar Altaic family has not died completely, despite the fact that the U paradigm has become the dominant one. In fact, after a period of confusion subsequent to the establishment of the U node, as described in the previous sections, the idea that all these languages are related after all, has come up again. However, the overall conception of the relationship has slightly changed as shown in Table 2.1. According to the Ural-Altaic theory, the language groups in question are now related through two separate, well-defined, independent nodes, the U node and the Altaic node. In other words, these are not any longer 'equal-level' language groups, even if there does not appear to be any work which specifically argues for this state of affairs.

The supporters of the Ural-Altaic theory, in the current sense of the term, are still a good number, even if some are more cautious than others. For instance, Ramstedt (whose model was Castrén), deals with this question particularly in his paper *Olemmeko mongoleja?* 'Are we Mongols' (1909: 180–5; see also 1946–7: 17–18). Joki touches upon this topic, among other occasions, in a lecture given at the 'Istituto Orientale', University of Naples, on the history of the cultural words of the U languages (1980).[35] Aalto (1969/ 87) lists various grammatical and lexical shared elements. Räsänen, through an extensive research, supports the Ural-Altaic genetic relationship, proposing a long list of similarities as well as correspondences in the field of (core) Lexicon and Morphology (1947a, 1953, 1955, 1957, 1963/4, 1963/95). Sinor, in a number of publications (1969, 1975, 1988, 1990), has proposed a rich list of shared features between the U and Altaic families, even if he has never really argued explicitly in favour of their genetic relationship. Poppe (1977b: 225, 1983) points out the weaknesses of the Ural-Altaic theory, whose etymologies should be revisited according to strict phonetic and semantic laws, but also points out the existence of a certain number of 'good' sound-correspondences between the U and Altaic languages (as illustrated in Chapter 6).

The same situation of complex, intermingled relations among the various branches conventionally classified as U and Altaic emerges from the research by Róna-Tas (see, for example, 1983; 1988a: 742–52). According to the author, the sound etymologies which span the borders of the U and Altaic nodes are not to be considered as proof of a genetic relationship, but rather as the result of (more or less) intense contacts. Menges (1968/95), on the other hand, lists many lexical and grammatical similarities between the U and Altaic languages, and considers them as genetically related. Collinder has summarised his viewpoint on the topic, which has been the focus of many of his publications (1947, 1952, 1965b, 1970), in the paper *Pro hypothesi Uralo-Altaica* (1977b: 73). Here Collinder states that 'Angesichts des Tatbestandes gibt es m. E. nur zwei theoretische Wahlmöglichkeiten: Urverwandtschaft oder *non liquet*'. Fokos-Fuchs, through an extensive literature (see, for example, 1933, 1937, 1960, 1961, 1962) deals mainly with the morpho-syntactic and typological features shared by U and Altaic, some of which are certainly of relevance for assessing genetic relationship (see Chapter 8).

Compare also, for example, Klose (1987), Malherbe ((ed.) 1995) and publication Series such as 'Ural-Altaic Series' (Bloomington) and 'Veröffentlichungen der Societas Uralo-altaica', Germany.

2.6. Conclusion

2.6.1. *Summary of the evidence*

Here is a summary of the key points in the establishment of the U paradigm.

- There are no historical records that refer to a U/F-U population, language or culture. These designations are purely linguistic creations from the second half of the 19th century.
- The few historical records that do exist are either inconsistent with the U paradigm, or are neutral. For example, the records that are supposed to be associated with the Hungarians, despite their ambiguities, all consistently consider the Hungarians purely and simply as Turkic people. The other historical sources refer only to individual people or languages which are now classified as U/F-U.
- Budenz attempted to apply the Comparative Method to his Hungarian/ Ugric parallels, but the method was still in its infancy, and thus could not be applied properly. He argued that Hungarian, while definitively belonging to the Ugric group, still shares some cognates with Turkic because both the Turkic and the Ugric languages go back to the same Altaic node.
- Budenz' work and methods were criticised by Donner, who argued that one can learn nothing from lexical analysis and sound-laws. He introduced the intermediate F-U node, but did not provide any reconstruction or any sort of justification for it. Following the example of then-recent studies in Indo-European languages, Donner concentrated on the analysis of morphological features, although, as we shall see in Chapter 8, the Comparative Method is not applicable to the Morphology of the U languages. He showed that Samoyed shared features with both the F-U and the other Altaic languages, but he concluded that, on balance, the relationship with F-U was 'closer'. In view of the rather inconclusive data he presents, it is unclear why he came to this on-balance conclusion.
- The works of Budenz and Donner use different methodologies, and their results are inconclusive or contradictory, even when taken on their own. This is particularly so in the light of modern knowledge. For example, examining a sample of Budenz' etymologies, only 19% are accepted as still valid by UEW.
- All the researchers in the late 19th century, despite their disagreements, were in agreement on one fixed point: namely that all of the languages now classified as U and Altaic are genetically derived from the same node, called at the time Altaic. However, during the early 20th century, there came about the predominant belief that there is no genetic connection between the languages belonging to the U node, and the other languages 'left behind' under the Altaic node. The observed similarities that contradict this model came to be explained as due purely to borrowing, or to

mere chance resemblance, although this appears to be based more on assumption rather than on systematic evidence. This belief is still reported widely in many textbooks on the subject and forms an important part of the U paradigm.

The status quaestionis, as summarised in the points listed above, supports the claim I made at the beginning of the chapter: the existence of the U family has not been established scientifically in the last decades of the 19th century, contrary to general belief.

To conclude this topic, I would like to make two final observations. Firstly, the correlations between Hungarian and Turkic are not restricted to the lexical level only. They also extend to some areas of Morphology (as shown in Chapter 8) and to Phonology. The phonological correlations are illustrated by Ligeti in his comprehensive volume of 1986, whose Chapter 2 has the title: *A török és a magyar hangtörténet konvergens fejlődése* 'the convergent development of the Turkic and magyar sound-history'[36] (see also Ligeti 1975a: 282[37]). For some examples of these convergent Turkic and Hungarian sound-developments see Note 38.

Secondly, the idea of a wider Eurasiatic relationship was also supported by the founder of studies on Hungarian prehistory, Gy. Németh. For example, Németh (1934: 162/1990: 85) stated that there is a way of solving the 'problem of the Ural-Altaic language family' ('Az urál-altaji nyelvcsalád problémája'). Instead of the Ural-Altaic basic language ('alap-nyelv'), whose existence nobody has so far been able to demonstrate, one should accept the concept of a chain of interconnected languages ('összefüggő nyelvlánc'), which extends from eastern Europe to middle Asia. The old connections among the members of this chain are based 'probably' on intense contacts, rather than on common inheritance.[39] He further claimed (1934: 84/1990: 161) that the Turkic character of the old lexical correspondences 'without doubt' is to be traced back to the times of the Uralic community.[40] On the whole, Németh was of the opinion that the model of a dialectal continuum of intersecting languages better suited this vast linguistic area than the family tree model.

2.6.2. *Political influence on the paradigm*

This historical review would be incomplete without a brief discussion of how the standard U paradigm came to be favoured by political forces, at least in the past and in some countries. I want to emphasise that the following is my personal interpretation, and that further research is needed in this area.

There are clearly forces at work associated with the power of an established paradigm. These forces are well attested (see, for example, Kuhn 1970), and they make it difficult for scholars to publish claims that contradict the prevailing paradigm. However, I have the strong impression that, in addition, there have been in the past also political and social forces at work, which favoured the U paradigm during its formation.

The beginning of the socio-political bias towards a purely U origin of the Hungarians may be traced back to Hungary and its position within the Austro-Hungarian Monarchy (1867–1918), the period of the so-called '*Ausgleich*'.[41]

Austria's ruling dynasty, the Habsburgs, had played a crucial role in ousting the Ottoman Turks at the end of the 17th century from the central part of the kingdom of Hungary, which the Turks had occupied for 150 years. Instead of restoring Hungary's independence, however, at first the Habsburgs imposed firm Austrian control over the country, provoking bitter disappointment among the Hungarians. Later on, in the 1860s, Austria, being threatened by Prussia, sued for a compromise with the Hungarians, a compromise which was accepted by their ruling class. As a result, a new state, called 'Austro-Hungarian/Dual Monarchy', was created, within which both the Austrian Germans and the Hungarians were allowed complete freedom and autonomy in the conduct of their internal affairs. This agreement with Austria launched the Hungarians on an unprecedented course of economic and political progress. Within this framework, for the new Hungarian élite the mention of the possible Turkic (or Turkish) ancestry of the Hungarians became politically embarrassing, and possibly disruptive. For the uninitiated layman, 'Turkic' was the same as 'Turkish', the name of an empire that both Austrians and Hungarians had faced as their enemy in the not-so-distant past. Also, at least some Hungarians gradually came to share the Habsburg prejudice against anything Balkan or Asian, and the Austrians themselves preferred the Hungarians to have descended from humble fish-fat smelling people (Róna-Tas 1978a: 264), rather than from formidable Asiatic warriors. Among the Hungarians, those who sought explanation for their historical and linguistic origin outside the F-U paradigm were usually explicitly or implicitly registering their desire for a more autonomous Hungary. Therefore, research into the question of Turkish/Turkic ancestry could be construed and interpreted as a form of protest against the political status quo. In the age of historical and literary 'Romanticism' and the growth of national consciousness, scientific research into the matter of ethnic and linguistic origins almost inevitably became affected by extraneous political considerations. Budenz and another relevant figure of the 'Ugric-Turkic battle', Pál Hunfalvy,[42] were German. It is easy to see that in such circumstances, they could have been politically motivated in their scientific analysis. This appears to be supported when 'reading between the lines' of Budenz' scientific papers (although, as already pointed out, genuine scientific beliefs have undoubtedly played their role). For example, on many occasions Budenz is so intent on denying linguistic connections between Hungarian and Turkic that he proposes alternative connections that must even at the time have seemed ludicrous, whilst denying obvious Turkic connections that presented no such problems (see examples (2.1) and (2.2) above, and more examples in Marcantonio, Nummenaho & Salvagni 2001).

In more recent times, during the period of Russian influence, it was dangerous for scholars to embrace the thesis of a Turkic origin of the Hungarians. In fact, under the influence of the former Soviet Union, the U paradigm received the *imprimatur* of the authorities. Those who advocated a Turkic origin of the Hungarians came to be associated with nationalists and right-wing propagandists. For example, Csillaghy (1977–81: 309) describes how the nazi-fascists adopted the thesis that Hungarians descend from the superior 'Turanic' race, basically identified with the Turks. This thesis in turn was used as propaganda against the Russians and the communists.

The picture of strong political influence is reinforced by my personal 'reading between the lines' of the works dealing with Hungarian prehistory. For example, some of the strongest pieces of evidence contradicting the U origin of the Hungarians come from the shared Hungarian and Bashkir proper names (and other lexical items[43]), and from the expedition of Friar Julianus, who could communicate in 'Hungarian' with a group of people living nearby modern Bashkiria. These data are systematically minimised or 'airbrushed out' from textbooks, and one finds explicit statements that the Hungarians have never lived in that area (see Appendix V). Another embarrassing element for the standard theory is the Hungarian/Avar connection, as documented in the *Annales* and analysed in Gy. László's research. However, one finds the results of this research mainly being simply rejected as 'wrong', without apparent good reason. It is hard not to conclude that this is a heavily biased interpretation.

Individual publications, however, are not dishonest. On my reading, it is as if the researchers were trying to be as honest as possible within the constraints imposed by both the paradigm and the social forces. A glance at the titles of the papers and books reported in the bibliography here (and there are many more), reveals that many of them are entitled: 'the question of . . .', or 'the problem of . . .', etc. Compare for example Ligeti (1976): *Régi török jövevényszavaink etimológiai problémái*, 'The etymological problems of our old Turkic loan-words', or Czeglédy (1945): *A IX századi magyar történelem főbb kérdései*, 'The major questions of Hungarian history in the 9th century'. Compare also the other Hungarian references containing the word *kérdés* 'question, query, problem, issue'. Finally, recall the problem of the Ural-Altaic relationship as stated by Németh (see Section 2.6.1 and also Németh 1928), or Sinor (1988). These scholars usually describe the counter-evidence to the paradigm in correct detail, but simply fail to draw what seems to be conclusions obvious to an external reader, that is, basically, that the U languages do not form a family.

In the last ten years or so, after the fall of the Berlin Wall, many publications have appeared that openly challenge the textbook position by reconsidering the Hungarian link with the Avars, the Huns, and others, that is, the Turkic populations mentioned in the historical sources.[44] Perhaps, this is more than a coincidence.

One does not have to 'read between the lines' to see that political and social considerations favoured the establishment of standard U theory in Finland. This fact is nowadays openly admitted, as is evident from the many discussions that appear even in popular newspapers and magazines. For example, in the magazine 'Suomen Kuvalehti'[45] (1997: 36), whose front cover has the title: Suomalaisten uudet juuret. Mistä me tulemme?, 'the new roots of the Finns. Where do we come from?,' one reads (my translation): 'The idea of our origin from around the Volga-bends fitted in well with the national thinking of the time [from 1880 onwards], because being Uralic emphasized our own personality and identity as different from that of the other Scandinavian people. This theory also made clear that there was no connection with the Slavic peoples either, since it was proved that: "we were here before you"'.[46] The reader may recall that Finland was under the influence of the Swedes first (from about 1200 until 1809) and of the Russians later on (1809–1917), before acquiring its independence in 1917. In contrast, the thesis of a genetic and cultural connection of the Finns with the Hungarians, and other populations living in central Europe, fitted better the desires and aspirations of the emerging Finnish intelligentsia of the 19th century (Laakso 1999b: 112).

The view that the area between the Volga-bends and the Urals was the original homeland of the Finns was canonised at the symposium of Tvärminne in 1980. This is reported in the Suomen Kuvalehti magazine (1997: 35) as follows: 'The first homeland was originally looked for in the area between the Urals and Central Asia. Anyhow, the Russian **Köppen** rescued the Finns, who were hypersensitive to any talk about their Mongolian origins'.[47] Köppen rescued the Finns through the following argument: the region east of the Urals could not have been the original homeland, because on that side of the Urals there were at the time neither bees nor honey, whilst the F-U languages do contain the names referring to these elements.[48] The same admission of 'hypersensitivity' by the Finns to the idea of their possible Asiatic origin is expressed by the following sentence, apparently often used by the famous scholar M. Räsänen: 'Suomalaiset ja turkkilaiset kielet ovat sukua, mutta siitä ei saa puhua',[49] 'the Finnic and Turkic languages are related, but of this, one cannot talk'.

3

MODERN INTERPRETATIONS OF THE URALIC PARADIGM

There are not many elements in the Uralic languages that carry
sufficient weight to allow a genetic relation to be proposed
between languages that contain them, as the same features tend
to occur in other languages of the Northern Eurasian zone[1]

János Pusztay

According to mainstream interpretation and textbooks, the U languages form a consistent genetic family tree that is unrelated to any of the surrounding languages. We shall examine in the next chapter the specific, modern linguistic evidence on which this model is based. However, before we do so it is important to understand the context in which this generally accepted model resides. As we shall see, there is a significant debate within the field on the most appropriate way to account for the correlations existing among the U languages.

In fact, many variations to the mainstream and textbook interpretation have been published in the literature, motivated by its limitations or by its actual inconsistencies with the linguistic evidence. They range from minor variations to the family tree, through acceptance that the Uralic family is part of a wider family group (Ural-Altaic, Uralo-Yukaghir or others), to the rejection of the validity of the very genetic relationships on which the Uralic family is supposedly founded. It is remarkable that these variations usually go unreported in the textbooks and, often, even in the specialist literature.

The purpose of this chapter is to review this debate. We have already introduced in Chapter 1 some references for and against the conventional paradigm. Here I shall review this paradigm and its alternatives in some detail.

3.1. THE TEXTBOOK INTERPRETATION – THE 'STANDARD URALIC THEORY'

The textbook interpretation is basically as follows. In the north-eastern area of Europe, in a zone which extends from the Baltic sea deep into north-eastern Russia, between the Ural mountains and the Volga river, and beyond the Urals, with eastern limits on the Taimyr peninsula and along the Yenisei and Ob rivers, about thirty (or more) between languages and dialects are spoken, which form the U/F-U family. This family includes Finnish, Estonian, Mordvin, Cheremis, Zyrian, Samoyed, Vogul, Ostyak and (at the time of its formation), Hungarian. The terms 'U' and 'F-U' are often used as synonyms; however, in the current linguistic practice they indicate different nodes within the family, as evident from the family tree diagrams (Figure 1.1). In this book, the term 'U' will be used to make reference to the entire family, as well as to the 'U node' proper.

The U family is generally claimed to have originated somewhere in the area of the Ural mountains, where the P-U close community is supposed to have lived about 8,000/6,000 years ago. Some researchers consider more plausible the idea of an 'extended homeland', between the Ural mountains and the Volga river, or between the Urals and the Baltic coasts. For example, Abondolo ((ed.) 1998: 1) states that 'the proto-homeland of the speakers of the language from which all Uralic languages come is unknown, but a relatively large and sparsely populated region at or near the southern end of the Ural mountains is likely'. The modern U languages are claimed to have formed as the result of subsequent, linear, binary splits (see for example Hajdú 1966, 1981; Gy. Décsy 1990), according to the requirements of the conventional family tree diagram. The first split supposedly gave rise to two major sub-groups, one of which migrated eastwards, forming the Samoyed languages/dialects (northern and southern), spoken mainly to the east of the Urals, whilst the other migrated westwards, forming the F-U branch. The Ugric group in turn split further into Hungarian on the one hand and the Ob-Ugric languages (Vogul /Mansi and Ostyak/Khanty) on the other, these last languages/people being now located east of the Urals. The Finnic branch split into two major sub-groups: Finno-Volgaic and Permian (~ Permic). The Finno-Volgaic group is formed by the Finnic sub-group proper, which includes the Balto-Finnic languages and Lapp (/Saami) according to some researchers at least, and the Volgaic group, which includes only Mordvin (/Mordva) and Cheremis (/Mari). The Permian branch is formed by Zyrian (/Komi) and Votyak (/Udmurt). For the geographical distribution of the U languages and people see the map given at the end of the book.

As mentioned, the family tree diagram reproduced in this book is the one usually provided in most specialist and non-specialist literature, even though several diverse U tree diagrams have so far been proposed, even within the conventional paradigm (see in this regard, the review by Sutrop 2000a, 2000b; see also Sutrop 1999 and discussion below). For example, the position of Lapp within the conventional family tree is very much disputed, as well as the existence of the Ugric node (Sauvageot 1976; Kálmán 1988). The same holds for the Volgaic node, given that several researchers (Collinder 1965a; Bereczki 1980b and 1988) deny the existence of a special relationship between Cheremis and Mordvin, on the basis of lack of evidence. Similarly, T. Itkonen (1997) claims that early on the 'Finno-

Volgaic' group must have consisted of four, relatively independent P-Languages: P-Finnic, P-Lapp, P-Mordvin and P-Cheremis.

There are at least five proposals concerning the sub-grouping of the constituent branches of Finnic:

Table 3.1 Internal classifications of the Finnic languages (from Ruhlen 1987: 69)

Collinder 1965a	Austerlitz 1968	Sauvageot & Menges 1973
FINNIC:	**FINNIC:**	**FINNIC:**
I Mordvin	I PERMIC	I BALTIC FINNIC
II Mari	II VOLGAIC	II SAAMIC
III BALTIC FINNIC	III NORTH FINNIC:	III VOLGAIC
IV SAAMIC	A SAAMIC	IV PERMIC
V PERMIC	B BALTIC FINNIC	

Harms 1974	Voegelin & Voegelin 1977
FINNIC:	**FINNIC:**
I PERMIC	I PERMIC
II Mari	II FINNO-VOLGAIC:
III WEST-FINNIC:	A VOLGAIC
A Mordvin	B FINNO-LAPPIC :
B NORTH FINNIC:	1 SAAMIC
1 SAAMIC	2 BALTIC FINNIC
2 BALTIC FINNIC	

With regard to the estimated period of separation of the various branches, although there are different views, with some researchers refusing to give an estimated time at all, the following dates for the major splits can be considered a kind of 'standard':

- The first split, which gave rise to the F-U and Samoyed P-languages, is held to have taken place during early Neolithic, some 6,500 years ago, or even before;
- P-F-U supposedly was still spoken along the Volga-bends round about 2500–2000 BC (Hajdú 1969b, 1975a, 1975b); according to this view, its disintegration must have taken place after 2000 BC at least. Sammallahti (1988: 481) claims that 3500/3000 BC is more probable;
- On the other hand, according to some researchers at least, the split of P-F-U into P-Finno-Permian and P-Ugric cannot be very much older than the split of P-Finno-Permian into Permian and Finno-Volgaic. According to Sammallahti (1988: 520), 'an approximate date would be somewhere between the disintegration of Proto-Finno-Ugric at 3500–3000 BC, and the introduction of the 'Battle-Axe' culture at 2500–2000 BC, if it is at all possible to date the different phases of the process. It is quite obvious that

the processes of disintegration in the different parts of the area overlapped chronologically and that differences – dialects – evolved inside of diverging areas already before these became different languages';

- The disintegration of the Ugric community and the split of P-Ugric into P-Hungarian and P-Ob-Ugric has been dated to the beginning of the first millennium BC by Honti (1982a: 14, 1975). According to Sammallahti (1988: 499), it must have begun, if not been completed, much earlier, given the relatively small number of words shared by the Ugric languages (Lehtiranta[2] 1982).

In particular, Raun (1956) and Hajdú (1975c: 50), using the method of Glottochronology (Swadesh 1971), suggest the following: the common P-U period ended about 6,000 years ago; P-F-U diversified about 4,500/4,000 years ago; P-Finno-Permian and P-Finno-Volgaic about 3,500 years ago; and finally P-Balto-Finnic about 2,500 years ago. T. Itkonen (1984: 350) suggests the date 2500 BC as the latest period before the end of the P-F-U community, the date 1500 BC for Finno-Volgaic and the date 1000 BC at the latest for Balto-Finnic, whilst considering uncertain the end of the Finno-Permian period. Of the same opinion as Itkonen seems to be Korhonen (1984a, 1984b). P-Samoyed is generally considered to have remained unified until the last millennium BC. Notice however that the method of glottochronology is rather controversial.

As one can see, all the estimated dates, despite internal disagreements, point toward the assumption of a great antiquity for P-U and its branches, the youngest ones being at least more than 2,000 years old.

3.2. CRITICISM OF THE TEXTBOOK INTERPRETATION AND PROPOSED ALTERNATIVES

Many authors recognise that there are data conflicting with (one or the other) tenets of the standard U paradigm, or with the conventional family tree. Some authors try to account for them by varying the details of the family tree; others classify U as a sub-node of wider language groups. More radical approaches, such as the rejection of the genetic affinity of the U languages, have been proposed too. These approaches are outlined in the following sections.

3.2.1. *Variations to the conventional family tree model*

The authors proposing variations to the family tree basically claim that, although the similarities among the U languages are to be interpreted as the result of genetic relationship, the conventional family tree diagram is not good enough to account for them. In particular, it cannot represent faithfully the complex convergences and divergences that occur among these languages. This general point of view is well summarised by K. Häkkinen (1996: 60). She argues that the traditional concept of the U family tree is more a conventional way of thinking rather than a collection of linguistic facts ('on pikemmin totunnainen ajattelumalli kuin kokoelma lingvistisiä faktoja'). This traditional way of thinking does not agree either with the results of the other fields of research dealing with the past. When there are several possibilities of representing a language family, it is nearly despotism ('mielivalta') to dress historical developments in the shape of a family tree without giving linguistic foundations to the chosen solutions.

In what follows, I shall present some of the major weaknesses of the conventional tree as identified by several authors, such as Häkkinen, Hajdú, Salminen and Viitso.

Häkkinen (1983: 378–83) is concerned with the following two major issues:

(a) the criteria adopted to identify lexical correlations;
(b) the absence of evidence in support of the traditional intermediate nodes of P-U, and related long time-scale of development of the daughter languages.

Regarding the issue (a), the author warns that none of the criteria adopted in the etymological research – family tree, phonological criteria, distribution – can be applied on its own in a decisive manner to establish the degree of certainty and the chronology of the U correspondences. On the contrary, each etymology has to be weighted in the light of all these criteria, criteria which could turn out to be neutral, or even in contradiction with each other. All in all, the actual correspondences are far from being ideal, and respectful of the model. Therefore, one must be 'elastic' ('joustavia'; 1983: 379) in the use of these criteria, and conclusions can be drawn only by taking all of them into account. Given the restricted amount of material the reconstruction of P-U is based upon, the sound history cannot be considered as definitive and illuminating as it should be, according to the Comparative Method. This in turn means that the phonological criteria within U cannot be granted that privileged position they normally hold over the other criteria available.

Regarding the issue (b), Häkkinen observes that, in estimating the chronology of the original Lexicon one has to make recourse to criteria which are so weak that its stratification into layers, based on these criteria only, is rather precarious. In fact, although the reconstructions of the oldest nodes of the U family tree are hypotheses based originally on the method of comparison, they become 'axioms' when investigating the developments of the intermediate nodes, given that there is no direct evidence for them. The conventional family tree model, in order to better reflect the results of present-day research, should be transformed into a 'bush-model' ('pensas-malli'), or a 'comb-model' ('kampamalli'), as it has been re-named by Korhonen (1984c: 360). These models are neutral from the point of view of chronology, and, in fact, they admit the possibility that the daughter languages developed from P-U through a period of time shorter than generally assumed so far (see also Laakso 1999a: 54). Figure 3.1 shows Häkkinen's 'bush-model'[3]:

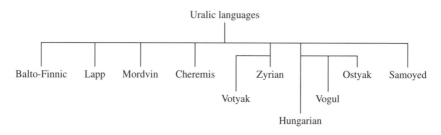

Figure 3.1 Häkkinen's 'bush-model' diagram (1983: 384)

Häkkinen foresees the utility of a statistical approach to help to individuate the genuine cognates and their chronology, wherein the distribution of the parallels should be analysed bypassing the intermediate, unrealistic nodes. She also provides a small scheme indicating the number of etymologies in common among the various branches, and remarks how the numerical relations do not correspond to the traditional assumptions about distantly or closely related languages (see also Honti 1993, for similar results[4]). Notice, however, that in Häkkinen's bush-model the Ugric node is maintained.

Hajdú, a strong supporter of the genetic affinity of the U languages, has repeatedly warned about the absolute inadequacy of the genealogical tree to represent the complex, intricate ('bonyolult') historical processes which have brought forth the modern U languages (see, for example, Hajdú & Domokos[5] 1978: 67). Hajdú (1969a) has also envisaged the existence of a north Eurasian language conglomerate/*Sprachbund* ('nyelvi szövetség'). In a later work (1975a: 37, 42), the author tried to represent some shared salient features of the U languages – presence of Dual, phonological length, local suffixes etc. – by means of isoglosses, and he came up with the following two schemes (see also Hajdú 1976 for a diagram consisting of concentring circles and segments) (see Figures 3.2 and 3.3).

By and large, it appears at first that there is a certain correlation between the linguistic and geographic closeness of the various languages. For example, the circles diagram highlights the following factors:

• The Ob-Ugric languages, which in the conventional family-tree are represented as forming a genetic node with Hungarian, are in fact closer to Samoyed;
• Cheremis, Mordvin and the Permian languages are very close to each other;
• Hungarian is nearly as close to Permian as it is to Ob-Ugric.

Figure 3.2 Hajdú's diagram of isoglosses (1975a: 42; after Sinor[6] (ed.) 1988: XVI)

However, the isoglosses diagram also highlights a striking contradiction to the just stated equation 'geographical closeness = linguistic closeness': certain features are shared by geographically, as well as (supposedly) genetically distant languages. For example, the Dual is present in Lapp, Samoyed and Ob-Ugric; quantity correlation is present in Lapp and Finnish on one side, and Hungarian on the other side. Furthermore, it is self-evident that such a scheme, based on isoglosses, cannot be converted either into a family tree type of scheme, or into the various versions of U family trees proposed so far, as pointed out by Hajdú himself (1975a, 1975b, 2000: 257).

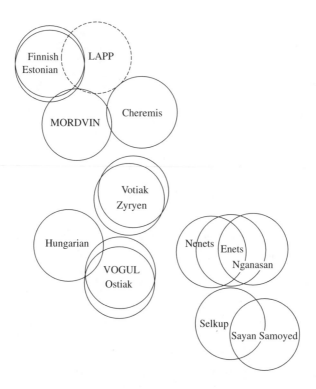

Figure 3.3 Hajdú's circle diagram (1975a: 37; after Sinor (ed.) 1988: XV)

This factor on its own should be enough to cast some doubt on the validity of the conventional family tree.

Salminen (1999: 20) claims that the U languages form a chain whose reciprocal relations can be represented by a 'ball-diagram' ('pallokaavio') (see Figure 3.4).

Kulonen (1995: 50), whilst recognising the positive aspects of the 'bush-model', believes that its information value is quite small, and that languages can also be grouped with the help of isoglosses, by incorporating them inside

Figure 3.4 Salminen's 'ball-diagram' (1999: 20)

circles of different thickness, whereby the thickness of the circles reflects the quantity of shared features. She calls the reader's attention to an 'isoglossi-malli', actually drawn first by M. Korhonen (see Figure 3.5).

Viitso (1997a, 1997b: 223) proposes a revision of the standard family tree according to which the break-up of the F-U node began in the west, with the separation of a 'West Finno-Ugric' and an 'East Finno-Ugric' branch. Here, the most noticeable 'deviations' – as it were – from the traditional tree can be considered to be: (a) the absence of the Ugric node (Vogul, Hungarian and Ostyak belong to three different sub-branches); (b) the sort of isolated position of Ostyak; (c) the grouping together, under the Central Finno-Ugric node, of Permian, Mordvin, Cheremis, Vogul and Hungarian (see Figure 3.6).

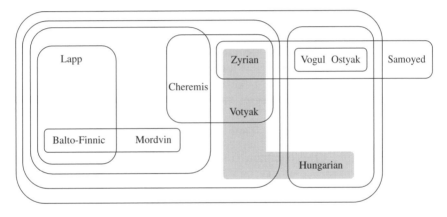

Figure 3.5 Kulonen's 'isogloss-model' diagram (1995: 50)

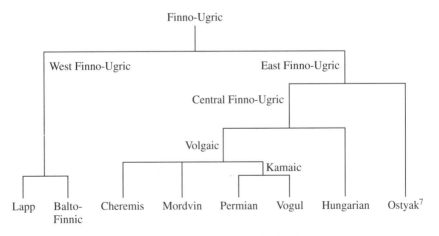

Figure 3.6 Viitso's family tree diagram (1997b: 223)

Among the other authors who have proposed alternative family trees, which (like Häkkinen's tree) one might classify as 'unrooted', to use Sutrop's (2000a: 178) definition, one may quote here the following: Uesson (1970: 116); Östman & Raukko (1995: 58), whose tree model is based on language contact theories; Taagepera (1997, 2000), who proposes a 'forest' type of tree, with diverging and converging branches and with (possibly non-Uralic) roots and non-unitary stem.

For more detail on alternative U family trees compare Künnap (1998a) and Sutrop (2000a, 2000b).

3.2.2. Rejection of the genetic affinity

The underlying claim of those scholars who (more or less strongly) deny a common origin for the U languages is that the observed, shared similarities are neither good enough nor numerous enough to maintain the thesis of the genetic relationship. As Suhonen (1999: 248) puts it, 'the existence of a uniform Uralic Proto-Language is logically improbable'. The shared similarities of the U languages are held to be better explained as the result of contact/Sprachbund. This point of view is well represented by researchers such as Tauli (1966), Pusztay (1995, 1997), Künnap (1995, 1997a, 1997b, 1998a). Consider, for example, Tauli's words (1966: 11; see also 1955):

The origin of all the common traits of the U languages is so far not known. The existence of a certain grammatical category or morpheme in separate languages need not indicate that this originates from a common proto-language or a parallel development of different languages which is the classical point of view, but may be due to the spreading of the phenomenon from one language to other contiguous languages

Similarly, Pusztay (1997: 17–18) states that:

There are not many elements in the Uralic languages that carry sufficient weight to allow a genetic relation to be proposed between languages that contain them, as the same features tend to occur in other languages of the Northern Eurasian zone (e.g. the suffixes denoting local cases or the markers of number) . . . The Uralic languages . . . form together with the Palaeo-Siberian languages (and those belonging to the Altaic group) an extensive, typologically highly uniform area in which the majority of the linguistic categories are formed in both structurally and materially highly similar ways . . . It follows from this that there were probably many languages (language formations) among those located across the Northern Eurasian zone like the links in a chain that could be interpreted in retrospect as having served as the Proto-Language, but only two or perhaps three of these (one in the Baltic region, one in Western Siberia, and possibly one lying between these) can be related to the present-day

Uralic languages . . . Again, I regard a chained structure as a more probable alternative . . . The interstices between the links in the chain of places of origin were probably occupied by wandering peoples that did not belong permanently to any definable community. I was inclined earlier to regard the Lapps as one such group, but more recent genetic research suggests otherwise. The languages of the western and central groups are typical Finno-Ugric ones, but those of the eastern group are of Siberian origin

Pusztay stresses several times that, contrary to the general, current opinion, those elements that are present only in some U languages should not be traced back to a common P-Language. Furthermore, the present status of the morphological and morpho-syntactic research leads us towards the conclusion that one cannot talk about a P-Language in the classical sense of the term. The following language chain diagram would better reflect the status of the correlations among the U and Palaeo-Siberian languages (see Figure 3.7).

As one can see, Mordvin, which is normally classified as belonging to the Finno-Volgaic branch, is here located in the same link which contains the Ugric and Samoyed languages. This is because Mordvin is the only western language that exhibits certain features which are actually typical of the eastern languages (such as the split Definite vs Indefinite Conjugation, reflection of the Plurality of the Object in the verb structure, etc.). This means that, on the basis of these features at least, there is a typological boundary running between the central and eastern groups, and a genetic boundary running at the east of the eastern group.

Several scholars, including Wiik (through a number of papers; see Chapter 7), Künnap (1997a, 1997b, 1998a) and Taagepera (2000), have further interpreted the *Sprachbund* type of link among the U languages in terms of lingua franca. In other words, if a P-Language did exist, it must have been a sort of lingua franca of the hunter-gatherer people of north-eastern Europe. This interpretation would fit better the reality of the social and geographical situation of Eurasia. As Taagepera (2000: 384) puts it:

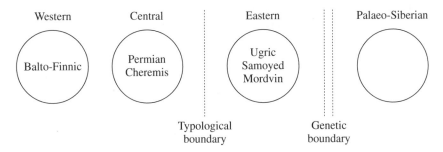

Figure 3.7 Pusztay's language chain diagram (1997: 13)

How can various features within a *Sprachbund* spread over large distances? . . . Areal diffusion would explain similarities between geographically contiguous populations, but how could features diffuse over four thousand kilometres, even over thousands of years? This is where the hypothesis of a Uralic lingua franca, instead of a proto-Uralic home language, comes handy.

3.2.3. *Wider language families*

To account for the similarities the U languages appear to share with other language families, and which are interpreted as mere borrowings or accidental 'look-alikes' within the conventional paradigm, the following interpretations have been proposed:

(a) **Ural-Altaic theory**, which holds that the U languages are a branch of the wider Ural-Altaic family, as already discussed in the previous chapter.

(b) **Uralo-Yukaghir theory** (supported by researchers such as Collinder 1940; Ruhlen 1987: 64), according to which there is a genetic relationship between U and Yukaghir only, with Altaic being excluded. This is despite the fact that U, Altaic and Yukaghir appear to share more or less the same quantity and quality of features.

(c) **Nostratic/Eurasiatic theory**, held by the 'Nostraticists'(see, for example, Pedersen 1933; Illič-Svityč 1971–84; Shevoroshkin (ed.) 1971), and Greenberg (2000) and his group, according to which the Ural-Altaic family is in turn part of an even wider macro-family, called respectively 'Nostratic' and 'Eurasiatic'. These macro-families, which partially overlap, include Indo-European, Afro-Asiatic, Yukaghir, Eskimo-Aleut, Kartvelian, Dravidian, Korean-Japanese-Ainu. Apart from some well-known methodological differences (the Nostraticists work with P-Languages, Greenberg operates with 'mass-comparison'), both Nostraticists and Greenberg base the establishment of their families on the recognition of about 600/700 etymologies, grammatical and lexical, which, again, partially overlap. A list of 'Nostratic' etymologies can be found in Dolgopolsky (1998a); see also Dolgopolsky (1998b). Notice however that of the 124 etymologies listed in Dolgopolsky (1998a), 61 do not exhibit a P-U parallel.

(d) **Uralo-Dravidian theory**, according to which there is a genetic relationship between just the U and the Dravidian languages. A linguistic relationship between U and Dravidian has been suspected for many years, although it has failed to attract wide attention. After the publication of the *Dravidian Etymological Dictionary*, by Burrow & Emeneau (1961), a more systematic investigation of the relevant material has been possible. As a result, Tyler (1968) has compiled a corpus of 153 'correspondences' between U and Dravidian, including basic vocabulary and a few grammatical formants, using for U the *Fenno-Ugric Vocabulary* by Collinder (1955). The Dravidian P-forms are claimed by the author (1968: 798) to be related 'by systematic phonemic correspondences' with the equivalent U P-forms. Menges (1964) discusses a number of morphological and syntactic similarities between Altaic and Dravidian. Similarly, Bouda (1953) lists 137 pairs of Dravidian-Altaic etymologies, together with 28 Dravidian-Ural-Altaic common etymologies, the majority of which appear in Tyler's work. These facts, according to Tyler, can probably be considered as evidence in favour of the existence of a macro-family consisting only of Dravidian, Altaic and U.

For a critical review of the Uralo-Dravidian relationship see Larsson (1982).

(e) **Uralo-Indo-European theory**, according to which there is a genetic relationship between U and Indo-European only. This position is held or at least favoured by several linguists, belonging to different schools.
(f) **Mixed languages theory,** held by scholars such as Wiik (see Chapter 7), Künnap (1997c), Taagepera (2000); according to which P-U was basically the lingua franca of the hunter-gatherer people of north-Europe, whilst the Balto-Finnic languages were 'mixed' languages, originated from the mixing of the P-U lingua franca with the language(s) of the expanding Indo-European people.

As one can see, there are basically two major trends of thought, both contrasting with the conventional paradigm. Some scholars, a minority, deny the existence of the U family altogether, claiming that the not-too-many shared features are basically the result of areal convergence. Others, the majority, do accept the validity of the U node, and therefore of the U family, but do not accept one or the other of the traditional tenets. In particular, several scholars believe that the U language family is related to other language families, although they may disagree as to which family U is related to.

3.3. Conclusion

The very existence of the debate outlined above, which proceeds in parallel with the textbook and mainstream position, suggests that the conventional paradigm has at least a case to answer. The key issue to emerge from the debate is whether the correlations traditionally identified within U are good enough and numerous enough to demonstrate a genetic relationship. Similar questions have been raised regarding the correlations that have been identified between the U and non-U area.

We have seen in this short review how different researchers have used the same data and the same methods of analysis (the Comparative Method and related family tree), and yet have reached contradictory conclusions on the origin and classification of the Uralic languages. How can this be the case? Logically, there are two possible causes:

- There is something wrong with the way the Comparative Method is applied to these languages, or
- The method itself is 'not even wrong' – that is, the U theory (and its competitors) are so flexible that they can be adjusted to account for almost any data.

The answer to this question will become clearer by systematically examining the detailed evidence. This is the process that is about to start in the next chapter, beginning with phonological and lexical data. But, whatever the answer, the fact remains that the Comparative Method is not easily applicable to the U language family, not only because of the reasons expounded in the Introduction, but also because of another crucial factor, as evidenced in the appropriate chapter: the absence of a common, complex morphological system.

4

RECONSTRUCTING THE SOUND STRUCTURE AND LEXICON OF THE URALIC FAMILY TREE

The historical development of all of these families has been established, by means of the comparative method, to a degree of precision which is both predictive and productive.[1]

Daniel Abondolo

The starting point for most modern reconstructions of the Uralic family tree is the reconstruction due to Janhunen (1981a). Strictly speaking, this corpus should be referred to as the P-Finno-Permian-Samoyed node, after the languages that are compared. Nevertheless, it is labelled, and usually referred to, as a reconstruction of P-U, even though the key P-Ugric node is not included in the systematic comparison.

As we shall see in Section 4.1, this corpus contains a large number of sound-rules and a small number of etymologies. If one counts only etymologies that obey the sound-rules regularly (that is, as they are stated) then the sound-rules outnumber the etymologies. In other words, this corpus does not meet the 'significance criterion' of the Comparative Method – that each sound-rule should be supported by a significant number of regular etymologies – and therefore the reconstruction does not qualify for the high level of confidence that is sometimes inherited when the Comparative Method is used. Accordingly, one cannot tell whether the corpus represents genuine linguistic relationships or is instead the result of chance resemblances.

In Section 4.2 we shall examine the modern reconstruction of the rest of the U family tree, particularly the Ugric node. As we saw in Chapter 2, the belief in the existence of the Ugric node was originally founded on a coincidence of proper names – a similarity between the words *Yugria* and *hungarus*. Since that time, this node has defied all attempts to reconstruct it based on the primary linguistic evidence and, as Abondolo (1987: 185) remarks:

Hungarian has no close relatives; the Ob-Ugric languages, traditionally bundled together with Hungarian into the Ugric subgroup of the Uralic family, are radically different from Hungarian in their phonology, syntax and vocabulary.

See also Hajdú[2] (1987: 306) and Sammallahti[3] (1988: 484) for similar remarks.

Nevertheless, in 1988 Sammallahti introduced a new method to reconstruct the entire U family tree, including the Ugric node. He started from
Janhunen's reconstruction of P-Finno-Permian-Samoyed, which he equated
with P-U and assumed to be at the top of the conventional family tree
including the Ugric node. He also started from Honti's (1982a) reconstruction of P-Ob-Ugric. His method was to 'bridge the gap' between the
assumed starting-point reconstructions (P-Finno-Permian-Samoyed and
P-Ob-Ugric) by 'interpolating' the assumed intermediate P-Finno-Ugric
and P-Ugric nodes. Although this paper is often presented as being a
definitive reconstruction, the author in fact warns clearly that this is not
the case, saying for example that (1988: 486) 'the details are far from
settled'.

As we shall see in Section 4.2, there are several problems with this
programme. Firstly, it inherits the difficulties of the P-Finno-Permian-
Samoyed corpus on which it is based. More seriously, there is a
methodological problem: reconstructions (rather than actual attested
forms) are usually compared against other reconstructions; in this sense
they are neither provable nor disprovable. Since the very purpose of the
reconstructions is to 'bridge the gap' between word-forms, it is perhaps not
surprising that the resulting chain of reconstructions *seems* to be relatively
regular.

The completeness and regularity of this reconstruction of the entire family
tree becomes idealised when it is presented in textbooks. Textbooks
commonly report the 'correspondences' as if they were 'predictive and
productive'. To take a recent example, Csepregi (1998: 14) describes the
highly regular nature of the correspondences between Finnish and Hungarian, and illustrates this with four examples where Finn. *p-* systematically
corresponds to Hun. *f-*, from P-U *p-*:

Finnish	Hungarian	Meaning
pää	*fej ~ fő*	'head'
puu	*fa*	'tree'
pelkää	*fél*	'he/she fears'
pääsky	*fecske*	'swallow (bird)'

This apparent regularity of the reflexes of *p-* might seem, as presented, as
if it were typical of the complete picture; however, in reality only the first
sound in these words is (arguably) regular. For example, P-U *p-* also
develops into Hun. *b-*, as shown in example (4.34) below. Further, only one
of the listed examples (*pelkää/fél*) is classed as regular according to the
original reconstruction of Janhunen (1981a), as shown in example (5.9) in
the next chapter. The other correspondences (*puu/fa* and *pää/fej*) show
recognised difficulties, including the presence of an 'unspecified' segment, as

shown in examples (4.17) and (4.50) respectively, or they are not included in the original P-U corpus at all (*pääsky*/*fecske*).

In this chapter, the reconstructions are analysed in their own terms, that is, using the Comparative Method. Wherever possible I shall always compare the etymologies against primary linguistic evidence through specific examples. I shall leave it to the next chapter to consider alternative statistical methods to analyse the linguistic correlations.

4.1. JANHUNEN'S CORPUS: PROTO-FINNO-PERMIAN-SAMOYED

The principal reconstruction that is called 'P-U' is due to Janhunen (1981a). Despite its nomenclature, this reconstruction is in fact based on P-Samoyed and P-Finno-Permian. The Ugric node is not taken into consideration systematically because no suitable reconstructions of it are available. This limited reconstruction is justified as a 'simplified but very useful approximation' of P-U on geographical grounds. As Janhunen (1998: 461) puts it

> as there still seem to be considerable taxonomic and reconstructional problems to be solved for the eastern branches of Finno-Ugric, a simplified but very useful approximation of proto-Uralic can be obtained in the meantime by comparing proto-Samoyedic with proto-Baltic-Fennic . . . as these two branches represent opposite geographical extremes of the Uralic language family, it may be assumed that any diachronic feature shared by proto-Samoyedic and proto-Baltic-Fennic is likely to derive from proto-Uralic

4.1.1. *The number of sound-rules and etymologies*

With regard to the sound-rules on which the corpus is based, the vowel-rules for first and non-first syllable are listed fully, but the consonant-rules are not all listed. For instance, based on typical etymologies, initial **k-* remains (in most cases) unchanged in going from P-U to P-Samoyed. This rule is not listed and it must be inferred from the examples.

Overall, the paper lists 58 sound-rules for vocalism and 12 sound-rules for consonantism. In addition, the author introduces an 'unspecified' consonantal segment '**x*' to account for some particularly problematic parallels. As he says (1981a: 246, my translation)[4]:

> One must note that all the assumptions presented concerning the independent phonematic status and distribution of **x* are totally tentative. There are certainly several other possible explanations. In particular it is quite problematic to distinguish **x* in the etymological material from the

occlusive *k and from the nasal *η, as well as from the semi-vowels *w and *j, which also had the tendency to disappear

Turning to the etymological material, there are 132 listed etymologies, 7 pronouns and one duplicate in this corpus. The author regards the first 94 of the etymologies as sound-wise regular and semantically plausible (1981a: 246, my translation)[5]:

> Although many phonological details allow the possibility of alternative interpretations, one can be fairly sure that all the above-listed correspondences, which have been classified according to the vowel-relations (numbers 1–94) are, from the point of view of proto-Uralic and the closest lower-level proto-languages, sound-wise regular and semantically plausible, and are therefore etymologically irreproachable . . . The corpus is not large, but it is enough to give at least a general picture of the sound-structure of the proto-language.

Fifteen of these 94 etymologies, numbered (80)–(94), are established on the basis of the tentative multiple-value segment *x. For many of the remaining etymologies, there is ambiguity as to their regularity. For example, the following are extracts from the author's comments on the etymologies numbered (1) to (30), which are apparently among the best of these good etymologies:

Etymology number	Author's comments
4	semantic difficulties
6	presence of irregular sound variations in P-Finnic
9	secondary semantic development in Finnic
12	vowel irregularities in Balto-Finnic and Ugric
14	different meanings, possibly the result of areal innovation
15	variation in sound and meaning at the F-U level
20	vowel irregularities
21	narrow distribution, perhaps a hypothetical correspondence
23	exact semantic reconstruction impossible
24	confusion between two etymological sets (see item (86))
25	much sound and meaning variation, possibly a *Wanderwort*
26	secondary consonantal change in Early-P-Finnish

Excluding etymologies with identified difficulties of this sort, only 65 of the 132 etymologies obey the sound-rules regularly (that is, as they are stated). This number would be further reduced if one excluded etymologies that rely on the tentative segment *x. Approximately a quarter of these 'obedient' etymologies are associated, according to UEW and Tyler (1968), with non-U languages.

In summary, this corpus contains more sound-rules than regular etymologies. We have seen that there are 71 stated sound-rules (more if one counts the unstated consonant-rules); and there are 65 etymologies that obey the sound-rules regularly (fewer if one does not count etymologies that are based on the segment *x).

This exercise highlights the subjectivity in the way the Comparative Method is usually applied. It has become common practice in the field for the number of etymologies obeying a given set of sound-rules to become largely a matter for personal interpretation, rather than of objective testing against the stated rules. For example, the reported number of etymologies in the U corpus might be increased if one neglects difficulties such as those reported in the scheme above.

4.1.2. *The 'cumulative effect' of the Comparative Method in the Proto-Uralic corpus*

The use of the Comparative Method is sometimes held to endow etymologies with a high level of statistical confidence, because it is unlikely that a large number of etymologies should all obey the same sound-rule consistently and regularly. This is called the 'cumulative effect' of the Comparative Method. In this section we undertake a more detailed test for the cumulative effect in this corpus.

As mentioned, Janhunen's (1981a) P-U reconstruction contains a complete and clear set of sound-rules for vocalism, and it is possible to use it to test for the cumulative effect at least for vocalism in this context. The consonantal rules are not all stated, so that this test cannot be applied so easily to consonantism.

In this test, I counted the number of etymologies that support each of the vowel-rules. The results of this counting are shown in Tables 4.1a and 4.1b and in the graphs shown in Figures 4.1a and 4.1b.

As an aid to interpreting these tables, let us take the case where we wish to count all 132 etymologies (that is, including the etymologies that do not obey the sound-rules as they are stated). This corresponds to Table 4.1a. On the

Table 4.1a The etymologies supporting the vowel-rules in P-Uralic

All 132 etymologies (excluding pronouns and duplicates)		
Number of etymologies supporting the rule	Number of rules	
1	19	34%
2	19	34%
3	5	9%
4	9	16%
5	2	4%
7	2	4%

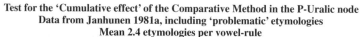

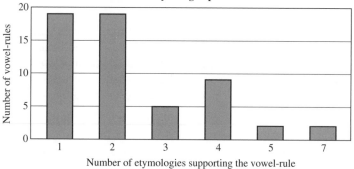

Figure 4.1a The etymologies that support each vowel-rule in P-Uralic

Table 4.1b The 'good' etymologies supporting the vowel-rules in P-Uralic

The 65 'good' etymologies (those that obey the sound-rules as stated)		
Number of etymologies supporting the rule	Number of rules	
0	20	36%
1	17	30%
2	12	21%
3	5	9%
4	1	2%
5	1	2%

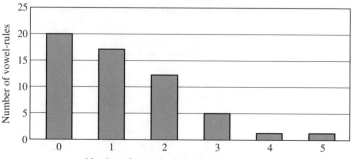

Figure 4.1b The 'good' etymologies that support each vowel-rule in P-Uralic

first row we see that there are 19 rules that are supported by only a single etymology. The second row tells us that 19 of the rules are supported by two etymologies, the third row tells us that 5 of the rules are supported by three etymologies, and so on.

As will be clear from these tables, there is no evidence for a 'cumulative effect' of the Comparative Method (where many etymologies all obey a given sound-rule systematically) in this corpus. For example, more than half of the sound-rules are supported by two etymologies or fewer, whether one takes all the etymologies or just the 'good' ones.

4.2. THE RECONSTRUCTION OF THE UGRIC NODE

According to the conventional family tree, the Ugric node is an intermediate-level node, bringing together Hungarian and P-Ob-Ugric, which in turn comprises Vogul (/Mansi) and Ostyak (/Khanty).

As we saw in Chapter 2, the belief in the privileged relationship between the Ugric languages was originally founded on a similarity of proper names (*hungarus–Yugria*), and nothing that would nowadays be considered as actual evidence was involved at the time. Subsequently, the founder of the field, Budenz, adopted a relatively flat family tree that did not postulate an intermediate node of this nature at all. Modern researchers also recognise many difficulties with the Ugric node. It has long been recognised that Hungarian does not fit comfortably within this theoretical structure, and this has prevented the Ugric node from being reconstructed by conventional means. We shall review this evidence in Section 4.2.1 below.

The conventional paradigm has not been amended to take account of this conflict between model and evidence, and it has remained unchanged to this day. It was (and is) simply assumed that the Ugric node must be valid and that Hungarian must be part of it. This conflict was finally 'resolved' in 1988 by Sammallahti, who used an 'interpolation' to bridge the gap between P-Finno-Permian-Samoyed (the assumed top-level node) and P-Ob-Ugric. This resolution identified supposedly regular sound-changes leading all the way from P-Uralic to Hungarian via the P-Finno-Ugric and P-Ugric nodes, thus apparently establishing the U tree to a high level of precision. I shall critically examine this method in Section 4.2.2.

4.2.1. *Hungarian recognised as an isolate*

It is widely stated in the literature that, whilst there is sufficient evidence to group Vogul and Ostyak together into the so-called Ob-Ugric node, the relationship of Hungarian to the rest of the Ugric languages is 'rather loose' (Sammallahti 1988: 500). For instance, as we have seen above, Abondolo (1987: 185) observes that Hungarian is radically different from the Ob-Ugric languages in Phonology, Syntax, and vocabulary. He later reaffirms this analysis (Abondolo 1998b: 428):

> Although typically Uralic in many respects (broadly agglutinating, with vowel harmony, postpositions, possessive suffixes, and minimal noun-phrase agreement), Hungarian is also strongly deviant in certain regards, in particular in the development of its vowels and in the details of its noun and verb finite paradigms

The common features that are mentioned – broad agglutination, vowel harmony, postpositions, possessive suffixes and minimal noun-phrase agreement – are widely considered to be either the result of *Sprachbund* processes or as simple 'implications' of the 'Universals of language' (see Chapter 8 for a discussion of these features). Whatever the interpretation, these features are not usually considered relevant for the purpose of assessing genetic relations. Accordingly, to account for the 'deviant' character of Hungarian, Abondolo (1998b: 428) says:

> What is traditionally termed 'Ugric' may itself have been more a *Sprachbund* than a node in the Uralic family tree

Viitso (1995, 1997a, 1997b) also shares the view that Hungarian and the Ob-Ugric languages do not form a genetic node, as illustrated in Figure 3.6. Whilst not all authors go as far as this, most authors confirm the view that Hungarian is an 'isolate'. For example, Sauvageot (1971: 28) says that Hungarian is:

> une langue d'origine finno-ougrienne sans que nous puissions dire s'il est plus proche de tel autre idiome du même groupe. Les traits que nous lui découvrons nous font apparaître qu'il a dû prendre à date très ancienne une allure particulière qui l'a vite distingué des autres langues finno-ougriennes . . . Cette allure 'indépendante' du hongrois peut s'expliquer par le fait qu'il se serait détaché de très bonne heure de l'ensemble finno-ougrien ou qu'il se serait trouvé d'emblée situé sur la périférie

Likewise, Hajdú & Domokos (1978: 82–7) observe that it is impossible to speak of a close linguistic connection between the Hungarian and the Ob-Ugric communities. Salminen (1997b: 86) also calls the connection between Hungarian and the Ob-Ugric languages into question:

> while Sami [*sic*], Finnic, Mordvin, Mari, Permian, and Samoyed are beyond doubt as historical linguistic entities, with a host of common innovations in each, the same is far from being true about the alleged Ugrian branch, consisting of Hungarian, Mansi [Vogul] and Khanty [Ostyak]

The 'deviant' nature of Hungarian (which will be evidenced through the phonological, lexical and grammatical data presented later in this book), poses a central difficulty in Uralic studies: the inability to reconstruct the Ugric node in turn means that it is not possible to reconstruct the Finno-Ugric and therefore the Uralic node (that is, at least within the framework of the conventional tree). As Helimski (1984b: 253) puts it:

> The Ugric proto-language, essentially important as the potential *tertium comparationis*, remains on the whole beyond our reach as long as we have no adequate Proto-Ugric phonological reconstruction

For further information on the difficulties posed by the Ugric node see also Sauvageot (1976) and Kálmán (1988).

4.2.2. *A riddle solved*

Despite the fact that Hungarian resisted all conventional linguistic attempts to match it to the Ugric node and therefore to the Uralic tree, there remained a powerful belief in the linguistic community that the question of the Ugric origin of Hungarian had been (scientifically) settled in the final decades of the 1800s. Hungarian had to be a Ugric (and Uralic) language. It is as if researchers believed that the fault lay in their lack of ability or inventiveness in achieving a convincing reconstruction, rather than in an objective mismatch between the model and the primary data that it is supposed to explain.

In 1988, Sammallahti 'solved' the riddle by devising a way to bridge the gap between the existing reconstructions in Uralic and thus to reconstruct the entire U family tree. This method made it possible to reconstruct the Ugric node, whilst bypassing the uncomfortable mismatches in primary evidence from Hungarian, Vogul and Ostyak. In this work, Sammallahti began by recognising these fundamental mismatches (1988: 513):

> Hungarian vowels and consonants participate in complex morpho-phonemic alternations, which makes it difficult to trace the development of different sounds

However, after 'bridging the gap' by interpolating the intermediate nodes, Sammallahti listed a set of derived sound-laws leading all the way from the top-level node, through P-Finno-Ugric and P-Ugric, to Hungarian. As presented in this paper, these sound-laws appear to be relatively regular and thereby to confirm the method.

4.2.3. *A riddle truly solved?*

The first weakness with this interpolation is that the original problem has not gone away. There is still a mismatch between the primary data and the model, and no amount of reconstruction can make it appear to researchers who examine the actual languages that Hungarian shares a privileged relationship with Vogul and Ostyak.

The second weakness with the method, and the central one in my view, is that it is not directly testable against primary evidence. It does not connect primary linguistic evidence with other primary linguistic evidence. Instead, reconstructions are compared against other reconstructions in most cases. Since the very purpose of a reconstruction is to achieve regularity between the end-forms, with so many links in the chain it should not be surprising if the matches between the reconstructed forms are thus able to seem relatively regular: one is not constrained to the same extent by direct evidence at the many points in the chain that involve reconstructions. Accordingly, Sammallahti (1988: 515 f.) is able to report that the reconstructed correspondences are relatively regular. There is a list of P-Ugric vowels which are described as having 'regular reflexes' in Modern Hungarian. As to the consonants, there is a list of P-Ugric consonants that underwent 'more or less regular changes' towards modern Hungarian, but the author identifies a significant degree of variation here (1988: 515–20). This reported (basic) regularity is in contradiction to the statement made by the author a few pages earlier, that the parallels between the original languages are problematic (see quotation in the previous section).

The third problem with this method is that it is based on evidence that is recognised to be irregular, but that is reported and analysed as if it were instead (essentially) regular. About 50% of the words in both the consonant and vowel lists consist of etymologies which are classified as problematic or irregular in Janhunen's corpus or (contrary to Sammallahti's stated method) are absent from that corpus altogether. Further, most of the etymologies which are used to substantiate a given sound-change are (arguably) regular in only the one sound-change under consideration and do not display systematic regular correspondences across the entire word, as would be demanded by a proper application of the Comparative Method. The problematic character of many of these etymologies is discussed in various places in this book, please see (quoting from English): 'father-in-law', 'sinew', 'arrow', 'liver', 'under', 'mother', 'ice', 'tongue, language', 'side', 'winter', 'eye', 'tree', 'six', 'five', 'two', 'three', 'urine', 'to die', 'to drink', 'moon, month', 'to bring', 'elm', 'give, sell', 'to cook', 'willow', 'wave, foam', 'heart', 'metal', 'knot', 'woman', 'bee', 'to drink'.

Finally, since this reconstruction is based on Janhunen's (1981a) corpus, it suffers from the same weaknesses identified for that corpus, namely that one cannot tell whether it is the result of a true linguistic connection or of chance resemblance.

4.3. OUTLINE OF THE PHONOLOGICAL STRUCTURE OF THE URALIC LANGUAGES

What follows is an essential description of the phonemic inventory and general phonological structure of the U languages. This overview concentrates on those features, such as vowel harmony, consonant gradation etc., that are relevant for the historical analysis I am about to present, and which will allow the reader to follow and appreciate the current status of the 'reconstructed' P-U sound structure (for a detailed and up-to-date description of the sound structure of the U languages see the quoted book by Abondolo (ed.) 1998; see also Abondolo 1994; Comrie 1988 and Janhunen 1981b).

4.3.1. Phoneme inventory

Within the vowel system the most salient characteristic of a large number of U languages is the presence of front round and/or back (or central) unrounded vowels. All the U languages distinguish at least 5 vowel qualities (*i, e, a, o, u*), such as Erzya Mordvin, but most U languages have much richer systems, including reduced vowels. Finnish has *ü*[6] *ö ä* front vowels. Front round vowels (often associated to vowel harmony) are found also in most Balto-Finnic languages, in Cheremis, in Hungarian, in Vakh-Ostyak, in Samoyed (Samoyed Tawgi and Selkup). Non-front unrounded vowels are found in Estonian, Votic, Livonian, Cheremis, most dialects of the Permian languages (where mid *ę* and *į* play a significant role), in some dialects of Ob-Ugric, and in Samoyed. The most prolific vowel system in terms of qualitative opposition is that of Vakh-Ostyak, with an inventory of 13 vowels, including front full round/unrounded vowels and back full round/unrounded vowels, + 2 reduced front vowels (round/unrounded), and two reduced back vowels (round/unrounded) (Tereškin 1961: 9). Diphthongs occur mainly in Balto-Finnic and Lapp, but are prominent also in some dialects of Vogul and in Samoyed Tawgi. In general, the vocalism of the U languages, particularly in the Ob-Ugric languages and in the Lappic languages, is very rich and varied.

The smallest consonant inventory may be found in Balto-Finnic. For example, Finnish has obstruents at only three points of articulation: *p t k*. At the opposite extreme there is Samoyed Selkup with *p, t, t́, č, k, q*. Most languages fall somewhere between these extremes, with the presence of a separate palatal (or palatalised alveolar/dental) articulation series in most of the languages, with the exclusion of Balto-Finnic. Opposition of voice is rare, being fully developed only in the Permian languages and Hungarian. Mordvin is unique in allowing frequent initial consonant clusters in native vocabulary. The U languages lack prosodic phonological opposition at the word level, the stress being in fact predictable, at the beginning of the word, in most languages (with the obvious exceptions due to borrowing). However, the following languages deviate from this rule: Cheremis, where the stress, non-phonemic, falls generally on the last phonologically full vowel (Kangasmaa-Minn 1998: 224); Mordvin, where the stress is free and non-distinctive with regard to grammar and Lexicon (Zaicz 1998: 190); the various Samoyedic languages, which present quite a complex, variegated situation in this regard (see the chapters on the Samoyedic languages in Abondolo (ed.) 1998: 457–601).

4.3.2. Quantitative opposition

Quantitative vowel opposition, in one form or another – short vs long, reduced vs full – is found in all U languages (save Erzya Mordvin and most of Permian), even if how this is realised phonetically varies greatly from language to language. For example, in Finnish, vowel length is distinctive in all positions: tuuli 'wind' vs tuli 'fire'. The long vowels are mostly to be considered as an innovation,[7] if one assumes that length distinction was not a P-U feature (see Abondolo 1998a: 150 and discussion below). The Estonian quantity system is quite complex, as shown by Hint (1997). Here it might suffice to quote Viitso (1998: 119): 'In standard Estonian all vowels in primarily stressed syllables and most consonants . ... have both short and long counterparts. Second, there exists in stressed syllables a tripartite correlation of distinctive syllabic quantities, usually referred to as quantity 1, quantity 2, and quantity 3.'

4.3.3. Morpho-phonological alternations

The major alternations to be found in the U area are vowel harmony (VH) and consonant gradation (CG). In addition to these alternations, which will be described briefly below, there are other – paradigmatic and lexical – minor vowel alternations of one kind or another, which are language specific, and are more or less extensive and/or systematic:

- long vs short vowel alternations of the type: Finn. maa 'land (Nominative)' vs ma-i-ta 'land-(Plural-Partitive)'; Hun. szél 'wind (Nominative)' vs szele-t 'wind-(Accusative)';
- vowel quality alternations of the type found in Lapp: Nominative gietta 'hand' vs Illative gittii; in Samoyed Yurak: Nominative ja 'earth' vs Accusative Plural jo; in Finnish: palaa 'to burn (intransitive)' vs polttaa 'to burn (transitive)'; in Hungarian: hal- 'to die' vs holt 'dead'.

In Hungarian there is an articulated vowel alternation restricted to a closed set of items. Consider the following examples where a different 'oblique stem', as Abondolo (1987: 194–5) calls it, appears in connection with certain suffixes: dal 'song' vs fal 'wall' exhibit a different stem in the

Accusative: *dal-t* vs *fala-t*. The same is true for the following pair: *gyomor* 'stomach' and *nyomor* 'misery', whose respective Accusative is: *gyomro-t* vs *nyomor-t*. Nouns with the oblique stem in -*a* or -*e* may also be involved in other kinds of alternations, as shown by the following pair: *falu* vs *falva-k* 'village vs village-Plu.', *kapu* vs *kapu-k* 'gate vs gate-Plu.' In a word, the oblique stem occurs only to the left of certain suffixes. Such a distribution reflects, according to Abondolo (ibid.), the historical fact that most names which now exhibit oblique stems date from at least Ugric and often F-U or even U times. Indeed, as we will see below, some researchers have postulated the existence of alternations already at the F-U period.

In Eastern Ostyak, vowel alternation is more extended and systematic and is both of qualitative and/or quantitative character. There are qualitative alternations such as: *i* ~ *ä* (*ämp* ~ *imp-əm* 'dog ~ dog-my'), which occur both in substantives and verbs, and to which only full vowels can participate. There are purely quantitative alternations such as: *ə* ~ *e* (*wer-* ~ *wəri* 'to make ~ make-it !'), which occur in certain verbs only. There are other alternations such as: *o* ~ *ă* (*toγə̂r-* ~ *tă̆γrĭ* ! 'to lock ~ lock-it'), which are at the same time of a quantitative-qualitative character and are known in verbs only (Gulya[8]1966: 39–44).

One interesting factor to observe here from the point of view of historical investigation is that pointed out by Honti[9] (1998a: 340; see also 1982a and 1983):

> Forms showing the alternations have not completely supplanted the older, non-alternating forms, with the result that there is much superabundance and many parallel forms are attested in different degrees and in different lexical items, across the dialects. In Vvj [Vakh and Vasjugan], for example, the first-person singular form of *äämp* 'dog' is either *äämpääm* or *iimpəm*. High vowels optionally replace low ones in parallel fashion in the formation of the imperative and the past tense built with -∅, e.g. V *lääwətləm* 'I feed', *lääwtää* or *liiwtää* 'feed!', *lääwtəm* or *liiwtəm* 'I fed'

Morpho-phonological alternations are much less extended and systematic in Vogul, where nominal stems ending in a vowel do not alternate, in contrast to consonant final nominal stems and verbal stems, which all alternate. In Finnish, the instances of morpho-phonological or lexical gradation are rather limited and are normally considered exceptions to its normal, mechanical operation (see below).

Regarding the Samoyedic languages, it is worth mentioning that Samoyed Tawgi presents such an abundance and complexity of morpho-phonological alternations, including glottal stop alternation, truncation, two types of gradation, vowel harmony and accommodation, stem alternation etc., as to be absolutely unique within U (Helimski 1998a: 487).

Phenomena of sandhi across word boundaries are characteristic only of individual languages, such as Nenets.

4.3.3.1. *Vowel harmony*

Vowel harmony (VH) is the term used when all the vowels of a single word must be of the same quality. In the U languages VH is mainly 'palatal' in kind, that is, the vowels of a word must be either all front or all back in quality. VH is found in most Balto-Finnic languages, in Mordvin, in Cheremis, in Hungarian and in Vakh-Ostyak, but not in Vogul, with the exception of the Tavda dialect. According to Keresztes (1998: 397), 'The present-day dialects of Mansi have lost Vowel Harmony. The Southern (Tavda) dialect data collected at the turn of the last century show that this form of Mansi was archaic in this respect.'

VH is of a highly idiosyncratic type in Samoyed, where it is a productive process only in Samoyed Tawgi, whilst related phenomena are present also in Samoyed Yurak and Yenisei. Curiously enough, VH is not present in Lapp, Estonian and Livonian, and is not present in all Vogul and Ostyak dialects. For example, in Estonian, in non-initial syllables, the vowel oppositions *a* vs *ä*, *e* vs *õ*, *u* vs *ü* are neutralised in favour of *a*, *e*, *u*, so that only these three vowels and *i* can occur in non-initial syllable. If one interprets VH as a combination of neutralisation and assimilation, as proposed by Comrie (1988: 454–6), then Estonian can be considered similar to the other Balto-Finnic languages in having neutralisation of the front vs back opposition in non-initial syllables, but different from them in lacking assimilation. VH thus represents another of those U features which does not correlate with the conventional internal genetic groups.

VH may extend to suffixes (Case endings, possessive endings etc.), as well as to epenthetic vowels, as shown in the following examples: Finn. *talo* 'house' $\longrightarrow$ *talo-ssa* 'house-in', but *kylpy* 'bath' $\longrightarrow$ *kylvy-ssä* 'bath-in'; Hun. *kert* 'garden' $\longrightarrow$ *kert-be* 'garden-into', but *konyha* 'kitchen' $\longrightarrow$ *konyhá-ba* 'kitchen-into'; *ember* 'man' $\longrightarrow$ *ember-e-m* 'man-Ep.Vow.-my', but *asszony* 'lady' $\longrightarrow$ *asszony-o-m* 'lady-Ep.Vow.-my, madam'.

Vakh-Ostyak has a particularly rich vowel system and a very consistent palatal VH, compare for example: *i* vs *į*; *ü* vs *u*; *ö̆* vs *ŏ*; *ə* vs *ə̑*. Here are some examples: *vəri!* 'make it!' vs *pän̥į!* 'put it!'; *köt-ö̆γ* 'hand-our' vs *kut-ŏγ* 'house-our' (Gulya 1966: 37–8).

In some languages, such as Hungarian and East Cheremis, there are also a few instances of Labial Harmony. For example, in Hungarian some suffixes have a third, labial variant: *e / o /ö*, to be used when there is a labial vowel within the word. Compare *ház-hoz* 'house-toward', *víz-hez* 'water-toward', but *gyümölcs-höz* 'fruit-toward'. The variant *ö* is also available for the ephentetic vowel, as in *gyümölcs-ö-t* 'fruit-Ep.Vow.-Acc.' In Finnish and in Hungarian the vowels *i* and *e* are neutral from the point of view of VH.

4.3.3.2. *Consonant gradation*

Contrary to common perception, consonant gradation (CG) is not a general characteristic of the U languages. And, in fact, opinions about its origin, its chronology and its 'U nature' may diverge greatly, as can be seen from the different opinions held by Setälä[10] (1912/14), Helimski (1995), Ravila[11] (1951), Sammallahti[12] (1984: 138), Hajdú[13] (2000: 261). For example, Helimski (1995) shares with Setälä the opinion that CG is an old U feature which has been lost in most languages (through a process of 'de-gradation'). The author basis his claim on the fact that CG is present in the more external languages of the U area, Samoyed Yurak and Balto-Finnic. Furthermore, the Finnic and Samoyed CG, and related linguistic and extra-linguistic phenomena, are argued by the author to be very similar in kind.

The reality is that CG is missing in most U languages and the details of the phenomenon vary considerably from language to language. CG is present only in Balto-Finnic (but not in Veps and Livonian) and Lapp (but not in all the idioms). A different type of CG, even less homogeneous than that found in Balto-Finnic and Lapp, is present in Samoyed Yurak (Nenets) (Salminen 1997a, 1998: 257–9), in Samoyed Tawgi (Nganasan), and in southern Selkup. In Samoyed Tawgi two different types of gradation co-exist: syllabic gradation and rhythmic gradation (Helimski 1998a: 487–94). In southern Selkup the most characteristic alternation is that of nasal and homotopic stops: $m \sim p, n \sim t, \eta \sim k$ (Helimski 1998b: 554–5; see also Collinder 1960: 216).

CG can be essentially described, using Abondolo's (1994: 4855) definition, as 'alternation of strong vs weak consonant(ism) word-medially in open vs closed syllables'. The core of the CG can be seen and understood clearly in the stop consonants, the only type present in all the U languages that have gradation at all. Originally, the first sound of the pair, the so-called 'strong grade', appeared word-medially in an open syllable, whilst the second member of the pair, the so-called 'weak grade', appeared word-medially in a syllable which had become closed by adding grammatical and functional suffixes. The basic alternations are as follows:

- between a geminate and a single plosive: *kk* vs *k* (Finn. *kirkko* 'church' vs *kirko-t* 'church-Plu.');
- between a single plosive and the corresponding voiced fricative (or its language-specific reflex): *p* vs *v* (Finn. *papu* 'bean' vs *pavu-t* 'bean-Plu.');
- between a velar *k* and *Ø* (Finn. *laki* 'law' vs *lai-t* 'law-Plu.');
- between a voiceless and a voiced plosive: *t* vs *d* (Finn. *pöytä* 'table' vs *pöydä-t* 'table-Plu.').

When consonant clusters containing liquid or nasal are encountered, the following alternations normally happen:

- *lp* vs *lv* (Finn. *kylpy* 'bath' vs *kylvy-n* 'bath-Gen.');
- *mp* vs *mm* (Finn. *hampaa-n* 'tooth-Gen. vs *hammas* 'tooth-Nom.') .

In reality, CG is much more complex than this, with a lot of exceptions, also depending on which Case ending is added to the stem. However, a deeper analysis of this and other phenomena of phonological structure lies beyond the scope of this book (for an overview see Hajdú 2000: 259–61).

Although the original, basic conditioning factor for CG is the opposition between open vs closed syllables, subsequent phonetic and/or analogical changes may eliminate this conditioning environment so that in some languages (in some areas) a number of morphological forms can be distinguished only through the opposition between strong and weak grade. This is particularly evident in Estonian and in Lapp, and, to some extent, also in Finnish. For example, in Finnish, the alternation *jalka* ('foot-Nom.') vs *jala-n* ('foot-Gen.') vs *jalka-a* ('foot-Partit.') can be accounted for in terms of the phonetic opposition between open vs closed syllable. In contrast, in the corresponding Estonian forms Gen. *jala* (weak grade) vs Partit. *jalga* (strong grade), there is no Case ending closing the second syllable, therefore there is no phonetic conditioning on the basis of which to predict the occurrence of the weak grade. The same is true of the Estonian Partitive Plural *jalgu*, which can be understood if compared with the corresponding Finnish *jalko-j-a* ('foot-Plu.-Partit.'; the final vowel *o* instead of *a*, like in Nom. *jalka,* is a normal vowel alternation in this kind of environment). Compare the scheme in Table 4.2.

Table 4.2 Partial noun declension in Finnish and Estonian

	Nominative	Genitive	Partitive Singular	Partitive Plural
Finn:	*lehti* 'leaf'	*lehde-n*	*lehte-ä*	*lehti-ä < lehti-j-ä*
Est:	*leht*	*lehe*	*lehte*	*lehti*

In Estonian the loss of the final vowel in the Nominative has lead to the reanalysis of this vowel as an inflectional Case ending in the other cases. This fact, together with the loss of the conditioning environments for CG and vowel alternation, has created inflectional forms which are recognisable solely by alternations (though the alternations themselves are no more predictable from the form of the stem). They are, therefore, fusional rather than agglutinative forms.

4.4. ATTEMPTS TO RECONSTRUCT THE PROTO-URALIC VOCALISM

In this paragraph I shall discuss in some detail the major attempts that have been made in the modern literature to reconstruct the P-U vocalism, including the reconstructions by Janhunen and Sammallahti introduced in the sections above. We shall see that the evidence on which the reconstructed P-U vocalism is based does not in fact support the idealised picture that is usually reported in textbooks.

4.4.1. *Vowel alternation vs quantity correlation*

As mentioned above, neither quantity correlation nor the various vowel alternations scattered throughout the U languages represent a compact, consistent, systematic phenomenon in the languages in which they occur. Furthermore, they display a rather erratic distribution. The question therefore has arisen as to whether these phenomena are to be traced back to P-U times, or are to be considered as more recent, independent developments. Two major points of view have emerged:

(i)   the point of view of W. Steinitz (1944, 1950, 1955; see also Setälä 1912/ 14), according to whom vowel alternation was a common, old P-U phenomenon, and not a secondary, language-specific one. Vowel alternation can be traced back at least to the F-U period, although it appears sporadically nowadays – it is present in a more or less systematic way only in Ob-Ugric, Lapp, and, partially, in Hungarian. The author reconstructs a series of more or less regular paradigmatic alternations for the first syllable, of the type $a \sim o$, $a \sim \dot{\imath}$, $a \sim u$/$\ddot{a} \sim i$, $\ddot{a} \sim e$, $e \sim \bar{\imath}$ etc. These alternations are held to be able to account particularly for irregular correspondences; in fact, they are used by the author as an overall, pervasive explanatory force. The starting point is the vocalism of Eastern (Vakh-) Ostyak and Hill Cheremis, languages that Steinitz considers as the most archaic with regard to vocalism. Both these languages present the same phenomenon: next to a system of full, normal vowels with three tongue-heights, there is a system of reduced vowels, with one vowel only, the difference between the two sets being both phonetic and phonological. According to the author, these features cannot be considered as a coincidence, since these two languages are not closely related within U either genetically or geo-graphically; therefore, these features must be considered inherited from the P-L. Compare the following etymological matches between Ostyak and Cheremis containing reduced vowels:

(4.1) Ost. *kŏs-* 'to urinate'/Che. *kə̑ž-* (UEW 210)

(4.2) Ost. *kŏṇč* 'nail'/Che. *küč* (UEW 157)

(4.3) Ost. *ńĕlə* 'four'/Che. *nə̑l* (UEW 315–16)

In general, to the Vakh Ostyak reduced vowels *ŏ, ȫ, ĕ* are supposed to correspond the Hill Cheremis reduced vowels, *ə̑, ü, ə*. This is good enough for the author, even though in another (more eastern) Cheremis dialect the relevant correspondences are with the following full vowels respectively: *u, ü, i*. These vowels would have derived, in a further development, from the reduced vowels, despite the fact that this is not quite a 'natural' process. The reconstructed P-U vocalic system must have contained therefore, according to the author, the opposition: 'full vs reduced vowels' together with a series of alternations, but not quantity correlation as such. The long vs short opposition must have been a concomitant factor in the realisation of the full vowels (as it still happens in a way in Ostyak, where the long vs short realisation of the vowel of first syllable depends on the structure of the syllable and the quality of the vowel of second syllable).

However, there are several weaknesses in Steinitz' analysis, in addition to the mismatch between full and reduced vowels in other Cheremis dialects (as observed by the author himself): (a) there are only very few relevant matches to support such an analysis; (b) there are too many reconstructed vowel alternations; (c) there are counter-examples, as shown by Ost. *nem* 'name' (full vowel) vs Che. *ləm* (reduced vowel; UEW 305; see also Abondolo 1996: 2). Furthermore, Bereczki (1968, 1969), examining the reduced vowels of Cheremis, has come to the conclusion that they have nothing to do with those of Ostyak, but represent an independent development. This is reminiscent of the parallel developments in the nearby Turkic languages Tatar and Chuvash (in Chuvash central, illabial short *ĕ* and non-front illabial *ă* seem to correspond to Che. *ÿ* and *y* respectively (Manzelli 1993: 562). In other words, these reduced vowels would be a typical result of *Sprachbund* convergence.

(ii)   the opposing point of view of E. Itkonen (1939, 1946, 1954, 1960, 1962, 1988). The author, whilst questioning the assumed regularity of Steinitz' alternations, considers the Balto-Finnic group, particularly Finnish, as the most conservative languages with regard to sound-structure. This view is based on the fact that several supposedly old loan-words in U have been preserved in Finnish in a shape closer to the reconstructed form than the corresponding term of the donor language itself, or any other corresponding term within U. For example, the term for 'king' in Finnish is *kuningas,* which is reminiscent of the Germanic form **kuningaz* more than Swedish *konung, kung.* Similarly, the Finnish term for '100': *sata* is closer to the reconstructed Indo-Iranian form **śata* than Zyr. *śo*/Ost. *sot, sat*/Hun. *száz* (UEW 467). Furthermore, certain Finnish words – whether borrowed or originally U – have not changed at all, judging from the (generally accepted) reconstructed P-forms[14] : *kala* 'fish' < P-U **kala; maksa* 'liver' < P-U **maksa; nime-* 'name' < P-U **nime; pesä* 'nest' < P-U **pesä; mene-* 'to go' < P-U **mene-; pata* 'pot' < P-U **pata,* and many others.

Itkonen reconstructs the vowel structure of the P-Finno-Permian node by additionally taking into account the conditioning factor of the vocalism of second syllable, a factor generally neglected in previous reconstructions. He starts with Balto-Finnic and Lapp, and then carries on with Votyak, Mordvin, Cheremis and Zyrian. The reconstruction contains only full vowels, together with quantity correlation (only for the mid vowels), a feature which is indeed typical of Balto-Finnic, as mentioned above. Itkonen goes also a step further, claiming that the vocalism of the languages belonging to the Permian, Volgaic, and Balto-Finnic nodes can be derived from the same reconstructed vocalic system, so that, at least in this area, it does not seem necessary to posit several intermediate P-Languages. In practice, Itkonen considers the reconstructed Finno-Permian vocalism as substantially identical with that of the F-U node, even if the vocalism of the western languages does not really match that of the Ugric branch (see below). Vowel alternations of the Ostyak type are not included, being considered a recent, independent development; this is because paradigmatic (and derivational) vowel alternations are almost non-existent in Finno-Permian, particularly in Finnish.

Among the difficulties encountered while equating *de facto* the Finno-Permian vocalism with the F-U vocalism is the question of quantity correlation, which can be traced back to P-Finno-Permian only. The quantity opposition found in other languages, such as Hungarian, Vogul and Samoyed, seems to have developed during the independent lives of the languages, as indicated by the frequent mismatch between long and short vowel counterparts in the relevant correspondences. For example, a long vowel (in first syllable) in Hungarian may correspond to a short one in Vogul and vice versa: Hun. *négy* vs Vog. *ńila* 'four' (UEW 315); Hun. *fészëk* vs Vog. *piít* 'nest' (UEW 375); Hun. *öl* vs Vog. *äl* 'to kill' (UEW 566–7; notice however that in this case there are also Vogul variants with short vowel). The view that long vowels are an innovation, at least in Hungarian, seems to be confirmed by the old texts, where the difference between long and short, if it did exist, was not marked (see Bárczi 1958a: 84). Similarly, Collinder (1965a: 102) remarks that:

> it is not so that a Fennic word with a long vowel . . . has a Hungarian counterpart with a long vowel and that a Fennic word with a short vowel has a Hungarian counterpart with a short vowel. . . . The Hungarian counterpart of Fi. *liemi* 'broth' is *lé*, asg. [Accusative Singular] *levet*; the Hungarian counterpart of Fi. *veri* 'blood' is *vér*, asg. *vért* (note the short vowel in the derivative *vërës, vörös* 'red')

The case of Samoyed seems again to support the view that quantity correlation is not to be considered as an original P-U feature. In fact, the type of quantitative correlation found in the Samoyed languages, which consists of a sequence of any full vowel of the paradigm followed by an invariable, reduced vowel segment, has been reconstructed only for P-Samoyed, and differs from other types of quantity correlation. It is not clear how these two phenomena – Finno-Permian systematic (non-combinatory) quantity correlation vs Samoyed vowel sequence – are to be interpreted from the point of view of the reconstruction of P-U. This topic will be discussed in detail in the sections below.

Serious doubts about the U origin of the Balto-Finnic quantity correlation have also been expressed by Lehtinen (1967), Rédei (1968) and Hajdú (2000: 258), whilst the validity of this view has been re-proposed in Itkonen (1969).

To summarise, and also to note some agreements, both Steinitz and Itkonen reconstruct 11 vowels: 7 short and 4 long (Itkonen); 8 full (with three tongue-heights) and 3 reduced (Steinitz). In correspondence to the reconstructed reduced vowels of Steinitz – *$\breve{u}$, * $\breve{\ddot{u}}$, *$\breve{\imath}$ – Itkonen reconstructs the short vowels *u, *$\ddot{u}$ and *i. The difference is that in Steinitz' reconstruction vowel alternations play an essential role, whilst in Itkonen's reconstruction they are dismissed as a secondary, language-specific phenomenon, and vice versa for quantity correlation. Steinitz bases his analysis mainly on the eastern languages, whilst Itkonen analyses only the western languages, leaving in turn Ob-Ugric and Hungarian untouched. Recall that according to the analysis of vowel alternation in Eastern Ostyak, as proposed by Honti (1982a, 1983, 1998a; see above Section 4.3.3), forms with alternation are co-occurrent with 'older' forms without alternation, so that, judging from this analysis at least, vowel alternation can be interpreted as a recent, language-specific, development.

Recently, the view that paradigmatic alternations can be traced back to P-U, although in moderation, has been re-proposed in the 'rotation' model of Tálos (1987) and Abondolo (1995, 1996). Basically, the rotation model proposes a re-transcription of the previously reconstructed P-U vowels, but only with **two** tongue-heights and **with** quantity correlation. However, as already mentioned with regard to Steinitz, the basic weakness with this kind of approach is that alternations contain too much explanatory power; in other words, the more alternations one postulates for the P-Language, the easier it is to establish correspondences (see also below).

4.4.2. *Simplification of the Uralic family tree*

As a follow-up to E. Itkonen research, Korhonen, in a series of publications (1974, 1976, 1981, 1984a, 1984b, 1986, 1988c, 1989) proposes a considerable simplification of the conventional family tree. The author argues that, due to the scarcity of material suitable for reconstruction, the qualitative differences (in vocalism and consonantism) that can be observed among the oldest nodes of U do not appear to be either numerous or relevant, despite the temporal difference which is supposed to have occurred. That is, a qualitative stratification into layers becomes slighter and slighter as one attempts to reconstruct older nodes. For example, the reconstructed Late-P-Finnic differs notably from Early-P-Finnic, but the changes in Early-P-Finnic itself are but a few. The changes to be traced back to P-Finno-Volgaic are restricted to no more than a couple of sound-changes. At the level of P-Finno-Permian and at the level of older P-Languages, no one single sound-change can be safely reconstructed. And, in fact, the reconstructions of P-Finno-Permian, P-F-U and P-U usually reported in the literature do not fundamentally differ from each other. The same holds true for the reconstruction of P-Finno-Volgaic and Early P-Finnic.[15] In principle, it may be possible for sound-changes to proceed very slowly at some points in time, as shown by those borrowed words (*kuningas* and *sata*), or those U words that have been so preserved in Finnish as to remain exactly the same as the reconstructed forms (see the examples in the previous section). However, it cannot be explained how a language could have remained the same, sound wise, in each single sound relation, for several millennia.

After observing that a stratification into several chronological layers is not really justifiable for U on the basis of phonological innovations, Korhonen argues that a stratification based on morphological innovations – which can be important as well – is certainly justifiable. However, to support his claim, the author can only find two examples: a) the ending -*s*, used to form local Case endings, as in Finn. *talo-ssa* (< *talo-s-na*) 'house-in' and *talo-sta* (< *talo-s-ta*) 'house-out=of', an ending which seems to be a Finno-Volgaic innovation; b) the constructions of the type Finn. *raha-tta* 'money-without', *leivä-ttä* 'bread-without', which seem to go back to the Finno-Permian period.

This state of affairs leads Korhonen to some interesting considerations about the Comparative Method and the nature of the reconstructed P-Language. He states that reconstructions cannot provide us with any information which is not already visible in the daughter languages. Then he wonders whether the P-Language (and related P-forms) obtained as a result of the Comparative Method and/or the method of internal reconstruction shouldn't be regarded more as a synchronic, rather than a diachronic linguistic entity. In other words, the author (1974: 254) thinks[16] that the P-Language may be regarded as a 'synchronic meta-language', upon which the characteristics of related languages are projected in accordance with certain principles of 'naturalness'. This statement was not meant to deny the merits of historical reconstructions, but simply to note that reconstructions can tell us only one part of the history of languages, and that reconstructions of every single aspect of a P-Language may not be obtained.

After these methodological considerations, Korhonen analyses the morpho-phonemic alternations known to have existed in P-Finnish (P-Balto-Finnic and P-Lapp), such as the alternations in stem-final vowels and the phonematic consonant alternations. These alternations existed in addition to consonant gradation proper (which operates mechanically; see Section 4.3.3.2 above[17]), and are reflexes of non-alternating forms posited for Early-P-Finnish, as shown in Table 4.3 (adapted from Korhonen 1974: 245).

Table 4.3 Morpho-phonemic alternations in Proto-Finnish

$i \sim e$	nimi	'name'	vs	nime-n	'name-Gen.'	<	*nime	vs	*nime-n
$a \sim o$:	kala	'fish'	vs	kalo-j-a	'fish-Plu.-Partit.'	<	*kala	vs	*kala-j-ta
$a \sim e$:	kota	'house'	vs	kot-i-a	'house-Plu.-Partit.'	<	*kota	vs	*kota-j-ta[18]
$ä \sim Ø$:	pesä	'nest'	vs	pes-i-ä	'nest-Plu.-Partit.'	<	*pesä	vs	*pesä-j-tä
$s \sim t$:	käsi	'hand'	vs	käte-nä	'hand-Ess.'	<	*käte	vs	*käte-nä
$n \sim m$:	ydin	'nucleus'	vs	ytime-n	'nucleus-Gen.'	<	*üðem	vs	*üðeme-n

Korhonen then remarks that it is impossible, through the methods of historical linguistics, to obtain a reliable reconstruction of any morpho-phonemic alternation assumed to have existed in P-Finno-Permian, P-F-U or P-U. In other words, it seems unlikely that consonant gradation was already present at the F-U and/or at the U phase. In Balto-Finnic, Lapp, as well as in Samoyed Tawgi and Selkup, gradation is a superficial phenomenon, whose phonetic origin is still transparent. If this feature had existed in earlier phases, it would have left some kind of fossilised traces at least in some of the related languages. In contrast, the F-U vowel alternations postulated by Setälä (1896) and Steinitz (for which see Section 4.4.1 above), seem to fulfil better the requirements established for an old type of alternation. In Ostyak, as already mentioned, the process is a bit more productive in the eastern dialects, although its original conditioning factors cannot be reconstructed. In most languages this phenomenon appears to be sporadic and fossilised (recall: Hun. *hal-* vs *holt*, Finn. *palaa* vs *polttaa*). Nevertheless, all in all, the available F-U material relevant for the reconstruction of vowel alternations is so scanty that no safe conclusion can be drawn, one way or the other. In this regard, the Comparative Method proves powerless ('vertaileva menetelmä osoittautuu voimattomaksi' (1974: 252)). One can have an idea of what the past vowel alternations and irregularities might have been, but it is difficult to reconstruct their exact quality and character.

The difficulties encountered in reconstructing original, P-U alternations are pointed out also by Janhunen (1981b: 27), who states that:

A consequence of the phonotactic restrictions is that only two distinctive stem types could occur in the word roots: å/ä-stems and ə-stems. A characteristic of the latter is that the stem final high (reduced) vowel ə could alternate with zero before suffixes comprising a whole syllable, provided the restrictions on consonant distribution were not violated. This phenomenon (the so called consonant stem) is actually one of the very few morphophonemic alternations that can be reconstructed in PU.

There have been attempts to reconcile some of the major problems related to the reconstruction of the P-U vocalism. For example, Décsy (1969a, 1969b) and Hajdú (1969c) share two basic starting points: it is not safe to reconstruct the vocalism of P-U only on the basis of a few dozen etymologies. Next to etymologies, attention should be paid to other features, such as typological trends in Phonology, frequency in the occurrence of sounds etc. For example, the velar illabial *ę* and *į* (which have been reconstructed by some researchers, such as Steinitz, Collinder and Janhunen, see below), as well as the palato-labial *ü* and *ö*, occur quite rarely, so that one might well assume that they have developed, independently, in more recent times. In other words, in theory it is plausible that the complexity and diversity of the vocalic system of the U languages might have developed from an original, very simple system, containing only the fundamental vowel (*a o u e i*), plus the very frequent *ä*. From such a basic system, all the other vowels could have derived through the ordinary, natural processes of velarisation (*ę, į*), palatalisation (*ü, ö*), reduction (*ə, ŏ*), labialisation (*å*), lengthening etc., not excluding the possibility that sounds such as *ü* and *ę* might have been allophones of *i* and *e* respectively.

This is fine and plausible; however, if we accepted this view, how would we distinguish P-U vocalism from any other?

4.4.3. Sammallahti's reconstruction of the Proto-Uralic and Proto-Finno-Ugric vocalism

Sammallahti (1988) has proposed a reconstruction of the P-U vocalism based on Janhunen (1981a) which is often reported as a 'standard' reconstruction (see, for example, Campbell (1997: 832)) (Table 4.4). According to the author, instead of *å*, *a* is also possible, or even more probable from a typological point of view.

Sammallahti (1988: 486) has also 'sketched' a reconstruction of the P-F-U vocalism. He states that this reconstruction is:

Table 4.4 Sammallahti's Proto-Uralic (initial and non-initial) vocalism (1988: 481)

	Back vowels	Front vowels
Stressed Position	/ *u i* *o* *å*	*ü i* *e* *ä* /
Unstressed Position	/ *i* *i* *ä* *ä* /	

an attempt to bridge the gap between the existing reconstructions of Proto-Uralic (Janhunen 1981a), Proto-Ob-Ugric (somewhat modified from Honti 1982a), and P-Finno-Permic (Itkonen 1954). The details are far from settled

The author argues that the postulation of a distinctive P-F-U vocalism, as opposed to the P-U vocalism, is supported by five 'systematic changes' in vocalism of first syllable (apart from the preservation of *i). These changes, however, are 'the same as proposed by Janhunen for Proto-Finno-Permic' and are each substantiated by one etymology only. Furthermore, four of the five listed etymologies belong to those problematic etymologies for which Janhunen has introduced the unspecified segment '*x'. The etymologies in question are: 'arrow' (see example (4.5) below), 'tongue', 'spruce' (see example (4.4) below) and 'wing/feather' (see example (7.10) below). The reconstructed P-F-U vocalism is as follows in Table 4.5.

Table 4.5 Sammallahti's Proto-Finno-Ugric (first syllable) vocalism (1988: 486)

	short				long		
/u	i	ü	i		/uu	ii	ii
o			e		oo		ee/
å			ä/				

According to the author (1988: 486), in the second syllable the opposition *i vs *i was probably already neutralised in the P-F-U phase and only *i remained. This change eventually led to the abolition of *i (and *ii) also in the first syllable, and gave an impetus to the reshaping of the vowel system.

4.4.4. The 'reconstruction' of the P-Ob-Ugric vocalism

The reconstruction of the P-Ob-Ugric vocalism, generally neglected in major attempts at reconstruction of the P-U sound structure, has been the object of extensive research by Honti (1979, 1982a, 1982b, 1983, 1984) and Abondolo (1995, 1996). Compare also the 'Umlaut hypothesis' for the Ostyak 'Ablaut' recently suggested by Helimski (1999).

Honti (1982a) selected on a principled basis the etymologies to compare, which is in itself a great achievement, considering the highly divergent dialects of Vogul and Ostyak. He has also argued in favour of the secondary origin of the Eastern Ostyak vowel alternations (see Section 4.3.3 above). However, among the long-standing problems one can mention the following: (a) the author concentrates on the vowels of first syllable; (b) the author reconstructs Ob-Ugric internally, disregarding evidence from outside; (c) up to 17 P-Ob-Ugric vowels are reconstructed; (d) the proposed sound-developments may not always be strict in terms of phonetic/phonological criteria.

Abondolo, on the other hand, does take into account the U cognates through an extensive etymological material, but he recognises only two tongue-heights by eliminating the mid vowels. According to the author (1996: 11–12), the elimination of the mid vowels from the reconstruction 'shifts the burden of explicitness onto quantity, which must always be a variable in any language, and not only in stress-timed ones'. Therefore, Abondolo assumes the presence in P-U of the vocalic quantitative opposition, which is supposed to have 'collapsed' just before the break-up of common P-Ob-Ugric, yielding the merging of long and short vowels, of the type $*ii/*i > *i, *ää/*ä > *ä,$ etc. (Notice that Sammallahti (1988: 500) is of the same opinion with regard to vowels of first syllable.) However, without taking into account the question of the two tongue-heights, it is perhaps safer not to consider quantity opposition as an original P-U feature, as highlighted above (see Section 4.4.1). Furthermore, there is no independent evidence for a 'collapse' of quantity opposition in P-Ob-Ugric. Last, but not least, as already mentioned, Abondolo's approach is too powerful, because of the presence of alternations in the P-Language.

Despite the efforts and the achievements, one may still safely state that the Ob-Ugric vowel correspondences remain obscure.

4.4.5. *Matching Proto-Samoyed with Proto-Finnic: Janhunen's corpus*

We have already introduced Janhunen's comparative corpus in Section 4.1 above. In the following three sections I shall discuss this corpus in detail.

As we have seen, there is a mismatch between the vocalism of the western U languages and that of the Samoyed languages. We have also seen that there were no proper, complete reconstructions available for the conventional family tree. As Janhunen says (1981a: 219, my translation)[19]:

> the traditional Uralic family tree might be founded more on a kind of rough 'finger-feeling' than on an exact analysis of the material,

Janhunen tried to bridge this gap between the Finnic and Samoyed sound structure, and to overcome the absence of an 'exact analysis of the material'. The author first reconstructed the vocalism (and, partially, consonantism) of P-Samoyed (1977), a reconstruction which can be considered *grosso modo* achieved. Then he compared the P-Samoyed vocalism with the P-Balto-Finnic/P-Finno-Permian vocalism. The consonantal structure was also taken into account. The Ugric branch, however, was left out of the systematic comparison (for the reasons expounded in Section 4.1 above), so that the P-Finno-Permian node was, *de facto*, equated with the P-F-U node.

Janhunen's research (a follow-up to Sammallahti's 1979 basic work on

P-U reconstruction) shows how difficult it can be to match just the Finnic branch – let alone the P-F-U node – with the Samoyed branch. In addition, Janhunen's detailed analysis of the Finno-Permian, Samoyed, and (sometimes) Ugric sound structure uncovers a degree of irregularity which is diffuse and pervasive, and it is certainly much higher than normally depicted in the general and specialist literature.

In what follows I shall report some of the 'P-U' etymologies as reconstructed by Janhunen (1981a). I shall choose obviously the lexical items which best fit the purpose of this work, without therefore closely respecting the author's way of arguing and grouping of the material. In particular, the lexical items listed in Section 4.4.5.1 illustrate the question of quantity correlation from the perspective of a proper P-U (as opposed to P-F-U) reconstruction. The lexical items listed in Section 4.4.5.2 illustrate the problem of the velar illabial vowels. Examples of (more or less) irregular correspondences either in vocalism or in consonantism, or both, will be reported in Section 4.4.5.3. The majority of these etymologies represent the very core of the etymological material upon which the establishment of the U family has been based. Juxtaposing the reconstructions proposed by Janhunen with those proposed by other sources will help to clarify the variety of opinions, interpretations, analyses of what has been defined as the '*daedalus*' of the investigation of the P-U vocalism (Gheno & Hajdú 1992: 175).

4.4.5.1. *The question of Proto-Uralic quantity correlation*

The following examples basically show how distant the P-Samoyed etymologies can be from the P-Finno-Permian etymologies, whilst sometimes being closer to the Ugric etymologies, even if a systematic comparison with the Ugric parallels, as mentioned, is not provided:

(4.4) P-F-P *kōsi* vs P-S *kåət* 'spruce, *picea excelsa*': Finn. *kuusi* /Sam. Yu. *χādī*/Sam.Ye. *kari, kadi*/Sam.Ka. *kot,* etc.; these are reconstructed as P-U *kåxsi̥* by Janhunen (1981a: 240, item (80)) but as P-U * *kuse* ~ *kose* in UEW 222; the Balto-Finnic parallels are irregular in the vocalism of first syllable.

(4.5) P-F-P *ńōli* vs P-S ?* *ńęəj* 'arrow': Finn *nuoli*/Hun. *nyíl* /Zyr. *ńi̥l, ńęv* /Vog. *ńēl, ńāl* /Sam.Yu. *-ńi* /Sam. Se. *-ńī*/Sam. Ka. *nié*; these are reconstructed as P-U *ńi̥xli̥* by Janhunen (1981a: 241, item (83)) but as P-U *ńęle* (*ńōle*) in UEW 317. The Ugric languages are claimed by Janhunen to have preserved the distinctive quality of the vowel of first syllable better than their cognates. The same holds true on other occasions, see for example Hun. *íj* 'bow' (item (96) in Janhunen).

A similar kind of vowel counterpart between P-Samoyed and P-Finno-Permian holds for other basic lexical items, such as: Finn. *kieli* 'language', reconstructed as P-U *käxli* by Janhunen (item (81): 240); Finn. *tuomi* 'bird-cherry', reconstructed as P-U *d'ixmi* (item (82): 240); Finn. *koivu* 'birch', reconstructed as P-U *koxji* (item (84): 241); Hun. *toll* /Mor. *tolga* 'feather/wing', reconstructed as P-U *tuxli* (item (85): 241); Finn. *kuolla-* 'to die', for which see lexical item (4.20) below.

(4.6) P-F-P *kakta* vs P-S *kitä* 'two': Finn *kaksi*/Hun. *két*/Vog. *kit*/Sam. Yu. *śid'e*/Sam.Ye. *sire* etc.; these are reconstructed by Janhunen as P-U *kektä* ~ *käktä* (item (113): 258) but in UEW 118–19 as P-U *kakta* ~ *käktä* (the Samoyed forms are considered very uncertain). Here again both the Samoyed and the Ugric languages are claimed by Janhunen to have preserved the original front vowel of first syllable, so that in P-Finno-Permian a sporadic change *ä* > *a* must be assumed. The mismatch in the vocalism of the two branches is ascribed to the 'sound lability' typical of terms indicating numerals ('tyypillistä äänteellistä labiiliutta'; (Janhunen 1981a: 258)).

(4.7) P-F-P *śüdäm(i)* vs P-S *sejə̂* 'heart': Finn. *sydän* (Gen. *sydämen*)/Hun. *szív* (dialectal *szű, szü*) / Sam.Yu. *śej*/Sam. Ka. *sī*; these are reconstructed as P-U *śäd'ä* ~ *śüdä* by Janhunen (item (117): 258) but in UEW 477 as P-U *śiδä(-mɜ)* (*śüδä(-mɜ)*). According to Janhunen, the reduced vowel of second syllable in Samoyed could point to an original sequence of open vowel +syllable final semivowel. The word presents however other irregularities: the loss of original *d* (or *d'*) in Ugric: Vog. *sim* /Ost. *sĕm*/Hun. *szív*; and the illabiality of the first syllable: Ug ? *śidäm*. (Note that this is one of the few lexical items on the basis of which an intermediate *δ has been postulated).

In pairs such as (4.4) and (4.5) a vocalic sequence in P-Samoyed seems to correspond 'fairly regularly' (1981a: 239) to a long vowel (in initial syllable) in P-Finno-Permian. This sequence consists of an ordinary, full vowel + a reduced vowel, of the type *Vø. The reduced vowel is to be traced back to P-Samoyed, being a distinctive unit in its vowel paradigm (Janhunen 1981a: 239f.). These etymological pairs seem to add weight to the view that a quantity correlation of some sort was an original, P-U feature: on one side there is vowel length, which is typical only of Balto-Finnic; on the other side there is the Samoyed vowel sequence, which is to be interpreted as a bi-syllabic sequence having a hiatus instead of a consonant at syllable border (of the type *VCø at the P-Samoyed period). Unfortunately, the number of the relevant etymologies (exactly 5 items are listed in the corpus), is not sufficient to draw any safe conclusion. And, in fact, Janhunen seems unsure about how to interpret these phenomena and their mutual relationship from the point of view of the reconstruction of P-U. Neither can he decide which of the two features should be considered original and which secondary: the Finno-Permian vowel length or the Samoyed post-vowel reduced vowel.

Besides the possibility exists that both these features are secondary developments, reflexes of a still unknown P-U segment (from the phonotactic point if view, the question revolves around the nature of the consonant at syllable border). According to the author, this last interpretation seems to be the most neutral and the most promising one. Therefore Janhunen introduces a symbol which will hence be part of the reconstructed consonantism of P-U among several authors: he traces back the reduced vowel of the Samoyed vowel sequence to a distinct P-U consonantal segment, which, being unknown, he marks as '*x'. We have already reported Janhunen's view on the status of this segment (see quote in Section 4.1.1 above). This analysis is basically confirmed in Janhunen (1998: 463). The author states that the consonant in question 'is probably to be classified as a velar glide, paradigmatically parallel to the other two glides *w *y '. He then adds[20] that 'The non-syllabic origin of the reduced vowel in vowel sequences explains the absence of any such sequences with a full vowel as the latter component'.

At this point Janhunen remarks that there are in the U lexicon several words consisting of one syllable, of the type CV in Samoyed, and CVV in Balto-Finnic, which also seem to correspond etymologically 'fairly' often (1981a: 245–8). This type of word is traditionally interpreted as having been originally a two-syllables root, although the problem is of course the phonological definition and reconstruction of the internal consonant.[21] One possibility in the identification of this phoneme could be to connect it to the consonantal segment x . This would allow us to state that at the P-Finno-Permian phase (or at the P-F-U phase?) the vowel preceding the intervocalic x has become long, exactly as happens to the vowel preceding x of syllable final position in examples (4.4) and (4.5) above. In any case, the syllable final consonant *x would always have merged with the vowel, whilst the intervocalic *x would have been preserved sometimes as an independent segment. Examples of these one-syllable roots are: Finn. *myy-* 'to give, sell', whose reconstructed forms could be: P-F-P ? *mexi-* vs P-S *mi-* < U *mexi-* (item (91): 245); Hun. *fő-* /Mor. *pije-* 'to cook, prepare', reconstructed as P-F-P ? *pexi-* vs P-S *pi-* < U *pexi-* (item (92): 245); Finn. *nai-nen* 'woman' (*nai-da* 'to marry', *naa-ras* 'female')/Hun. *nő* 'woman', reconstructed as F-P ? *näxi* vs P-S *ne* < U *näxi* (item (94): 245). However, as Janhunen points out on several occasions, all the assumptions about the phonological status and the distribution of this segment *x are precarious, particularly because *k, *$ŋ$, *w and *j too show the tendency to fall together with the vowel in similar contexts.

The question of the existence of a P-U quantity correlation can be concluded with the following words by Helimski (1984a: 13):

> The numerous differences formed in the course of separate development [of the Samoyed languages] exclude the possibility of accounting for the 'quantity in Samoyed' as a whole.

As is evident from the examples, in UEW the P-U segment *x as reconstructed by Janhunen (1981a) and adopted by Sammallahti (1988), is totally missing.

The above listed examples also illustrate the mismatch in the vowel counterparts of the various branches of U. Consider for example the etymological set of (4.7). Here the Samoyed and Ugric parallels point to something close to an original *i (notice however that Janhunen considers the Ugric *i as irregular), whilst other parallels point to a labio-palatal vowel. The same seems to hold true in the following parallels: Hun. köt 'to bind, tie'/ Vot. kïtkï- /Finn. kytke-, which seem to point again to a labio-palatal vowel. However, Old Hungarian has ket-nie[22], whilst Vogul has kät-, so that something close to an original *e could be reconstructed as well (UEW 163).

The etymological set in (4.5), in addition to the question of quantity correlation, also illustrates the debated question of the existence in P-U of an independent velar illabial ï of first syllable. Its existence was first postulated by Steinitz (1955), and is supported, among others, by Collinder (1965a). In examples of the type of (4.5) the Ob-Ugric and/or Permian languages have velar illabial ï or ẹ, Hungarian has i (reflex of velar illabial ï[23]), whilst in the western languages various velar vowels appear. Janhunen, as we have seen, reconstructs P-U *ńïxlï. However, not everybody accepts this reconstruction, as shown by the alternating P-forms proposed by UEW 317: *ńẹle (*ńōle). Another example of this type is Finn. suoni/Hun. ín 'sinew, tendon', to which correspond on the one hand Vog. tẹ̄n, tān and Zyr.-Vot. sẹn/Sam.Ye. ti, etc., but also Ost. lan, jan, ton, with no illabial vowels, on the other hand. For this set UEW 441 proposes the alternating forms *sẹne (*sōne).[24]

4.4.5.2. The question of the velar illabial vowels

The controversy regarding the velar illabial vowels extends to other etymological sets. According to Janhunen (1981a: 227–37), the P-U nature of this vowel, which is supposed to have merged later on with P-F-P *a, is reinforced by the existence of some Ob-Ugric and Samoyed parallels containing the same illabial vowel (another phonological convergence between the two U branches). In contrast, one finds a in Finnish as well as in Hungarian, as shown in the following examples:

(4.8) P-S *ïlȝ vs P-F-P *ala 'under': Finn. ala, alla (SSA I, 66)/Hun. al (alatt, etc.)/Ost. ïl/Sam.Yu. ŋilna; these are reconstructed by Janhunen as P-U *ïlå (item (38): 227) but as P-U *ala in UEW 6.

(4.9) P-S *mïtȝ vs P-F-P *maksa 'liver': Finn. maksa/Hun. máj /Vog. majȝt /Sam.Yu. mit; these are reconstructed by Janhunen as P-U *mïkså (item (41): 228), but as P-U *maksa in UEW 264.

According to E. Itkonen (1988: 326–7), however, there seems to be only one correspondence of this kind involving at the same time Vogul, Ostyak and Samoyed, the term for '*pinus-cembra*': Vot. *susį-pu*/Ost. *lįyəl* /Vog. *tȩ̄t*, *tāt*/Sam Yu. **tidə?* < P-F-P **saksi*. These are reconstructed by Janhunen as P-U **sįksį* (1981a: 236, item (70)) but by UEW 445 as P-U **soksз* (*saksз*, *sęksз*). Therefore, the claim that between an **a* (present in Finno-Permian and Hungarian) and illabial **į* (present in Vogul, Samoyed and Ostyak), the second vowel should be considered original, cannot really be maintained. On the contrary, it is *į* that should be considered as a development from **a*, as shown by Hun. *ipa*, which is a dialectal variant of *apa* 'father (-in-law)'. One could postulate the change **a* > **į* > *i*, starting from an original F-U **appe*. Janhunen (1981a: 236, item (71)) on the other hand reconstructs P-S **-әpә* vs P-F-P **appi* (Finn. *appi*), from P-U **įppį*, and claims that Hun. *ipa* clearly points to the original, illabial vowel. However, there are, here too, several variants within Ugric: compare Ost. *up*, *op* and Vog. *apā*, *up* etc. (UEW 14).

As is evident from the examples listed above, the Hungarian vocalism at times lines up with the Ob-Ugric vocalism (at least with one of the Ob-Ugric languages) and/or with the Samoyed vocalism, and at other times it lines up with the Finno-Permian vocalism.

An example of the first case is the term for 'arrow' (Hun. *nyíl*; example (4.5) above). Here Hungarian, according to Janhunen, has clearly preserved the original quality of the initial vowel, the illabial vowel, together with Samoyed. The same is true for Hun *íj*/Finn. *jousi*/Sam.Yu. *ŋin*/Vog. *jäwt*, *jawt*/Ost. *joyəl* 'bow', for which Janhunen reconstructs P-S **jįntә* and P-U **jįŋsį* (item (96): 253), whilst UEW 101 reconstructs P-U **joŋ(k)sз*.

As examples of the second case compare Hun. *al, alatt* (example (4.8) above), and Hun. *máj* (example (4.9) above), where the Hungarian vocalism lines up with that of Finnish, whilst the Vogul and Ostyak vocalism oscillate between the Samoyed and the Finno-Permian vowel quality.

The difficulties of matching the Finno-Permian (/F-U) and the Samoyed node mainly with regard to vocalism (but also with regard to consonantism) have been pointed out also by Sammallahti (1979: 50–8). In addition to the question of the uncertain match between the Samoyed vowel sequence and the Finno-Permian quantity correlation, the author highlights the following problems: the question of the four P-S vowels: **ö*, **e*, **i* and **ә*, unknown to P-F-U; the overall different vocalic phonotaxis between the two branches and the fact that to P-S **ә* corresponds, mainly, the following set of vowels in P-F-U: **u* (about 20 cases), **a* (about 4–7 cases), **o* (3 cases), **i* (3 cases), **ō* and **ū* (2 cases).

4.4.5.3. *The status of the Proto-Uralic sound-structure*

The etymologies listed in Janhunen's corpus, according to the author, can be divided into three groups from the point of view of reconstruction (1981a: 252):

(a) stems whose sound-quality can be reconstructed in a clear way, despite the irregularities, given that the irregularities can be somehow justified;
(b) stems for whose reconstruction the P-Languages of the lower levels give way to alternative choices;
(c) stems whose P-U original sound-shape remains unclear for several reasons.

I shall list below some of these etymologies, obviously reproducing Janhunen's reconstruction, without, however, respecting his order of presentation. The following examples belong to Group (b):

(4.10) P-S *emä vs P-F-P *emä 'mother, female, woman': Finn. emä /Hun. eme 'sow' (Old Hun. 'female')/Sam. Se. ämä/Sam. Yu. ńeb'e etc.; these are reconstructed as P-U *ämä ~ *emä (item (110): 257; UEW 74). The author remarks that in this case the sound irregularity might be caused by the affective nature or (approximate) likeness typical of child language ('luonteenomainen affektiivisuus tai lastenkielenomaisuus').

(4.11) P-S *meńä vs P-F-P *meńä 'daughter-in-law, young woman', reconstructed as P-U *mäńä ~ *meńä (item (111): 257). Compare Finn. miniä /Hun. mëny /Vog. miń, mäń/Sam Ye. mē. The Balto-Finnic parallels point to an initial closed vowel *mińä (UEW 276)

(4.12) P-S *wiŋə vs P-F-P ? *wäŋiw 'son-in-law',[25] reconstructed as P-U *weŋiw ~ *wäŋiw (item (114): 258). Compare: Finn. vävy /Hun. vő / Mor. ov/Che. wiŋγə/Ost. woŋ/Sam.Yu. jīj /Sam.Ye. bī. UEW 565 reconstructs *wäŋe, whilst pointing out the irregularity in the vowel correspondence of Finnish, Lapp, Mordvin and Cheremis, probably due to the 'affective character' of the term (and also to the velarising influence of -ŋ-). Janhunen makes the same remark with regard to 'affective character'.

(4.13) P-S *tiwə vs P-F-P ? *täwiw 'lung', reconstructed as P-U *tewiw ~ *täwiw (item (115): 258). Compare: dialectal Finn. tävy, täky, täty/ Vot. and Zyr. ti̯ /Hun. tüdő (dialectal tidő)/Sam. Yu. ĭ̄wāk /Sam. Ka. tu. This etymology presents the same vowel relationship as the previous one, in which case one has to assume a change from P-U into P-F-U of the type: *ä ~ e > *ü > *i̯[26] (UEW 519).

As one can see, Janhunen has proposed two reconstructed variants for each etymological set, but, in his opinion, there are no definitive criteria to decide which of the two represents the oldest state of affairs.

To this group too belong the following terms: the term for 'heart' (item (4.7) above); the term for 'two' (item (4.6) above) and the term for 'lake, sea': Hun. tó (Acc. tava-t)/Vot. and Zyr. ti̯ /Sam.Ye. to, etc., for which Janhunen reconstructs P-U *toxi̯ ~ *tuxi̯ (item (109): 257), whilst UEW 533 reconstructs *towɜ.

The following lexical items belong to Group (c). According to Janhunen[27] (1981a: 259), this group contains a number of P-U roots whose reconstructions are still connected to unsolved sound-problems or otherwise uncertain features. The majority of the 'Uralic correspondences that flood the etymological literature' can be allocated to this group. The criteria by which the lexical items are chosen are their 'sufficient phonological and semantic similarity',[28] and their belonging to the basic vocabulary:

(4.14) P-S. *nåtɜ- vs P-F-P *natɜ(-) 'younger sister of man or woman, wife of the brother': Finn. nato/Che. nuðɜ/Sam.Yu. nādū, nātū; these are reconstructed as P-U *nåtɜ- (item (118): 259). Here the difficulty consists in tracing back the vowel of the second syllable (UEW 299).

(4.15) P-S ? *je̜ 'pine-tree, pinus silvestris' vs P-Ob-Ug. *jɜɣ 'tree'. Compare: Ost. juχ 'wood'/Vog. jiw /Sam. Yu. jeʔ (item (120): 260). Here there seems to be irregularity at the Samoyed level, and there is still uncertainty in the reconstruction of Ob-Ugric. The most likely reconstruction is P-U *jɜxi, or perhaps *ji̯xi̯, from which at least the Samoyed forms can be derived. Janhunen also thinks that these might be innovative forms, given their restricted distribution. UEW 107 reconstructs P-U *juwɜ.

Other words included in this group are: Finn. vyö 'belt', which is irregular in many respects (item (121): 260); Finn. uida 'to swim', which presents irregularities in the consonantism in Samoyed and in the vocalism in Balto-Finnic (item (122): 260); Finn. kymmenen 'ten', which exhibits the 'variation typical' of the terms indicating numbers (item (124): 261).

The following words (forming a special sub-group within the previous one) are considered by the author 'particularly troublesome' ('erityisen hankalia' (1981a: 261)), because to an (apparent) common sound representative at one level an 'unexplained variety' ('selittämätön kirjavuus') seems to correspond at another level. This is particularly evident in a group of quite compact Balto-Finnic etymologies, such as: luu 'bone', puu 'tree, wood', suu 'mouth', kuu 'moon, month':

(4.16) P-S *le̜ vs P-F-P ? *luxi 'bone', which could be reconstructed as P-U *li̯xi̯ ~ *luxi̯ (item (125): 261). Compare: Finn. luu /Che. lu /Zyr. and Vot. li̯/Ost. lŏɣ/Vog. luw /Sam.Yu. lī /Sam. Se. le̜ /Sam.Ta. latā. According to Janhunen, in Samoyed and in Ob-Ugric an internal w and even x could be postulated. However, in Finno-Permian even w is questionable. Another difficulty is the preservation of initial lateral in Samoyed, instead of the expected palatalisation (> *j). UEW 254 reconstructs U *luwe. Sammallahti (1988: 502) proposes F-U *luxi, which is supposed to change into P-Ug. *lugĭ. The change * x > *g is supposed to be a common Ugric innovation.

(4.17) P-S *pä vs P-F-P ? *puxi 'tree, wood', reconstructed as P-U ? *pɜxį (item (126): 262). Compare: Finn. *puu* / Hun. *fa* / Sam.Yu. *pā* / Sam.Ye. *fe*. In this word it seems impossible to reconstruct even approximately the quality of the vowel of first syllable (although it must have been a back vowel), because of the divergence in the various P-Languages: alongside P-S *ä, as reconstructed above, in P-F-P it seems to be *u, whilst in Ob-Ugric it seems to be *a (? *påxį). Regarding the intervocalic consonant, judging (for example) from Hun. *fa*, *w seems at first justified, as indeed proposed by UEW 410: *puwe. However, Janhunen observes that such a sound would normally have been preserved in Samoyed, as in P-U *kåwį > P-S *kåw 'ear' (item (97): 253). Sammallahti (1988: 539) reconstructs: P-U *pu/o/äxɨ/li; P-F-U *puxi; P-Ug. *pŭgĭ.

A similar situation with regard to the internal consonant holds for the following set: Finn. *suu* /Sam.Yu. *śo,* etc. 'mouth', for which P-U *śuxį ~ *śoxį could be reconstructed, judging from P-F-P *śuxi, but perhaps *śuwį could be reconstructed, judging from Hun. *száj* (Janhunen 1981a: 262, item (127)). Compare the reconstruction *śuwe in UEW 492.

(4.18) P-S *kįj vs P-F-P ? *kuɲi 'moon, month', reconstructed as P-U ? *kįjį ~ *kuɲį (item (128): 262–3). Compare: Finn. *kuu* 'moon, month'/ Hun. *hó-(nap)* 'month'/Ost. *χŭw* /Sam. Ka. *ki*. Here the contrast between Samoyed intervocalic *-j- on the one hand, and the generally assumed P-F-P/P-F-U *-ŋ- on the other, is evident. UEW 211 reconstructs *kuŋe, from which at least Mor. E. *koŋ* and perhaps Hun. *hó-* (3rd Person Singular Possessive *hava*) could be derived. On the other hand, on the basis of the Ostyak dialect 'Tremjugan', which has *kŏγ*, one could reconstruct *k or *x (? *kuxį). In any case, Janhunen concludes that the word remains uncertain both in vocalism and consonantism.

(4.19) P-S ? *kįnsɜ- vs P-F-P ? *kunśɜ 'star', reconstructed as P-U ? *kįnśɜ ~ *kunśɜ (item (129): 263). Compare: Vot. *kiźil'i*/Hun. *húgy*/Sam. Ma. *kindži-*. This word presents the same (first syllable) vowel relationship as the previous word. The reconstruction proposed by UEW 210, *kuńćɜ ~ *kućɜ, does not take into account the quality of the Samoyed initial vowel.

To conclude this list, I shall present one etymological set which, according to Janhunen (1981a: 263), belongs to the 'most troublesome' group of U etymologies sound-wise ('kaikkein hankalimpia äänteellisesti'). In this set, the Samoyed parallels exhibit the vowel-sequence *(C)Vǝ(-) in stem final position:

(4.20) P-S *kåǝ- vs P-B-F *kōli- 'to die', which could be reconstructed as P-U ? *kȝ(x) (l)ȝ- (item (130): 263). Compare: Finn. *kuolla* (~ *kuole-*)/ Hun. *hal-*/Vot. *kul-*/Ost. *kăla-*/Vog. *kāl-*, *χōl-*/Sam.Ye. *kā-*, etc. In all the F-U parallels there is an intervocalic lateral, for which there is no clear reflex in Samoyed. The vowel of first syllable in Balto-Finnic is long, but in the parallels of other F-U languages it can be derived from a short vowel as well. Some Finno-Permian parallels seem to presuppose an original open vowel for the final syllable (? *kola-*). On the other hand, the vowel sequence in Samoyed is, according to the author, unquestionable. UEW 173 reconstructs *kola-*.

The same kind of problems (for which the author proposes several solutions) are to be found, for example, in the etymology for Finn. *nuolla-* (~ *nuole-*) 'to lick', reconstructed as P-S ? *ńåǝ-*, as P-B-F *nōli-* and as P-U ? *ńȝ(x)(l)ȝ-* (item (131): 264). UEW 321 proposes *ńole-* (*ńōle-*).

To conclude this section, a quick look, without going into details, to some less problematic items, the items belonging to Group (a): Est. *kõba* 'skin, bark' (item (95): 252); Finn. *jousi* 'bow' (item (96): 253); Finn. *korva* 'ear' (item (97): 253); Hun. *köd* 'mist, fog' (item (100): 254); Hun. *szügy* 'chest' (item (101): 254); Finn. *kyynel* 'tear' (item (102): 255); Lapp *vuoŋâs-* 'mouth, opening' (item (103): 255); Finn. *ylä-* ~ *yli-* 'upper part, above' (item (105): 256); Finn. *ime-* 'to suck' (item (106): 256).

4.4.6. Conclusion on vocalism

As we have seen, whilst it may be possible to reconstruct, with varying degrees of accuracy, the vocalism of a few branches of U (Balto-Finnic, Finno-Permian, Samoyed), these reconstructions cannot be traced back to the same common source, unless one postulates a high number of rules, each of which is supported by a small number of etymologies. Even if one were to accept these reconstructions, there remains the problem of the irregularity that characterises many of the etymologies involved. This picture is further complicated by the omission of the Ugric node from the systematic comparison.

To conclude this line of thought, I would like to note the conclusions from two works by E. Itkonen. In Itkonen (1946: 337), the author says:

In allen diesen Sprachen erscheinen neben der regelmässigen Vertretung auch Ergebnisse sporadischer Vokalentwicklung, und zwar im Lappischen und Mordwinischen in etwas stärkerem Ausmass als im Ostseefinnischen. Dies versteht sich von selbst, wenn man die gründliche Neubildung berücksichtigt, der das ursprüngliche System in jenen Sprachen unterworfen wurde. Auch der vierte Vertreter der finnisch-wolgaischen Gruppe, das Tscheremissische, hat deutliche Züge der Vertretung der Ursprache bewahrt. Die Hauptlinien der Entwicklung lassen sich auch dort verhältnismässig leicht feststellen, aber die Erklärung der Einzelheiten ist vor allem wegen der Knappheit des etymologischen Vergleichsmaterials oft recht beschwerlich

In (1954: 342–3), Itkonen says:

Sehr gewöhnlich ist es, dass neben der 'lautgesetzlichen', d.h. durchweg einheitlich vor sich gegangenen Entwicklung der Elemente des früheren vortscheremissischen bzw. vorpermischen Vokalsystems, auch viel lautliche Spaltung vorkommt, die oft völlig unregelmässig erscheint, wenn man die Sache vom Standpunkt jenes früheren Systems betrachtet. Das beste Beispiel für eine im wesentlichen ausnahmslose Entwicklung eines bestimmten einzelnen Bestandteiles des Vokalismus der Ursprache bietet sowohl im Tscheremissischen als auch in den permischen Sprachen die Geschichte des urspr. kurzen *u. Dagegen weisen urspr. *a und urspr. *$ä$ eine starke Spaltung auf; beispielsweise aus *$ä$ sind in der tscheremissischen Sprache sogar drei verschiedene Vokale entstanden, die man dennoch alle als normale Vertretungsweisen des *$ä$ betrachten kann. . . . Der letztgenannten Beobachtung müssen wir jedoch hinzufügen, dass eine mechanisch regelmässige Entwicklung der eizelnen Vokale lediglich dann erwartungsgemäss ist, wenn im Aufbau des Vokalsystems selbst keine grösseren Veränderungen eintreten. Eine derartige Regelmässigkeit ist solchen Lautveränderungen eigen, die sich in nur wenig voneinander verschiedenen Mundarten einer Sprache vollziehen. Wenn hingegen im Lauf der Zeiten das Vokalsystem der Ursprache von Grund auf durcheinander kommt und zerbricht, so dass z.B. die Entwicklung der Vokalqualität zu einem erheblich vermehrten Formenreichtum führt – wie es gerade in den von uns untersuchten Sprachen geschehen ist – , dann ist vielfache Spaltung unausbleiblich. . . . Also ist die ausnahmslos regelmässige Entwicklung irgendeines ursprünglichen Lautes im Leben der Sprache kein Selbstzweck, wie man es sich früher auch in der finnisch-ugrischen Sprachforschung oft vorstellte, sondern zweckmässig ist nur das, was der Ganzheit, dem System dient . . . Die Erforschung der finnisch-ugrischen Vokalgeschichte dürfte für einen Forscher, der nicht zugibt, dass ein scheinbar unregelmässiger Lautwandel in Wirklichkeit teleologisch sein kann, zu einer unlösbaren Aufgabe werden

As one can see, Itkonen does not seem prepared to give in to the idea of the existence of 'teleology' in language developments, and correctly so, even if the temptation seems to be there.

4.5. ATTEMPTS TO RECONSTRUCT THE PROTO-URALIC CONSONANTISM

When textbooks and the specialist literature refer to the 'reconstructed P-Uralic consonantism', it is often difficult to disentangle exactly what is meant by this term. For example, the systematic work of Janhunen (1981a) lists all the vowel-rules, but only some of the consonant-rules, and it is necessary to infer the rest of them from the examples that are given. For other sources, the phrase refers to a type of reconstruction which 'bridges' the assumed P-Uralic node with the assumed lower-level nodes. This process is again usually only implicit, but the first explicit attempt to do so systematically was by Sammallahti (1988). This process was introduced above and will be discussed in detail below. Other sources may be referring to less quantitative 'correspondences', such as the supposed first-consonant matches between Hungarian and Finnish reported in Csepregi (1998: 14) and reproduced in the introduction to this chapter.

In this paragraph I shall try to make explicit the list of the generally accepted (and often implicit) P-Uralic consonants, their reflexes in the modern languages, and the sound-rules through which they are held to have developed through the intermediate nodes down to the modern languages. Previous authors have been concerned primarily with reconstructed forms only. Here, I examine these consonants systematically by cross-referencing the reconstructed sounds and sound-rules with the primary data – that is, with the actual attested languages. In this analysis, I shall attempt to be clear on the regularities, the variations and the exceptions that are encountered.

We have already seen in the previous paragraph that several 'correspondences' have to be established by postulating an unspecified consonantal segment $*x$ – a type of 'joker in the pack' – to match particularly difficult etymologies. When we examine the consonantism in detail below, the following picture will emerge:

- The overall picture is one of a significant amount of variation and exception. This is particularly evident in the reflexes of the medial clusters. This variation is occasionally acknowledged in textbooks and in the specialist literature.
- In some cases there is evidence that a supposedly ancient change is in the process of 'diffusing', that is, it is not implemented in all the relevant cases. For example, the change P-Finno-Ugric $*k$- $\longrightarrow$ P-Ugric $*\chi$- (in a given context) is usually reported to be a specific 'Ugric innovation'. However, this change is fully implemented only in Hungarian, whilst it is in the process of diffusing in Vogul and Ostyak. It is possible that the spreading of the change will come to completion, in which case the end result will be a regular sound-change. However, the change is not regular at present, so that the primary data appear to be inconsistent with the presumed reconstruction.

- The generally accepted reconstructions appear to be inconsistent with the presumed depth of the family tree. For example, although P-Uralic and P-Finno-Ugric are supposed to be clearly distinct nodes at great linguistic depth from one another, there are only three or four postulated consonantal differences between them. We shall see that the evidence is scarce even for these few differences, as recognised by Sammallahti (1988: 490). A similar situation holds for the lack of changes between the P-Finno-Ugric node and its lower nodes, P-Ugric and P-Finno-Permian. As we have seen in Chapter 3, this state of affairs is occasionally recognised in the literature. Some scholars have in fact proposed a 'flat' family tree, which is neutral from the point of view of chronology (see Figure 3.1).
- The distribution in the modern languages of the few identified consonantal changes does not match the binary stratification of the conventional U tree. For example, the change P-Uralic *p- to f- is supposed to occur between P-Ugric and Hungarian, but it can also be observed between P-Uralic and Samoyed.

As mentioned, I shall also point out the changes that do appear to proceed regularly. For example, the change from P-Uralic *-t- to Hun. -z- appears to have no identified exceptions. It is unclear how to interpret these regular changes. For example, the change in question is supported by eight examples in Sammallahti (1988: 516) but only one of these (the term for 'water') is listed in the original reconstruction due to Janhunen (1981a).

4.5.1. The 'reconstructed' Proto-Uralic consonantism

Below I shall present a list of the traditionally reconstructed P-U consonants, taking into account only those consonants whose reconstruction does not appear to have attracted much controversy (for more detail see Raun (1971: 1–44); Sammallahti (1988: 479–554); Gheno & Hajdú (1992: 164–8); Janhunen (1981a: 250–2, 1981b); Helimski (1984b) and Abondolo (ed.) 1998: 1–42)):

- the (voiceless) plosive *p, *t, *k;
- the glides *w and *j;
- the (voiceless) sibilants, generally three: *s, *ś, *š; or two: *s and *ś;
- the ordinary as well as palatalised liquids *r, *l/*ĺ and nasals *m, *n/*ń ;
- the affricates, generally one *č, or two, *č and the palatal(ised) *ć.

The status of the reconstructed affricates however is uncertain, for two reasons; firstly, the reflexes of initial affricates can hardly be distinguished from those of initial sibilants; secondly, their occurrence is more frequent in internal position. In fact, some scholars think that affricates and sibilants might have been variants in the P-Language (Hajdú 1969a: 70–1; Gheno & Hajdú 1992: 165). Janhunen (1981b: 24) states that:

The affricate *c probably differed from the dental stop *t both in release (affrication) and in place of articulation (cacuminal). It is not clear which of these two phonetic features was phonologically more important, and dialectal differences may also complicate the picture. If, however, it was cacuminality that was the distinctive characteristic, then it would be plausible to postulate other cacuminal phonemes as well. A cacuminal (retroflex) sibilant *š, at least, was a distinctive unit in PFU, but it cannot be reliably traced using C[ommon] U[ralic] etymological material

Similarly, Abondolo ((ed.) 1998: 12) claims that it is possible to reckon without ć, explaining correspondences that would derive from it as 'affective variants' of ś. Compare however Honti (1972), who argues that the confusion typical of the reflexes of affricates and sibilants is of second natures; this in turn is the effect of (mostly regular) processes of disaffrication. Compare also Katz (1972).

Some researchers (such as Janhunen 1981b), express concern also regarding the reconstruction of the palatal series *ś, *ń, *l̦ (and *δ'/*δ which are not mentioned in the list above), due to the scarcity of relevant etymological material. For the same reason, Sammallahti (1979: 24) claims that the presence of *ś at the P-U phase is uncertain. Doubts have also been expressed regarding the existence of *γ, *ŋ (not mentioned in the list above) and *r, whose occurrences seem to be confined to internal position only.

Some authors, such as Sammallahti (1988: 482), include the 'unspecified' consonantal segment *x introduced by Janhunen in the list of the reconstructed consonants (see Section 4.4.5.1 above). All in all (as we have seen in the previous paragraph) this segment can be defined as a 'cover symbol' (Abondolo (ed.) 1998: 12) for several phenomena, such as the lengthening of the preceding vowel in Finno-Permian and the vowel sequence in P-Samoyed. Sammallahti basically shares Janhunen's view about the nature of this segment. In fact, Sammallahti (1988: 482) states that 'the phonetic nature of /x/ is unclear', although, on the basis of Ob-Ugric evidence, such a segment could represent two different sounds: a laryngeal sound, which would yield a long vowel in P-Ob-Ugric, and a velar sound, which would give rise to the correspondent spirant. The segment *x could even be a pure syllable boundary, reconstructed for certain types of contexts. As mentioned, this consonantal segment is totally missing from the reconstructions in UEW.

Consonant clusters have been reconstructed only for internal position. The most frequent clusters are 'sonorant + sonorant' and 'sonorant + plosive'. The reconstruction of geminates, because of the scarcity of etymological material, is more uncertain. According to Korhonen (1986), it is likely that the Comparative Method introduces a bias in this area of reconstruction, because more marked consonant clusters can be somehow reconstructed, whilst less marked types, including geminates, are rare or cannot be reconstructed at all. All in all, the situation of the assumed medial clusters appears uncertain, as already evidenced by some examples reported in the previous paragraph (see examples (4.6) and (4.19)).

In general, the plosive occurred more frequently in (initial) strong position, whilst liquids and glides occurred more frequently in weak position (word-final, syllable final position), that is, they occurred *in coda*. As Abondolo ((ed.) 1998: 13) puts it:

> the relative age of medial cluster, geminates, and the distribution of (geminate) affricates complicate the picture, as does the role of affective vocabulary and loans.

Finally, the phonological structure of the P-U stems has generally been reconstructed as follows (from Sammallahti 1988: 480):

(C)V(C)C V ((C)C(V))-.

Table 4.6 from Sammallahti (1988: 482), often quoted in the literature as a kind of 'standard reconstruction', can indeed be used to illustrate the generally agreed-upon reconstructed P-U consonantism, although variations exist.

Table 4.6 Sammallahti's Proto-Uralic consonantism (1988: 482)

/p			m			w
t	s	c	n	d	r l	
	ś		ń	d'		j
k			ŋ			
						x /

According to Sammallahti the following holds: *d* / *d'* were probably spirants; the absence of initial *d* in the reconstruction is probably coincidental, since its marked counterpart *d'* is present, although its presence is not extensive; *c* was retroflex (cacuminal); *r*, *ŋ* and *x* were apparently confined to word internal position.

4.5.2. *The sound-changes in consonantism*

In the following sections I shall illustrate the quantity, quality, distribution and level of irregularity of the sound-changes traditionally identified within U consonantism. The parallels reported from the actual languages and most reconstructions are quoted from UEW, according to the adopted policy (see 'Transcription and References'). If the meaning of the parallels in the various languages is not (grossly) different from the reconstructed meaning, it will not be reported. If it is relevant for the discussion of the sound-changes, dialectal variants of the same language may be reported, but not necessarily the name of the dialects.

4.5.2.1. *From Proto-Uralic to the modern languages*

In this section I shall examine the correlations between the reconstructed consonants of P-U as listed in Section 4.5.1 above and their reflexes in the modern languages. We shall see that there is no evidence for a rich stratification or other time-depth of the family tree, since there are very few differences between the reconstructed consonants and their actual reflexes. In particular, we shall see that there are no significant differences in the consonantal structure between the P-U and the P-F-U phases. This is in accordance with recent observations in the literature. For example, as discussed in detail in the next section, Sammallahti (1979: 43) states that the consonantism of P-U is basically identical with that of P-F-U. Similarly, Honti (1975: 133) states that:

> we do not know how to separate from one another on the basis of phonetic points of view the Finno-Ugric and the Uralic proto-language

See also Gheno & Hajdú (1992: 162) and Hajdú (1981) for similar remarks.

(a) development of initial sibilants and affricates. The distribution of the sibilants in the U languages is highly intricate. Their reflexes in the various languages are basically the same, irrespective of whether they are supposed to derive from the P-U or the P-F-U period:

(4.21) ? P-U *s- / *sile (*süle) 'lap, bosom': Finn. *syli*/Hun. *öl*/Vog. *täl*/Ost. *tĕt, lŏl, jŏl* /Zyr. *sịl*/Vot. *sul*/Che. *šŭlö*/Mor. *seĺ* /Lapp. *sâllâ-*/? Sam. Se. *tii* /? Sam. Yu. *čīb'e* (UEW 444)

(4.22) P-F-U *s-/*säppä 'bile': Finn. *sappi* /Hun. *epe* /Vog. *tãp* /Vot. and Zyr. *sẹp*/Mor. E. *sepe*, M. *šäpä*/Lapp. *sappe* (UEW 435)

(4.23) P-U *š-/*šurɜ- 'to cut, divide': Hun. *irt-* (Old Hun. *ort-*) 'exterminate'/Ost. *tărt-, lŏrt-, jŏrt-*/Zyr. and Vot. *šịr-*/Sam. Yu. *tār-*/Sam. Se. *taara-* (UEW 503–4)

(4.24) P-F-U *š- /*šiŋe-re 'mouse': Finn. *hiiri* /Hun. *egér*/Vog. *täŋkər*/Ost. *teŋkər, löŋkər, jöŋkər*/Zyr. and Vot. *šịr*/Mor. E. *čejeŕ*, Mor. M. *šejer* (UEW 500)

(4.25) P-U *ś-/*śilmä 'eye': Finn. *silmä*/Hun. *szëm*[29]/Zyr. and Vot. *śin* / Mor. E. *śeĺme*/Che. *sənzä, šińća*/Vog. *sam, šäm*/Ost. *sem*/Sam. Yu. *sew, häem* /Sam. Ta. *säime* /Sam. Se. *sai, hai* etc. (UEW 479)

The developments of the P-U and P-F-U initial sibilants into the various daughter languages follow the same route. From P-U and/or P-F-U *s-* we have: Ø- for Hungarian, *t*- for Vogul and some dialects of Ostyak as well as some dialects of Samoyed and *s*- for other languages. From P-U and/or P-F-U *š- we have again Ø- for Hungarian, *h*- for Finnish, again *t*- for Vogul, some dialects of Ostyak and Samoyed; finally, we have š- for Zyrian and Votjak. It is clear that *s- and *š- fall together in Hungarian, Ob-Ugric and Samoyed, but their reflexes in Ob-Ugric are consistently distinct from those in Hungarian, and instead they are identical to those of (some) Samoyed languages. This is, however, not a surprise; as mentioned above (Section 3.2.1), Samoyed and Ob-Ugric are in several respects closer to each other than Hungarian and Ob-Ugric. Notice that the parallel merging of Hungarian and Samoyed *s- and *š- seems to point to the existence of only two sibilants, *s- and *ś- in P-U, rather than three.

The example (4.25) above and the examples (4.26) and (4.27) below show how the various sibilants/affricates, rather than being the result of specific sound-changes, are in fact coexistent variants, as one would otherwise expect for these kind of sounds:

(4.26) P-F-U *č-/*čukkз (čokkз) 'thick': Hun. *sok* 'many'/Zyr. *čẹk*/Vog. *šaw, sāw* /Che. *čakata* (UEW 62–3; note also Turkic *čoq* 'many'/ Mon. *čoүča* 'pile, quantity'/Tun. *čokčo* 'hill, pile')

(4.27) P-F-U *ć-/*ćolme 'knot, to tie': Finn. *solmi* (Gen. *solmen*), *solmu, solmi-a* 'to tie'/Hun. *csomó*/Mor. E. *śulmo* /Lapp *čuolbmâ* (UEW 38)

Hungarian *cs*- (/č/) is claimed to represent the 'normal' development of P-U/ P-F-U *ć-, as shown in (4.27) above, even though *s*- (/š/) is to be found too, as in the following examples: *süly* 'skorbut' < U *ćiklä* 'wart, nipple' (UEW 36) and *ős* 'ancestor' < U *ićä* 'father' (in internal position; UEW 78). On the other hand, Modern Hungarian *s*- is the reflex 'mainly' of the affricate *č-, as shown in (4.26) above. On this point, Abondolo (1998b: 436) comments that:

> The asymmetry of the pU s(h)ibilant/affricate system, $*s :: *s^j :: *c^j :: *č$, is perhaps reflected in two kinds of Hungarian doublets involving *š* which have been ascribed to internal borrowing: (a) those with **s**- ~ **š**-, such as *szöv*- 'weaves' ~ *sövény* 'hedge', . . . and (b) those with **š**- ~ **č** -, such as *sajog*- ~ *csillog*- 'glitters, shines'[30].

Figure 4.2, from Gheno & Hajdú (1992: 169) shows the main tendencies of development of the sibilants in some U languages. As one can see, the authors correctly reconstruct a sound-change, marked as *ϑ-, shared by Samoyed and Ob-Ugric, whilst normally this is reported to be a specific 'Ugric innovation' (as discussed in Section 4.5.3.1 below).

Other examples of reflexes of ordinary and palatalised affricates in initial position will be given below. The instability, the messiness and the high level

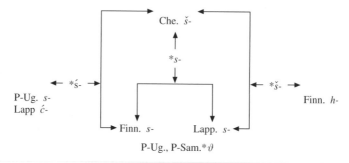

Figure 4.2 Gheno & Hajdú's sibilants diagram (1992: 169)

of variation associated with sibilants and affricates is highlighted also by the examples reported by Collinder (1960: 51–61; 1965a: 77–9).

(b) development of initial plosives. Like the sibilants, the development of the initial plosives *k-, *t-, *p-, whether (supposedly) derived from the P-U or the P-F-U period, gives the same results. The distribution of their reflexes, again, is not consistent with the conventional stratification of the U family tree.

These consonants generally remain unchanged in the daughter languages. However, *k- spirantises in Hungarian, some dialects of (Eastern) Vogul, (Western) Ostyak and Samoyed, if it is followed by a velar vowel. Similarly, *p- spirantises in Hungarian and in some dialects of Samoyed:

(4.28) P-U *k- / *kala 'fish': Finn. kala / Hun. hal / Vog. χūl, kul / Ost. χul, kul / Sam.Yu. χāle, kare / Sam. Se. qel, kel / Sam. Ka. kola (UEW 119; compare also Orok and Gold χolto). See the developments of *k- also in the U etymology *kola- 'to die', given below.

(4.29) P-F-U *t- / *tälwä 'winter': Finn. talvi / Hun. tél (Acc. tele-t) / Vog. tāl / Ost. tĕləγ / Zyr. tel / Mor. E. tele (UEW 516)

(4.30) P-U *p- / *puwe 'tree, wood': Finn. puu / Hun. fa / Vog. -pä / Zyr. and Vot. pu / Che. pu / Sam. Yu. pā / Sam.Ye. fe / Sam.Ta. fā / Sam. Ma. cha (UEW 410; compare also Mon. hoi 'wood, forest' (< *poi) / Orok pe / Man. f'a 'birch' (see example (4.17) above and (6.4) below)

The examples listed above show the following developments: *k-, if followed by velar vowel, changes into *χ- > *h- in Hungarian and, independently (see below), into χ- in some dialects of Vogul, Ostyak. The same development is to be found also in Samoyed (and in Tungusic). *p- changes into f- in Hungarian (although there are exceptions, see below), but also in some dialects of Samoyed (northernmost and southernmost dialects). Notice the same development in Tungusic.

As mentioned above, *t- remains generally unchanged. However, in Hungarian there are exceptions:

(4.31) Hun. *daru* 'crane', from P-F-U *tarɜ-kɜ (~ tarkɜ) / Ost. *tarəɣ* / Vog. *tē̮rəɣ, tāriɣ* (UEW 513; compare also Turkic *turna* / Mon. *toɣuriɣun*)

(4.32) Hun. *dob-* 'to throw', from P-Ug. *tV₁mpɜ- 'hit, beat' / Vog. *tā̮mp-* (UEW 896)

(4.33) Hun. *domb* 'hill', from P-Ug. *tV₁mpɜ / Vog. *tōmp* (UEW 896; this etymology is written in italics)

Also initial *p- may have exceptional reflexes in Hungarian, that is, this sound too may become voiced, instead of evolving into the expected *f-*, as shown below:

(4.34) Hun. *bőr* 'skin', from P-U *perɜ 'skin, bark': Ost. *pĕr* /Sam. Yu. *pīrʔ* (UEW 374; compare also Man. *feri* 'skin of donkey, shaved horse'). Compare also Hun. *borjú* 'calf', for which see Chapter 6 (example (6.7))

In fact, Hungarian has developed a full series of voiced plosives in initial position, standing almost alone in this respect within the family (see below).[31] In particular, Hungarian has developed a well-established correlation of voice which extends to plosives and fricatives. The introduction of initial voiced dental, for example, is generally considered to be the result of two combining factors. Firstly, the occasional spreading into that position of already existing intervocalic voiced stops, which in turn developed from the simplification of the cluster 'nasal + stop' (see below). Secondly, the influence of words (supposedly) borrowed from Turkic, such as *disznó* 'pig', *dió* 'nut', *dara* 'coarse (ground) meal', *dér* 'frost, rime', etc.[32]

From the above listed examples the following emerges:

(i) The various identified sound-changes may be shared by languages which are not supposed to belong to the same node, as shown, for instance, by the changes in common between Hungarian and Samoyed (see example (4.30)).

(ii) Competing variants, such as Vog. *χūl ~ kul*, Ost. *χul ~ kul* and Sam. *χāle ~ kare* (in example (4.28)), as well as the Samoyed competing variants *pā ~ fe* (in example (4.30)) suggest that the changes *k- > χ- and *p- > f- are in the process of 'diffusing', affecting only certain dialects at a time. It is possible that the spreading of these changes to all the dialects will eventually come to completion, thus yielding regular sound-changes; however, there is no a priori guarantee about the end results. Therefore, these changes cannot be classified as 'regular' at the moment. I shall come back to the topic of 'changes in progress' below.

(iii) Regarding the change *k- > *χ- > h- in Hungarian, one might observe that the sound χ is generally marked in the literature by the asterisk of reconstruction – as I did above following the tradition. This fact could lead the reader to believe that such a sound-change must have taken place in a very old, non-attested phase of development of the language. However, the sound χ, or perhaps γ (Imre 1988: 429), is actually attested in Old Hungarian. In fact, the oldest Hungarian text, the famous *Halotti beszéd* 'Funeral Oration'[33] (dated between 1192 and 1195 AD), presents the sequence of letters *ch-* to indicate what has become a laryngeal in Modern Hungarian. Compare the following examples: *chol-* > *hal-* 'to die'; *chol-t-a-t* 'die-Perf.-his-Acc., his having died, his death' > *holt-á-t*.[34] We also find in the text several other words containing the sequence *ch-*: *chomuv* > *hamu* 'ash(es)', perhaps from a Ugric form *$k u \delta$'m$\mathfrak{z}$* (UEW 194); *charm-ul* > *három-szor* 'three-times'[35] (*három* 'three' < F-U *kolme*; UEW 174); *uro-m-chuz* > *ura-m-hoz* 'Lord-my-to, to my Lord'.[36] These data clearly indicate that this is quite a recent change, although obviously it is older than the equivalent changes in Vogul, Ostyak and Samoyed. Therefore, it is clear that these are all independent changes. Notice that in the *Halotti beszéd* the word 'to die, death' is also written with initial *h-*: *halal-nec* 'death-to', *halal-ut* 'death-Acc.' In a later text, *A tihanyi apátság alapítólevele* 'The Foundation Charter of Tihany Abbey'[37] (issued in 1055), we find the term for '3' written *harmu*, and the term for 'sand' written *kumuc ~ humuc* > Modern Hun. *homok*. These data can be interpreted indeed as a sign of instability due to the change in progress $\chi \sim \gamma > h$. It is not certain when the fricative completely disappears in favour of the laryngeal, but a good guess would indicate the 14th century (for further details about the sound structure of P-Hungarian and Early Hungarian see Imre 1988).

(iv) These consonantal changes are not unique to the U languages. For instance, the examples (4.28), (4.30) and (4.34) illustrate how the changes *p-* > *f-* and *k-* > *χ-* (before velar vowel) take place in the Altaic languages within parallels similar in sound-shape and meaning. Compare also equivalent sound-changes within and outside the U area in example (4.26). Finally, compare the following developments within Altaic:

- P-Turkic *s* $\longrightarrow$ *h-* in Bashkir and *s* $\longrightarrow$ *$\emptyset$-* in Yakut;
- P-A *p-* is preserved as *p-* in Ulcha and Gold but may develop into *f-* in Manchu and in Mongolian (Poppe 1965: 7 and 26, 1977b, 1983; Manzelli 1993: 553–70).

For other similar developments see Poppe (1965: 36) and Tekin[38] (1994: 83). These (well-known) facts prompted several researchers, such as Collinder (1952), to attempt a reconstruction of at least some P-Ural-Altaic consonants. Compare also Sinor (1975: 260–1), who makes a list of 'sound correspondences' between 'U (or F-U)' and northern Tungusic, whereby the shared etymologies are interpreted as representing a 'very old layer' of borrowing.

Whatever the case and whatever the interpretations, if the U paradigm had developed differently, and if, for instance, the U languages and the Tungusic languages, or the U languages and the Turkic languages had been 'assumed' to be genetically related, these shared changes would have certainly been cited as evidence in favour of the (pre-established) relationship. I shall come back to the question of the shared sound-developments between U and Altaic and the question 'borrowed vs cognates' in Chapter 6.

(c) development of initial nasals and liquids. The development of initial nasals will not be dealt with in detail, since it remains basically unchanged. The same is true for *$\acute{n}$-, even if depalatalisation may occur in some languages. Regarding this, Joki (1965: 355–6) asks himself whether palatalisation in this and in the *$\acute{s}$-, *$\acute{l}$- sounds can really be considered a U phenomenon, given that one finds a 'whole bunch of mysterious cases of oscillations' ('koko joukko arvoituksellisia horjuntatapauksia'). For example, some languages are to be traced back to *n-, some others to *$\acute{n}$-, although the contextual vocalism or consonantism cannot justify a secondary palatalisation, as in the term for 'to lick': U *$\acute{n}ole$- (*$\acute{n}\bar{o}le$-; UEW 321). The author's conclusion is that at least some palatalised sounds might have been allophones, which started to be used in 'expressive' words, the category to which the verb 'to lick' belongs. This oscillation is present also in the Altaic languages.

Similarly, r- remains unchanged (with some rare exceptions). The same holds for the ordinary lateral, which however sometimes in some languages may have several variants, including its palatalised version, or j- and t- in some dialects of Ostyak . The dichotomy l-/$\acute{l}$- is interpreted sometimes as a preservation of the original, P-U dichotomy. Little can be said for the palatalised lateral, due to scarcity of material, but see below.

(d) development of initial glides. *j- remains generally unchanged, but, when it does change, its reflexes are not always predictable. Compare the terms for 'ice': F-U *$j\ddot{a}\eta e$, which in Vogul can have the variants $l\ddot{a}\eta$, $j\ddot{a}\eta k$, and in Hungarian the variant (dialectal) $gy\acute{e}g$ (gy = voiced palatal stop /d'/), alongside $j\acute{e}g$ (UEW 93). Compare also the terms for 'to drink': F-U *$ju\gamma e$- (*$juke$-), which in Cheremis has the variant $d'\ddot{u}a$- alongside $j\ddot{u}\ddot{a}$-, and in Votyak the variants $\acute{l}uktal \sim juktal$. In Hungarian *$j$- is lost because of the following -i-: iv- (i-, isz-; UEW 103); this is a regular change. Compare also the term for 'foot': F-U *$jalka$, where j- is preserved everywhere, except in Hungarian, where again the voiced palatal stop appears: $gyalog$ 'by foot' (UEW 88–9).

Initial *w- is generally preserved in the Ob-Ugric languages and in Cheremis, although there are exceptions, as shown by the absence of initial w- in Ostyak in (4.38) below. It changes elsewhere into v-, but it disappears in Finnic before short *o*, *u* and *ü*. If followed by a labial vowel, the reflex v- may or may not be dropped in Hungarian (and some other languages). There is a variety of developments in Samoyed, whereby some changes 'affect only a few words' (Collinder 1960: 64–6):

(4.35) F-U *w-/*wire 'blood': Finn. *veri*/Hun. *vér* /Vot. *ver, vur* /Che *wür* / Ost. *wĕr* /Vog. *wür* (UEW 576)

(4.36) F-U *w-/*witte 'five': Finn. *viisi* /Hun. *öt*/Mor. *veíe* /Che. *wić* /Ost. *wet* /Vog. *ät*/?? Sam.Yu. *jūt, jū?* 'ten'/Sam.Ta. *bī?* 'ten' etc. (UEW 577)

(4.37) U *w-/*wäŋe 'son-in-law': Finn. *vävy* /Hun. *vő* (3rd Person Possessive *vőj-e* ~ *vej-e*)/Lapp ? *vivvâ-* /Mor. *ov* /Che. *wiŋγə*/Sam. Yu. *jīj, wij*/Sam.Ye. *bī* (UEW 565; see item (4.12) above). Compare also F-U *wajće 'a type of duck', which gives in Hun. *vöcsök* (UEW 552)

(4.38) F-U *w-/*wilä (*wülä) 'surface, the upper part': Finn. *ylä* /Ost. *eləl* Che. *wəl-* (UEW 573–4)

(e) development of internal plosives. Like the initial plosives, the reflexes of internal plosives, whether supposedly derived from P-U or P-F-U, are the same.

The following examples show the development of internal P-U and/or P-F-U *-k-*:

(4.39) P-U *- k-/*joke 'river': Finn. *joki*/Est. *jõgi*/Lapp *jokk* /Old Hun. *-jó*/ Ost. *-jaγ, jaχ-*, Vog. *jā, jē* etc. / Zyr. and Vot. *ju* / Mor. E. *jov* ('the Mokša river') / Sam.Yu. *jaχā* / Sam.Ye. *d'aha* / Sam. Ma. *čaga* (UEW 99)

(4.40) P-F-U * -k-/*jikä (*ikä) 'old age, year': Finn. *ikä* / Est. *iga* / Lapp. *jâkke-* 'year' / Hun. *év* (Old Hun. *é*) / Che. *i(j)* / Mor. E. *ije* (UEW 98)

(4.41) P-F-U *-k- / *teke- 'to do, make': Finn. *teke-* / Est. *tege-* / Hun. *tëv-* (*të-, tësz-*) / Mor. E. *íeje-* (UEW 519; compare also Mon. *tege-*)

Inter-vocalic *-k-*, whilst preserved in Finnish (in the strong grade), becomes voiced and/or spirantises, and/or tends to disappear in the other U languages. It changes into -χ- in some Samoyed and Ostyak dialects, and into -γ- in other Ostyak dialects. It merges with the preceding vowel, which therefore becomes long, in Hungarian (probably through the process $k > \chi > w/v$), as shown by Old Hun. *-jó < jou* in (4.39). Notice however the absence of lengthening in Zyrian and Votyak in (4.39). Notice also that -v- has been preserved in Hungarian as shown in (4.40) and (4.41), and in Mordvin as shown in (4.39).

The developments of intervocalic *-t- are illustrated by the terms for 'water': P-U *wete (UEW 570): *-t- is preserved in Finnish: Nom. vesi vs Gen. vede-n (< *vete-n); it normally weakens in Hungarian: víz (Acc. vize-t), perhaps through the stage *-δ-. The same kind of weakening takes place in Mor E. & M. ved'. Internal -t- disappears in Zyr. va and Vot. vu, but also in Sam. Ma. bu. Once again, Hungarian diverges from the other two Ugric languages, presenting instead the same sort of development as Mordvin and the Permian languages. Vogul in contrast preserves the original *-t- (wit), in this lining up with Finnish and some Samoyed dialects (Sam. Se. yt/Sam. Yu. wit). In the following example both Vogul and Ostyak, unlike Hungarian, preserve intervocalic -t-: P-U *käte > Finn. käsi (Gen. käde-n) vs Hun. kéz, whereby -t- weakens in Mor. E. ked' and is preserved in Vog. kāt and Ost. köt (UEW 140). Compare also the word for '100', borrowed from Iranian: Finn. sata and Hun. száz, but Vog. sāt, šāt, and Ost. sat; in this case Mordvin and Cheremis behave as expected, being respectively śado and šüðə (UEW 467).

Notice that the change -t- > -z- seems to be one of the few changes in Hungarian which have been accomplished with no exceptions (Bereczki 1980a: 48).

Further variation can be found in Samoyed and Ostyak: for example Samoyed Selkup can have -t-, -tt-, -d-; Ostyak (North Obdorsk dialect) can have -d-; the change into d/d' occurs in Samoyed Kamas (Collinder 1960: 80).

Intervocalic *-p- is either preserved, or is changed into -v-, as in Hungarian, Cheremis (which can also have the variants -j- and -Ø-) and Mordvin:

(4.42) P-F-U *-p-/*repä (~ -ćз) 'fox': Finn. repo /Hun. ravasz 'shrewd'[39]/ Mor. E. ŕiveś /Che. rəwəž/Zyr. ruć (UEW 423; note the irregularity of first syllable a in Hungarian < Old Hun. u)

To summarise, the reflexes of *-k- *-p-, *-t- are not always clear-cut and do not always respect the conventionally established intermediate nodes.

(f) development of internal nasals and liquids. Intervocalic -m- (like initial m-) is generally preserved everywhere, although here too variation is encountered.

The Hungarian reflexes are not always predictable: -m- tends to develop into - v- (< *-w-) as shown by név 'noun, name' < P-U *nime (UEW 305), although often -v-/-w- merges with the preceding vowel, as in fű (Acc. füve-t) 'grass' < P-Ug. *pimз (UEW 879). If inserted in a consonantal cluster, the reflexes of -m- oscillate between -m- and -v- in an unpredictable way, as shown in the pair szëm 'eye'/három 'three' vs nyelv 'tongue, language'. In szëm (< P-U *śilmä; UEW 479) and három (< P-F-U *kolme; UEW 174) -m- is preserved, probably receiving support from the preceding consonant. In contrast, in nyelv (< F-U *ńälmä: Che. jəlmə/Ost. ńäläm; UEW 313) -m-changes into -*v*-, despite the fact that the context is the same. As Bereczki (1980a: 51) puts it, there is no rule in Hungarian regarding the preservation of internal -*m*- vs the change -*w*-/-*v*-. It is possible that this variation is the reflex of different conditioning environments present in a previous stage of development, as is often claimed. However, apart from the fact that this remains an unverifiable assumption, the thesis of a pure and simple instance of variation seems more plausible. As Collinder (1960: 140) says:

> In a **few words** at least, intervocalic *-*m*- has changed into -*v*- in Hungarian. The same development has **sometimes** taken place in Fennic (after a long vowel ?), and Mordvin. In Cheremis *-*m*- has **occasionally** disappeared after a labial vowel [bold is mine].

Internal *-*n*-, *-*ń*- and *-*r*- remain unchanged; the same is true for the liquids, here, too, with occasional depalatalisation of *-*ĺ*- in the western languages. Compare also the loss of -*l*- in Hun. *szëm* < *śilmä mentioned above.

(g) development of internal glides. *-*j*- tends to have two reflexes. It is either preserved or it is changed into -*Ø*- in almost all the U languages (Collinder 1960: 111). In Hungarian *-*j*- has more than two reflexes: it may develop into a voiced palatal stop (like in initial position): *kígyó* 'snake', but see dialectal *kijó* < P-U *kije (*küje) (UEW 154); it may be preserved in words such as *vaj* 'butter' < P-F-U *woje 'fat' (compare Finn. *voi*; UEW 578); or it may get lost in a few cases, such as *ú-sz-* 'to swim' < P-U **uje-* ~ **oje-*: Finn. *ui-da* (Hun. -*sz*- is an obscured frequentative suffix, according to UEW 542).

The etymological material regarding internal *-*w*- is rather scanty and its reflexes are not always predictable, although the following major tendencies can be observed. In Finnic it develops into -*v*- or -*Ø*-; in Lapp, Mordvin and Hungarian into -*v*-; in Permian and Samoyed into -*Ø*-; in Ostyak, into -*w*- in some dialects and into -*γ*- in others (Collinder 1960: 115); see also the discussion in Section 4.5.3.1, point (e).

(h) development of internal sibilants and affricates. The distribution of internal sibilants and affricates exhibits the same kind of messiness and variation as their initial counterparts, but there is less etymological material available for the investigation. For example, *-*s*- is claimed to have been generally preserved, but there seems to be only one clear testimony for it: Hun. *fészëk* 'nest' (*sz* = /*s*/)/Finn. *pesä*, but also Ost. *pĕl* and Vog. *piť* < P-U *pesä (UEW 375). Internal *-*ś*- usually becomes -*s*- or -*ź*-, as shown in the term for 'twenty': P-F-U *kuśȝ (*koje-ćȝ) > Hun. *húsz* /Vot. and Zyr. *kįź*/ Ost. *kos* (UEW 224). Regarding the reflexes of -*š*- see Section 4.5.2.2 point (a) and Section 4.5.3.1 point (a) below. Regarding the reflexes of internal *-*č*- see the term for 'knife' again in Section 4.5.3.1, point (b).

The following examples illustrate the various reflexes of the palatalised affricate. In Hungarian one can have also the voiced palatal stop, which in internal position can be the reflex of -*j-, as discussed in the previous subsection, and of several other palatalised sounds (*-ĺ-, *-ć- *-ńć-, *-δ'-):

(4.43) P-F-U *-ć-/*ečɜ 'younger brother/sister': Hun. öcs 'younger brother'/Vog. ēś, ĭčī/Ost. iťəki (UEW 70; compare also Turkic eči 'older brother'/Mon. ečige 'father'/Gold eče 'younger brother of the father')

(4.44) P-F-U *-ć-/*kećä 'a type of fish': Finn. keso, kesämä 'a small type of fish, cyprinus blicca' (SSA[40], I 349)/Hun. keszeg 'white-fish'/Vog. kāsew (UEW 141)

(4.45) P-F-U *-ć-/*wića- 'to see, look at, watch (out)': Est. viisa-/Hun. vigyáz- /Vot. voź- etc. (UEW 571). Compare also the term for 'father': P-U *ića (UEW 78)

(i) development of some internal clusters. We have already discussed the status of the consonantal clusters in Section 4.5.1 and illustrated one type in point (f) above. The following examples show the developments of some of the most frequent U and/or F-U clusters and for which somewhat more predictable reflexes can be found: 'nasal + stop'. Generally, some languages preserve the nasal, some others loose it, with consequent sonorisation of the following sound. Once again, the distribution of the changes does not necessarily match the boundaries of the traditional family tree, and the same changes may also take place in similar, non-U words:

(4.46) *-mt-/P-U *tumte- 'to feel, to touch': Finn. tunte-/Hun. tud- 'to know'/Zyr. tęd-/Vot. tod-/Sam. Ye. tudda-/Sam. Yu. tumtā – 'to know' (UEW 536)

(4.47) *-mt-/P-F-U *amta- 'to give': Finn. anta-/Hun. ad-/Zyr. and Vot. ud-/Mor. E. and M. ando- (UEW 8)

The following example, whilst illustrating the developments of the clusters -mp-, also exemplifies the variety of reflexes one can have among the various languages as well as within the same language:

(4.48) *-mp-/P-U *kumpa 'wave': Finn. kumpu 'hillock, mound'/Hun. hab 'foam'/Mor. M. komba/Zyr. gɨb-/Ost. kŏmp/Vog. kop, kump, χop, χump /Sam. Yu. χāmpa/Sam.Ye. kaba (UEW 203; compare also Turkic qōm)

As in other circumstances, in this case too Hungarian lines up with the Permian languages and some Samoyed languages, rather than with the Ob-Ugric languages. The Hungarian terms dob- and domb mentioned above (examples (4.32) and (4.33) respectively), with their different reflexes, also belong to this class of examples.

The third frequent cluster of this type is -ŋk-, whose reflexes are illustrated in example (4.49) below. The Hungarian term presents the initial voiced stop as in *dob-*, *domb*, instead of the expected *t-*; the reflex -χ- in Vogul is also an irregular reflex, for which one should assume a development of the type: *-ŋk- > *-ŋχ- > -χ-:

(4.49) *-ŋk-/F-U *tuŋke- 'push, get through, stuff, stick': Finn. *tunke-*/Hun. *dug-*/Mor. E. and M. *tongo-*/? Vog. *tokr-*, *toχr-* (UEW 537; compare also Altaic: *tïŋ- ~ *tïγ- ~ *tïq-*: Turkic *tïγ-*/Mon. *čigji-*)

The changes shared by Hungarian and Permian – rather than the predicted Hungarian and Ob-Ugric – have attracted several explanations. For example, according to Abondolo ((ed.) 1998: 5), the relative chronologies of the two shared sound-changes reported above (weakening of intervocalic *-t-* and the change *-mt-/-nt- > -d-*) are different in Hungarian and in Permian. Therefore these two shared innovations must be considered as evidence of 'secondary' areal contact at best, and not as evidence of a genetic relationship between Hungarian and Permian closer than that of Hungarian and Ob-Ugric. This is certainly a plausible explanation, and I am certainly not advocating a closer genetic relationship between Hungarian and Permian just on the basis of these shared innovations. However, I would like to point out that no safe conclusion about the nature and the timing of these changes can be drawn from the available data. In fact, any conclusion of this sort, in the absence of old records, can only be based on a set of interlocking assumptions which might even be correct, but whose validity we shall never be able to verify (see Note 41 for more details on this issue).

4.5.2.2. *From Proto-Uralic to Proto-Finno-Ugric according to Sammallahti*

As mentioned in the previous section, Sammallahti observes that the U consonantism remained fundamentally unchanged between the P-U and P-F-U phase. This observation is at variance with the assumed great time-depth of the family tree, and so the author tries to identify some sound-changes. He states that (1988: 490):

> The consonantal paradigm of PFU contained the sounds already present in PU with a few additions. There was one systematic change

The author then lists these additions, whilst pointing out that their status is uncertain, due to the paucity of reconstructable material:

(**a**): *š-*, whose evidence is 'scarce but probably conclusive (1988: 490)'. However, two of the four listed etymologies are not present in all the Ugric languages: *pišä-* 'to prepare food' is not found for sure in Hungarian and *mekši* 'bee' is not found in Ob-Ugric.

(b): *$*\acute{c}$* (palatalised affricate), which again has been established on the basis of few etymologies. Sammallahti (1988: 491) observes that:

> Of the Hungarian words beginning with *s-* [/*š*/], only one has a satisfactory Ob-Ugric etymology pointing to an earlier *$*\acute{c}$*-, but even here the Ob-Ugric vowel seems younger than Proto-Ugric and the initial consonants do not match (*sert-* 'to hurt': Proto-Ob-Ugric *$*\acute{c}ääreg$*- id.). On the other hand, only one of the regular Ob-Ugric etymologies with an initial *$*\acute{c}$*- listed by Honti (1982[a]: 130–1, items 74–88) has possible cognates elsewhere (*$*\acute{c}ääreg$*-), so they seem to be either loans or neologisms. Yet, many of the Hungarian words beginning with *cs-* have satisfactory etymologies in Permic and other north-western languages (e.g. *csap, csegely* [. . .] *csomó, csupor*[42]).

The author continues that in order to explain the features shared by Hungarian and the north-western (Finno-Permian) languages, one should probably add another level to the family tree, a level intermediate between P-Finno-Permian and P-Finno-Ugric. 'This proto-language could be called Proto-Finno-Hungarian'. However, Sammallahti decides not to pursue the matter any further.

(c): *$*\acute{l}$*-, which has been established on the basis of one satisfactory etymology only: P-U *$*lupså$* 'moisture'; this, however, is not found either in the Ugric or in the Permian branch.

The single 'systematic change' from P-U to P-F-U mentioned by the author is formulated as follows (1988: 490):

$$*V_x > *VV \text{ before a consonant (PU } *kåxs\dot{i} > \text{PFU } *koosi \text{ 'spruce')}$$

We have already discussed in detail the etymologies containing the segment *$*x$* and the problems associated with it (see Section 4.4.5.1; see in particular examples (4.4) and (4.20) above). Furthermore, as pointed out by Janhunen, the relevant (P-Samoyed and P-Finnic) correspondences, rather than 'systematic', are 'fairly regular', and their number is limited.

Finally, still according to Sammallahti (1988: 492), the phonotactics of the P-F-U consonants was again rather similar to that of P-U consonants. In summary, as observed by Häkkinen (1990: 186), the F-U words do not appear to differ in any significant way, in either their structure or their meaning, from the U words.

Regarding the difference in consonantism of first syllable between the P-F-U node and the lower-level nodes, yet again, no major sound-changes have been identified. This state of affairs is evident from the examples listed above, and is acknowledged by several modern sources. For example, Korhonen (1981: 126) remarks that there are no significant sound-changes between the consonantism of P-F-U and that of early P-Finnic. Sammallahti (1988: 523) states that 'The consonantal paradigm in PFP [P-Finno-Permian] remained largely the same as in PFU'. And, in fact, at p. 524 the author presents the reconstructed P-Finno-Permian consonantism, which is exactly the same as the reconstructed P-F-U consonantism presented on his p. 491, with only one change: P-F-U $*w$ > P-F-P $*v$ (see Table 4.7).

Table 4.7 Sammallahti's Proto-Finno-Ugric and Proto-Finno-Permian consonantism (1988: 491 and 524)

/p			m				v
t	s		n	d	l	r	
	š	č					
	ś	ć	ń	d'	(ĺ)		j
k			ŋ				
							x /

Sammallahti further remarks (1988: 532) that the P-Finno-Permian consonant system has undergone only minor changes. In particular, in word initial positions the consonants have retained their original qualities (apart from a few irregular cases).

4.5.3. The 'Ugric' innovations

Despite the total lack of any evidence in support of the Ugric node (see Section 4.2.1), there are still attempts at identifying innovations typical of the Ugric level only. In the following sections I shall illustrate some of the best 'evidence' that has been quoted in the literature to support the establishment of the Ugric node (see, for example, Sammallahti 1988: 500 f.; Décsy 1965: 212 f.; Honti 1979, 1998a: 332–3, 1998b).

4.5.3.1. Ugric consonantal sound-changes

The following are claimed to be specific, common 'Ugric innovations':

(a): P-F-U $*s$- and $*š$- fall together and change into P-Ug. $*θ$-, from which the following three developments are held to have derived: P-Ug. $*θ$- > Hun. Ø-; P-Ug. $*θ$- > Vog. t-; P-Ug. $*θ$- > Ost. t-, l-, j-, as shown in the examples (4.21) to (4.24) above. Another etymology usually quoted in this context is the etymology for 'tendon' (see Section 4.4.5.1): Hun. ín (~ ina-)/Vog. tān, tē̮n / Ost. (Demjanka dialect) ton/Ost. (Vakh and Obdorsk dialect) lan/Ost. (Vasjugan) jan, but also Sam.Ye. ti/Sam. Ta. taŋa/Sam. Se. čăn ~ tsăn etc. (UEW 441).

However, there is no independent evidence to support the reconstruction of $*θ$, except for the desire to create a common 'Ugric innovation'. In fact, $*θ$ is only needed to explain the odd presence of t- in Vogul and in part of Ostyak. Regarding the other Ostyak variants, it needs to be asked whether a *θ sound can really be the appropriate intermediate node.[43] It would be simpler and more consistent with observations from other language groups to assume that each development in each of the languages involved has instead been achieved independently. For example in Hungarian the process might have been the natural, and quite frequent lenition *s- / *š- > *h- > Ø-.[44] Besides, several Samoyed languages show the same developments as Ob-Ugric, as also illustrated in Figure 4.2.

As a consequence of the (presumed) merging of *s- and *š-, the resulting gap is assumed to have been re-filled in P-Ugric by the depalatalisation of P-U *ś-, as shown in the etymology for 'eye': P-U *śilmä > P-Ug. *sĭmä (according to Sammallahti (1988: 502); see also Honti (1979) and (1998a: 333); see example (4.25) above). According to this analysis, the Ugric languages are all claimed to present, as a common innovation, the same reflex s-. However, s- is also present in Sam. Yu. sew and Sam. Ka. sima, whilst in some other dialects of Vogul we find again š-: Vog. (Konda and Pelymka dialect) šäm (UEW 479).

(b): the existence of a common Ugric sound *č (Décsy 1965: 212; see also discussion in Section 4.5.2.1 above). This sound is then assumed to have changed into *š (note that the U/F-U *š is supposed to have merged with s). In reality, in support of this change there are few examples and relatively many exceptions, as shown by the following set: Hun. kés 'knife'/Ost. köčəγ, kesi/Vog. kāsi < F-U *kečɜ (UEW 142; Sauvageot 1976: 128).

(c): Honti (1998a: 353) states that:

> Already in proto-Ugric, *k had markedly different allophones in front-vocalic versus back-vocalic environments. The result was the development, albeit separately in each of the three Ugric languages, of *k > x (< h- in Hungarian) in back-vocalic words.

However, as discussed in Section 4.5.2.1 (and also remarked by Honti), this change has come to completion only in Hungarian (although not long ago) and is now in the process of diffusing in some Ob-Ugric languages/dialects. Furthermore, this very same sound change also occurs in some Samoyed languages. Therefore, this change is a 'relatively' new dialectal process (as also remarked by Gheno & Hajdú (1992: 172) and Sauvageot (1971: 22)) and cannot be classified as a 'Ugric innovation'.

(d): the so-called Ugric velar strengthening in intervocalic position: P-F-U *-ŋ- > P-Ug. *-ŋk-, as shown by the etymology for 'ice': P-F-U *jäŋi > P-Ugr. *jäŋkĭ (according to Sammallahti 1988: 502; compare Ost. jöŋk /Vog. jāŋk /Hun. jég /Finn. jää /Mor. E. ej, Mor. M. jäj (UEW 93). However, Sammallahti (ibid.) also observes that: 'There seem to be a number of cases where PFU *ŋ was preserved in PUg'.

(4.50) Vog. (Lower-Konda and Pelymka dialect) *päŋk*, but also Vog. (Tavda dialect) *päŋ* /Hun. *fej, fő* < P-F-U **päŋi* 'head' (Sammallahti 1988: 502; UEW 365)

(4.51) Ost. *lŏŋ* /Vog. *toj, tuw* /Sam.Yu. *tā?*/Sam. Ta. *taŋa* /Finn. *suvi* (Gen. *suve-n*) < P-F-U **suŋi* 'summer, thaw' (Sammallahti 1988: 502; UEW 451). Compare also the etymology for 'son-in-law', reconstructed as P-F-U **wäŋiw* by Sammallahti (ibid.; see example (4.12) and (4.37) above).

(e): non-initial P-U/P-F-U **-w* changes into P-Ug. **-γ*, to revert then to *-w* (*-v* in Hungarian) in certain dialects and environments (Honti 1985, 1998a: 353). Evidence in support of this change is claimed to be, for example, the term for 'stone': P-U **kiwe* (UEW 163), the term for 'winter': P-F-U **tälwä* (UEW 516), and the term for 'bone': P-U **luwe* (UEW 254; see above example (4.16)). However, there is no independent evidence on the basis of which the above-described process can be postulated, so that the reflexes *-γ* and *-w*/*-v* found for example in the term for 'stone' (Ost. *köγ* / Vog. *käw*/ Hun. *kő* (Acc. *köve-t*)), can also satisfactorily be explained as independent developments. Furthermore, the etymology for 'bone' presents problems, as discussed above. Regarding the etymology for 'winter' **tälwä,* one may observe that, alongside Ostyak *tēlǝγ*, there is Vogul *tāl* and Hun. *tél* (Acc. *tele-t*), where there is no trace of **-w* or **-γ*.

(f): Honti (1998a: 353) considers the reflex of the velar illabial vowel **i̯* (**ï* in his transcription), present in the Ugric languages, as another piece of evidence in favour of the existence of the Ugric node. Compare: Hun. *nyíl* vs Finn. *nuoli* 'arrow' (see above example (4. 5)). Indeed, as the reader may recall, Janhunen (1981a) observed that the Ugric languages may at times be quite conservative in vocalism. However, quite apart from that there is no way to establish the 'relative archaicity' of the 'reconstructed' vowels, the real problem is that – yet again – the Ugric languages are not consistent in presenting the reflexes of the illabial vowels. This fact has been illustrated while discussing this sound in Section 4.4.5.2. To give a further example, the Ostyak correspondences of Hun. *nyíl* 'arrow' are *ńal, ńot* (according to UEW 317) so that Honti (ibid.), in order to maintain a coherent development in Ob-Ugric, is forced to postulate an otherwise unmotivated change P-Ost. **ïï* > Ost. *aa.*

In a another article (1998b), Honti reaffirms that there are least two 'deep-rooted' ('syvällekäyviä') sound-changes that clearly differentiate the Ugric languages from the western, Finno-Permian languages: the developments of initial sibilants, and the spirantisation of **k-* before a back-vowel. A distinct Ugric feature is also assumed to be the change **-w* > **-γ*, and the preservation of velar illabial **i̯.* As one can see, there is nothing new, so that the above-reported problems cannot be considered overcome. Honti is however correct when, to defend the paucity of the shared Ugric sound innovations, he observes that the Finno-Volgaic and the Finno-Permian shared innovations are not numerous either.[45]

(g): Hajdú & Domokos (1978: 82–7) claim that Ob-Ugric and Hungarian share a relatively large new vocabulary, among which figure the following etymologies: the term for 'horse', Hun. *ló*; the term for 'saddle' (Hun. *nyerëg* / Ost. *nöγər* / Vog. *naγər*; UEW 874); the term for 'bridle' (Hun. *fék* / Ost. *päk* / Vog. *behch* 'habena'; UEW 878), the term for 'second-grass horse', that is, 'two-year old horse': Hun. *'másod-fű ló'*, to be compared with the isomorphic Vogul expression *'kit pum lu'* with the same meaning. However, the term for 'horse' is not a specific Ugric term, as discussed in Chapter 6, whilst the two isomorphic expressions are not unique to Hungarian and Vogul, but represent a typical way of building phrases in most U (and Altaic) languages.

4.5.3.2. *The presumed borrowing in the 'Ugric period'*

It is often argued that the postulation of the Ugric node is supported by the existence of words of non-U origin that have been borrowed into this distinctive layer. Among the most quoted examples is the term for '7', considered to be of Indo-European origin, and a group of words considered to be of Turkic origin, as discussed below:

(a): the Ob-Ugric equivalents of Hun. *hét* 'seven' are Vog. *sāt, sāt* and Ost. *låpət, tåpət.* (UEW 844). These parallels are usually assumed to have been borrowed from an Indo-European language at the time of the undivided Ugric community (compare San. *saptá* / Ave. *hapta* (Joki 1973: 313, item (138)). However, the vowel relations suggest that the P-Ob-Ugric terms and the Hungarian term have been borrowed separately (Sammallahti 1988: 504). Note also that in Vogul we find the irregular initial **s-* and in Hungarian we find the irregular initial *h-*, instead of the expected reflexes (recall that: **s-* > Hun. Ø- and Vog. *t-*; the Vogul, Hungarian and Ostyak reflex *s-* presupposes instead an initial **ś-*).

(b): some Turkic loan-words are claimed to have entered Hungarian at the time of the still undivided P-Ugric community. This claim in turn is supposed to be supported by the fact that these loan-words share the innovations typical of the Ugric phase. One of these (alleged) Ugric innovations has been discussed in the previous section (point (c)): the change **k-* > **χ-* > *h-*. This innovation is supposed to be visible in the following Hungarian words of Turkic origin:

(4.52) Hun. *hattyú* / Ost. *kŏtəŋ, χŏtəŋ,* / Vog. *χotəŋ, kotəŋ* 'swan' < Ug. **kottзŋз*.[46] Compare Cha. *qotan,* but also Mon. *χutan, qotan* 'pelican', *chodang* '*pelicanus onocrotalus*' (UEW 857; Ligeti 1986: 138–9). Note that, according to TESz II, 75, this is 'probably' a Turkic loaning in Ugric times.

(4.53) Hun. *homok* 'sand', which derives from 'Ancient Turkic *qumaq*' according to Róna-Tas (1988a: 750). Compare also Mon. *qumaki* (Ligeti 1986: 80). Note however that there seem to be no parallels in Ob-Ugric. TESz II, 139 claims that the word belongs to the oldest contacts between Hungarian and Turkic.

(4.54) Hun. *hajó* 'boat'. The borrowing is 'probably' from Turkic *qayiq* 'rowing boat' according to UEW 169. Compare also Yak. $\chi ay\bar{\imath}q$ and Mon. *qayaγ* (Ligeti 1986: 28). According to TESz II, 26, the origin of the word is disputed, but a U origin is also probable; its presumed Altaic connection requires further investigation. As in the previous example, there do not seem to be parallels in Ob-Ugric.

Conversely, those Hungarian words of Turkic origin which have not been affected by this change are supposed to have entered Hungarian after the disintegration of the Ugric community. This is the case of the following words, where the initial **k-* of the donor language is preserved: Hun. *kapu* 'front-door', for which compare Chu. *qapu* and Tur. *kapu* (TESZ II, 367; Ligeti 1986: 77–8); Hun. *kos* 'ram', for which compare Tur. *koç* and Cha. *qočqar* (TESz II, 585); Hun. *karvaly* 'sparrow-hawk', for which compare Tur. *qïrγui* but also Middle Mon. *kirγui* (Ligeti 1986: 71; this word is 'probably' of old Turkic origin, according to TESz 395 and presents serious sound difficulties according to Ligeti).

However, the situation is not clear, as is already evidenced by the absence of the expected Ob-Ugric parallels for Hungarian *homok* and *hajó*. Indeed, as pointed out by Róna-Tas (1988a: 751) 'we are far from being on solid ground in supposing an early Turkic influence on P-Ugr[ic]'.

For example, with regard to Hun. *homok* 'sand', Róna-Tas (1988a: 750) observes that the change 'back vocalic *q-* > *x-* did occur in Chuvash, only its chronology is unclear', although it seems to be quite a late change, around the tenth century. According to the author, this means that (ibid.) 'the Hung *h-* reflex of T[urkic] *q-* can be explained also by assuming that the borrowed T[urkic] form had already *x-*'.

The same type of analysis holds for Hun. *hajó* 'boat' and *hattyú* 'swan'. The other words, less than a dozen, which have been classified as belonging to the 'Ugric layer' of borrowing from Turkic, present again all sorts of problems (see the list and related comments in Róna-Tas 1988a: 749–51).

Similarly, Ligeti (1986: 136–7) observes that it is difficult to identify a specific layer of borrowing from Turkic at the 'Ugric level', also because of the absence of old Turkic records (the oldest going back to the 8th century). The author (1986: 80) observes, for instance, that the etymology of *homok* is unclear because of the presence of final -*k* as opposed to initial *h*-. He further comments (1986: 26–7) that words of this type can equally well be accounted for in both ways, that is: either as borrowing from a Turkic language early enough to participate to the sound-change in question, or as borrowing from a Turkic language which itself has already implemented the change *q*- > *χ*-.

I shall come back to the topic of the borrowing from Turkic into Hungarian in Chapter 6.

4.5.4. *The position of Lapp*

At this point a mention has to be made about the position of Lapp within the U family, without going into details.

The position of Lapp within U, as well as the origin of the Lappic people, is highly controversial. Lapp is most often classified as belonging to the Finnic node (Ravila 1935; E. Itkonen 1955, 1960; Sammallahti 1984, 1995). In this case, Lapp and Balto-Finnic are generally claimed to derive from a common P-Language, called 'Early-P-Finnic', which is supposed to have split into P-Lapp and Middle-P-Finnic about 1000 BC at the latest, or possibly much earlier. However, the contradiction between the linguistic affinity and the cultural and racial divergences between the Lapps and the Balto-Finns have convinced several researchers to frame the hypothesis of a language switch. The Lapps might have not been U people; they might have been instead of a different race (probably an arctic race, like the Samoyeds) and might have spoken a different, non-U language. At some point, they might have adopted the language of the Balto-Finns after coming into long, intense contact with them (Setälä 1926; Toivonen 1949/50; Carpelan 2000: 29).

Regarding the complex phonological, lexical and morphological structure of this language group it suffices here to quote the following remarks by Sammallahti (1998: 44):

> Saami differs from Fennic in a number of features. In phonology, the vowel system has undergone a radical reorganization whereas the consonant system has retained many old features, such as palatalized consonants, which were lost in Fennic as a consequence of the Indo-European contacts which ultimately helped bring about the disintegration of the Fennic-Saamic protolanguage. In morphology, Saami has retained the dual number in its personal pronouns, personal endings, and possessive suffixes, . . . Saami lacks the external local cases which Fennic developed after the disintegration of the protolanguage

See also the complementary descriptions by Korhonen (1988a, 1988b).

The lexical, phonological and morpho-syntactic features of Lapp are such that this language group does not really fit into any of the traditionally established nodes. Tauli (1955: 25) has classified Lapp as a 'mixed language *par excellence*', since it seems to share features with several, different language groups. Austerlitz (1987) considers the Lapp branch as an isolate, as evident from his family tree (1987: 178). As a matter of fact, Lapp is similar to the Indo-European languages at the syntactic/typological level. It is quite close to the Balto-Finnic languages at the lexical level, even if there is a strikingly high number of Lapp indigenous (?) words, which are not shared with Balto-Finnic, especially in the areas of 'fishing', 'hunting' and 'natural environment' (Lehtiranta 1982, 1989).

Recently, the question of the origin and nature of this language group has arisen again through the opposing views of T. Itkonen (1997) and Korhonen (1981: 33) on the one hand, and Sammallahti (1999) on the other. T. Itkonen (1997: 260) questions again the existence of the 'Saami-Finnic (~ Finno-Lappic)' P-Language, by arguing that the presumed phonological, morphological and lexical evidence normally brought forward in favour of this node is rather scanty. He concludes that:

> Thus the notion of a Finno-Lappic intermediate protolanguage should be abandoned as a useless operational tool; the special similarities between Finnic and Lappic should rather be understood as a result of a continuous loan

In contrast, Sammallahti (1999) argues in favour of the existence of this intermediate P-Language ('varhaiskantasuomi' 'early-P-Finnic'), by trying to demonstrate that the reported elements of counter-evidence are not convincing. He argues also that the split of this node must have taken place before the P-Baltic period.

4.5.5. *Sound-changes in progress*

We have observed above (Section 4.5.2.1) that some consonantal changes appear to be in the process of diffusing. For example, we have observed the diffusing of initial fricative velar (before a back-vowel) in some dialects of Vogul, Ostyak and Samoyed. Another example of sound-change in progress is represented by the diffusing of the correlation of voice in Permian. As described by Riese (1998: 255):

> the main difference between pFU [P-F-U] and pPN [P-Permian] is the appearance, in pPN, of voiced analogues for most of the pFU obstruents. About one-sixth of inherited pFU words appear with voiced initial obstruent in pPN.

Compare the following examples: P-F-U *perä* 'back (part)' > Finn. *perä*, but Zyr. *bẹr*/Vot. *ber* (UEW 373); P-F-U *kinče* (*künče*) 'nail' > Zyr. *gįž*/Vot. *gįžį* (UEW 157).

Instances of changes in progress can also be identified in the area of vocalism. For example, we have already seen that the words exhibiting vowel alternation in Ostyak co-exist with the assumed older forms without vowel alternation. We have hinted at the loss of stem final vowels, generally reconstructed for P-U as *-a, *-ä, *-e, although there are different opinions (Korhonen 1988c and Collinder 1960: 192). This process has affected most languages, including (partially) Finnish, Lapp (only in polysyllabic stems and in suffixes), Cheremis and Mordvin, and is *in fieri* in Estonian. Compare, for example, the etymology for 'water' *vete, which has lost its final vowel in Hun. *víz* / Mor. M. and E. *ved'* / Che. *wǝt* / Vog. *wüï*, but not in Finnish, where, however, the short, final vowel has changed: Nom. *vesi* vs Gen. *vede-n* (< *vete-n*). Compare also Finn. Nom. *lumi* vs Gen. *lume-n* 'snow', but Mor. E. and M. *lov*/Che. *lǝm* etc. (< F-P *lume (UEW 253)). This sound-change, at least in Hungarian, has been accomplished quite recently in historical times (around the 12th/13th centuries), and is rather well documented. In fact, final vowels, probably already reduced (Bárczi, Benkő & Berrár (eds) 1967: 148–52; Hajdú 1972: 51–2), are still present in the oldest Hungarian documents, where they have developed into -i, -ị, -u, -ü; compare for example Old Hun. *hodu* > Modern Hun. *had* 'army, troops'. We also have clear cases of co-occurrence of the two competing forms: Old Hun. *ut* vs *utu* 'road' > Modern Hun. *út* (both examples are from the text 'The Foundation Charter of the Abbey of Tihany'; see below Chapter 8). This process is still retrievable in alternations of the type: *nyíl* 'arrow' vs *nyila-k* 'arrow-Plu.'; *kéz* 'hand' vs *keze-t* 'hand-Acc.', vs *keze-s* 'guarantor' (-s is a derivational suffix).

In Vogul and Ostyak too the loss of final short vowels seems to be quite recent, although probably less recent than in Hungarian.

4.5.6. *Conclusion on consonantism*

In terms of quantity, only a few sound-changes have been identified within the U consonantism between the assumed P-Language and the daughter languages. In terms of distribution, these changes do not respect at all the conventional, intermediate nodes. In terms of quality, we have observed (in this and in the previous paragraph) instances of irregular reflexes, variation, correlations established through the adoption of the unspecified consonantal segment *x*. Even those changes which appear at first as proceeding regularly, such as *k- > χ- or *p- > f-, are not that regular after all, because they are in the process of diffusing for example in Vogul, Ostyak and in Samoyed. These sound-changes might eventually be accomplished regularly in all the dialects, this being the inevitable end result of the dynamics of sound-changes, at least according to some interpretations (Labov 1994; Lass 1993). However, they cannot be claimed to be regular at the moment.

4.5.7. *Common phonological features in Eurasia*

At this point it must be pointed out that the phonological features discussed in this chapter are not specific to the U languages. On the contrary, vowel harmony, consonant gradation, reduced vowels, vowel alternations of one sort or other, are fairly widespread phenomena in one or other of the Altaic/ Palaeo-Siberian languages:

- Vowel harmony is present in the Turkic languages and Classical Mongolian, where it has developed into velar (or post-palatal) vs palatal (or pre-palatal) opposition, with some cases of labial harmony in Turkish. This, in turn, is generally considered to be the source of the instances of labial harmony in Hungarian and East Cheremis. Besides this, at least in some Turkic languages too, the vowels *i* and *e* (with their specific phonetic realisations) are neutral, as in Finnish and Hungarian. It is to be noticed that VH does not appear exactly in the same form in the languages in which it is present, neither in U nor in Altaic. In other words, it is not a 'perfect', consistent phenomenon. In Altaic, as well as in U, it is present in a random way. For example, VH is present in Turkish; in Chuvash, although it is present, it is not as superficially obvious as in the other Turkic languages; it is well developed in Yakut. Furthermore, only the Turkic and Mongolian languages have the kind of horizontal (front/back) opposition that is characteristic of several U languages. Tungus has a different system, a vertical system, contrasting high and low vowels. The random distribution and the uneven character of VH could lead to the assumption that it was not an original U feature (see however for a different opinion Korhonen[47](1993: 329) and Abondolo[48] (1998 (ed.): 18)), but developed independently in the various languages. This assumption is supported by the fact that in the first Hungarian and Turkic documents VH is not yet fully developed (see the relevant Hungarian examples in Chapter 8). Both the Altaic and U languages share therefore at least the 'tendency' to develop VH. Even if it is a 'borrowable' feature[49], and, as a type of assimilation, it is present in other languages of the world, VH is certainly a feature that ties together U and Altaic within Eurasia.
- Both consonant gradation and vowel gradation are found in non-U languages of Asia: CG, which is fully developed only in Finnish, Lapp and Samoyed Tawgi, is also found in Mongolian and Eskimo, where it extends to all the consonants. VG, found in different forms in Vogul, Ostyak, Estonian, and, to a lesser extent, Samoyed, is also present in the Eastern Palaeo-Siberian languages.
- Reduced vowels of the types found in Samoyed Yurak, Cheremis and Ostyak, also exist in the Turkic languages Chuvash and Tatar, although in this last case there are contrasting analyses of the vowel length (Tauli 1955).
- As remarked by Räsänen (1963/4: 184), both the Altaic and U languages possess the following features: a) the richness of the vowel system, compared with the relative paucity of consonants; b) the restrictions on consonant clusters, which are not allowed in initial position, are rare in

final position and possibly avoided in internal position; c) the phonotactic simplicity of the reconstructed P-Languages (simplicity which, however, may be a distortion of the method; see Korhonen (1993: 33)).

- Finally, as pointed out by Janhunen (2000: 68), the vowel system of P-Finnic and P-Samoyed – the 'two extremes of the [U] language family'– are rather similar to each other. However, these two U systems are also rather similar to the vowel system reconstructable for the Altaic P-Languages, including P-Turkic and P-Mongolian (as well as P-Tungusic and 'P-Koreanic'). This, according to the author, suggests 'a prolonged Post-Proto-Uralic areal continuum'.

4.6. CONCLUSION

4.6.1. *The status of the reconstructions*

In this chapter we have analysed in detail the various attempts to reconstruct the P-U sound-structure and the intermediate nodes of the U family tree. We have seen that, contrary to general belief, the nodes of the conventional family tree have not been reconstructed in accordance with the conventional Comparative Method:

The P-U node
- Contrary to general belief, the P-U node has not been reconstructed from its putative constituents. The node that is usually referred to as the P-Uralic node is in fact based on the systematic comparison of P-Finno-Permian and P-Samoyed only, and it omits the key Ugric node.
- We observed that this reconstruction of P-Finno-Permian-Samoyed has a large number of sound-rules and a small number of etymologies. The significance of this is that the reconstruction cannot be associated with a high level of confidence, contrary to what would normally be expected with a proper application of the Comparative Method. In other words, it would be consistent with the evidence to interpret the entire reconstruction as due to chance resemblance.

The P-Ugric node
- It is generally believed that the existence of the P-Ugric node was established historically by the end of the 19th century. However, this is not the case. The belief in the existence of the Ugric node was based solely on a coincidence of similar names (*Yugria* and *hungarus*) as discussed in Chapter 2, and, in fact, there has emerged no scientific evidence to support this node.
- The P-Ugric node has resisted all conventional attempts at its reconstruction, due to the vast differences between Hungarian and the Ob-Ugric

languages. Some mainstream authors conclude from this that the Ugric node should be interpreted as the result of a *Sprachbund* convergence, rather than as a conventional genetic node.

The P-Finno-Ugric node
- It is generally believed that the P-Finno-Ugric node was established by the founders of the field by the end of the 19th century. In fact, as we saw in Chapter 2, the P-Finno-Ugric node was introduced by Donner (but was not adopted by Budenz). However, no reconstruction – at any level of language – was provided by Donner to justify its establishment.
- Subsequently, there have been no systematic attempts to reconstruct this node using conventional methods.

The reconstruction of the entire Uralic family tree
- A systematic attempt to reconstruct the P-Finno-Ugric and P-Ugric nodes was made in 1988 by Sammallahti. This author used what may be called a 'reverse reconstruction' method. It was assumed that the conventional U family tree had been established beyond doubt. It was further assumed that the reconstructed P-Finno-Permian-Samoyed node was identical to the top-level P-Uralic node. Using these assumptions, the method was to attempt to 'bridge the gap' between the P-Uralic node and the P-Ob-Ugric node.
- We have noted a number of specific problems with this type of reconstruction. Many of the postulated (intermediate) sound-changes are based only on one or two assumed reconstructed etymologies, and therefore they could be considered to be ad hoc. Also, the entire reconstruction is based on the P-U node, which, as we have mentioned, could have been due to pure chance resemblance.
- We have also noted a methodological problem. The overall reconstruction does not compare primary linguistic evidence directly. Instead, comparisons are generally made between reconstructions, and these are therefore not directly verifiable against the actual data. The method might, in this sense, be 'not even wrong'.

However, our analysis of consonantism above has identified some ('mostly') regular sound-changes, for example P-U *p- > Hun. *f-, as commonly reported in textbooks. Although these changes are generally embedded within etymologies that are irregular in other respects, and therefore should be rejected according to a strict application of the Comparative Method, there is the possibility that some of these changes do represent a pattern that requires explanation. We have not undertaken this analysis in detail here and this will be examined in the next chapter.

4.6.2. *A possible interpretation of the evidence*

Taking all these points into consideration, we could conclude that the U etymologies, in the vast majority of the cases, are 'similarities' rather than 'correspondences'. This means that, according to the Comparative Method as it is normally applied, the U languages, at least at the level of phonological structure, do not form a language family. There is no evidence that P-U is a valid node. One may speak of the principal language groupings, namely Balto-Finnic, (Finno-) Permian, Ob-Ugric, Hungarian, Samoyed and Lapp, as forming a dialectal continuum, but there is no convincing evidence that they all derive genetically from the same node, the P-U node, as traditionally conceived.

The thesis that the U languages may form a dialectal continuum is not new. We have already discussed the idea of the language chain as proposed by Németh and Pusztay (in Chapters 2 and 3 respectively). Similarly, Hajdú (1987: 310), after pointing out the lack of convincing reconstructions for most intermediate nodes, and the relative character of the sketched P-U features, states that P-U might not have been a unitary language. P-U might have been instead a set of languages and dialects which formed an areal dialectal chain:

> Die Hauptstrukturzüge der uralischen Grundsprache lassen sich in großen Linien dennoch skizzieren, doch muß man mit der Relativität der diesbezüglichen Ergebnisse rechnen . . . [und daß] die Grundsprache eigentlich nichts anderes war als eine areal zusammenhängende Kette von einander nahestehenden Sprachen und Sprachinseln,

The interpretation of a dialectal continuum does not necessarily imply that the U languages are not related at all among themselves (as claimed by some researchers), but it certainly means that their mutual relations are not as close to justify the conventional U node and family tree. Besides, other language groups could well be included within the same dialectal continuum, as discussed in the following chapters. Similarly, Viitso (1997a) has suggested not using the term 'family' for the U languages, given that such a term should be restricted to more compact families, such as Indo-European or Turkic. For the U languages, a more appropriate term is thought to be 'language *phylum*'.

Bearing in mind the nature, the quantity and quality of the sound-changes within U, it should now become clear why the various periods/layers traditionally established for it are based mainly on distributional, rather than on phonological criteria. Indeed, usually a reconstructed lexical item is classified as U – that is as belonging to the (presumed) oldest layer of the family – if parallels are found both in the F-U branch and in the Samoyed branch. It is classified as F-U if parallels are found in at least one Finnic language and one Ugric language, but not in the Samoyed languages. It is classified as Ugric if parallels are found only in Hungarian and/or the Ob-Ugric languages, etc. This classification is done regardless of whether or not any significant sound-changes have occurred, or any other 'new' lexical/grammatical features have emerged. This state of affairs, however, does not have to be ascribed to bad practice, but merely to the factors individuated in this chapter: the sound-changes and differences typical of the various U branches are neither numerous, nor particularly relevant, nor evenly spread over all the relevant items, so as to allow a qualitatively significant stratification. This aspect has been recently pointed out in the literature; compare for example Koivulehto (1999: 208), or the following quote by Häkkinen[50] (1990: 57–8, my translation; see also 1984a):

> The grading of the [U] lexicon into several layers is impossible with the help of sound marks. For this same reason the role of the distributional criterion has been for a long time past decisive in estimating the age of single words: it has been the only possible criterion.

4.6.3. *A possible interpretation of the evidence within the paradigm?*

One reads of two principal explanations in the literature to account for the paucity and the high level of irregularity of the P-U comparative corpus.

(i) Basic words (which constitute most of the P-U established etymologies) are highly unstable because of their presumed 'affective character' and 'frequency of use'.

(ii) There is evidence to support the assumption that the P-Language is very ancient; therefore one might expect a substantial degree of irregularity and the fading away of many correlations over a long period of time.

Regarding the first explanation, the 'affective character' and 'frequency of use' of basic words, it is of course possible that this is the case in the U languages. However, the assumption that this type of words is unstable appears to be contrary to evidence from other languages. In fact, there is no evidence that the two factors in question should cause 'instability' and therefore irregularity – and no explanation is found within the U literature. Rather, it seems to be the other way round. For example, Bynon (1977: 43) examines English words such as *tooth, foot, mouse, man, woman, to be, to go, to eat, to drink, will, can, do,* etc. These words are almost the same as the 'affective' words found within U. She remarks as follows:

> Perhaps their **stability** and **resistance to change** is due to their very high frequency of occurrence in discourse and to the fact that their forms are therefore acquired by the child at an early stage before the respective grammatical rules have been acquired [bold is mine].

Regarding the second explanation, the presumed great antiquity of the P-Language, we shall examine this in Chapter 7.

4.6.4. *Counter-evidence tends to be minimised*

The claim that most of the U etymologies should be classified as 'similarities' rather than 'correspondences', is clearly at odds with most of the relevant literature where the term 'correspondence' is consistently used or, at least, assumed. Some scholars, such as Collinder and Aalto, recognise that the U etymologies may indeed be problematic:

> The anomalies involved in the following system [the U vowel-system] are numerous . . .The scarcity of the etymological material makes it difficult to arrive at strict 'sound-laws' (Collinder 1960: 151).

> Though for instance, the genetic affinity of the Uralic languages is established beyond any doubt and is generally accepted, the actual number of reliable-looking reconstructions is still rather limited (Aalto 1975: 258).

Similarly, Mikola (1976: 211–12) observes that among the U languages there are a good number of etymologies whose meaning, but not sound-shape, is stable; he proposes therefore a conciliatory view between 'strict sound-laws' and 'laxer correspondences'. He concludes that in U historical linguistics the phonological criteria cannot hold that privileged position they normally hold within comparative linguistics. Finally, Häkkinen (1996: 53) observes that, even at a cautious estimate, at least half of the established U etymologies are either uncertain or controversial.[51]

However, in general, the question of the high level of irregularity within U tends to be minimised, through that process of 'dilution' or 'idealisation' described in the Introduction (as well as at the beginning of this chapter). This process is sometimes explicitly stated, so that the (often hidden) contradictions involved come into light. For example, Sammallahti (1988: 491) says:

> For the time being and for the sake of this presentation, this line [that is, the links between Hungarian and Permian, instead of between Hungarian and Ob-Ugric] is not pursued further: it is assumed that the Ob-Ugric languages as well as Hungarian originate from a common Proto-language, called Proto-Ugric.

And, later on (1988: 499–500):

> Although this grouping [Ugric] has been questioned frequently, it will be used in this presentation . . . This is justified by the fact that it is possible to build unitary reconstructions for Proto-Ugric and Proto-Ob-Ugric. This is done mostly on the basis of the Ugric languages: the Hungarian reflexes of

the PFU vowels are not as clear. The relationship of Hungarian to the rest of the Ugric languages is therefore rather loose,

Within this context perhaps one should also quote the book by Décsy (1990), whose title, *The Uralic Protolanguage: a Comprehensive Reconstruction*, clearly contradicts the picture presented in this book. This 'comprehensive reconstruction' is based on the 472 P-U etymologies reconstructed in UEW; however, we shall see in the next chapter that these etymologies could be the result of chance resemblances. Décsy (1990: 17) also defends the postulation of a distinct P-F-U node, arguing that there are indeed 'considerable differences' between the P-U and the P-F-U phase. However, the 6 sound-changes and/or features listed by the author to illustrate these differences (features 2 to 7) are the very same as those illustrated in this chapter, from which the opposite conclusion has been drawn.

The process of minimisation of the counter-evidence in Phonology might have been supported by the fact that in other language families too the reconstruction of (areas of) the sound structure can prove problematic, particularly vocalism. This is also the case for the Indo-European vocalism (at least according to some positions). One could also correctly object that the lack of convincing reconstructions of major sub-branches is not in itself a serious problem, given that this is encountered also in well-established families. For example, within Indo-European it is not really possible to reconstruct Common Baltic (let alone Balto-Slavic!), or Common Italic. Similarly, within Germanic, the concept of 'West Germanic' is difficult to define, and so on. To these objections one may answer that if the elements of counter-evidence were restricted to the phonological level only, whilst extensive, unequivocal evidence was available at other levels of language – for example Morphology – one might and perhaps even should disregard the counter-evidence within Phonology. However, this is not the case with regard to U, as will emerge from the remainder of the book.

The reality is that the high degree of variation encountered within the U languages (particularly in Ob-Ugric and Samoyed), is in direct contrast, indeed absolutely incompatible with the idealised, monolithic P-Language presupposed by the family tree model. The high degree of variation typical of the U languages is faithfully and extensively illustrated, for example, in Collinder (1960, 1965a). In the chapters on Phonology the author highlights how the various sound-changes under discussion may occur 'sporadically', in 'a few words', 'sometimes', in 'some dialects', in 'some words' and 'some contexts' etc. One may indeed wonder why Uralists insist in analysing these languages by only applying the Comparative Method – the only one available until not so long ago, but not nowadays – rather than the methods of Dialectology, or the 'diffusionist' ideas, despite the achievements and the recognition obtained by these disciplines in recent times (Lass 1993: 179). Perhaps, a diffusionist approach, or a statistical approach of the type applied by Labov (1994), might even reveal a kind of order, some kind of pattern, within variation, something like the 'orderly heterogeneity' of Weinreich et al. (1968).

Similar thoughts about the opportunity for utilising a dialectal and/or a diffusionist approach have been expressed by Róna-Tas (1991: 22–4) to account for the many phonologically 'contradictory' correspondences to be found in Turkic (Doerfer[52] 1971). Róna-Tas states that :

> In the Early Ancient Turkic period there was what might be called a heterogeneous linguistic unit . . . Many of the isoglosses coincided and formed bundles, but some did not, they simply crossed the others. Unless we keep in mind this finding of modern dialectology, we will be unable to understand the problems connected with the reconstruction of Proto-Turkic . . . Language never changes in an instant . . . This tendency [to change] affects most of the words in the given category. Sometimes it affects all members of the given category, in other cases only most of them. But even those members which are affected do not change at once. Frequency of use, more stable occurrence in frequently used expressions can delay the change.

5

FALSE MATCHES OR GENUINE LINGUISTIC CORRELATIONS?

*Any claim that a similarity between two human languages is
significant must be supported by a demonstration that it could
not be the result of sheer chance*[1]

Don Ringe

In any given list of lexical parallels, there will be some parallels which are the
result of chance resemblance. These are called 'accidental look-alikes' or 'false
matches'. As we saw in Chapter 4, there is no evidence in the Uralic corpus for
a 'cumulative effect' (where a large number of etymologies all clearly obey the
same sound-rule), and therefore the Comparative Method does not provide
us, in this context, with the tools to distinguish false matches reliably from
true lexical correspondences. A new method is therefore required.

In other language groups, several authors have also come to the conclusion that probabilistic reasoning is better able to quantify the number and
distribution of false matches, especially in a context of scarcity of comparative material,[2] such as Ringe (1995, 1999), Baxter & Manaster Ramer (1996,
1999: 41), Manaster Ramer & Hitchock (1996), Hymes (1973), Sankoff
(1973: 95), Kroeber (1958: 455), Anttila (1989: 397), Embleton[3] (1991, 1999/
2000: 323–4) and McMahon, Lohr & McMahon (1998).

Therefore, the purpose of this chapter is to quantify the rate and
distribution of false matches in the reconstructed U Lexicon. This chapter
follows the method introduced by Ringe (1995, 1999). It compares the
reconstructed lexicon against a 'control case', equivalent to random words
that are matched against statistically equivalent correspondence rules.

After an introduction to the method, using a simple example, I describe
the method in detail. I shall then examine two separate samples of P-U
Lexicon in this way: the body-parts reported in UEW, and Janhunen's
(1981a) reconstruction of P-U. As we shall see, in each case the reconstructed etymologies are in reasonably good agreement, both in number and
in distribution, with the expected distribution of false matches. This confirms
our earlier result, that one cannot tell whether these reconstructions are the
result of a true linguistic relationship or of chance resemblances.

Looking at the results in more detail, we shall see that a total of about 15
words in our samples (about 10% of the lexical items) lie outside the
expected distribution of false matches. Given the approximations involved
and the small number of words, this is not a definitive result and it is only

suggestive of a relationship. Nevertheless, these words are the best candidates for having statistical significance. We shall see that all but two of these words are also reported as being present in other language groups such as Altaic, so that, if they are truly significant, they suggest a wider relationship than just the Uralic area.

Alternative methods to those adopted in this chapter, which are not discussed here, include lexicostatistics (Lees 1953, Swadesh 1971; see a review of this method in Fox 1995) and computer simulation of sound-changes that have occurred in the U languages (see Bátori 1980).

5.1. INTRODUCTION: THE SIGNIFICANCE OF THE PROTO-URALIC NUMERALS '1' TO '10'

By way of introduction to the method, which is based on that of Ringe (1995, 1999), this section describes a greatly simplified example. Its purpose is to orient the reader and to introduce the key concepts. We use this example to explain our treatment of the vowels and of the component Ø.

In our simple comparison, we shall examine only a small sub-set of the Lexicon, namely the numerals '1' to '10'. We shall compare Janhunen's (1981a) P-Uralic corpus with Modern Hungarian. This example is intended for illustration only, and it is not meant to be a conclusive test.

If two languages are completely unrelated, we might nevertheless expect they would have some words in common because of accidental look-alikes. Putting this more quantitatively, there are approximately nine distinct reconstructed P-U consonants (see Table 5.3 below for details), so there is approximately a 1 in 9 probability that, in a comparison of P-U with another language, there will accidentally be a matching consonant at any given position.[4] For example, we might expect the initial consonant to match in one of the numerals (actually a little more than one, in fact 10 times 1/9). Likewise we would expect the second consonant to match in one numeral, and so on.

How does this compare with the numerals reported in U studies? There are only two reconstructed numerals in Janhunen's P-U corpus. As the author (2000: 60) says:

> The lexical material clearly suggests that the P-Uralic numeral system comprised only the items for '2', and '5' or '10'.

These correspondences are in Table 5.1.

Could these correlations have occurred by chance if the languages were completely unrelated?

Looking firstly at the initial consonant, there is one clear match, that is, the initial *k*- in '2'. As discussed above, we would expect approximately one

Table 5.1 The numerals '1' to '10' in Proto-Uralic and Hungarian[5]

Hungarian	P-U	Reconstructed meaning
két ~ kéttő	*käktä ~ *kakta ~ kektä	'2'
öt	*witte ~ *wixti ~ *witti ~ *witi	'5' or '10'

match at this position to have occurred by chance if the languages were unrelated (see example (4.6)).

One might argue that there is a second match at the first position, that is, in the word for '5' or '10' (for which see example (4.36)), since it is generally reported that an original *w can sometimes develop into a Ø in Hungarian (see, for example, Sammallahti 1988: 519). However, one finds (Sammallahti 1988: 515–19) that the Hungarian Ø can also correspond in various positions with any of the reconstructed consonants: *s, *š, *w /*v, *k, *m, *j, *l, *p, the 'unspecified' segment *x, the specific 'Ugric innovations' *θ and *g (if these reconstructions are accepted, see Section 4.5.3.1) and, of course, to Ø. Some of these matches for Ø have been illustrated in Chapter 4; see the examples (4.21), (4.23), (4.36), (4.39) and the examples in points (d), (f) and (g) of Section 4.5.2.1. Whatever the interpretation, in this sense the form Ø is a sort of 'wild card' that, statistically, does not restrict the matches very much if at all. Therefore, in order to obtain statistically consistent results, a Ø must be treated as if it is not a match.

Looking next at the second, internal consonant, the situation is less clear. Strictly speaking there are no unambiguous matches in this position, but there are some approximate matches and we can attempt to take them into account. In the term for '2', Hungarian -t- ~ -tt- is a not-always consistent reflex of the P-U internal cluster *-kt- (see, for example, Collinder 1960: 82–3; Sammallahti[6] 1988: 519–20). As Janhunen (1981a: 258) puts it, 'the irregularities in this word ['2'] reflect the sound lability typical of the numerals'. For illustration only, and not intending to be totally quantitative at this stage, we might count the second consonant in the term for '2' as 'half a match'. Similarly, the internal -t- in the term for '5' is not really a match because of the two different meanings of the word ('5' or '10') which doubles the chance of a match. It is also an ambiguous reflex, for which there are a variety of P-U reconstructions proposed, as can be seen in Table 5.1. Again, for the purpose of illustration only, we might count this as approximately 'half a match'. Overall, one finds arguably about two half-matches in the second consonant position, and this is again in reasonable accord with the one match that we expect to occur if all the matches were by pure chance alone.

Looking now at the vowels, these have a low statistical significance for the reasons discussed in Chapter 4, that is, there are almost as many vowel-rules as etymologies within the P-Uralic corpus. In this situation, almost any vowel combination can be accepted as a 'match' according to one or other of the rules, so that this criterion does not significantly alter the chances of a match. It is therefore appropriate to ignore vowels in this kind of analysis. Researchers in other fields have also recognised that, over long time-scales, vowels are more unstable and might be removed from statistical comparison. For example, Ringe (1999) discusses this regarding the Amerindian languages.

Finally, we consider the effect of phonotactic constraints on the statistics. These are quantified in Ringe (1999). The most significant (and simplest) effect is associated with the frequency of use of consonants in various languages. This alters the probability of a false match, but Ringe argues the effect is relatively small. Regarding the possible existence of more sophisticated combinatorial patterns, these have not been unambiguously identified in the P-U corpus, and there is a debate on this topic; see Korhonen (1986), Honti (1981), Sammallahti (1988: 492–4), Bakró-Nagy (1988, 1990a, 1990b, 1992), Ringe (1998: 176–7).

How can one interpret this information? It needs to be said at this point that, even if this analysis were rigorous or statistically significant (which it is not), it would not prevent anybody holding the opinion that the numerals '1' to '10' in Hungarian are linguistically related to those in the P-U corpus. What this analysis does show, however, is that this (limited) data does not constitute scientific evidence in favour of this relationship, because the correspondences might in all probability have occurred by chance.

This analysis is of course not complete. It is only intended to illustrate the issues involved. A better calculation would define clear quantitative criteria as to what is meant by a 'match' and by a 'half-match'; it would factor in the property that it is less likely for several matches all to cluster in one word; it would involve multiple comparisons of several languages and/or language groups across the Uralic area; and it would require more data in order to have greater statistical significance. This is the type of analysis that is embarked upon in the next section.

5.2. The method

The method that is employed here is based on that introduced by Ringe (1995, 1999). It is related to the method that is used to test medical drugs, where one compares the effects of the drug against the effects of a placebo, and seeks a significantly different response in the two trials. In the case of the reconstructed Lexicon, we compare the reconstructed etymologies against a 'control case' which is equivalent to random words that are matched against the same comparison criteria. Again, one seeks a significant difference between the two cases. A simplified example of the application of this method has been given above.

In a comparison against a control case such as this, the exact method of analysis usually does not matter very much, as long as it is reasonably well correlated with the behaviour one seeks. This is because any changes in the method of analysis would affect both the control and the reconstructed etymologies in the same way and would therefore not affect the overall comparison. One is therefore free to choose a method of analysis that is as clear-cut and unambiguous as possible.

Therefore, in this test, following Ringe (1995), I compare the 'distribution of matches', that is, the percentage of matches that are present in 2 language groups, the percentage of matches that are present in 3 language groups, and so on. This test has the advantage that its results can be easily predicted and it can identify 'outliers', that is, sub-sets of words that do appear to be statistically significant, even if the average number is not statistically significant.

In the trials, I compare two separate sets of etymologies against their relevant control cases. These sets of etymologies are as follows:

- all the etymologies referring to body-part terms which are listed in UEW;
- all Janhunen's (1981a) etymologies up to the number (94), that is, the ones the author considers the best.

This choice has been motivated by the following two factors: body-part terms are widely regarded as being amongst the least 'borrowable' terms within basic Lexicon; Janhunen's corpus is based on stricter phonological criteria than any other U corpus, and is generally considered as the most reliable one. Janhunen does not systematically report matches from groups outside of Balto-Finnic/Finno-Permian and Samoyed, and therefore in my analysis Janhunen's etymologies have been cross-referenced with UEW, to identify their distribution in the other language groups.

I classified each etymology according to whether it was reported as present in the following language groups (the number of languages and dialects is according to UEW) (see Table 5.2).

Table 5.2 The language groups used in the statistical analysis

Group	Number of languages in group
Balto-Finnic	8
Permian/Volgaic	5
Ob-Ugric	2 (several dialects)
Hungarian	1
Samoyed	4
Lapp	1 (several dialects)

These groups have been chosen for the following reasons. Hungarian is analysed on its own due to its isolated position within the U family tree (as discussed in Section 4.2.1). Lapp is also analysed as a group on its own, because it in fact consists of many languages or dialects, and also because of its controversial position within U (see Section 4.5.4). With regard to Balto-Finnic and Permian-Volgaic, these can be considered one single group (as argued in Chapter 4), but it is split into two for the purposes of this analysis because it would be otherwise too large for statistical calculation.

Table 5.3 calculates the probability of a false match for words with 1, 2 and 3 consonants. The following factors should be noted:

- In calculating the probability of a false match, I compare the consonants, and do not compare the vowels in the words. As was described in Section 5.1 above, the vowels have little or no effect on the probability of a false match.
- In calculating the probability of a false match, the form Ø is considered not to be a match, because the Ø does not count statistically as a consonant, as described in the previous section. Etymologies that include words with a Ø are counted as having one fewer consonantal match.[7] For example Finn. *suoni* 'vein' is equivalent to Hun *ín*, and this 'correspondence' is here considered to be a one-consonant match.
- A certain amount of personal intuition and subjectivity is required on the part of the compiler of the etymologies in assessing whether two words are sufficiently similar in meaning, sound etc. Because of this, the calculation can only be approximate.

Armed with these estimates of the probability of a false match, it is possible to predict the percentage of false matches we expect to appear in exactly 2 language groups, the percentage of false matches we expect to appear in exactly 3 language groups, and so on. The distribution is the so-called 'binomial' distribution. Notice that, in our case, the words are pre-selected to appear in at least one language group (these form the initial candidates for the Uralic word-lists), and so the binomial distribution must be calculated in relation to the extra groups in which the word appears. For example, the probability that a one-consonant word (62% probability of a false match) appears in all six language groups, is calculated as the binomial factor for selecting 5 out of 5 language groups at 62% probability each. The calculated percentages are shown in Table 5.4.

The main sources of error in this predicted distribution of false matches are as follows:

- The calculation of the probabilities of a false match are based on approximate figures only. I compare the observed distribution with the above distribution for false positives, but one must identify clearly those differences that are sensitive to errors in the probability, and those that are

Table 5.3 Calculation of the probability of false matches

Criterion used in UEW	Effect	Probability of false match (approximate)		
		1 cons't	2 cons't	3 cons't
In practice, the dictionary considers that words match if the consonants match (see discussion above). Excluding rare occurrences (such as *r,* particularly in initial position), unsafe reconstructions, variants and affricates (these last sounds being hardly distinguishable from sibilants (see Section 4)), one may use for the purpose of analysis the following 9 distinct, common consonants, namely *w/v, j, p, t, k, l, m, n, s/š* (there are only very few F-U words and no U words with initial **r* listed in UEW; the U and F-U words with initial **l* are much more numerous, over 20 items; only 1 U and a few F-U words with initial *š* are listed)	If one chooses (say) the first consonant of a word in language A, then there is about a 1 in 9 chance that the corresponding word in an unrelated language B will have the same consonant.	11%	1.2%	0.13%
The dictionary considers that words match if they contain the same number of consonants, OR if some of them contain additional consonants (which in some etymologies are assumed to be dropped). In the matches for body-parts reported by UEW, 23% of the matches contain one consonant (plus, in some cases, a second or third dropped consonant), 70% contain two (plus in a few cases a third dropped consonant) and 7% contain three consonants.	There is a reduced probability of a false match with words that contain one or three consonants, because short or long words are rare. I take the reductions as 1/4 for one consonant, and 7% for three consonants.	reduced to 2.8%	reduced to 1.2%	reduced to 0.01%
The dictionary accepts a wide range of meanings for each word. To take one example: 'sky, weather, wind, world, air, heavy snowfall, snowstorm' (Carlson[8] 1990). There are typically between 2 and 4 different reported meanings for each P-Word; a few are reported to have 1 meaning or 5 meanings.	The wide variety of meanings (taken as 3) increases the probability of a false positive. (in fact, the factor is slightly less than 3[9]).	increased to 8%	increased to 3.6%	increased to 0.03%
The dictionary accepts more than one reflex for a given P-Phoneme (see Chapter 4.). This increases the probability of a false match by increasing the range of sounds that are accepted as a match.	The variety of consonant matches (taken as 2) increases the probability of a false positive. The calculation is similar to the above.	increased to 15%	increased to 7%	increased to 0.06%
There are several languages/dialects in each group, and a word is counted as belonging to a group if it appears in only one of the languages/dialects of the group.	The variety of languages in each group (taken as 6) increases the probability of a false positive. Calculation as above.	increased to 62%	increased to 35%	increased to 0.4%

Table 5.4 Expected distribution of false matches

Number of language groups in which a chosen word appears	Words with 1 consonant (binomial distribution at 62% probability)	Words with 2 consonants (binomial distribution at 35% probability)	Words with 3 consonants (binomial distribution at 0.4% probability)
2	7%	35%	99%
3	21%	38%	1%
4	35%	20%	0
5	28%	6%	0
6	9%	1%	0

not. I only analyse in detail those differences that are not sensitive to errors in this probability.

- The groups must be of about the same size if the binomial distribution is to give a good approximation to the expected distribution of false matches. However, our groups are not the same size, most notably because they include Hungarian which is an isolate. This is likely to alter the distribution a little from that shown. In practice, this alteration is relatively small, because each group did in fact contain approximately the same number of matches (mean 44, standard deviation 11). One possible interpretation of this phenomenon is that Hungarian might be selected more often than other languages as the 'pre-selected' language, since the authors of UEW were mainly Hungarian in origin. In fact, the conclusions we show below were essentially unchanged when the analysis was re-calculated excluding Hungarian.

5.3. RESULTS

In this section I shall analyse first the etymologies for body-parts present in UEW, and then the etymologies from Janhunen's corpus.

5.3.1. *Body-parts terms reported in UEW*

Appendix I lists the terms for body-parts reported in UEW, showing in a tabular form the language groups to which each term belongs. The appendix includes only the 'safest' matches, that is, it excludes questionable matches as reported by UEW (i.e. any items marked with one or two '?' symbols). The list also excludes three words that were reported as present in only one group. The total number of etymologies is 69.

The graphs in Figure 5.1 compare the distribution of these words with the expected distribution of false positives. As can be seen from the graphs, the

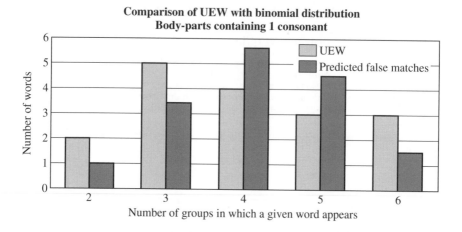

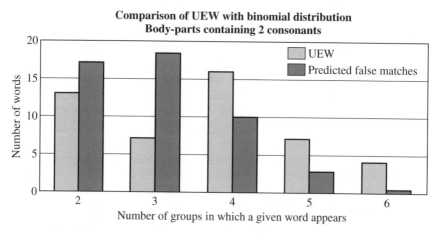

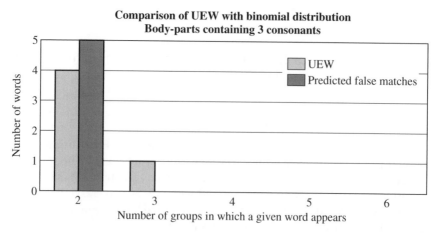

Figure 5.1 Graphs of the mathematical analysis of UEW body-parts

body-parts terms reported by UEW display a remarkably good fit to the predicted distribution of false matches. Most of these words are indistinguishable from random chance resemblances, at least using this measure.

However, this analysis does identify some deviations from the random distribution, and the following deviations must be explained:

• There are too many two-consonant words that are represented in all six language groups (4 words, compared to just 0.3 if all the matches were due to false positives). These are marked in bold in Appendix I and are discussed below. This number is significant statistically.

• There are also too many two-consonant words that are present in five language groups (7 words, compared to 2.6 if all the matches were due to false positives). These are marked in italics in Appendix I. It might be possible to account for this because of the approximate nature of the estimate of the probability of a false match, or because of sampling error, or both, and so, although these words might have some significance, they are not selected for particular attention and discussion.

• There is one three-syllable word that is present in three language groups (there would be none if the distribution were purely due to false positives). This word is marked in italics in Appendix I. The meaning of the reconstructed word is mainly 'hair' or 'stem', but there are other minor meanings too. The word is represented in both Balto-Finnic and Permian (the two groups that are most closely related to one another), so this anomaly probably indicates simply what is already known, that Balto-Finnic and Permian are closely related. The word is present also in Lapp, which I have considered as an isolate.

• In the distribution of two-syllable words, there are too many words that are present in four language groups and not enough words present in three language groups. Most of the words that are present in four language groups are represented in both Balto-Finnic and Permian, so this anomaly also probably indicates simply that Balto-Finnic and Permian are so closely related as to form one single group, as indeed argued by some researchers (see Chapter 4).

5.3.2. *Janhunen's corpus*

One can perform a similar analysis using the word-list from Janhunen's (1981a) corpus. These words are listed in Appendix II. From the 94 etymologies identified by Janhunen as 'good', I have excluded duplications, items marked with a '?' by Janhunen himself, and the items that are not recognised in UEW, leaving a total of 77 for analysis.

In a similar fashion to the above, one can compare the distribution of matches with the prediction of false matches. This is shown in the graphs in Figure 5.2.

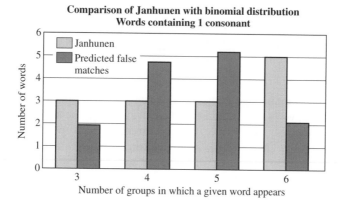

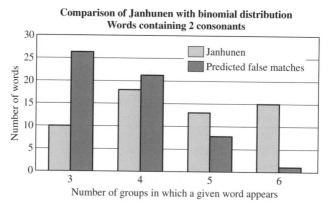

Figure 5.2 Graphs of the mathematical analysis of Janhunen's corpus

In the above graphs, the calculation of the distribution of false positives differs slightly from the case of UEW because Janhunen's list is pre-selected for words that are present in 2 groups, Samoyed and Finno-Permian (equated with F-U), instead of only one group as in UEW. The random matches are associated with the 4 extra language groups (instead of 5 in UEW). The same predicted false match probabilities are used (i.e. 62% and 35%), because the matches outside this pre-selection are identified with the aid of UEW. For example, the predicted number of false positives for two-consonant words represented in all 6 languages is the binomial distribution at 35%, for 4 out of 4 languages.

As can be seen from the above graphs, the data reported by Janhunen also displays a remarkably good fit to the predicted distribution of false matches. Most of these words are again indistinguishable from random chance resemblances, at least on this measure.

However, this analysis too does identify some deviations from the random distribution, and the following deviations must be explained:

- There are too many two-consonant words that are represented in all 6 language groups (15 words, compared to just one if all the matches were due to false positives). These are marked in bold in Appendix II. This appears to be significant statistically, and is discussed in detail below.
- There are too many one-consonant words that are represented in all 6 language groups (5 words, compared to 2 if all the matches were due to false positives). These are marked in italics in Appendix II. It might be possible to account for this result because of the approximate nature of the estimate of the probability of a false match, or because of sampling error, or both; so that, although these words might have some significance, they are not selected for particular attention and discussion.

5.4. THE SIMILARITIES THAT APPEAR TO BE STATISTICALLY SIGNIFICANT

The words present in both samples which clearly deviate from the random distribution are summarised in Table 5.5 (reconstruction as given in UEW).

This table excludes the one three-consonant word that appears in three languages, because it attracts a particularly wide a range of meanings, and it is of very limited occurrence: the term for 'hair/stem': P-U *kalke*, which presents slightly different meanings in the three languages in which it appears: Finn. *kalki* (Gen. *kaljen* 'hair, stem'/Lapp. *guolgâ* 'hair (but not the hair on the head of human beings; coat, covering of hair)'/Mor. E. *kalgo* 'tip (of grass or grain)' (UEW 644; SSA II, 286). This is the only word with three consonants actually preserved in all the languages.

The details of the two-consonant items from UEW present in all 6 language groups are as follows:

(5.1) The term for 'eye': Finn. *silmä* /Hun. *szëm* (UEW 479). This item does not have parallels in Altaic or Yukaghir, but in Dravidian, according to Tyler ((1968); item (55)). It is present in Janhunen's corpus (item (30): 225), where it also belongs to the class of the significant items. According to Janhunen's analysis, this term is the only occurrence of the following (first and second syllable) vowel correspondence: P-Sam. *ϑ-ä* ~ P-F-P *i - ä*.

(5.2) The term for 'egg/testicle': Finn. *muna*/Hun. *mony* (UEW 285). This item is present in Janhunen's corpus (item (19): 285) and does not present irregularity; it has a parallel in Dravidian according to Tyler ((1968), item (49)).

(5.3) The term for 'liver': Finn. *maksa*/Hun. *máj*, which has been encountered several times in this book (UEW 264). It is also present in

Table 5.5 The lexical items that might be statistically significant

Meaning and reconstruction	Comments	Present elsewhere?
*śilmä 'eye'		Dravidian
*muna 'egg/testicle'		Dravidian
*maksa 'liver'		Turkic, Tungusic
*kuńće ~ kuće 'urine'		Tungusic
*waśke 'some kind of metal/ ?copper	several meanings. Wanderwort	
*sile (*süle) lap/bosom	several meanings. Janhunen considers the word to be present in Samoyed but UEW says this is uncertain.	
*pura 'drill (to drill)'	probably a modern word	Turkic, Mongolian, ? I-E
*pesä 'nest'		
*pele- 'to fear'		
*pälä 'half/relative/side'	several meanings. Janhunen says 'confused with another etymology'	
*nime 'name'	Wanderwort	
*mene- 'to go'		Yukaghir
*kumpa 'wave'	several meanings	Turkic
*kala 'fish'	Wanderwort	
*kaδ'a- 'to let go, drop'		Turkic

Janhunen's corpus (item (41): 228), where it belongs to the class of the statistically significant items. It appears in Turkic and Tungusic, with the same meaning. This etymology presents the problem of the velar illabial j as illustrated in example (4.9): compare P-Sam. *mįtə̂ vs P-F-P *maksa. Janhunen himself claims (1981a: 227) that there is no contextual explanation why an open, back vowel in Finno-Permian (in first syllable) should correspond to a more closed one in Samoyed. Notice also that all other language groups, including Hungarian and the non-U languages, present open vowels.

(5.4) The term for 'urine': Finn. kusi /Hun. húgy (UEW 210). This term is present also in Janhunen's corpus (item (65): 236), and in Tungusic. It does not seem to present any phonological problem in vocalism; however, according to UEW, two alternative reconstructions have to be proposed to account for the variation in the development of the internal consonants.

The statistically significant words from Janhunen's corpus, which contain two consonants and are present in all 6 language groups (excluding the ones in common with the UEW list, and therefore already quoted above), are as follows:

(5.5) The term for 'some kind of metal, ? copper': Finn. *vaski*/Hun. *vas* 'iron' (item (25): 225; UEW 560). This is a well known *Wanderwort*.

(5.6) The term for 'lap, bosom': Finn. *syli* /Hun. *öl* (item (60): 234). According to UEW 444, the Samoyed correspondences are considered uncertain, and marked with one '?' See example (4.21).

(5.7) The term for 'drill, (to drill)': Finn. *pura ~ pora, puraa- ~ poraa-*[10]/ Hun. *fúr-* (item (36): 226; UEW 405). This item has parallels in non-U languages according to UEW: Turkic *bur-*/Mon. *burɣui-* 'a piece of wire used to clean a smoking pipe'/Lat. *forāre*/Ger. *bohren* (the I-E connection is considered uncertain by UEW).

(5.8) The word for 'nest': Finn. *pesä* 'nest'/Hun. *fészëk* (item (28): 225; UEW 375). This item does not present irregularities and it is present within U only.

(5.9) The word for 'fear, (to fear)': Finn. *pelko, pelkää-*/Hun. *fél-* (item (56): 234; UEW 370). Like the previous one, this item does not present irregularities and it is present within U only.

(5.10) The word for 'half, relative, side': Finn. *pieli*/Hun. *fél* (item (24): 224; UEW 362). The problem here is the variety of meanings, and, as pointed out by Janhunen, the etymology has got confused, at least in the etymological literature, with the similar word *pieli* 'edge, external side, corner'; compare *suu-pieli* 'mouth-corner, corner of the mouth'. Compare also SSA[11] II, 347–8.

(5.11) The word for 'name': Finn. *nimi*/Hun. *név* (item (58): 234; UEW 305). Another well-known *Wanderwort*.

(5.12) The term for 'to go': Finn. *mene-*/Hun. *mën-* (3rd Sin. *mëgy*), (item (55): 234; UEW 272). According to UEW this item has an equivalent in Yuk. *män-* with the meaning 'to jump'.

(5.13) The term for 'wave, etc.': Finn. *kumpu* (Gen. *kummun*) 'hill, hillock, mound', *kumpua- ~ kumpuu-* 'to spring (of water out of a source)'/ Hun. *hab* 'surf, foam, spume'/Ost. *χump* 'wave'/Vog. *kop, χump* 'wave' (item (12): 222; UEW 203). In this etymological set there is a mismatch in vocalism; notice also the variety of meanings. According to Janhunen, in this case the Ugric languages have better preserved the original sound-shape, although the diachronic details of vocalism remain unclear. Compare also example (4.48).

(5.14) The term for 'fish': Finn. *kala*/Hun. *hal* (item (7): 222; UEW 119). A well-known *Wanderwort* (compare example (4.28)).

(5.15) The term for 'to let go, drop, let': Finn. *katoa-* (compare *kadota* 'to disappear')/Hun. *hagy-* (item (2): 221; UEW 115). This item has a parallel in Turkic *qal-* 'to remain (behind)'.

The following words, again from Janhunen corpus, are those with one consonant only – according to the method adopted here (see Section (5.1)). Though analysed in detail here, they are not reported in the table above, because they are not so significant statistically:

(5.16) The term for 'arrow': Finn. *nuoli*/Hun. *nyíl*/(item (83): 241; UEW 317). This item presents the problem of illabial *i̯*. There are parallels in Turkic and Tungusic; see, for discussion, example (4.5).

(5.17) The term for 'river': Finn. *joki*/Old Hun. *jó* (item (15): 223; UEW 99). This item is not present elsewhere; see, for discussion, example (4.39).

(5.18) The term for 'to live': Finn. *elä-*/Hun. *él-* (item (27): 225; UEW 73). Like the previous one, this item is not present elsewhere.

(5.19) The term for 'father-in-law': Finn. *appi*/Hun. *ipa* 'father-in-law', *apa* 'father'/Ost. *up* (item (71): 236; UEW 14). This item presents again the issue of the velar illabial vowels. UEW does not mention the Samoyed parallels (see Section 4.4.5.2).

(5.20) The term for 'lower part, space under': Finn. *ala-(osa)*/Hun. *al, alatt* (item (38): 227; UEW 6; see example (4.8)). The word is present in Yukaghir and Turkic, where it is also grammaticalised to function as a postposition, like in the U languages.

As one can see, according to this investigation, from the terms present in the table only the terms for 'nest' and '(to) fear' are impeccable correspondences which are also uniquely U. From the terms not reported on the table (because containing one consonant only) only the terms for 'river' and 'to live' are impeccable correspondences which are not present elsewhere.

To conclude this section, one may notice that the number of the P-U and P-F-U etymologies turns out to be very low even when they are examined in the light of the conventional classification, that is, according to their mere distribution throughout the conventionally established nodes. In fact, the P-U etymologies which are represented in all the U languages – the '100 % etymologies', to use Häkkinen's (1998: 193, 1999: 168) definition – and which are regarded as relatively safe in UEW and in other etymological dictionaries, number only 17. They are, quoting from Finnish:

(5.21) *ala, alla* 'under', *ku(ka)* 'who', *maksa* 'liver', *me* 'we', *mi(kä)* 'what', *minä* 'I', *niellä* 'to swallow', *nimi* 'name', *nuolla* 'to lick', *nuoli* 'arrow' (see example (4.5) and (5.16) above), *pesä* 'nest' (see example (5.8)), *punoa* 'twist', *silmä* 'eye' (see example (4.25) and (5.1) above), *suoni* 'vein', *sydän* 'heart' (see example (4.7)), *tuo* 'that', *uida* 'to swim'

However, of these words, 5 are pronouns; they are too short and irregular to be useful for the purpose of assessing relationships. Eight words are held to have parallels in other languages: *ala, maksa, nimi, nuolla, nuoli, punoa* (for which see Yuk. *pun* and Got. *spinnan*; UEW 402), *suoni* (for which see Old Ind. *snåvan-*; UEW 441) and *uida* (for which see Tungusic **uju-*; UEW 542). Only the remaining 4 words are purely U: *silmä, sydän, pesä* and *niellä* (UEW 315), of which only *pesä* is an impeccable correspondence, as discussed above.

Similarly, the etymologies where a parallel is either missing or uncertain in one U language only – 'the 90% etymologies' (Häkkinen 1998: 193 f., 1999: 168) – only number 22:

(5.22) *jää* 'ice', *kaksi* 'two' (see example (4.6)), *kolme* 'three', *kuolla* 'to die' (see example (4.20)), *kusi* 'urine' (see example (4.1) and (5.4) above), *kuusi* 'six', *kuusi(-puu)* 'pine(-tree), spruce, *picea excelsa*' (see example (4.4)), *kyynär* 'elbow', *käsi* 'hand', *mennä* 'to go', *neljä* 'four', *pelätä, pelkää-* 'to be afraid, to fear'(see item (5.9) above), *sarvi* 'horn', *sata* '100', *syli* 'lap/bosom' (examples (4.21) and (5.6) above), *talvi* 'winter', *tämä* 'this', *vaski* 'a kind of metal/?copper' (item (5.5) above), *veri* 'blood' (see example (4.35), *viisi* 'five/ten' (for which see Note 5), *voi* 'fat, butter', *ydin* 'marrow'

Here too, 11 etymologies are held by other sources to have parallels in the Altaic languages and/or Yukaghir, or in Dravidian: *jää, kaksi, kusi, kuusi(-puu), mennä* (for which see (5.12) above), *neljä, talvi, kyynär(ä)* (for which see Tun. *īčēn, īkēn*, Lat. *genu* and Got. *kniu* 'knee' according to UEW 158), *voi* (for which see Turkic **bai*: Bas. *mai* (UEW 578)), *kuolla* (for which see Tyler (1968) item (38)), *käsi* (for which see Tyler (1968) item (73)). *Vaski* is a well-known *Wanderwort*, *sarvi* and *sata* are loan-words from Indo-European (see Chapter 7). We are left with only 8 etymologies which are purely F-U. However, most of these F-U lexical items are problematic, one way or the other, as reported in the appropriate sections of Chapter 4.

5.5. Conclusion

In the previous chapter I have argued that the U languages do not form a family and that P-U is not a valid node on the basis of phonological arguments. However, it was important to go into statistical detail in this chapter because this might have disproved my conclusion. On the contrary, though, we found that the vast majority of the reconstructed etymologies (within two chosen samples) are in reasonably good statistical agreement with the expected rate of false matches. At this point I would like to emphasize that this **does not** mean that **all** these etymologies are false matches. What this does mean is that one cannot rely on these etymologies to prove a linguistic relationship, because this number are likely to have occurred by chance alone.

Looking closer, the statistical analysis does permit us to identify a handful of words that do not match the random distribution and therefore need to be explained. These words have been listed in detail (see Table 5.5 and related discussion), but their explanation remains open. They might be understood as *Wanderwörter*, as widely represented ancient Eurasiatic words, as an artefact of the method, or – I believe less likely – as truly U words.

Personally, I am attracted to the concept that these words are part of a wide lexical stock, spanning the whole Eurasiatic area, but with the exclusion of the Indo-European languages. In fact, in Table 5.5, under the heading 'Present elsewhere?' the classification 'Indo-European' on its own does not appear: the etymologies that P-U shares with Indo-European ('drill' and 'name') are also shared with other language groups. This means that the statistically most relevant etymologies have no parallel in the Indo-European languages taken on their own. This in turn seems to be in agreement with what I shall claim below (Chapter 7), based on totally different arguments, that is: the lexical connection between U and Indo-European appears to be less strong than the lexical connection between U and the Asiatic languages under discussion.

I am convinced that a fuller analysis of the parallels involving all the language groups in question, avoiding the bias imposed by the assumption of separate U, Altaic and Yukaghir nodes, may well yield interesting results. If it were eventually demonstrated that such an Eurasiatic lexical stock did exist, and if I were allowed further speculation, I would speculate that the relationship between these lexical items is to some extent of genetic nature. And this simply on the basis of the observation that several of these statistically significant words belong to basic Lexicon, and are therefore rather resistant to borrowing. Obviously, language contacts too must have played an important role. However – and this is my the central point – at this stage it is impossible to distinguish borrowed features from inherited features within this wide linguistic context (as will be argued in the next chapter).

Supposing that genetic relations are indeed involved within this lexical stock, I would certainly not interpret them in 'Nostratic terms', as it might appear to be the case. By 'Nostratic terms' I mean an interpretation based on the traditional model of an ancient P-Language, which develops through the traditional, ordered, binary splits. The family tree model and the Comparative Method are simply not applicable in this linguistic context; instead I believe I have shown that these languages are best analysed using the methods of Dialectology.

Speculation apart, there is one inescapable conclusion to be drawn from this analysis. If there were truly a U node, we would expect the data to display decisively more statistical significance than this. A handful of significant words is simply not enough to establish a language family, particularly when these words are also present elsewhere. Whilst statistical analysis must be understood in a wider context of analysis, it has to be said that the very lack of significance supports the conclusion that P-U is not a valid node, as was argued in the previous chapter on the basis of pure linguistic investigation.

6

BORROWED OR INHERITED?

les comparaisons . . . ouralo-altaïques sont dépourvues de la
rigueur systématique qui est l'une des exigences les plus fonda-
mentales de la linguistique comparative[1]

Robert Austerlitz

There are recognised to be lexical parallels between the U languages and other languages outside the group. As we saw in Chapter 2, some of these parallels were cited by early researchers such as Budenz as evidence for a genetic relationship between what are now called the Uralic and Altaic groups. However, some time in the 1900s, the paradigm shifted, and it came to be assumed that U and Altaic were unrelated. Accordingly, these parallels had to be re-interpreted as 'borrowings', or just 'similarities'.

In line with the dominant Neo-grammarian view at the time, it was believed that inherited words obeyed regular sound-laws whilst borrowed words were in most cases 'irregular'. Accordingly, the parallels outside the U family had to be 're-classified' as irregular, and there emerged an extensive literature attempting to identify the donor language and chronology for those words that were supposed to be borrowed.

In this chapter we examine a sample of the Uralic basic Lexicon. We find that 90% of the items listed in the sample are reported in the literature to have an association with non-U languages. On average, each of the U etymologies is associated with 2.2 non-U languages. We also find that the patterns of 'regularity' vs 'irregularity' do not appear to respect the conventional boundaries of the U area. We conclude that the linguistic evidence, at least in this context, does not allow us to distinguish borrowed words from inherited words. In order to illuminate the (possible) relations, one is drawn into considering the isoglosses that are to be observed.

We find that there are strong isoglosses that intersect the conventional boundary of the Uralic area. For example, in the North there are isoglosses encompassing Tungusic languages and some northern U languages; in the South there are isoglosses encompassing Hungarian, Chuvash, Mongolian and Common Turkic languages; and in the North-East there are isoglosses encompassing Samoyed and Yukaghir. Some authors, such as Ligeti (1986: 53–8) and Sinor (1975: 251), express surprise that some of these parallels can be so 'flawless' in sound and meaning. However, when it comes to interpret- ing these 'flawless' correlations using the Comparative Method, they are not considered as evidence of a genetic relationship, since such an interpretation would contradict the a priori established families. Instead, they are interpreted as the result of 'convergent development' or of regular 'direct borrowing'. These interpretations are in direct contradiction to the adopted Neo-grammarian principle that borrowed words can easily be identified because of their irregularity. This contradiction should not be a surprise because, as we shall see, this Neo-grammarian principle has been superseded by modern linguistic evidence.

6.1. METHODOLOGY

As we shall see in repeated examples in this chapter, reasonably good parallels are usually interpreted differently according to the context. If the U parallel is with another language within the U area, any regularity is interpreted as evidence of genetic inheritance. But if the U parallel is with a language outside the U area, any regularity is usually attributed to 'convergent but independent development' (Ligeti 1986: 53–8) or to what is termed regular, direct borrowing.

One should not be surprised that there are difficulties in distinguishing borrowed from inherited words in the Uralic context, because this has also been encountered more generally outside the Uralic field. The Neo-grammarian principle that borrowed words can be identified because, unlike inherited words, they are mostly 'irregular', is contradicted by modern research. In fact, borrowed words tend to become integrated into the phonological, semantic and morpho-syntactic structure of the recipient language after only a few generations, if not at the very time of the borrowing. I would like to quote in this regard a passage by Lass (1997: 193–4), who is making a general point that happens to be illustrated with Finnish examples, borrowed from (Northern)·Germanic:

> Usually borrowings are . . . phonologically reconfigured to match the requirements of the borrowing language. Speakers . . . do not accept foreign phones, but in various ways accommodate them to the 'nearest' native ones . . . the unmarked case is that a foreign phone will be replaced by a native one, and a phonotactically inadmissible sequence will be replaced in the same way (hence Fi *pelto* 'field' < Gmc **/felð-u-/*, *Risto* 'Christopher', *ranta* 'bank, shore' < Gmc **/stranð-/*, *kinkku* 'ham' NGmc *skinka*, etc.: Finnic historically has no voiced stops or */f/*, and does not allow initial clusters)

As one can see, there are no linguistic clues, there is no 'atypicalness' (Lass 1997: 191) in the Finnish terms *pelto, kinkku, Risto* and *ranta* on the basis of which one could identify them as borrowed words. We know this from other types of information. There is an extensive literature on the topic of the integration of borrowed words into recipient languages. See for example Gamillscheg (1911: 162), Schuchardt (1925: 28), Bloomfield (1933: 450), Haugen (1950), Weinreich (1953), Paul (1960: 396 f.), Gusmani (1981: 21–43) and Labov (1994: 332 f.).

Furthermore, according to Martinet (1959: 145 f.), Weinreich (1953) and Klajn (1972: 42 f.), the assimilation of borrowed words is particularly efficient where most of the languages involved share phonological and structural similarities or where the borrowing is extensive. As is discussed in this chapter, in Section 4.5.7 above and in Chapter 8 below, these conditions all apply in the U/Altaic/Yukaghir context. This general observation means that, particularly on the long time-scales that are assumed to be involved in the U context, most if not all of the presumed borrowed words will by now behave in all respects and in all contexts like inherited words.

Moving on to the specific data within the field of Uralic studies, textbooks simply assert that the non-U correlations are distinguishable because they are irregular, but this question has attracted a large number of learned articles in the field. The quantity of publications betrays the unsettled nature of this topic. In particular, the evidence often seems to be at variance with the model, as we saw in the quote from Sinor reported in Section 1.3.3 (and repeated below in the appropriate context). As mentioned, there has been no actual research that systematically demonstrates the assumed irregularity of all the non-U parallels. Indeed one might expect such a demonstration to be extremely difficult, if not impossible, to complete since, as we saw in Chapter 4, there is a high degree of irregularity within the U comparative corpus itself. We saw too (and shall see again below), that some U and Altaic languages share a number of basic phonological features and even some apparently common sound-developments. In this situation, one would have to demonstrate that the correlations with languages outside the U family are in some sense 'more irregular' than those within the U family, but it is unclear what specific criteria might be applied to such a classification.

In this chapter we examine the semantic areas of body-parts and flora and fauna in detail. As we shall see, in these samples each U etymology is associated in the literature with 2.2 non-U languages on average. There is much disagreement on the chronology and donor languages of these parallels, if they are assumed to be borrowed, and we shall illustrate the level of disagreement that exists using some examples. We shall see that the actual, case-by-case evidence to classify the parallels as 'borrowed', 'inherited' or 'chance resemblance', is simply not clear. Indeed, this chapter will demonstrate that clear-cut, safe classifications of these parallels cannot be obtained in the Uralic context because of the general and context-specific reasons expounded above.

After a description of the general situation, this chapter will discuss in more detail the topic of the lexical correlations between U and Altaic, Hungarian and non-Uralic languages, U and Yukaghir. It will also introduce the topic of the U correlations with Indo-European, which will be dealt with more fully in the next chapter.

6.2. THE PARALLELS WITH NON-U LANGUAGES

As we saw in Chapter 4, a proper 'P-U' comparative corpus does not exist, the best and most comprehensive reconstruction being based on the Finnic and Samoyed branch only. We also saw that even this limited corpus contains many problematic correlations. Further, the mathematical analysis carried out in Chapter 5 confirmed that the criteria generally adopted for establishing etymologies within U are rather lax. It is not surprising therefore that a large number of U etymologies have been associated in the literature with etymologies from other language families. On several occasions a given U etymology has been associated at the same time with etymologies from language families as distant as Indo-European and Altaic. It is unlikely that both of these interpretations are correct (unless one believes in the Nostratic hypothesis), so that it is reasonable to conclude that the reported literature probably contains a significant number of accidental look-alikes.

6.2.1. Body-parts and flora and fauna

The tables and graphs in the following pages illustrate the extent of the associations that have been made in the literature. The sources used in compiling these tables are restricted to dictionaries and recognised sources: Szinnyei (1927); Paasonen (1912/13–1916/17, 1918); Collinder (1952, 1955, 1957, 1960, 1977a, 1977b); Räsänen (1920, 1947a, 1947b, 1953, 1955, 1963/5, 1969–71); Joki (1944, 1952, 1973); Poppe (1960b, 1960c, 1977b, 1983); Koivulehto (1987, 1991); Campbell (1990a); Róna-Tas (1983, 1988a, 1991); Sinor (1965, 1969, 1970, 1973, 1975, 1988, 1990); Tyler (1968); Friedrich (1970); Doerfer (1963–75); Clauson (1972); Hajdú (1954, 1963, 1964, 1969b, 1975c); Hajdú & Domokos (1978); Janhunen (1977), Ligeti (1938); Watkins (1985); K.Vilkuna (1950); Hakulinen (1979); and Rédei (1999a).

The tables and graphs below show the flora and fauna terms and the body-parts terms that are discussed in the quoted literature and that are present in at least two U languages. For each word, the tables show the number of non-U languages with which the U word has been associated. These non-U languages belong to the following families: Indo-European, Altaic, Palaeo-Siberian, Dravidian.

On average, each of the U etymologies is associated with 2.2 non-U languages. Only 6 of the 60 etymologies examined do not have an external association reported in the literature examined.

It can be noted here that the terms for flora and fauna include a significant number of items which have been identified as forming a unique 'U culture', whose bearers were supposed to be a Stone Age hunting, fishing and gatherer population (Hajdú 1975a, 1975b, 1975c). These terms also illustrate

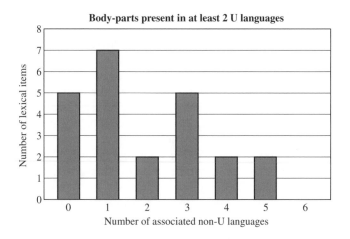

Figure 6.1 Uralic body-parts and their external associations

Table 6.1 Uralic body-parts and their external associations

U only	Heart
	Foot
	Bile (Alternative a)
	Nail
	Blood
U plus 1 other	Eye
	Hand
	Spleen
	Bile (Alternative b)
	Horn
	Udder
	Kidney
U plus 2 others	Tongue, language
	Intestine
U plus 3 others	Skin/bark/film (Alternative a)
	Peel /skin/bark/film (Alternative b)
	Navel
	Lip
	Opening/ mouth /estuary
U plus 4 others	Egg/testicle/penis
	Liver
U plus 5 others	Head
	Urine

that there are several words available within the whole area to indicate the
same and/or similar tree, or animal. Both tables illustrate the variety of
meanings which are often accepted in order to establish a connection,
whether within U only, or between U and non-U languages.

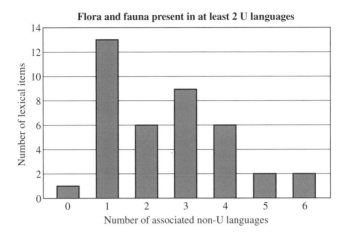

Figure 6.2 Uralic flora and fauna and their external associations

6.2.2. *Typical examples*

Space does not permit to deal in detail with all the items reported in the tables and graphs. Therefore, this section reports just some typical examples, to illustrate the situation depicted numerically above.

As can be seen from the examples below, a word will typically have a variety of associated meanings in the various languages (for example: 'mouth/lip/opening/estuary/muzzle'), and only one or two matching sounds, both within U and with external languages. These factors suggest that one must consider seriously the possibility that many of the parallels will be accidental 'look-alikes'. Indeed, it is sometimes suggested in the literature that this is the case, although there does not appear to be any systematic work to substantiate this claim, or to distinguish the possible 'look-alikes' from the possible 'borrowed' elements (with the exception of Ringe's work; see below). As discussed, most scholars use the Comparative Method to analyse this linguistic area, and, accordingly, attempt to classify the similarities either as 'borrowed' or as 'inherited'. If a word is interpreted as borrowed, one often finds a variety of interpretations regarding the possible donor language, direction and chronology of the borrowing, as shown below:

(6.1) P-F-U *$\check{s}ola$ 'intestine' (UEW 483–4; SKES 113–14, Räsänen 1955: 23). According to Poppe (1983: 192–3) this etymological set presents 'good' U and Altaic correspondences with regard to the initial sibilants. According to Koivulehto (1987: 204–8), this word is borrowed from Indo-European. Sinor (1975: 257) comments that 'the absence of the Samoyed data is rather surprising.' Compare Finn. *suoli* /Mor. E. *śulo* /Vot. *śul* /Ost. *sol, sut*/Yuk. *šole* /Tungusic *$\check{s}ilu\text{-}kta$: *silukta, hilukta*

Table 6.2 Uralic flora and fauna and their external associations

U only	River	
U plus 1 other	Dog/drone (male bee)/male reindeer	Reindeer alternative
	Reindeer/elk	Reindeer alternative
	Horse	
	Ox/leading reindeer	Reindeer alternative
	Reindeer	Reindeer alternative
	Mouse	
	'A type of duck'	
	'A type of fish'	
	Mole/mouse	
	Otter	
	Ash tree	
	Sponge/fungus	
	Feather	
U plus 2 others	Male elk/deer/reindeer/sacrificial animal	Reindeer alternative
	Birch	
	Beaver	
	Berry	
	Grass	
	Conifer	Tree alternative
U plus 3 others	Domesticated reindeer	Reindeer alternative
	Lizard	
	Partridge	
	(Relay) horse	
	Pine (*pinus cembra/pinus sibirica*)	Tree alternative
	Tree/wood	Tree alternative
	Stalk/stem	
	Juniper	
	Aspen/poplar/willow	Tree alternative
U plus 4 others	Pine/tree/picea	Tree alternative
	Spruce/pine	Tree alternative
	Bird-cherry/ *prunus padus*	
	Domesticated reindeer/sheep/cow	Reindeer alternative
	Male elk/reindeer/camel	Reindeer alternative
	Bark (of tree)	
U plus 5 others	Poplar/ aspen	Tree alternative
	Mountain ash/rowan/*sorbus aucuparia*	Tree alternative
U plus 6 others	Spruce/tree/forest	Tree alternative
	Fish	

(6.2) P-U *aŋe* 'opening, mouth, estuary, lip, muzzle, etc.' (UEW 11). This word presents some sound-difficulties and a variety of meanings both within U and in the nearby languages. For example, the initial vowel seems to be *ä*, and not *a*, in P-Samoyed (Janhunen 1977: 20; Sammallahti 1979: 27). Janhunen (1981a: 255; item (103)) reconstructs P-U *åŋi*. According to Hajdú (1954: 42, 135) the initial *ń*- (typical of several Samoyed forms) is secondary. In Hungarian a sporadic development of the type *$*\eta > *\gamma > j$* should be assumed. Compare:

Hun. *aj* 'depression, notch', *ajak* 'lip' etc./? Che. *äŋ* 'mouth, estuary, opening'/Vot. *įm* 'mouth'/Zyr. *vom* 'mouth, estuary'/Ost. *oŋ, ŏŋ* 'mouth, estuary, etc.'/Sam. Yu. *ńaʔ* 'mouth'/Sam. Ye. *êʔ* 'mouth, estuary', etc. UEW proposes a comparison with P-A **amŋa*: Turkic *aɣïz* 'mouth'/Chu. *văr* 'opening'/Mon. *ang* 'opening', *aman* 'mouth, estuary'/Tun. *amŋa* 'mouth, estuary' (see also Poppe 1960c: 94). Róna-Tas (1983: 241) observes that 'we find in this word *ŋ* > *ɣ* in the Ugric and *ŋ* > *m* in the Permian languages but these are late and independent changes. Should T[urkic] *aɣïz* be in connection with the U word this would be possible only if it were a Ugric loan. So we have in this case a U word with M[anchu]-T[ungus] and M[ongolian] connections if we accept that P-Sam. *ä* is secondary. If not, then it is only a PFU – M[anchu]-T[ungus]-M[ongolian] **correspondence**'[bold is mine]. According to Sinor (1975: 254–5) two different forms can be reconstructed for Tungusic: **ang* and **am*. Therefore, the U words could be considered borrowed from this language group, although with reservation. In this case, within U only the Ob-Ugric and the Cheremis parallels would show agreement with Tungusic.

One may wonder on which grounds the assumed 'late' chronology of the changes *ŋ* > *ɣ* in Ugric and *ŋ* > *m* in Permian can be established. Notice also that, according to UEW, there is no Vogul parallel, so that it not clear what the 'Ugric' reflex might have been.

(6.3) P-Sam. **kün* 'navel'/Old Turkic *kin-dik*/Mon. *küyi* (< *kügi*)/Hun. *köldök* (from Róna-Tas (1988a: 744), whose transcription has been adopted; it is not listed in UEW). In Chapter 2 we saw that Budenz connected this word to F-U words meaning 'tongue/language', a connection which is now rejected. Within U, this word is present in Samoyed and Hungarian only. According to Róna-Tas, the various Samoyed parallels are derived from Ancient Turkic *küŋ* (see also Joki (1952: 124) and Ligeti (1938: 199)). If the Mongolian and the Turkic forms were to be considered related, the common form would be **küŋi* (according to Róna-Tas), in which case the borrowing could well have taken place from Mongolian, or, more generally, from Altaic. The Hungarian form is considered by Róna-Tas as borrowed from Turkic *kindik*. The same origin is proposed in TESz II, 606.

(6.4) P-U **puwe* 'tree, wood, forest, etc.' As discussed in Chapter 4, this is a problematic etymology within U, and, in fact, according to Janhunen (1981a), its reconstruction should contain the segment '*x*' (see examples (4.17) and (4.30)). For this item, there are competing associations with parallels from Indo-European and Altaic. Compare Finn. *puu* /Hun. *fa* /Cher. *pu* /Zyr. *pu* /Vog. *-pä* /Sam. Yu. *pā* / Sam. Ye. *fe*/Mon. *hoi* (< * *poi*) 'forest'/Tun. *hijika* 'forest'/Orok *pe*/Gold *pia*/Man. *f'a* 'birch-tree' (UEW 410). According to Poppe (1983: 195–6) in this etymological set the initial P-U *p- has 'regular' correspondences with initial P-A *p-. According to Campbell ((1990a: 161), whose transcription is reproduced) a connection can be made with I-E *pwk' ~ *pewk' 'pine, spruce': Gre. *peuke* 'spruce, pine, spruce forest'/Lit. *pušìs* 'spruce, pine'/OHG *fiuhta* ~ *fiehta* 'spruce', etc. Koivulehto (1991: 56–7), like Campbell, proposes an Indo-European origin, but from a different root: *b^huH- ~ *b^howH- 'to grow, flourish'. This etymology, together with similar others, are supposed to be indicative of very old contacts between U and Indo-European peoples (see in Chapter 7 example (7.9) and related discussion).

(6.5) P-U *juwɜ 'pine-tree (*pinus silvestris*), wood'. This etymology is another problematic one within U (see example (4.15) and related discussion in Chapter 4). Like the previous item, it has been associated with several different languages and language groups. Compare: ? Che. *yäkte* 'any tall tree, wood'/Vog. *jiw* 'tree, wood'/Ost. *juχ*/Sam. Yu. *je ʔ*/Sam. Ka. *d'ȫ* / Tun. *jagda* 'pine'/Man. *jakdan*/Chu. *yaxta* 'spruce, pine' (UEW 107; Paasonen 1912/13–1916/17, item (337); SKES 122). Sinor (1975: 251) observes that the ending -*te* of Cheremis has been analysed in the literature as a word suffix. Therefore, one can reconstruct P-U *yVk (V= vowel); this form corresponds to the Tungusic forms reconstructable as * *jVk-* ~ *jVg- (-*kta*, -*gda*, or -*ta*, -*te* etc. are suffixes often present in Tungusic tree-names). Then the author comments:

I find it hard to believe that a correspondence as flawless in form and meaning as that existing between the Uralic and Tunguz forms could be coincidental . . . I would not like to exclude the possibility that the Cheremis and Chuvash words – or at least one of them – are direct borrowings from Tunguz.

UEW does not mention the non-U similarities, which are here quoted from Sinor, and does not include the Cheremis parallel in its etymological set because of the cluster -*kt*-. Räsänen (1920: 240) believes that the Chuvash parallel is a loan from Cheremis. According to Campbell (1990a: 168–9) the U parallels are 'strikingly similar' to I-E *eywo- 'yew', although this root means 'yew' consistently only in Germanic and Celtic (the reconstructed form is from Friedrich (1970: 121); compare OHG. *īwa* and Ger. *Eibe* 'yew(-tree)'). Furthermore, Campbell also includes in the U set Finn. *juko*(-*puu*) and Est. *juka* ~ *juha*(-*puu*) 'yew'. According to SSA I, 245–6 Finn. *juko* ~ *jukko* derives from Germ. *juka*, and appears to be only Finnic in distribution.

(6.6.) P-Ug. *luwɜ (*luγə) 'horse'. Compare Hun. *ló* (Acc. *lova-t*)/Vog. *low*, *luw*, *lo* /Ost. *loγ*, *law* / Tur. *ulaq* 'Kurier'/Kir. *lau* (UEW 863). The U etymological set has been traditionally considered as borrowed from

Turkic, and it is supposed to constitute another testimony of the existence of the Ugric community and node (see Section 4.5.3.2 for the (alleged) borrowing into the 'Ugric period'). However, the whole matter is quite problematic. According to Róna-Tas (1988a: 749–50): 'The Vocalism . . . is unclear and the dropping of the initial *u-* in P-Ugr is not motivated . . . The loss of an initial vowel in Chuvash is known, but is very recent. The Turkic word is in fact a Eurasian cultural term for post-horse, relay horse, transport horse, the earliest data in the Chinese sources are from the year 629 and in this meaning it entered many languages as Persian, Arabic etc.' Other authors have basically come to the conclusion that it is very difficult to define and classify these correlations. For example, UEW 863 thinks possible an 'unknown language', as the donor language of both the Ugric and Turkic forms. According to Sinor (1965: 312–15), the P-Ugric form **laγ* (as the author reconstructs it) is at the root of the Turkic and Mongolian forms *lav, lau, ulaγ(a)*. Given that the word is not restricted to Turkic, a purely Turkic etymology has to be discarded, a fact which, to use Sinor's words (1965: 314–15) 'touches upon the vexed and most controversial question of the horse-breeding of the Ugrians in general and the Hungarians in particular . . . *Yunt* [Old Turkic and Samoyed term for 'horse'] and *ulaγ* are thus Altaic words going back to a non-Altaic substratum, which may have been Uralic, but could just as well have been one of unknown substance, which left its trace on what was to become respectively Ugric and Turkic'.

A similar situation holds for the 'vexed' etymologies equivalent to Hun. *hattyú* 'swan', *homok* 'sand', *hajó* 'boat' (for which see Section 4.5.3.2 above), *nyár* 'summer', *nyak* 'neck' (see again Róna-Tas (1988a: 750f.) and discussion below), and many others. One may also notice here, as in other occasions, the easy recourse to the '*deus ex machina*' or, as P. Michalove jokingly suggested,[2] to the '*lingua ex machina*', when data are not 'well behaved'.

6.3. THE CORRELATIONS BETWEEN URALIC AND ALTAIC

The relationship between U and Altaic has been discussed already in Chapter 2, and will be returned to in Chapter 8. Therefore, in this section I shall make only a couple of brief remarks.

Judging from the lexical items examined in the previous section and from the distribution of several, major Altaic phonological isoglosses (see next section), the status of the Altaic etymologies does not appear to be too different from that of the U etymologies. Many of them seem to be 'similarities' rather than 'correspondences', given that they present phonological and/or other types of problems and a high degree of variation. This state of affairs has indeed been pointed out by several researchers, including Sinor (1963) and Doerfer (1968, 1971). Recall, for example, the problem of the 'contradictory' Turkic correspondences, mentioned above (Section 4.6.4). The many instances of 'bad' sound-correspondences are in fact the major reason – coupled with the presumed absence of sufficient shared Lexicon – why several scholars have altogether denied the validity of the Altaic node and family (Clauson 1956, 1969; Doerfer 1985; Janhunen 1984a; Unger 1990). As Sinor (1963: 144) puts it:

> As for the comparative study of the vocabulary of the Altaic languages, it seems to show that an Altaic *Ursprache* is not only theoretical: it is also imaginary

Compare however Vovin (1994, 1998), Greenberg (1997) and Miller (1989/ 91, 1991) in defence of the Altaic node.

This being the situation, one possible way out, or at least a useful exercise, would be the application of a mathematical method of analysis to the whole area, but bypassing the conventionally established nodes. Such an analysis would help to unveil the genuine linguistic correlations and their distribution, whilst separating them from the accidental 'look-alikes'.

We have seen in Chapter 4 (Section 4.5.2.1) and in the examples (6.1), (6.4) and (6.5) above that there are shared phonological features and several matching sounds or sound-developments across the U and Altaic linguistic area. We have also pointed out on several occasions that this would certainly have been interpreted as strong evidence in favour of the genetic unity of the U and Altaic languages, if the presumption of genetic unity were as alive today as it was between the end of 19th century and the beginning of the 20th century.

In a similar way, Sinor (1975) observes that some northern Tungusic and U lexical parallels are closer to each other than to those of languages within the traditional boundaries. Some U and Tungusic languages also share particularly strong grammatical isoglosses, as discussed in Chapter 8 (Section 8.5.3.4). In particular, Sinor (1988: 739; see also 1975: 261) argues that:

> a semantic analysis of the Uralo-Tunguz word correspondences show that their majority belong to what may be called an arctic vocabulary

The author (1975: 248–60) lists 37 Uralo-Tungusic lexical parallels, some of which appear to be reasonably good and quite widely represented both within the U and the Altaic area. We have already seen some of these parallels in example (6.5) above. Other parallels of this type include various terms for 'ice', 'snow', 'ski', 'sledge', 'knife', 'boot-leg', 'blunt arrowhead', etc. (for further examples see also Sinor (1970: 543f.)). Sinor concludes that these parallels are indicative of 'direct' borrowing between U and Tungusic, as pointed out above (see also Introduction).

However, Sinor also remarks that the mutual relations of the languages involved are rather intricate, to the point that the exact nature of the lexical correlations – borrowed vs inherited – cannot, in fact, be easily ascertained. This is illustrated by the following two quotes, the first of which is from Sinor (1975: 261–2), and the second is from Sinor (1988: 738; see also Section 1.4):

> The Uralo-Tunguz equations here presented must be set against a different background. When not presented on the model of a family tree, the five stocks which constitute the Uralo-Altaic group are usually thought of, as it were, in a linear way: Samoyed–Finno-Ugric // Turkic–Mongol–Tunguz. . . . I think to have shown the existence of a lexical interchange between Tunguz and Uralic and that some of the **contacts were made directly between PTU** [Proto-Tunguz] **and PFU** . . . If we project on a map the present geographical locations of the five Uralic and Altaic stocks, we notice that they fall into a roughly circular pattern:

> | | | |
> |---|---|---|
> | Samoyed | | Tunguz |
> | Finno-Ugric | | Mongol |
> | | Turkic | |

> Northern Tunguz and Uralic are in many respects closer together than Tunguz and Mongol. Mongol and Southern Tunguz show morphological similarities which are shared neither by Northern Tunguz nor by Turkic. The relationship of these groups with one another is much more involved than it has hitherto been envisaged. When one considers the fact that the position of Germanic among the Indo-European languages is still the subject of controversy, the obscurity of the Uralic and Altaic relationships becomes less surprising. . . . The meticulous study of the isoglosses running through Central Eurasia will, I am certain, reveal the existence of linguistic areal units which, whether or not related genetically with the neighbouring regions, share with them a number of morphological and lexical elements

> I am quite certain that if from all the Uralic and Altaic languages only the [Altaic] **Northern Tunguz** and [Uralic] **Ob-Ugric** were known, no one would deny their **genetic relationship** [all bolds are mine]

6.4. THE CORRELATIONS BETWEEN HUNGARIAN AND NON-URALIC LANGUAGES

In this section I shall examine the main correlations that have been reported in the literature between Hungarian and other non-Uralic languages, especially Common Turkic, Chuvash and Mongolian. We shall see that there are strong correlations among all these languages at the phonological and lexical level. These correlations – several of which are certainly genuine – stand in stark contrast to the acknowledged very poor correlations between Hungarian and the other Uralic languages, which was discussed in Chapter 4.

I shall also attempt to describe the mainstream 'textbook' interpretation of the origin of these correlations. I have to confess that I find this topic especially 'Gordian', and therefore it will be particularly difficult to disentangle clearly the chain of evidence, assumptions and interpretations that is involved. I shall do my best to separate these out from one another, but I must beg the reader's indulgence if anything in this section appears to be inconsistent or differs from the interpretations that are held by most of the practitioners in the field.

According to the conventional paradigm, the words of non-Uralic origin present in Hungarian are all borrowed, and for the majority of them the donor language has been identified as Old Bulgar Turkic (borrowing of the 'Chuvash type'). However, this textbook interpretation is contradicted in the specialist literature. The status, classification and chronology of the Turkic loan-words in Hungarian is still a debated topic (Gheno & Hajdú 1992: 13–25; Ligeti 1975a: 279). Consider for example the inconclusive and even apparently self-contradictory summary of this question from Róna-Tas (1988a: 755):

> Beyond doubt the Hungarians borrowed words in pre-Conquest times also from Turkic languages not of the Chuvash type. Whether they were of the Oghuz or the Kipchak type is very difficult to say. T. Halasi-Kun tried to show that many T[urkic] loanwords in the earliest layer were of Kipchak origin (1975[3]) . . . Some of the pre-Conquest **Turkic loanwords** in Hungarian are ultimately of **non-Turkic origin**. [bold is mine]

Indeed. An examination of the primary evidence in this section will confirm the interpretation that it is usually not possible to identify the donor language of these loan-words on the basis of linguistic evidence (taking as good that the words in question are in fact borrowed).

In the standard theory it is held that there is clear evidence that the words of non-Uralic origin in Hungarian are borrowed rather than inherited – this claim represents in fact one of the corner-stones of the U paradigm. Not surprisingly, this is the topic that has attracted perhaps most pages of learned articles in the field of Uralic and non-Uralic correlations, and it is therefore appropriate to discuss it here.

It is supposed that the Hungarians had long and close contact with Turkic tribes that could be clearly identified, namely, they were all of Old Bulgar Turkic character, starting from the On-ogurs down to the Khazars (see Section 2.1.2.6 for details). However, as we saw in Chapter 2, there is no independent evidence, no historical corroboration of this story, so that the only evidence for any of this is linguistic, namely, the presence of loan-words in Hungarian from an identified Bulgar Turkic source – the very feature that needs accounting for!

The conventional linguistic argument for the presence of loan-words in Hungarian from an identified Bulgar Turkic source runs as follows, as far as I can determine. The Khazars, in contact with whom the Hungarians are supposed to have spent about 300 years, were a multi-ethnic and multi-lingual society, with a major Turkic component (Golden 1990a: 264 f.; Franklin & Shepard 1996: 95); their language is now held to be extinct with no survivors. Only isolated names, toponyms and titles are preserved, and even these are obscured by poor transcription. And, in fact, there is no agreement among scholars as to whether the Turkic component of the Khazar society was of Bulgar type or not.[4] As Golden (1990a: 263–4) says, 'The long-standing debate over whether the Khazars spoke a form of Oghur or Common Turkic cannot be resolved.' Accordingly, this language is not taken into account in the argumentation.

The Old Bulgar Turkic languages are also extinct, and they must be reconstructed from their assumed only modern survivor, Chuvash. Since, clearly, more than one source is needed in order to make a reconstruction, the presumed loan-words in Hungarian are also used in the reconstruction, presumably as if they obeyed regular sound-laws – this presumed regularity is in direct contradiction to the presumed borrowed status of these words. Furthermore, the use of Hungarian in reconstructing Old Bulgar Turkic may result in a circular argument. For example, as we shall see, some of the etymologies have no Chuvash parallel at all, so that the only source for the reconstruction is the assumed loan-word in Hungarian; this word is then cited as evidence for the borrowing from Old Bulgar Turkic. For further discussion of the circularities involved in this area see also Csillaghy (1977–81: 312) and Sinor (1969: 276).

Finally, it is claimed that the source of the loan-words can be identified through the distribution of two isoglosses that are held to be characteristic of Bulgar Turkic. As Johanson (1998: 81) puts it, the Bulgar languages differ from Common Turkic:

> by regular phonetic representations such as *r* and *l* instead of *z* and *š* in certain words

However, these same isoglosses are also shared with Mongolian. Further-more, in some words the expected 'regular phonetic representations' do not take place (see example (6.7c), (6.7d) and (6.9c) below), and other words simply do not contain the relevant sounds. This means that, in the majority of cases, these criteria do not suffice to establish the source of the borrowing. As Golden (1990b: 244) says:

> many of these 'Bulghar' Turkic loanwords are **neutral** in terms of those characteristics which would permit us to classify them within Turkic.

Indeed, with regard to some of them we may only say that they are **Altaic** [bold is mine].

The detailed analysis presented below is based on the following references: Németh (1921a, 1921b, 1930/91, 1934/90); Ligeti ((ed.) 1943, 1935, 1960, 1961, 1975a, 1976, 1977–9; 1978, 1986); Gombocz (1908, 1912, 1921, 1960); Bárczi (1958b, 1965, 1966); Benkő (1967: 280–3); Poppe (1960a); Róna-Tas (1981, 1988a); Räsänen (1955, 1939); Halasi-Kun (1975); Gheno & Hajdú (1992); Johanson & Csató ((eds) 1998).

6.4.1. When and from which language did Hungarian borrow?

As discussed above, according to the textbook interpretation Hungarian borrowed words essentially from Turkic languages (specifically, from Bulgar Turkic), and not from other Altaic languages. This borrowing took place before the conquest of the present-day Hungarian territory, which is traditionally dated at 896 AD, as discussed in Chapter 2. This layer of borrowing is generally referred to as the 'pre-conquest' layer, and is considered to be the oldest layer of borrowing from Turkic.

6.4.1.1. The classification of the Turkic languages

In order to understand the conventional classification of the 'pre-conquest' Turkic L-Ws in Hungarian, a quick look at the classification of the Turkic languages relevant to this discussion is in order.

The Turkic languages, on the basis of phonological criteria, are divided into two major groups:

- Languages of the 'Chuvash type', that is, Chuvash and Old Bulgar Turkic (generally classified as western Turkic). The Bulgar languages are assumed to be closely related to, possibly the ancestors of, Chuvash (Johanson 1998: 81; Clark 1998: 434). Chuvash[5] in turn is generally considered to be the only modern representative of the Bulgar branch; therefore, in most (but not all) classifications it is given an isolated position, see for example Comrie (1981: 45), Katzner (1995: 3). However, in Baskakov's classification (1969) Chuvash is classified as a coordinate member of what the author calls the 'western Hunnic' group (together with Turkish, Bashkir, Tatar etc.), against an 'eastern Hunnic' group.
- 'Common Turkic' languages, that is, all the other Turkic languages (generally classified as eastern Turkic), which formed after the early split of the P-Bulgar languages from pre/Proto-Turkic.

As mentioned, this classification is based on a few isoglosses, the most relevant of which are the presence of *r* vs *z* and the presence of *l* vs *š* in Chuvash and Common Turkic respectively[6] (Räsänen 1969–71, I : 77, 424; Benzing 1959: 710–11; Johanson 1998: 81).

Textbooks usually claim that, on the basis of these isoglosses that separate Chuvash from all the other Turkic languages, one can also establish whether a given Turkic L-W in Hungarian derives from a 'Chuvash type' of language (namely Old Bulgar Turkic, P-Chuvash and, possibly, Khazar), or, alternatively, from a 'Common Turkic' language. It is also usually claimed that the majority of the Turkic L-Ws in Hungarian are of 'Chuvash type'. However, this apparently straightforward classification of the Turkic languages and therefore of the Turkic L-Ws in Hungarian presents two major weaknesses.[7]

Firstly, the classification of Chuvash itself within Altaic is controversial, being in turn connected with the 'controversy over the Altaic hypothesis', to use Comrie's (1981: 45) words. In fact, (ibid.):

> on the basis of some of the isoglosses that separate Turkic from Mongolian . . . Chuvash falls on the Mongolian side of the line

These isoglosses include the very presence of *r* and *l* where all the other Turkic languages have *z* and *š*. In other words, the crucial isoglosses on the basis of which the 'Bulgar origin' of the Turkic L-Ws in Hungarian is supposedly identifiable, are not shared by Chuvash and Hungarian only. They are also shared by the Mongolian languages, and, to some extent, by the Tungusic languages.

Secondly, as mentioned, the 'regular phonetic representations' *r* and *l* instead of *z* and *š* are not that regular after all, because, as Johanson remarks, these representations are implemented in 'certain words' only, whilst they are missing in other words. This situation is illustrated by the examples listed below:

(a) *r* vs *z* isogloss: (the examples are cited from Johanson (1998: 104f.), whose transcription is adopted; see also Comrie (1981: 45); for more examples of this type see Ligeti (1986: 14–15)):

(6.7) a Common Turkic *buzāγu* / Chu. *paru* / Bur. *buruu* / (Classical) Mongolian *biraγu* / Hun. *borjú* 'calf'

  b Common Turkic *ekiz* /Chu. *yěker*/Mon. *ikire* /Man. *ikiri* /Hun. *iker* 'twin'

  c Common Turkic *qār* /Chu. *yur* 'snow'

  d Common Turkic *tīz* 'knee' → *tirsgek* 'elbow, knee joint' (< *tiz-ge-k)/Hun. *tér-d* (< **tir-*) 'knee' (from Róna-Tas 1998: 72)

If taken at face value, examples such as (6.7a) and (6.7b) suggest that there is some sort of connection between Hungarian, Mongolian and Chuvash. However, such a connection would be contrary to the conventional paradigm and contrary to the assumed historical peregrinations and related contacts of the Hungarians.

Accordingly, Ligeti (1986: 14–16) attempts to show by linguistic reasoning that Hungarian has borrowed directly from Chuvash and not from Mongolian. In order to show this, he asserts that Hungarian 'rhotacism' derives directly from Chuvash 'rhotacism'. His evidence is based on two words where the process of rhotacism has been implemented in Hungarian but not in the Mongolian equivalents. However, for both of these words the Chuvash equivalent is missing! The author explains this contradiction by 'assuming' an original, unattested P-Chuvash form in r. These two words are the following (from Ligeti 1986: 15):

(6.8) a Hun. *karó* 'stake, pale, post'/Common Turkic *qazuq* '*idem*' ~ *qadaq* 'peg, pin, spike'/Tat. *kazak* ~ *kadak* 'nail, pin'/Mon. *qada-* 'to drive in, knock in'
       b Hungarian *iró* 'buttermilk'/Tat. *yåz-* 'to churn'/Bas. *yað-* 'to churn'

As mentioned, the overall situation is further complicated by the fact that the expected isogloss does not always materialise within the Turkic area, as shown in the examples (6.7c) and (6.7d), where r is present both in Common Turkic (in certain contexts) and in Chuvash.

(b) *l* vs *š* isogloss. Exactly the same situation applies to the isogloss Chu. *l* vs Common Turkic (non-initial) *š*, as shown in the following examples (from Johanson (1998: 105); for more examples of this type see Ligeti (1986: 16–17)):

(6.9) a Common Turkic *tāš* /Chu. *čul*/Mon. *čila-* 'stone'[8]
       b Common Turkic *köšek*/Mon. *gölige*/Hun *kölyök* 'young [of animal], puppy'
       c Common Turkic *yōl* / Chu. *śul* 'way'

This isogloss is implemented in a small number of cases; in fact, many of the relevant Turkic parallels present the same reflex *l*, as shown in (6.9c), or the same reflex *ś/š*, as shown below (in examples (6.10)). Similarly, as pointed out by Ligeti (1986: 16–17), the Hungarian words reflecting this isogloss are only four. In other words, this other supposedly crucial evidence in favour of the 'Chuvash character' of the borrowing in Hungarian is substantiated by four words only. Furthermore, two of these four Chuvash/Hungarian parallels have an equivalent in Mongolian; this is shown in example (6.9b), where, in fact, the expected Chuvash equivalent is, again, missing!

In addition to this, there is another element of complication. As Johanson (1998: 105) puts it, in some words there is 'an exception that complicates the picture', that is, Chuvash presents the reflex *ś* whereas Common Turkic has *š*. In this context the Mongolian reflex is the same as in Common Turkic, whilst the Hungarian reflex is -*lcs*- (*l-lčl*), or -*cs*- (*lčl*). Compare the following examples:

(6.10) a Common Turkic *bāš* / Chu. *puś* 'head' (from Johanson 1998: 105)
b Common Turkic *yimiš* / Chu. *śiměš* < *jimiš*/Mon. *jemiš* ~ *jimiš*/
Hun. *gyümölcs* 'fruit' (from Ligeti 1986: 17)
c Common Turkic *běšek*/Hun. *bölcső* 'cradle' (from Ligeti 1986: 17
and Johnason 1998: 105)
d Common Turkic *bošat-* 'release'/Chu. *pušat-*/Hun. *bocsát-* 'let go,
release' (from Ligeti 1986: 17 and Róna-Tas 1998: 72)

This primary evidence seems to suggest, again, that it is not possible to identify the exact origin of the borrowing in such an intricate context; it could have occurred equally from any of the sources in question. In fact, for example, according to some interpretations, in some cases Turkic *š* could be the reflex of an old **lč* (Johanson 1998: 105). However, Ligeti once again claims that the borrowing in Hungarian has taken place from Chuvash. This is justified by supposing that Hungarian has preserved the original *š* of the Chuvash donor language, the borrowing having taken place before the implementation of 'lambdaism' in Chuvash, that is, the change from *š* to *l*. As is evident from the examples, in the absence of old records or any other types of information, Ligeti's assumption of the 'borrowing from Chuvash' is neither provable nor disprovable.

(c) initial *ń-*. In addition to liquids and sibilants, also initial *ń-* presents another controversial issue (Johanson 1998: 105). For example, some Altaicists assume this sound to have existed in P-Altaic and to have developed into *y-* in Common Turkic. Compare the following examples, where, once again, Hungarian lines up with Mongolian, and not with Turkic, from which the word is traditionally claimed to have been borrowed (note that, according to Johanson (ibid.), the Hungarian parallel is a 'possible' L-W):

(6.11) Common Turkic *yāz* 'spring'/Mon. *niray* 'fresh'/Hun. *nyár* (/*ń-*/)
'summer'

The questions of lambdaism and rhotacism, and their interpretation for the purpose of reconstructing the assumed P-Phoneme within Turkic and Altaic are still a debated topic among scholars. For example, according to Janhunen (1996: 241), 'the basic framework is entirely clear, in that it is a question of phonemic split (**s* into *s* vs *z* > *r* and **sh* into *sh* vs **zh* > *l*)' in certain contexts. But there are different opinions, see for example Miller (1991: 311), Tekin (1986) and Róna-Tas (1998: 71–2); compare also Johanson (1998: 104–5) for a review of the debate. Furthermore, again according to Janhunen (1996: 241), lambdaism and rhotacism are a 'phenomenon . . . connected with the internal dialectology of Pre-Proto-Turkic' only, whilst, according to those scholars who support the Altaic theory, this phenomenon was already present in P-Altaic.

Keeping in mind this intricate social and linguistic environment, one can now review the debate revolving around the classification and chronology of the oldest Turkic L-Ws in Hungarian.

6.4.1.2. *The classification and chronology of the loan-words in Hungarian*

The oldest Turkic L-Ws in Hungarian, or at least the majority of them, were originally considered to be derived from Bulgar Turkic languages (mainly Volga Bulgar and P-Chuvash), and were assumed to have entered Hungarian in a period which varies between the 5th (or earlier) and the 7th/9th centuries AD (Gombocz 1912, 1921,1923 and 1960; Ligeti 1961). Indeed, some of the (presumed) borrowed forms present features which appeared at first to be alien to most of the Turkic and other Altaic languages, being instead proper only of Chuvash. In particular, Gombocz (1912) argued that before about 800 AD the Hungarians lived in the southern steppes of Russia, somewhere north of the Caucasus, in the vicinity of the Volga Bulgars, and that this date should be considered the *terminus ante quem* for the borrowing, even though in later works (1921, 1923) the author considered the middle of the 5th century AD more likely. According to Németh (1930/91: 126), the Bulgar Turkic influence on the Hungarians might have started already in the 1st century AD, although the 5th century could be an acceptable date too.

Subsequently, this picture has been called into question by several scholars. For instance, Poppe (1960a), on the basis of a previous study by Poppe (1927), stated that it would be a mistake to consider the Old Turkic elements in Hungarian as borrowed from Bulgar Turkic or P-Chuvash. To use the author's words (1960a: 140):

> The *r*- and *l*- forms are not necessarily Bulgarian in origin, but might have been taken from Hunnic and various languages and dialects at the Pre-Turkic stage

This means that the (oldest) Turkic L-Ws in Hungarian may be much older than it is generally assumed. Similarly, Räsänen (1949: 18–19; 1955), on the basis of parallels containing initial *ń*-, argued that Hungarian contains Bulgar Turkic elements considerably older than traditionally believed. These parallels include the above mentioned *nyár* 'summer' (EWUng[9] II, 1037), *nyál* 'saliva' (EWUng[10] II, 1036) and *nyak* 'neck' (EWUng[11] II, 1034).

Bárczi (1958b: 66, 72) on the other hand, claimed that several loans could have entered the language already at the time when the Hungarians were still living in the Uralic region, or even before (as already proposed by Németh, see Section 2.6.1), although the chronological aspect does not exclude the geographical aspect. In other words, the Hungarian reflexes of the relevant sounds (mainly Hungarian, Chuvash and Mongolian *r* vs Common Turkic *z*) could indicate two equally possible alternatives: (a) the loaning could go back to very old, Pre/Proto-Turkic times; and (b) the loaning could have originated much later, in the 'pre-conquest' times, in which case it would derive from a specific Turkic language: Chuvash.

Ligeti, on several occasions ((ed.) 1943: 45; 1961: 241; 1975a; 1977–9; 1986: 25–6) recognised that some Turkic L-Ws, including the much debated *nyár* and *nyak*, could have been borrowed rather early, in the area of the Uralic homeland. In other words, he admitted that for some of them one may only say that they are 'Altaic'. Nevertheless, Ligeti rejected the overall 'Altaic/Pre-Turkic' interpretation proposed by Poppe in favour of the traditional 'pre-conquest' interpretation. However, the rich documentation from the Altaic languages reported in his works, particularly the comprehensive book of 1986, if taken at face value, curiously does not always support his stated conclusions, as shown in the previous section.

Finally, regarding the question of the chronology of the Turkic L-Ws, one might also recall the discussion of the alleged layer of borrowing into the Ugric community, for which see Section 4.5.3.2.

6.4.1.3. *The 'Mongolian parallels' of the 'Turkic loan-words'*

We have already discussed in Section 6.4.1.1 the issue of the isoglosses shared by Hungarian, Chuvash and Mongolian, and we have shown some examples of Hungarian/Chuvash/Mongolian parallels. We have also seen in Section 2.1.2.3 that an important Hungarian word of supposed Turkic origin has, once again, a close parallel in Mongolian, so that, in reality, one cannot really tell which of the two language groups might have been the source of the borrowing. This word is Turkic *kündü* (Hun. *kündü* ~ *kende*), which has an exact parallel in Mon. *kündü*. Examples of this type are numerous. As Róna-Tas (1988a: 757) puts it:

> an unexpectedly great percentage of the Turkic loanwords in Hungarian has Mongolian parallels

More examples include (from Ligeti 1986: 48; see also 1986: 21): Hun. *alma* vs Mon. *alima* 'apple'; Hun. *búza* vs Mon. *buɣudai* etc. 'wheat'; Hun. *árpa* vs Mon. *arbai* vs Man. *arfa* 'barley'; Hun. *bátor* vs Mon. *baɣatur* vs Man. *baturu* 'courageous' etc. See also the examples (4.52)–(4.54) above. Ligeti (1935) considers these parallels as another of the 'unsolved questions' of the Hungarian/Turkic connection.

6.5 THE CORRELATIONS BETWEEN URALIC AND YUKAGHIR

6.5.1. *The position of Yukaghir*

Yukaghir is a language spoken in north-eastern Siberia by several hundred people. There are competing theories about its status that appear to encompass every possible classification. In most textbooks, Yukaghir is classified as an 'isolate'. Rédei (1999a) argues that the Yukaghir/U parallels are to be interpreted simply and purely as 'borrowed' words from U into Yukaghir. Collinder (1955: XII) claims that 'Yukaghir is **obviously** related to the Uralic languages' (bold is mine). Others, such as Paasonen (1907), Bouda (1940), Pusztay, (1980), Ruhlen (1987: 64) generally agree with this interpretation. But other authors such as Abondolo ((ed.) 1998: 8), are more cautious, speculating only that there might be a genetic relationship:

> The only truly credible candidate for productive, predictive comparison with Uralic is Yukaghir . . . If Uralic is related to Yukaghir, any superficial similarities between the two are unlikely to reflect an old, i.e. genetic, connection. The proof will have to come from analysis which goes much deeper, makes more daring hypotheses, and thereby incurs greater risks.

Examining the evidence, Yukaghir appears to share with some U languages, in particular Samoyed, some lexical, morphological and morpho-syntactic correlations (Collinder 1940, 1955, 1965a; Harms 1977; Sauvageot 1964, 1969; Hegedűs 1988; Audova 1996; Klesment 1996, Pusztay 1980). Collinder (1965a: 30) summarises the evidence as follows:

> The case system of Yukaghir is almost identical with that of Northern Samoyed . . . There are striking common traits in verb derivation . . . Yukaghir has half a hundred words in common with Uralic, in addition to those that might fairly be suspected of being loanwords . . . it is worth noting that all the Fenno-Ugric languages deviate more from Samoyed in their case inflection than Yukaghir does.

However, as with the other U and non-U parallels, there does not appear to have been any analysis to demonstrate that the observed correlations are of statistical significance. So we must add a fourth possibility, namely that the correlations are due in the main to chance resemblances.

Leaving to another chapter the discussion of the morphological similarities, I shall briefly comment here on the lexical similarities.

6.5.2. *The lexical correlations*

The U and Yukaghir lexical similarities identified in the literature include the following terms, quoting from the English translation (for a comprehensive list see Rédei (1999a)):

(6.12) 'mother' (UEW 74; Rédei 1999a: item (8)), 'father' (UEW 78; Rédei 1999a: item (9)), 'uncle' (UEW 34; Rédei 1999a: item (5)), 'sister-in-law' (UEW 135; Rédei 1999a: item (19)), ? 'head/hill' (UEW 365; Rédei 1999a: item (44)), 'intestine' (UEW 483–4; Rédei 1999a: item (82)), 'peel, skin, bark, film' (UEW 184; Rédei 1999a: item (66)), 'to

suck' (UEW 198; Rédei 1999a: item (10)), 'space under [something]'
(UEW 6; Rédei 1999a: item (1)), ? '(domesticated) reindeer' (UEW
387–8; Rédei 1999a: item (46)), 'white fir, silver fir, *abies*' (UEW 327;
Rédei 1999a: item (41)), 'to melt' (UEW 450–1: Rédei 1999a: item
(80)), 'to eat' (UEW 440; Rédei 1999a: item (79)), 'to be, become'
(UEW 243: Rédei 1999a: item (70))[12], etc.

As mentioned, Rédei (1999a: 25f.) argues that the Yukaghir/U parallels
are to be interpreted simply and purely as 'borrowed' words from U directly
into Yukaghir. In particular, in Yukaghir the following strata of borrowing
are supposed to be visible: a U stratum (Samoyed L-Ws); a Ugric/Ob-Ugric/
P-Ostyak stratum; a Samoyed stratum. However, the author himself warns
that one cannot rely on phonological criteria for drawing this classification,
given that one does not know the Yukaghir sound-structure and sound-
developments well enough. The Yukaghir etymologies display 'lautliche
Ähnlichkeit' (1999a: 25), rather than proper correspondences. Therefore,
as the author (1999a: 29) puts it:

> Diese Klassifizierung geschah in erster Linie nicht aufgrund von lautlichen
> Kriterien, sondern eher nach der Verbreitung der Wörter in den Geber-
> sprachen.

Another item of evidence to counter the 'borrowing' interpretation from
U into Yukaghir is provided by the U/Yukaghir parallels which in turn
appear to be shared with the Altaic languages. Rédei himself (1999a: 32)
recognises that this is a problem:

> Ein großes, bis auf weiteres ungelöstes Problem bedeuten die mandschu-
> tungusischen, türkischen und mongolischen Beziehungen der juka-
> girischen Wörter uralischer Herkunft: Von ihnen werden 11 Wörter mit
> empfohlenen mandschu-tungusischen, 10 mit türkischen und 6 mit
> mongolischen Entsprechungen verglichen.

As a matter of fact, how can one claim that the U/Yukaghir lexical
correlations are the result of direct, unidirectional influence from U
(Samoyed in particular) into Yukaghir, if a good number of them are to
be found elsewhere?

Once again, what these data tell us it that it is difficult, if not impossible,
to distinguish between 'borrowed' vs 'inherited' lexical items using the
Comparative Method in this linguistic area.

6.6. THE CORRELATIONS BETWEEN URALIC AND INDO-EUROPEAN

In the next sections I would like to make some general comments on the
topic of the relationship between U and Indo-European, leaving to the next

chapter a detailed discussion of the words of (presumed) Indo-European origin present in the U languages.

6.6.1. *Genuine correlations or accidental look-alikes?*

Most researchers consider the U and Indo-European lexical correlations as the effect of borrowing. However, there are a few researchers, including Nostraticists, who argue in favour of a genetic relationship. For example, Toivonen does not exclude the possibility of a 'Urverwandtschaft '' between the two families while discussing, for example, the F-U etymology for 'honey' (SKES 341): the similarity of F-U and I-E *mete* (for which see Chapter 7) can be considered as a proof of the Indo-European/U genetic relationship, even if this etymology is not present in Samoyed. Campbell's (1990a: 174–5) conclusion to his corpus of possible U and Indo-European tree terms (some of which have been examined above, see examples (6.4) and (6.5)) is as follows:

> While conceivably some of these compared forms are but fortuitously similar, the weight of the aggregate of comparisons is sufficient to support the conclusion that these two language families have a very old historical connection, one which reflects either a genetic affiliation or *Sprachbund* affinities, or perhaps both. The connection may involve diffusion, and indeed, certain of the forms presented here almost certainly involve borrowing . . . On the other hand, at this stage we cannot rule out the possibility that the similarities among some of the tree names explored here may perhaps reflect an old genetic relationship – a common ancestor.

However Ringe (1998), following Oswalt (1970), has applied a mathematical analysis to a sample of reconstructed U and Indo-European etymologies, to see whether they are indicative of chance resemblance or of a true linguistic relationship.[13] Ringe concludes (1998: 187) that:

> sober statistical testing of the relationship can barely establish it even probabilistically.

In his analysis, he compares a corpus of 100 reconstructed Indo-European and F-U words, using Sammallahti's (1988) reconstruction for F-U and his own reconstructions for Indo-European. The author observes that (1998: 183):

> Comparison of languages that are unarguably related generally reveals at least a few word-pairs in which appear two or more sound correspondences that might be significantly frequent

but he is able to find only three such word-pairs in his list. They are: the term for 'to bite': P-I-E *denk^y- vs P-F-U *puri-; the term for 'ice': P-I-E *yeg- vs P-F-U *jäŋi; the term for 'horn': P-I-E *k^{y}ron- vs P-F-U *s^{y}orwa. He observes that these three word-pairs are all problematic for one reason or the other: for example, the pair for 'ice' was introduced explicitly by the author because it seemed to be a good match, and therefore it is a biased datum point.

6.6.2. *The nature of the words of Indo-European origin*

Several authors consider the overall correlations between U and Indo-European as being of equal weight to the overall correlations between U and its eastern neighbouring languages, although some authors are more cautious than others. Manzelli (1993: 474) talks of the Indo-Uralic hypothesis as 'competing' with the Ural-Altaic hypothesis. Vovin (1994: 97) believes that:

> The relationship of Proto-Indo-European and Proto-Uralic is of the same nature, but more remote, than the relationship between English and Russian (see also Vovin 1998)

Korhonen (1989: 46) observes that there are similarities between U and Indo-European which are often interpreted as a sign of original genetic relationship, even though the basic structure of the U languages is closer to that of the Altaic languages and Yukaghir than that of the Indo-European languages. He then states that it will never be possible to establish whether the similarities shared by U with Altaic, Indo-European, Yukaghir, and, possibly, Dravidian are actually the result of genetic relationship or contacts. The author concludes that 'The horizon fades into the mist'. Greenberg (1991: 130) states that:

> I do not believe that there is a special close relationship between Uralic and Altaic, as was widely accepted in the nineteenth century, on typological grounds. In regard to the absence of a special relationship I agree with what I believe to be the general consensus at the present time. There is enough, however, in the way of concrete resemblances, to support the membership of both in the larger Eurasiatic family as I have outlined it here.

However, in my opinion, the evidence does not support setting the U/Indo-European correlations on the same level as the U/Asiatic correlations. Supposing for a moment that all the reported U and non-U lexical correlations are genuine correlations, one can observe some relevant differences regarding the nature and distribution of the identified Indo-European correlations vs the identified Asiatic correlations. For example, unlike the words of (presumed) Asiatic origin, the great majority of the words of (presumed) Indo-European origin belong to the 'cultural' domain, and not to basic Lexicon, with the exceptions to be found in the western U languages (see next chapter). Unlike the words of Asiatic origin, the words of Indo-European origin have a restricted distribution (if they are not totally absent) in branches such as Ob-Ugric and Samoyed, more distant from the European area. Instead, they have a much wider distribution in the western branches, particularly in Finnic and Balto-Finnic. The words of Indo-European origin present in the Finnic branch derive mainly from Germanic and Baltic, whilst those present in more eastern U languages derive mainly from eastern European languages. These general findings remain valid even in the light of the most recent researches in the field, as discussed in the next chapter. Therefore, these Indo-European/U parallels, if genuine, seem to be indicative of contact between single Indo-European languages and single U languages, rather than indicative of a genetic relationship between the two language families.

6.6.3. *On the nature of the morphological similarities*

The view that the Indo-European/U lexical correlations are better interpreted as acquired, and not as inherited features, is confirmed by the – I would dare to say – complete lack of morphological and morpho-syntactic similarities between the two language families. I believe that this is indeed the case, despite the fact that several morphological correlations are widely accepted: the (presumed) P-U Ablative/Locative *-$t(a)$ with P-I-E Ablative *-(V)d (Sweet 1900: 116); the P-U Accusative *-m with P-I-E *-m (notice, however, that P-U *-m is not a proper Accusative ending, see later); the Perfect/Tense suffix *-t with the P-I-E dental Preterite; the P-U Locative *-s with the (originally) P-I-E Oblique ending *-s (according to Orr 1997); the P-U Genitive *-n with *-n of oblique Cases of Indo-European heteroclitic declension (Hegedűs, Michalove & Manaster Ramer (eds) 1997).

I base my judgment on the undeniable relevant fact that the whole morphological and morpho-syntactic structure of the U languages differs enormously from that of Indo-European, as will become evident from Chapter 8. Similarly, the typological distance is equally great, a fact which certainly does have weight in assessing genetic relationship, as argued for by Di Giovine (1997); see also the discussion in Chapter 8. For example, the Indo-European Case system is intimately connected with gender, number, stem/root classes etc., whereby shared (sub-) systems are easily identifiable (for the structure and typology of Indo-European and related questions of reconstruction see, for example: Lehmann (1993); Belardi (1990)). None of this is to be found in U (nor in other Asiatic languages), where, on the contrary, one can observe: (a) the absence of gender, of noun classes, and, to some extent, of number; (b) the difficulty of retrieving and reconstructing shared morphological systems (or parts of systems); and (c) the simple nature of the few shared (primary) Case endings. These topics will be discussed in Chapter 8. Therefore, it may well be that the morphological connections identified in the literature are neither the result of genetic relationship, nor of borrowing, but simply the effect of chance resemblance, particularly in view of the simple, basic nature of the reconstructed Indo-European and U formants.

6.7. CONCLUSION

This chapter has examined the lexical parallels between the U languages and their neighbours. We found that these parallels are extensive. In the reconstructed U lexicon for body-parts and for flora and fauna, for example, each U reconstructed word was found to be associated with 2.2 external languages on average, and only 10% of the reconstructions had no external association.

In a study of the literature, we found little consensus in the classification of these external parallels. For example, although all of the words we examined have P-U reconstructions and are therefore supposedly inherited via the U family tree, we found several competing and often contradictory claims regarding how the words in question might have instead been borrowed.

Examining the words in detail, one finds that the parallels appear to be based on a large variety of meanings and a small number of matching consonants. This suggests that many of these parallels, both within U and outside it, are in fact accidental look-alikes. It does not appear to be possible to identify clearly the parallels that are more than chance resemblances without the appropriate methods of analysis. Even if one were able to do this for some specific words, it is not possible to distinguish between ancient borrowings and inherited words on linguistic grounds (as also shown by Sinor's analysis; see the quotes reported in Section 6.3), because borrowed words quickly tend to become assimilated into the recipient language.

Finally, it is evident that a model based on isoglosses is better suited than a family tree model to account for the intricate correlations observed in the Eurasiatic area, as also remarked by Sinor on several occasions.

7

THE ANTIQUITY OF PROTO-URALIC

*the irregularities present in the Uralic etymological corpus are a
natural consequence of the early dating . . . It is therefore no
wonder that there is hardly a single Proto-Uralic etymon that
would have a perfectly regular representation in every single
Uralic idiom*[1]

Juha Janhunen

It is usually assumed that P-U is between 8000 and 6000 years old.[2] The
purpose of this chapter is to examine the evidence for this assumption. In
order to review the evidence in its best light, I shall operate within the
paradigm, and assume in this chapter that the P-U language family and
community did exist.

It might be assumed that the high degree of irregularity that pervades U
linguistics can be taken as evidence to support the great antiquity of the P-
language. Over such a great span of time, one can easily expect many
irregularities and inconsistencies to creep into the languages. However, it is
more common for researchers to make the connection the other way round,
that is, to explain the high degree of irregularity by the assumed antiquity.
Independent evidence for the antiquity of this family is clearly needed in
order to avoid the obvious circularity.

The assumption of the great antiquity of P-U is not supported by
archaeological or ethnographic data, despite the many attempts made to
associate the P-U community with this or that particular material culture
(see a review in Carpelan (2000)). Neither are there old records. The
assumption is based instead on two kinds of evidence: (a) the reconstruction
of several tree-names, according to the method of Palaeo-linguistics; and (b)
the presence in the U languages of words of Indo-European origin, which
are supposed to be very old.

As we shall see in this chapter, the palaeo-linguistic evidence amounts to
five reconstructed words, and the evidence from early Indo-European
borrowings amounts to between five and fifteen words, depending on the
interpretation. Furthermore, there are problems with all these words. For
example, most of them have questionable reconstructions, or have parallels
outside the U and Indo-European areas.

In the first paragraph, I shall discuss the palaeo-linguistic evidence, that is,
the reconstructed tree-names; in the second paragraph, I shall examine the
evidence of the Indo-European Loan-words. Finally, I shall touch upon the

question of the supposed existence of a U substratum, which, if shown to be true, could constitute evidence in favour of the validity and the antiquity of the U family.

7.1. RECONSTRUCTED TREE-NAMES AND THE CHRONOLOGY OF PROTO-URALIC

The points (a)-(c) below summarise the 'palaeo-linguistic evidence' on the basis of which scholars have come to the conclusion that P-U is very old. This evidence has also been used to identify one of the many proposed U homelands, namely the more traditional one, located in the region of the Ural mountains. The relevant data have been put forward mainly by Hajdú (1964, 1966, 1969b, 1975a, 1975b, 1975c; Hajdú & Domokos 1978: 45–60; for Hajdú's homeland theory see also Koivulehto 1994: 143).

(a) the P-U community knew the name of the following trees:

(7.1) 'spruce, fir, *picea excelsa*': Finn. *kuusi* < P-U **kuse* ~ **kose* (UEW 222); see example (4.4)

(7.2) 'Siberian pine, *pinus cembra* ': Vot. *susi̯-pu* '*juniperus communis*'/Zyr. *sus* < P-U **soks3* (**saks3*, **sęks3*) (UEW 445; for a discussion of this etymology see Section 4.4.5.2)

(7.3) 'white fir, Siberian fir, silver fir, *abies*, etc.': Che. *nŭlγo*/Vot. *ńi̯l-pu*/ Zyr. *ńi̯l* /Ost. *ńălki̯*/Vog. *ńol* /Sam. Se. *njulg* etc. < P-U **ńulk3* (UEW 327)

(7.4) 'Siberian larch, *larix sibirica*': Zyr. *ńia*/Ost. *näŋk* /Vog. *ńik* < F-U **näŋ3* (UEW 302)

(7.5) 'elm, *ulmus*': Finn. *salava* 'crack willow, *salix fragilis*'/Hun. *szil* 'elm'/ Mor. *śel'ej* 'elm'/Che. *šol* 'elm' < F-U **śala* (UEW 458). Compare Latin *salix*

(b) the ancient distribution of all these trees, as established through pollen analysis, was as follows:
(1) all of them, with the exclusion of the 'elm', have always been part of the Siberian flora, as the names themselves clearly indicate (note, however that the term for 'Siberian larch' is missing in the Samoyed languages);
(2) the 'spruce' spread during the Early Holocene over the Urals up to the White Sea;
(3) the 'Siberian pine' and 'Siberian fir' appeared in Europe in the Middle Holocene (6000–500 BC), but their distribution remained limited to the area nearby the Urals;

(4) the 'Siberian larch', already widespread in Siberia, spread from the Urals toward the West only around 500 BC;

(5) the elm is of western origin, probably as old as the early Holocene, but started to spread toward the East, to reach and meet the conifer forest on the west side of the Urals, only in the Middle Holocene.

This picture suggests that the original U homeland was located where all these trees were present at the same time, which is roughly the area which includes the Middle Urals, with stretches into the North Urals, and the rivers Ob and Petchora. Regarding chronology, these data suggest that P-U must have been spoken after the period when the two types of pine and the spruce had already appeared in Europe. This period is identified with the Middle Holocene, the *terminus post quem* being 6000 BC.

(c) Because the F-U languages, but not Samoyed, have a term for 'elm' in their Lexicon the F-U period is held to have begun after the elm started to spread from its western, original environment to reach the Siberian forests on their western edges. The spreading of the elm in turn is assumed to have taken place between 6000 and 4000 BC (Hajdú 1969b; Campbell[3] 1997: 841). A later date has been suggested by Joki (1973: 330) on the basis of F-U terms for 'honey-bee' and 'honey', which are of Indo-European origin (see below). Apiculture is believed to have begun in eastern Europe around 2500/2000 BC. This could be, theoretically, a *terminus post quem*, even though the simple existence of words to indicate 'bee' and 'honey' does not necessarily imply the existence of proper apiculture, as also remarked by Joki.

The palaeo-linguistic evidence summarised in the points (a)–(c) above meets with several problems, without taking into account the fact that Palaeo-linguistics is not a reliable method of analysis (see, for example, E. Itkonen 1968a; Renfrew 1987). To start with, if this method were to be applied in an unbiased and consistent way, one should consider that three out of the five tree-names listed above have been associated in the literature with non-U languages. The same is true for several animal terms often used for the same purpose, such as the term for '*tetrao bonasia*, partridge' (Hajdú & Domokos 1978: 48). Indeed, most of the U flora and fauna terms refer to plants and animals that are found throughout a wide Eurasiatic area, some of them being typical of the Siberian flora, as indicated by the names themselves.

Secondly, the U languages are rather rich in names meaning 'pine/spruce/tree', etc., as shown in Figure 6.2 and Table 6.2 above. These 'alternative' names do not seem to attract much attention for the purpose of identifying the U *Urheimat* and related chronology, as also remarked by Hajdú & Domokos (1978: 54). This is the case, for example, for the following reconstructed items: P-U **juwȝ* 'pine tree, *pinus silvestris*' (UEW 107), which is only present in Vogul, Ostyak and Samoyed within U, although it has parallels in Turkic and Tungusic (according to some scholars); P-F-P *pečä ~ *penčä, which is present only in the Finno-Permian languages, compare Finn. *petäjä 'pinus silvestris'* (UEW 727); and the P-F-U term for 'spruce', present only in Hungarian (*fenyő*), Cheremis and Zyrian (UEW 416).

Thirdly, there is a high degree of variation, confusion and contamination in sound, meaning and/or both associated with most of the U (and non-U) terms indicating plants, as illustrated in Sections 6.2.1 and 6.2.2 above. This can make it quite difficult to individuate the exact plant referred to by these terms. For example, Finn. *salava* (example (7.5)) means '(crack) willow' and not 'elm', so that one 'must assume' that the current meaning is a 'secondary' meaning, as is assumed for example in UEW. In fact, the term *salava* has been considered by other sources as being of Germanic origin, and it has been connected to Finn. *halava* 'bay willow, *salix pentandra*', which in turn is believed to be of Baltic origin[4] (Suhonen 1989; SSA I,132). On the other hand, the proper term for 'elm' in Finnish is a different, but similar word: *jalava* (SSA I, 234 'Ulme'). This term, which cannot be derived from *$*šala$* because of the initial *j-*, seems to be an isolate (Räsänen 1955: 27).

Fourthly, one should assume not only that the P-U community and the other Asiatic P-communities shared the same, vast *habitat*, but also that all these communities are more or less equally ancient. However, several scholars, including Janhunen (1999: 31), claim that the Altaic languages are relatively young, mainly because the individual branches show very little diversity.[5] As Csillaghy[6] (1998) puts it, despite wanting to accept the idea of a genetic relationship and/or of long standing, close contacts between U and Altaic people, there remains still one 'unsolvable' obstacle: P-U goes back at least 6000 years, whilst P-Altaic cannot be traced back more than 2000 years, so that a relationship among relatives one of which is at least 4000 years older is quite unlikely. How can this (apparent?) contradiction be solved?

Apart from this, there is no guarantee that the reconstructed flora and fauna designations unequivocally indicated the very same plants and animals they refer to nowadays. But, even if this were the case, it does not necessarily follow that the people living in that area at that time spoke (already) a P-U language. Besides, the hunter-gatherer people are nomads, as is shown by the nomadic way of life of the hunter-gatherers who still live today in the Arctic/sub-Arctic zones. Therefore, the search for a *Urheimat* – if it is interpreted in the traditional terms – does not appear to make much sense in this context. Indeed, whilst some scholars believe that there was a U homeland, although they may disagree about its exact location (see Koivulehto 1999; Kallio 1999: 239), some others argue that the U homeland is unknown (Abondolo (ed.) 1998: 1; Cavalli-Sforza 1996: 194; Janhunen[7] 1999: 34–5), or that the very search for 'a' homeland is a hopeless activity, with no scientific foundation[8] (Korhonen 1993: 57).

To conclude this section, I would like to highlight that the palaeo-linguistic evidence brought forward to support the thesis of the great antiquity of U is strictly connected to, actually the very same as, the palaeo-linguistic evidence brought forward to individuate the P-U *Urheimat*, whose existence has been dismissed by several scholars.

7.2. INDO-EUROPEAN LOAN-WORDS AND THE CHRONOLOGY OF PROTO-URALIC

It is received wisdom that P-U contains loan-words (L-W) of Indo-European origin which are very old. More precisely, in the Lexicon belonging to the P-U period proper there are L-Ws which can be traced back to the P-Indo-European period, whilst in the Lexicon of the P-F-U period there are L-Ws which can be traced back to the P-Indo-Iranian (P-I-I) period, and so on. This means that:

• P-U must be at least as old as P-Indo-European, if not older;
• the conventional, binary stratification of the U family, established on the basis of internal evidence, receives further support from the fact that it matches the conventional, binary stratification of Indo-European.

However, on a closer examination of the relevant data and methods of analysis, these beliefs turn out to be difficult to maintain, because of the following reasons.

Firstly, the methods of historical linguistics cannot tell us much about 'absolute chronology', and this holds true also for Indo-European (Dixon 1997: 48–9; Ross 1996; Nichols 1992).

Secondly, no clear phonological criteria have been identified so far which would allow us to determine the exact donor language and the exact period of the borrowing from Indo-European into the U linguistic context. As Häkkinen[9] (1984a: 307) puts it:

it has recently begun to appear that in determining the period of borrowing and the relative ages of loans, the use of the sound and distribution criteria has been to some extent inconsistent

Indeed, the antiquity of the borrowed Indo-European word is usually established on the basis of its 'conventional' distribution within U, rather than on the basis of phonological criteria. In other words, a borrowed word is classified as belonging to the P-Indo-European layer of borrowing if it is present in all the branches of U, including Samoyed, that is, if it is present in P-U. It is classified as belonging to the P-Indo-Iranian layer if it is present in the F-U languages, but not in Samoyed, and so on. It is evident therefore that the whole matter of the great antiquity of P-U and its conventional stratification is connected with the question of the great antiquity of the

Indo-European L-Ws and their conventional stratification/classification in a rather circular way. For example, Trask (1996: 357), presumably unaware of the circularities intrinsic in this area, cross-checks some intermediate Indo-European nodes by making reference to some intermediate U nodes. He claims, correctly, that among the Indo-European L-Ws in U there is in Finnish *porsas* 'pig' and, in the distantly related Votyak, *pars*. He further claims that, judging from their phonological shape, these words must have been borrowed not from 'P-I-E *porkos*' but from 'P-I-I *parsa*'. Then the author states that:

> Uralic specialists **believe** they [Finnic and Votyak] must have separated from their common ancestor no later then 1500 BC . . . that means that Indo-Iranian must already have been in existence before 1500 BC, complete with its distinctive phonological developments [bold is mine]

Thirdly, even accepting and operating within this conventional framework, the evidence does not appear to support the thesis that borrowing from Indo-European took place already during the P-U period. In fact, no safe occurrences of Indo-European L-Ws have been identified in the Samoyedic branch, as it would be demanded by the model. As Joki (1973: 362–3, 373) puts it:[10]

- no single safe L-W from the P-Indo-European times can be found in the common P-U language;
- even when the Indo-European, particularly the Indo-Iranian origin of the loaning can be established, there are sometimes still difficulties in establishing the exact source and time of the borrowing;
- the oldest contacts with the U people can be traced back to the P-Iranian period, given that even the Indo-Iranian elements present in Samoyed derive from Iranian forms.

Similarly, Korenchy (1972: 42 f.) argues that it is difficult to establish phonological criteria on the basis of which one could distinguish the various layers of borrowing. This is also due to the fact that the P-Indo-European, P-Indo-Iranian and the P-Iranian periods are themselves difficult to delimit. In a later paper (1988: 673), after a careful examination of the phonological shape of the relevant words (mostly derived from Joki's (1973) corpus), the author states the following:

> Die Finnougrier aber – und das ist auch geographisch akzeptabel – haben ihre Lehnwörter aus der Sprache der alanischen Völkerschaften entlehnt. . . . Mit Hilfe der Arealhypothese können möglicherweise Wörter rekonstruiert werden, die man als 'alanisch' bezeichnen kann.

Korenchy also points out that there are just a few Iranian L-Ws in the oldest layers of U, with only 3 in Samoyed and 9 in the F-U layer, whilst their number increases in the single languages: 18 in Mordvin and 30 in

Hungarian, all of which are of Alanic origin. There are only 2 Iranian L-Ws in Ostyak and 4 in Vogul, and there seems to be no safe Iranian L-Ws in Balto-Finnic.

The view that no single L-W of Indo-European origin can safely be traced back to the common P-U period is shared by other Finnish scholars, such as Hakulinen (1979: 350).

In what follows, I shall illustrate the above outlined picture with a sample of the relevant data.

7.2.1. *The Proto-Indo-European period*

It is claimed that in U there are Indo-European L-Ws which are to be traced back to the P-Indo-European period because they are present also in Samoyed, that is, at the P-U stage. However, on a closer investigation, it turns out that the Indo-European L-Ws present in all the branches of U, including Samoyed, number just a few (Rédei 1986: 40–3; items (1)–(7)). Furthermore, and more seriously, their Indo-European origin is difficult to prove, given that similar words are present also in other, non-U languages, such as Altaic and Yukaghir. These words are (quoting from Finnish): *nimi* 'name'; *vesi* 'water'; *suoni* 'sinew, tendon'; *tuo-da* 'to bring, give'; *vaski* 'any metal/? copper'[11]; *myy-* 'to sell'; *kala* 'fish'; Hun. *mos* 'to wash'. Five of these words (*nimi, vesi, tuo-, vaski, kala*) are recognised cases of *Wanderwörter*.

7.2.2. *The Proto-Indo-Iranian period*

It is claimed that in U there are Indo-European L-Ws which are to be traced back to the P-Indo-Iranian period -18 according to Rédei (1986: 43–9; items (8)–(25)), because they are present in at least one Finnic and one Ugric language, but not in Samoyed. However, this is an idealistic picture, as evident from the two facts reported below:

(i) there are many L-Ws which sound-wise look rather archaic, possibly of Indo-Iranian nature, but whose distribution is quite restricted, in contradiction with the predictions of the model. The most-known examples are (quoting from Finnish): *mesi* 'honey', *mehi-läinen* 'bee', *porsas* 'pork, pig', *vasa* 'elk-calf', *marras* ~ *martaan* 'dead', *jyvä* 'grain', *sata* '100', *vasara* 'hammer', *taivas* 'sky', *varsa* 'foal, colt', *susi* 'wolf', *tosi* 'truth', *ora* 'thorn', *orpo* 'orphan', *osa* 'tail, part', *lapa* 'shoulder', *muru* 'crumb', *muurain* 'cloudberry', *oja* 'ditch', etc. For example, the distribution of *vasara* is limited to Balto-Finnic, Lapp and Mordvin (UEW 815), that of *vasa* is limited to Balto-Finnic. The borrowed words *porsas* and *jyvä* (UEW 633) are missing altogether in the Ugric languages.

Häkkinen (1990: 237) observes that, in the analysis of the old Indo-European words, one can clearly observe the 'striving/attempt' ('pyrkimys') to date as belonging to the F-U node those L-Ws whose distribution is not F-U, but is actually more restricted. Furthermore, some of the above-listed words, such as *jyvä*, *marras* and *porsas*, are classified by some authors as cases of 'multiple borrowing' (see below and Rédei (1986: 52 f.)).

(ii) the specific sound marks and sound-changes available for making such a subtle distinction between P-Indo-European and P-Indo-Iranian L-Ws are only two. Therefore, not only is it very difficult to distinguish between these two layers of borrowing, but one cannot use these L-Ws to support the existence of the two, supposedly different P-U and P-F-U nodes. The relevant sound-changes are (from Korenchy 1972):

(7.7) the P-I-E vowels **e/*o /*a* of first syllable normally merge into **a* in both P-Indo-Iranian and P-F-U, as shown in Finn. *vasa* < F-V **vasa* 'calf' (Joki 1973: 338, item (197)) or, according to other interpreta- tions < **wasa* (Rédei 1986: 63, item (61) and UEW 814) < P-I-I **vasa- ka* < P-I-E **u̯et-es-* 'year, annual' (IEW 1175). Compare Old. Ind. *vatsá-* 'calf';

(7.8) the P-I-E palatals change in both P-Indo-Iranian and P-F-U into sibilants, as shown in Finn. *porsas* '(young) pig, pork' < P-F-P **porśas* ~ **porćas* < P-I-I **porśos* (Joki 1973: 303, item (117); Rédei 1986: 56, item (42) and UEW 736) < P-I-E **pork'os* (IEW 841).

Rédei (1986: 43–9) divides his 18 P-F-U etymologies, borrowed from P-Indo-European and/or P-Indo-Iranian into two sub-groups on the basis of the above-listed phonological criteria. Group (1), the oldest layer, consists of those words – 12 – which have preserved the P-Indo-European trio **e*, **o*, **a*, as well as the P-Indo-European palatals. Group (2), a more recent layer, consists of those words – 6 – in which the above-mentioned sound-changes have taken place, that is: the vowels have merged into *a* and the palatals have changed into sibilants: **k'*, **k'h*, **g'*, **g'h* ⟶ respectively *ś*, *śh*, *ź*, *źh*.

However, once again, the situation is not a clear-cut one. For example, in the first sub-group (or in the second?) there are words such as Finn. *mehi-* (*läinen*) 'bee' < F-U **mekše-* (Mor. E. *mekš* / Vot. *muš* etc. / San. *mákṣā-* etc.; Rédei (1986: 45, item (13) and UEW 271), in which the consonantism and the vocalism contradict each other. In fact, the P-Indo-European vocalism has been preserved, so that, from that point of view, the word should be classified as archaic, but the consonantism has changed into the expected sibilants, therefore the word should be also classified as a younger loaning. The same is true for the term indicating 'pork, (young) pig' mentioned above (example (7.8)), for which compare the other U parallels: Zyr. *porś* / ? Vot. *parś* / Mor. E. *purcos* (UEW 736). Here, not only do the vocalism and consonantism contradict each other, but the consonantism itself is inconsistent, as shown by the Mordvin parallel, which is so reminiscent of Lat. *porcus*.[12]

In addition to these difficulties, there is the problem that similar 'P-Indo-Iranian/P-F-U' parallels are also to be found in other language groups. Compare for example: F-U *kota* 'hut' (Rédei 1986: 45, item (12)), which has parallels spread all over Eurasia and India (UEW 190); F-U *aja-* 'to drive, chase, travel', which has been associated with Altaic and Indo-European at the same time (Rédei 1986: 43, item (8); Joki 1973: 247, item (2)), and several others. Other etymologies, like F-U *arwa* 'value, price' (Rédei 1986: 43, item (9)) and F-U *mete* 'honey' (Rédei 1986: 45, item (14)), present all sorts of irregularities, and are instances of 'multiple borrowing'.

Regarding the second group, five of the six words listed by Rédei are classified as belonging to the P-Iranian layer of borrowing by Korenchy (1972).

However, the major difficulty in the attempt to identify L-Ws of P-Indo-European nature lies in the following fact: even the sound-changes above – the merging of P-Indo-European vowel trio and the change of P-Indo-European palatals into sibilants,[13] are not that reliable after all for the purpose of identifying the exact period of borrowing. In fact, as remarked by Korenchy (1972: 42), the change I-E *s > P-Ira. *h* probably occurred quite late, that is, P-I-E *s was preserved for a while also in P-Iranian. Therefore, if we find *ś* or *s* in P-F-U, and *s* or *h* in Iranian (instead of P-I-E *k'* or *s*), we cannot assume that we are necessarily dealing with a P-Indo-Iranian L-W: it could just as well be a P-Iranian L-W.

7.2.3. *Rédei's conclusion*

The overall situation can be summarised with the concluding comments made by Rédei to his work (1986). The author, being aware of the difficulties and contradictions outlined in the previous sections, recognises that the classification of the great majority of the Indo-European L-Ws present in the U languages can only be made on the basis of distributional criteria, and not on the basis of phonological criteria, because (1986: 25):

Es kann nämlich kein lautliches Kriterium festgestellt werden

7.3. BALTIC AND GERMANIC LOAN-WORDS IN THE FINNIC LANGUAGES

A detailed description of the nature, antiquity and the whereabouts of the Baltic and Germanic L-Ws in the Finnic languages, particularly Balto-Finnic, for which there is an extended literature, is outside the scope of this work (see an overview in Häkkinen 1996: 142–66). Nevertheless it is worth presenting an essential outline of the topic, just to illustrate how in most cases there are great difficulties in identifying the timing and the exact origin of the borrowing even within this restricted, highly investigated field. The reality is that in this, as in other areas of Uralic studies, opinions, assumptions, conclusions may vary greatly, and often contradict each other.

7.3.1. *The Baltic loan-words*

Sammallahti (1977, 1984) claims that the complex borrowing situation from the Baltic languages into Balto-Finnic, Lapp and Finno-Volgaic is best explicable if one assumes that the Baltic and pre-(Balto)-Finnic speakers constituted 'mixed' groups living in the same area, both of which were in more or less direct contact with their neighbours, the pre-Lapp speakers.

Recently, there has been an attempt by linguists (for example Sammallahti 1984), and archaeologists to connect the beginning of the Balto-Finnic/ Baltic contacts with the spreading of the so-called *vasara-kirves* ('battle-axe'[14]) culture in the area of the Baltic Sea, generally dated around 2500–2000 BC (but around 3200–2350 BC according to Carpelan 1999). However, such an estimate appears to be too old from the point of view of the sound-shape of the borrowed words, given that at least the majority of them seem to go back to P-Baltic, which is in turn considered to have started later than 2500–2000 BC. This means that the L-Ws which seem to reflect the 'battle-axe' culture would not be (yet) of Baltic origin, but of pre-Baltic or pre-Germanic origin, a finding which would fit in with the diffusion of the 'battle-axe' culture in a vast European area (including south Scandinavia, the north part of Middle Europe, south-western Finland and Estonia). Among the etymologies which are considered examples of unclear Baltic and/or Germanic origin, being quite archaic sound-wise, but very restricted in distribution, one can quote Finn *susi* 'wolf' and *tosi* 'true' (Koivulehto 1983a, 1983b, 1984; Korhonen 1976). This kind of pre-Baltic/pre-Germanic L-W is supposed to indicate, according to Koivulehto, that they are to be traced back directly to (late) P-Indo-European. The author argues that, in the absence of archaeological evidence, there is no reason not to connect the spreading of the still-uniform 'battle-axe' culture with the spreading of the still-uniform P-Indo-European language. In other words, the bearers of the battle-axe culture must have spoken a P-Indo-European dialect, and not a P-Baltic one, as claimed mainly by archaeologists (see, for example, Moora 1956). This very uniform P-Indo-European dialect is supposed to have been the donor language of the pre-Baltic/pre-Germanic L-Ws. Korhonen (1981: 32–4) has tried to match the contradicting archaeological and linguistic evidence, pushing the estimated date of the Finnic/Baltic contacts as far back as possible, around 1800–1500 BC. Opinions on this matter remain divided (see Sammallahti 1995: 149; Häkkinen 1996: 148–52; Kallio 1998).

Among the words of Baltic origin there are terms referring to kinship, body-parts, flora/fauna and natural environment, and terms referring to nationality. Here are just some examples, quoting from Finnish: *morsian* 'bride', *nepaa* 'cousin', *seura*, 'company/society', *heimo* 'tribe', *sisar* 'sister', *tytär/tyttö* 'daughter, girl', *hammas* 'tooth', *kaula* 'neck', *napa* 'navel', *reisi* 'thigh', *ankerias* 'eel', *harakka* 'magpie', *hirvi* 'elk', *härkä* 'ox', *lohi* 'salmon', *vuohi* 'goat', *heinä* 'hay', *herne* 'pea', *kuuro* 'shower', *lahti* 'bay'[15] (Posti 1977: 267–8), *meri* 'sea' (Kalima 1936: 137–8); *järvi* 'lake', *harmaa* 'grey', *virta* 'stream', *malo* 'opening/shore', *salo* 'wilds, a big forest, backwoods' (of unknown origin, according to some sources; see below and Suhonen 1984, 1988). The Baltic origin of these words is confirmed by the SSA dictionary, but see Ariste (1981a), who argues that most of the so-called Baltic L-Ws, such as *sisar* and *tyttö,* are in reality from old *satəm* dialects of Indo-European.

Note however, as pointed out by Kulonen (1999: 242), that the male kinship terms parallel to the female terms listed above do not share the same Baltic origin. For example, the term for 'boy, youngster', corresponding to *tytär/tyttö* 'daughter, girl', is considered to be of F-U origin; compare Hun. *fi, fiú* and Finn *poika* (UEW 390; SKES 590–1). The term for 'brother', Finn. *veli,* corresponding to *sisar* 'sister', is considered to be of very uncertain origin (the etymology is written in Italics in UEW 567, whilst no origin is indicated in SKES 1691). The term for 'groom', that is Finn. *sulhanen,* corresponding to *morsian* 'bride', has an uncertain etymology according to SKES[16] 1100–1. The same is true for Finn. *mies* 'man, husband', parallel to *nainen* 'woman, wife' (UEW 867 and SSA II, 166). In other words, the Finnish terms *veli, sulhanen* and *mies,* which are only Balto-Finnic in distribution, appear to be of unknown origin. To this list one can add words from the field of body-parts: *hiki* 'sweat', *huuli* 'lip', *koipi* 'leg, shank', *kuve* 'loins, side, flank', *kylki* 'side, flank', *liha* 'meat, flesh', *niska* 'back (nape) of the neck', *nenä* 'nose'. According to Ariste (1971: 255) these words are probably derived from unidentified languages spoken in the area before the arrival of the Balto-Finnic people (for more examples of Finnish words of unknown origin see Chapter 9).

7.3.2. *The Germanic loan-words*

The Germanic/Finnic contacts and related L-Ws have been generally considered to be of later origin than the Baltic/Finnic L-Ws (see for example Hakulinen 1979: 356–7). This view is based on the assumption that the Baltic, but not the Germanic L-Ws, have undergone the sound-changes typical of P-Balto-Finnic. In particular, it has long been claimed, since Collinder's works (1941), that the contacts between the Finnic and the Germanic people have been relatively recent in historical times. According to Collinder, these contacts could not have started prior to the first century BC. According to other researchers, such as Fromm (1957/8), Raun (1958) and Ariste (1981b), these contacts and therefore the penetration of the German L-Ws into the Finnic languages started during the first century AD, when the Germanic tribes settled along the mouth of the river Vistula and in present-day Estonia. This estimate has been confirmed by Rot (1988), who claims that 'four strata' of L-Ws entered the Finnic languages between the first century BC and the fourth century AD.

This traditional view has recently been challenged by Koivulehto (1980, 1981, 1984), whose underlying argument is that the earliest contacts between Finnic and Germanic tribes took place between 1500 and 500 BC, that is during the Nordic Bronze Age. In fact, according to Koivulehto (1981: 192 f., 1992/3), at least a sub-set of the oldest Germanic L-Ws seem to go back to P-Balto-Finnic, given that they presuppose the level of reconstruction pertinent to this stage (see also Joki 1988: 588). However, a definitive assessment of these L-Ws is difficult to achieve, once again because of the absence of sufficient, relevant phonological criteria. As a matter of fact, even the (First) Germanic Sound Shift, which could be a relevant, decisive criteria in this context, cannot be of much help, because the Finnic sound-changes which can be identified in connection with this Germanic feature, in most cases lack an exact correspondence in Balto-Finnic. Therefore, it is impossible to answer the still-debated question of whether a Germanic L-W has entered the target language before or after the time of the Germanic Sound Shift. This is because, if the L-W had originated after it, due to the tendency characteristic of foreign sounds to be assimilated into the target language (for which see discussion in the previous chapter) the borrowed word would have undergone those sound-substitutions which would have removed any trace of these typical Germanic sounds. For example, the Finnish word *pelto* 'field', considered to be one of the oldest Germanic L-Ws, can be explained as borrowed either from Germ. *pelto-*, before the Sound Shift, or from Germ. *felþa-*, after the Sound Shift. In this last case, the Finns, being unable to pronounce the two fricatives, would have substituted them with *p-* and *-t-* respectively, at the very time of borrowing (see in this regard Koivulehto 1983b: 111; Häkkinen 1990: 245–53).

Despite internal disagreements about the chronology of the borrowing, it is generally assumed that the Germanic/Balto-Finnic contacts were rather intense, to the point that Posti (1953), followed by Koivulehto (1984), claims that all the observed P-Late-Balto-Finnic changes, including consonant gradation, were caused by a Germanic Superstratum. More precisely, according to the author, consonant gradation was caused by the influence of Verner's Law. However, there appear to be inconsistencies with this analysis. For example, several sound-changes attributed to the influence of the Germanic Superstratum, can equally well be explained as independent, natural sound-developments, such as the change *$*\check{s} > h$* (Finn. *hiiri* 'mouse' < F-U *$*\check{s}i\eta e\text{-}re$* UEW 500). Furthermore, the Germanic Sound Shift has recently been dated as more recent than previously assumed, at the interface between the Bronze Age and the Iron Age (Schrodt 1976: 59–72 ; Koivulehto 1984: 201–2). To avoid the timing contradiction, Koivulehto & Vennemann (1996) have suggested that Posti's explanation of the consonant gradation improves if one assumes that the Sound Shift had not yet been implemented in the superstratal language. This means that consonant gradation should only be considered as arising during the Bronze Age, whilst the other sound-changes supposedly caused by the Germanic Superstratum should be considered as later, independent developments, going back to the Iron Age.

In addition to the chronological problems, which are of relevance here (and for which see also Kylstra et al. 1991–6), one may also notice that any theory of superstratum or of substratum within the U linguistic area meets with difficulties of social character. The Finnic people were (and still are) a small number, scattered over a vast territory, so that it is hard to imagine that there were the right conditions for bilingualism to arise, which is necessary for the implementation of interferences of this type.

The majority of the Germanic L-Ws refer to cultural objects and concepts, objects of everyday life, agriculture and institutions, as shown by the following Finnish examples: *kana* 'hen', *rauta* 'iron', *kulta* 'gold', *kansa* 'people', *kaura* 'oats', *aura* 'plough', *leipä* 'bread', *humala* 'hop, drunkenness, inebriation', *ruis* 'rye', *valta* 'power', *kuningas* 'king', *ruhtinas* 'prince'. Among the words in the semantic field of body-parts, one can quote: *hartia* 'shoulder', *hipiä* 'complexion', *otsa* 'forehead', *kalvo* 'membrane', *lantio* 'pelvis', *maha* 'stomach, belly', *nahka* 'skin (leather)'. To this list, one must add *äiti* 'mother', and the conjunction *ja* 'and'.

7.4. KOIVULEHTO'S INTERPRETATION OF THE INDO-EUROPEAN LOAN-WORDS

In recent research, Koivulehto has argued that the Indo-European L-Ws present in the U languages are much older than has previously been assumed. More precisely, many of the L-Ws of Indo-European origin, present mainly in Finnish and the other Finnic languages, but also in some other U languages, are to be traced back to the P-Indo-European phase (see also Anttila 1999/2000 for the same opinion). Koivulehto supports his analysis by arguing that certain P-U reconstructed sounds are the reflex of certain Indo-European reconstructed sounds typical of the P-Indo-European phase. These sound correspondences are supposed to be testimony of the very old age of the Indo-European/U contacts, and therefore, in turn, of the very old age of P-U. Koivulehto's analysis contrasts with the analysis of Joki, Rédei and Korenchy reported in the previous sections. In fact, these researchers concluded that the evidence seems to indicate not the P-Indo-European phase, but at least the P-Indo-Iranian phase, if not the Late Iranian phase, as the source of the oldest Indo-

European L-Ws. It is worth therefore taking a closer look at Koivulehto's data and argumentations.

7.4.1. *The Proto-Uralic segment 'x' and the Proto-Indo-European laryngeals*

According to Koivulehto (1991: 19 f.; 101 f.), among the relevant sound-correspondences suitable for identifying the oldest Indo-European L-Ws is the correspondence of the Indo-European laryngeals with the U consonantal segment x, as introduced by Janhunen (1981a) and adopted by Sammallahti (1988), for which see discussion in Section 4.4.5.1. More precisely, in the oldest Indo-European L-Ws the P-Indo-European laryngeals are held to have been substituted in P-U with the segment x (and occasionally with *k) in internal position, and with *k in initial position. As examples of substitution with the segment x (of which there are six in total[17]), consider the following (reconstructions according to Koivulehto, whose transcription is also used):

(7.9) P-U *$puxi$ (*$poxi/pVxI$[18]) 'wood, tree' vs P-I-E *b^huH- ~ *b^howH- 'to grow, flourish' (traditionally *$b^heu\partial$- ~ *$b^h\bar{u}$-; IEW 146 ff.). Compare Finn. *puu* 'tree'/Gre. φυή 'nature, character, etc.'/Got. *bagms* etc. (1991: 56 f., item (11); see also examples (4.17) and (6.4))

(7.10) P-U *$tuxli$ 'wind, mood, etc.' vs P-I-E *d^huH-li 'to spray, swirl, blow, smoke, smog, steam, etc.' (traditionally *$d^h\bar{u}$-li-[19]; IEW 261). Compare Finn. *tuuli* 'wind'/Lat. *$f\bar{u}li$- (> *f\bar{u}l\bar{\imath}go* 'soot') and *f\bar{u}mus* / Lit. *d\bar{u}lis* 'fog' (1991: 65–6; item (14)). Note that the etymology cannot be safely classified as U, given that the supposed Hungarian and Samoyed equivalents mean 'feather/wing' (see also Janhunen 1981a: 241, item (85)).

Koivulehto's analysis, however rigorous, in my personal opinion cannot be accepted, for two basic reasons. Firstly, it relies on a sound, the P-U consonantal segment x, whose phonetic/phonological nature is unclear – it was called x because its nature is 'unknown' – although the author believes that it could be identified with the traditional γ. Compare also Viitso (1992: 161), who expresses a similar point of view to mine. In addition, there is the problem of the controversial status of the 'laryngeal theory', due to the difficulty of finding evidence for the laryngeals and/or defining their precise nature (see Belardi 1958: 185; Cipriano[20] 1988: 124; Lehmann 1993: 107–10; Bammesberger (ed.) 1988; Vennemann (ed.) 1989). Therefore, one runs the risk of comparing two 'cover symbols'. Second, as Koivulehto himself points out (1991: 105–16), there are six L-Ws which look rather archaic, judging from certain sound-substitutions, but for which no laryngeal reflex (in initial position, before vowel) can be found, as in the following example:

(7.11) P-F-U *aja- 'to drive, guide' vs P-I-E *ag'-el o- (IEW 4); the substitution of -g'- with -j- seems to point to a very old L-W[21] (1991: 105–
6, item (1)). Compare Finn. aja-/Old Ind. ájati 'he drives'

Also words such as Finn. orpo 'orphan' and Finn. osa 'part', which were
by Rédei classified as L-Ws (probably) from the Indo-Iranian period (see
above Section 7.2.2), are supposed to belong to this older layer of borrowing
(Koivulehto 1991: 106, item (3); and 107, item (4) respectively): that is, they
are supposed to be very old L-Ws containing no reflexes of laryngeals in
initial position. Koivulehto believes that the absence of the expected reflex
('den "fehlenden" Laryngalreflex im Anlaut' (1991: 109)) may be explained
by assuming an innovative, probably central or western Indo-European
dialect as the source of these L-Ws, a dialect where the laryngeals had totally
disappeared or become very weakly articulated at the time of the borrowing.
This explanation seems to me to be ad hoc, and cannot in any case be
verified or falsified.

In addition to this, one may also note what follows: the U items under
discussion are problematic etymologies in several respects, as discussed in
Chapter 4; a wide range of meanings have to be accepted in order to
establish a lexical match between the P-Indo-European and the P-U form.

7.4.2. Early Uralic/Indo-European contacts and the Uralic Urheimat

In a recent paper, Koivulehto (1999) has reaffirmed the two basic claims put
forward in his previous research, whilst also providing a clear summary of
his most significant data. In particular, the author confirms that: (a) the
contacts between the U and the Indo-European people must have started
much earlier than ever assumed so far, that is, at the time of the still
undivided P-languages, round about 4000 BC; and (b) the existence of these
early contacts proves that the homeland of the P-U community must have
been located in the area between the Baltic Sea and the Volga river. As a
consequence, the hypothesis of an Asiatic homeland, or that of a homeland
located in the western side of the Ural mountains, should be rejected.

However, in this paper Koivulehto acknowledges that there may be
difficulties in establishing clear phonological criteria for the classification
of the Indo-European L-Ws, particularly the Iranian L-Ws (1999: 214), and
that there appears to be evidence counter to his two assumptions, but he
believes he can provide an explanation. The items of counter-evidence and
Koivulehto's explanations can be summarised as follows:

(a) the traditional model predicts that there should be a wide distribution
of the Pre-Indo-Iranian/early P-Indo-Iranian L-Ws at the F-U layer.
This wide distribution has not materialised. On the contrary, the
(presumed) Indo-Iranian L-Ws in the F-U layer number surprisingly
few, only 14 items ('Laajalevikkisiä (suomalais-ugrilainen levikki) on

oikeastaan yllättävän vähän' (1999: 215)). This piece of counter-evidence could be explained if it is assumed that some of these very old L-Ws might have disappeared or might have been borrowed only in some branches of U;

(b) the majority of these L-Ws seem to have spread particularly in the western languages only, the Finno-Permian branch, namely 19 items ('Enemmän näyttää olevan vain läntisiin (suomalais-permiläisiin) kieliin levinneitä, nimittäin 19 kappaletta' (1999: 215)). This other piece of counter-evidence can be explained by assuming that the homeland of the Indo-Iranian branch was located in a (relatively) more western place than the original Indo-European homeland. In this case, more western Indo-European peoples might have been able to move that far towards the north-west, into middle Europe, the Baltic areas and up to the southern part of Scandinavia and Finland (1999: 231), where the transfer of L-Ws must have taken place (see also Sammallahti 1977: 124 for similar ideas).

One could object that the assumption in point (a) is, once again, neither provable nor disprovable, and that there is no independent evidence whatsoever that (Indo-) Iranian tribes wandered that far toward north-west Europe.

7.4.3. *Indo-European loan-words, Asiatic loan-words,* Wanderwörter, *or something else?*

In the previous section I have pointed out what appear to me to be the major shortcomings of Koivulehto's analysis (for a positive comment see Kallio 1999). However, even if one accepted his analysis, there remains still a difficulty in accepting the overall idea of very ancient contacts between the U and Indo-European people: the majority of those few (13) etymologies which, according to Koivulehto (1999: 209–11), represent the oldest layer of borrowing (from P-Indo-European into P-U), are classified in a different way in other sources. That is, some of these 13 words are considered to have a parallel also in the Asiatic languages, as illustrated in examples (6.4) and (6.5) above. Others are not classified at all as of Indo-European origin; some others are well-known cases of *Wanderwörter*. In addition, many of these P-U/P-Indo-European parallels are rather problematic etymologies on the U side (they have been discussed in Chapter 4.). These factors have already been observed in relation to the Indo-European L-Ws listed by Rédei (1986), and, in fact, Koivulehto's and Rédei's lists by and large overlap (see above Sections 7.2.1 and 7.2.2). Given this intricate lexical and phonological constellation, as also illustrated in Chapter 6, one cannot be sure that the etymologies in question are safe, genuine instances of direct borrowing from Indo-European into U. Therefore, one cannot rely on these words to argue that the contacts between the U and Indo-European communities had already taken place at the times of their respective, undivided P-communities.

In order for the reader to realise the extent of this problem, I shall report below the list of Koivulehto's 13 P-Indo-European/P-U parallels[22], whilst indicating their possible parallels in other language groups. These 13 words are divided into two groups: in the first group (7.12) there are words (7) which are also present in Samoyed, and therefore are supposed to be the oldest L-Ws; in the second group (7.13) there are words (6) which are missing in Samoyed. The reconstructions of some of these parallels contain the segment x on the U side, and the laryngeals on the Indo-European side (quoting from Finnish, if available):

(7.12) *myydä* 'to give, sell' (UEW 275 confirms the I-E connection; see Section 4.4.5.1); Hung. *mos-* (UEW 289 confirms the I-E connection; see Section 7.2.1); *nimi* 'name' (*Wanderwort*); *pelätä* 'to be afraid, to fear' (it is not connected to I-E by UEW 370; see Table 5.5 and example (5.9)); *punoa* 'to twist, weave' (it is connected to Yuk. *pun* 'to tell' and Got. *spinnan* by UEW 402); *pura ~ pora* 'drill' (it is connected to Turkic *bur-*; the I-E connection is given as uncertain in UEW 405; see also Table 5.5 and example (5.7)); *vesi* 'water' (*Wanderwort*)

(7.13) *ajaa* 'to drive' (UEW 4 gives as uncertain the I-E connection; see example (7.11)); *salko* '(long) pole' (it is connected only to Yuk. *culgo-* 'crowbar' in UEW 460); *suoni* (UEW 441 confirms the I-E connection; see discussion in Section 4.4.5.1); *tuoda* 'to bring, give' (it is connected also to Yuk. *tadi* by UEW 529); *ostaa* 'to buy' (the I-E connection is uncertain according to UEW 585); *vetää* 'to pull' (UEW 569 confirms the I-E connection)

The same state of affairs holds true for those 14 (assumed) Indo-Iranian L-Ws which are present at the F-U level, and whose distribution, according to the traditional paradigm, 'should have been wider' than it actually is (Koivulehto 1999: 216):

(7.14) *arvo* 'value', **asera* 'gentleman', *juoda* 'to drink', *kota* 'hut', *mehi-läinen* 'bee', *mesi* 'honey', *sata* 'hundred', *sarvi* 'horn', *ora* 'thorn', *orpo* 'orphan', *suoli* 'intestine', *voi* 'fat, butter', *vuori* 'mountain, tall rock', *vuosi* 'year'

For example, *kota* is a *Wanderwort*; *suoli* has been connected also to Yukaghir and Tungusic (UEW 483); *voi* 'fat, butter' has been connected also to Turkic **bai* (UEW 578), *vuosi* is not connected to Indo-European at all by UEW 335. Moreover, some other of these etymologies are also instances of 'multiple borrowing' (*arvo, mesi, mehi-läinen,* etc.), and some others have been classified as later borrowing by other scholars, such as *asera*, which has been considered as late Iranian by Korenchy ((1972); see Section 7.2).

To conclude this section, I would like to point out that one cannot exclude a priori the hypothesis that at least several of the reported Indo-European/U lexical correlations are only the effect of chance resemblance, for the following reasons: (a) the lack of agreement among the various sources regarding the number, exact origin and chronology of the borrowing; (b) the reliance on correspondences of sounds whose nature cannot be specified; (c) the variety of meanings one has to accept in order to establish a match; (d) the results of the mathematical analysis carried out by Ringe (1998) and Oswalt (1970) on a sample of P-U and P-Indo-European roots (for which see Section 6.6.1); and (e) the result of the mathematical analysis of a sample of the U Lexicon (as carried out in Chapter 5), according to which most lexical correlations within U can actually be accounted for by chance resemblance.

7.5. The presumed Uralic Substratum

There is another intriguing aspect which, to an unbiased examination, should make researchers suspicious about the existence of a very old, close P-U language community: there is hardly any linguistic interference, at any level of language, from a U Substratum into the nearby Baltic, Germanic or Slavic languages, however much researchers have striven to find it (Gy. Décsy 1967; Veenker 1967; Kiparsky 1969, 1970; Thomason & Kaufman 1988: 238–51; Orr 1992; for a list of features from a 'possible Uralic substratum' see Künnap 1998a: 104–10).

In what follows, I shall briefly review this state of affairs, that is, I shall review the lexical, morphological/morpho-syntactic, and phonological interference, which, supposedly, point to the existence of U Substratum.

7.5.1. *Lexical interference*

There are no old Uralic L-Ws in either the Germanic, or the Baltic or Slavic languages. This is even more surprising when one considers that, in contrast, the lexical influence from these languages on the western U languages appears to be quite consistent (see Gy. Décsy 1988 and the discussion in the previous sections). It is certainly true that borrowing, unlike convergence, is usually a unidirectional process, representing the effect of the speech-form which has the higher social status. Indeed, scholars generally claim that, at the time of the contacts between the Indo-European and the (western) U people, the Indo-European were farmers who enjoyed a higher life standard and social status, and therefore did not borrow any words from the U languages (although they adopted some U phonological and morpho-syntactic features, see below). Nevertheless, the (apparent) total absence of borrowed U words remains, in my opinion, surprising, given that, when a more-prestige language spreads into an area of a less-prestige language, it does tend to borrow at least a few terms from the indigenous language for local flora and fauna, local artefacts, and, occasionally toponyms as well. However, this is not at all the case here.

7.5.2. Morphological and morpho-syntactic interference

In support of the existence of an ancient U Substratum, it has recently been claimed that there is morpho-syntactic interference from this substratum into the nearby Germanic, Baltic and Slavic languages, even if no traces of lexical interference are to be found. However, the reported cases of interference are highly restricted, and appear to be consistent with local contacts, rather than with a more exotic source. Here there are some examples (for more details see Künnap 1997b; Wiik 1999):

- loss of grammatical gender in Latvian, under the influence of Livonian;
- loss of the suffix of 3rd Person Singular for the verbs in the Baltic languages, under the influence of Finnic languages;
- development of the so-called second Genitive in Russian, a Partitive-type construction which arose through the reinterpretation of a vanishing noun-class distinction, and which is used also to mark the Object of negative sentences. This construction is claimed to have developed under the influence of Finnic languages. Compare for example Finnish, where in negative sentences the Direct Object takes the Partitive: *Pekka lukee kirja-n* 'Pekka reads book-Acc., Pekka reads the book' vs *Pekka ei lue kirja-a* 'Pekka does=not read book-Partit., Pekka does not read the book';[23]
- the use in Russian of an imperative suffix -*ka*, which is claimed to derive from the P-U suffix *-*k* (which is, however, not only U; see Chapter 8);
- the lack of the verb 'to have' and the use of the construction-type *mihi est* in Russian and Latvian, which has clearly derived from the influence of Finnic languages, not being present in Russian until the 15th century (Veenker 1967: 117–19; Orr 1989);
- the use of the 'Nominative Object' in infinitive constructions of the type '. . . I have to . . .' in Latvian and northern Russian; compare the Finnish construction: *minun täytyy ostaa kirja-Ø* 'I=Gen. has to=buy book-Nom., I have to buy a book', whereby the Object is unmarked, instead of having the Accusative marker -*n* (Orr 1994/5: 55; Klaas 1996; Mathiassen 1985).

The instances of morpho-syntactic interference reported here, in common with those usually reported in the literature, are restricted to the Germanic and Baltic languages, and the northern dialects of Russia (and, of course, the other Scandinavian languages), as target languages. The donor languages are the western, Finnic languages, particularly Balto-Finnic. In other words, this kind of interference does not seem to have anything to do with a P-U Substratum. Besides, it is well known that just finding the same feature in two different languages is not in itself unequivocal proof of contact, or of the contact-induced origin of the feature in question (Bednarczuk 1991). Indeed, many of the features generally brought forward to support the existence of a U Substratum can well be accounted for in terms of natural tendencies of language development.

7.5.3. Phonological interference

Regarding the phonological interference, I shall discuss, briefly, Wiik's model only, the other reported cases of phonological interference being too dubious and problematic to be worth mentioning (see some examples in Thomason & Kaufman 1988: 239–51).

Wiik argues in favour of the existence of a U Substratum in the Indo-European languages on the basis of phonological evidence only (1995, 1997a, 1997b, 1999 and 2000).[24] He believes in fact that phonological substratal interference on its own, without the corresponding lexical interference, is a possible linguistic phenomenon (contrary to what is commonly claimed), being supported in this by Thomason & Kaufman's similar statement (1988: 42–3).

Taking into consideration the relevant archaeological cultures and the assumptions concerning the languages used in these cultures, Wiik rejects the idea of a 'restricted' U homeland in the area between the Urals and the Volga river, claiming instead that P-U was spoken along a vast area in northern Europe. Around 8000 BC Europe was roughly divided into two areas of subsistence: in the North there was the 'culture of the forests', while the populations of the South were already engaged in agriculture and animal breeding/milking (goats). The common language of communication of the hunter-gatherers of the North was P-U, a kind of lingua franca, whilst the common language of the people practising agriculture was P-Indo-European. The borderline between the two worlds ran more or less from Holland, through Germany, Poland and Ukraine, up to the Black Sea. Around 5500 BC agriculture started to spread into the territories inhabited by the U people. The hunter-gatherers adopted the more stable and predictable way of life of the farmers, adjusting to their culture. Therefore, they gradually shifted their own lingua franca, that is, P-U, for P-Indo-European, in this way leaving in it a U Substratum. The P-Indo-European language in question could (tentatively, at least) be called the 'north P-Indo-European': it was the P-Language that later on (under various U and perhaps other language influence) split into the Germanic, Slavic and Baltic P-Languages. However, the Northern populations learned to speak Indo-European in a 'Uralic way', like in any shifting situation. In other words, they made mistakes in pronouncing phonemes and words, as well as in constructing phrases and sentences.

These very mistakes were the factors that triggered many significant sound-changes in the target Indo-European languages, in this way giving rise to phenomena such as: the transformation of palatal occlusives into sibilants in Balto-Slavic; the palatalisation of consonants in the Germanic-Balto-Slavic P-Language; all the typical P-Germanic sound-changes, including stress in initial position, the changes known as 'Grimm's Law' and 'Verner's Law', Umlaut etc.

Through his interpretation of the Germanic Sound Shift, Wiik is able to back up the thesis by Posti (1953), which holds that the Balto-Finnic consonant gradation is not an old, U phenomenon, but has arisen as a result of *Sprachbund*, under the influence of the Germanic languages. In fact, the relationship between Verner's Law and consonant gradation can now be seen as a 'back-and-forth movement (Wiik 1997a: 22)', in the sense that Verner's Law was originally a U Substratum feature based on initial stress, whilst consonant gradation was a Germanic and Scandinavian feature brought to the Finnic coasts by the Germanic and Scandinavian newcomers.

Wiik's model may sound appealing at first. Germanists have often claimed that P-Germanic was indeed formed under the impact of non-Indo-European speaking people, with whom they are supposed to have mixed after migrating into their southern Scandinavian locations, probably before 1000 BC (Hawkins 1987; Polomé 1986; Pokorny 1968). This claim is supported by the following two facts: (a) one third of the vocabulary of the Germanic languages is not of Indo-European origin, including basic-vocabulary terms;[25] (b) the typical Germanic consonantal sound-changes are indeed considered, for example by Hawkins (1987: 61):

unparalleled in their extent elsewhere in Indo-European and suggest that speakers of a fricative-rich language with no voiced stops made systematic conversions of Indo-European sounds into their own nearest equivalents, and that these eventually became adopted by the speech community as a whole

Unfortunately, the non-Indo-European words present in the Germanic languages are not of U origin, and, more seriously, P-U is not at all a fricative-rich language. Looking at the historical U languages, one certainly finds several fricatives, so that, if Wiik's analysis were to be proven plausible, the historical U languages, rather than P-U, even in its lingua franca vest, could be a better candidate for the job. Similarly, the single historical languages may well have provided the substratal material at the origin of the other Germanic, Slavic, and Baltic sound-changes – supposing for a moment that this is a plausible scenario. For example, regarding the shift of accent in first syllable in P-Germanic, the triggering factors might have been as well the contacts with single Balto-Finnic languages, and the change might well have taken place later than 3500 BC as postulated by Wiik (see also Taagepera 1994).

To conclude I believe that, even if it were possible to have phonological interference without lexical interference, and even if the typical Baltic/Slavic/Germanic sound-changes could be proven to have been triggered by a substratal linguistic element, there is still no evidence that this element was an ancient P-Language – supposedly P-U – rather than the actual, historical U languages.

7.6. SUMMARY AND CONCLUSION

There is a methodological problem in the techniques that have been used to estimate the age of the U family. Because there are no records, there is no evidence outside the linguistic sphere relating to the antiquity of the family. The only evidence is of linguistic nature. But it is widely recognised that linguistic methods (Palaeo-linguistics and historical linguistics) are unable to tell us the absolute age of a family. This general problem has been pointed out by, among others, Dixon (1997: 48–9), who questions even the traditional estimated date of around 6000 BP for P-Indo-European.

Leaving aside the methodological problem, palaeo-linguistic analysis refers to plants that are supposed to have been present on the Western side of the Ural mountains at a certain time in history. In fact, these plants were present over a wide Asiatic area (and even have corresponding names, such as 'Siberian Pine').

Again leaving aside the methodological problem, the analysis of historical linguistics is based on L-Ws from Indo-European. These L-Ws are problematic in many respects. For example, the entire evidence of great antiquity amounts to 13 words (Koivulehto 1999) or less, 7 words (according to Rédei 1986), or 6 (according to Koivulehto 1991), words which partially overlap. However, most of these words have been classified as having parallels in other Asiatic languages, and so the classification as Indo-European borrowing can be questioned. Furthermore, there is no agreement on the criteria to be used to determine the donor language and the time of a borrowing, and therefore to identify the age of the (assumed) oldest Indo-European layer of borrowing. For example, for some scholars it is not even possible to make the distinction between the Indo-European and the Indo-Iranian/Iranian layer. For some others, the use of unspecified segments, such as the P-Indo-European laryngeals and the 'unknown' P-U segment x, is good enough to support the very old age of a given L-W. As a result, a given word can have several, contradictory classifications. For example, a word that is used as evidence of antiquity by one scholar may be classified by another as evidence of more recent borrowing from Late Iranian. As Janhunen (1999: 35) puts it, this P-Indo-European/P-U lexical connection is still debatable from the point of view of establishing the age of P-U.

Finally, we have examined the attempts to find support for the antiquity of U in the presumed existence of a U Substratum, basically 'borrowings' from U into Indo-European. We have seen that researchers have failed to find any evidence at the lexical level. Researchers have found correlations at the level of Syntax and Phonology; however this evidence, if proven correct, suggests local influences rather than a U Substratum, because the correlations are highly localised geographically.

To conclude I would like to emphasise that, just because the reported evidence in favour of the great antiquity of U is wanting, one cannot exclude a priori the possibility that U (if it existed) is indeed a very ancient family. However, the fact remains that no convincing evidence has been identified to support this claim so far.

8

MORPHOLOGY

Standard comparative method, then, requires accidence of gram-
mar and such things as shared arbitrary lexical categorization as
evidence for an initial assumption of relatedness; it uses sound
correspondences as a way of describing the internal development
of a family, not as a primary evidence of relatedness for a family
as a whole[1]

Johanna Nichols

Textbooks commonly state that the Morphology of the Uralic languages has been reconstructed consistently. For example, a full reconstructed Case-system, comprising eight Case endings, is often reported, as shown in Table 8.1. However this simple picture is contradicted by the specialist literature. There are in fact only two Case endings that are widely represented in the modern Uralic languages, namely the Locative -*n* and the Locative/ Ablative -*t*. Both of these are also present, with similar functions, in the nearby Asiatic languages. Unlike Indo-European, one cannot reconstruct complete sets (or even sub-sets) of paradigms, such as nominal, verbal, pronominal, grammatical, etc. Nor does the literature contain any identified shared irregularities, 'idiosyncrasies', or instances of suppletion or syncretism of the type found, again, in Indo-European (Meillet 1967: 41). There are no accepted reconstructions in the field for Tense or Aspect. Where reconstructions have been proposed, there are sometimes several competing candidates. For example, there are at least four different candidates for the marker for Plurality (all of which happen to be represented in several of the nearby Asiatic languages). This picture means that the U languages are not 'Neogrammarian material' (Lass 1993: 180) at the morphological level of language, in the same way as we saw above they are not 'Neogrammarian material' at the phonological level of language. Within the traditional framework of the Comparative Method there is very little evidence from this area that qualifies to support the Uralic node, and, indeed, the little evidence that exists suggests that, if there is a relationship, it extends beyond the Uralic area.

One should not be surprised at the absence of significant common Morphology. As we shall see, it is recognised in the specialist literature that most of the Case endings, verbal endings and plural markers in the modern Uralic languages are innovations formed independently in the individual languages. For example, there is evidence that many of the Case endings were formed in historical times through the processes of Grammaticalisation and Exaptation.

Since the application of the Comparative Method to Morphology does not yield useful results, this chapter also includes a statistical analysis of some basic formants, whose purpose is to identify correlations that are demonstrably significant. The method is analogous to the one we adopted in Chapter 5 for the U Lexicon. The results of this analysis identify some correlations that are very unlikely to be the result of chance. The geographical distributions of these significant elements all extend beyond the Uralic area and into the nearby eastern languages. For example, there is a handful of significant formants that are spread widely across the entire Eurasiatic area.

These correlations appear to be good evidence for some sort of linguistic relationship, but they run counter to the conventional interpretation that the Uralic languages are independent of their neighbours to the East. The evidence appears to be more consistent with a model of intersecting isoglosses spanning a wide Eurasiatic area. If one accepts this interpretation, then it suggests that the correlations among the Uralic languages, as well as their correlations with the other Asiatic languages, can best be accounted for by adopting methods of analysis other than the Comparative Method.

8.1. CASE ENDINGS AND THE BASIC TYPOLOGICAL STRUCTURE OF THE URALIC LANGUAGES

In the modern U languages there are two different categories of Case endings:

- Case endings which can be traced back to a common ancestor. These are a small group of simple formants, consisting of the most basic, natural sounds which express spatial relations, topical Object marking, and perhaps a Genitive/Possessive relation. It is precisely these endings, appropriately called 'primary' by Tauli (1966), that have been traditionally reconstructed for P-U; they are analysed in detail in Section 8.2.
- Case endings which cannot be traced back to a common ancestor, for the simple reason that they have been created during the independent life of the historical languages, probably in parallel, but certainly separately in each language. These are new, complex, Case endings, or 'secondary' endings, to use again Tauli's (1966) definition; they will be illustrated in Section 8.3.

These endings, whether primary or secondary, are mainly suffixes, and their structure is mainly agglutinative. As Sinor (1978: 146) puts it: 'Normally, a word can consist of an invariable and meaningful root followed by one or several suffixes.' But I prefer to use here the term 'ending', because it is neutral with regard to the typological structure of the U languages. In fact, the agglutinative structure which is generally believed to be typical of U is actually not to be found in all the languages, or at least not in a consistent, 'pure' way. In reality, there is a variety of typological organisation, ranging from a consistent, agglutinative system, as found in Cheremis (Ivanov & Tužarov 1970; see an example in Note 2), to a more fusional one, as found in Estonian (as partially illustrated in Table 4.2) and Lapp. On the basis of this diversity in typological structure, Tauli (1966) has questioned the claim of a common origin for all the U languages (see also Comrie 1978/9; Austerlitz 1970; Korhonen 1996). Here, I shall not discuss this matter any further, because this is not strictly relevant for the topic of this book. However, I believe that the agglutinative structure can, after all, still be considered as the original typological structure for all the U languages, even if it appears as a defective system in several of them. In fact, the agglutinative system is present in quite a number of languages, whilst the most common deviations from it are still those derived from historical changes which operate on an originally agglutinative system. These changes have produced alternations of the type discussed in Chapter 4, some of which have later on become morphologically conditioned, after the loss of the original phonetic motivation (as shown indeed by Estonian). However, the origin of fusion in these modifications to the originally agglutinative system is, in most cases, still retrievable.

Syncretism and suppletion are certainly present in the U languages (see Abondolo (ed.) 1998: 30–2 and Hajdú 2000: 266), but these phenomena tend to be language specific, and it is hard to trace them back to a common source. Besides, at least some of the reported instances of syncretism and suppletion can be interpreted in a different way (see Marcantonio[3] 1983). The absence of shared syncretism/suppletion, the absence of shared irregularity, etc., is due to the fact that major, significant areas of Morphology are independent, language-specific innovations, as will become evident in the sections below.

8.2. Reconstructing the 'primary' Case endings

It is received wisdom that the U languages are very rich in Case endings (namely suffixes). Consequently, several 'primary' Case endings have been generally reconstructed. Table 8.1 represents a typical reconstructed Case system, although minor variations exist (Collinder 1960; 1965a; Tauli 1956, 1966; Janhunen 1981b; Hajdú 1966; Honti 1995b; Rédei 1998: 38; see Appendix III for the distribution of the Case endings within and outside the U area).

However, among these primary Case endings, those which are present in **all** of the U languages at the same time, and are therefore relevant for the purpose of comparison and reconstruction, are the local Cases only: Locative, Ablative, Lative. They typically reflect a three-way spatial opposition: 'stasis' vs 'movement' 'to' and 'from'.

Table 8.1 The reconstructed Proto-Uralic 'primary' Case endings

1 Nom.	*-Ø	5 Loc. II	*-t
2 Gen.	*-n	6 Abl.	*-ta ~ -tä
3 Acc.	*-m	7 Lat./Dat. I	*-ń ~ *-n
4 Loc. I	*-n, *-na ~ *-nä	8 Lat./Pro. II	*-k(V)

In the languages with rich Case system, this basic opposition may be implemented with various sub-categories, of the type: 'stasis in' or 'motion (toward/from)' the 'inside', 'surface', 'vicinity' of something etc. (see Cardona 1976, 1985). In contrast, the other Case endings, such as Genitive, (so-called) Accusative, and other, more or less abstract Case endings, are present only in some of the languages. Furthermore, the grammatical Subject is always marked -Ø, as it is the Direct Object, given that what is normally called 'Accusative' is in reality a kind of Topical marker. There-fore, it is evident that the only 'Arguments' of the verb which are consist-ently codified by a Case ending in all the U languages are those which express 'directionality' and 'location'. This situation is actually found in some U languages/dialects. There are only two Case endings in the Sherkal[4], Obdorsk and Nizyam dialects of Ostyak (three if one counts the marker -Ø for the Subject): Lative and Locative. There are five endings in Northern Vogul: Lative, Locative, Ablative, Instrumental, Translative (assuming that Instrumental can be considered 'Argument' of the Verb). Compare Table 8.2, which presents the Case system (in the singular) of Nizyam Ostyak[5], illustrated by the noun *xååp* 'boat' (Abondolo 1998c: 361), and the Case system (in the singular) of northern Vogul, illustrated by the noun *ala* 'roof' (Keresztes 1998: 410).

Within the specialist literature, opinions about the number and the nature of the reconstructed Case endings may differ from the reconstruction above. For example, Abondolo (1998 (ed.): 18) states that:

There were [in P-U] also at least three local cases, including a Locative *-nA, a Separative *-tA ~ *tI, and perhaps the Latives *-k (and /or *-ŋ) and *-c^j (and/or *-n^j).[6]

Table 8.2 The Case system of Nizyam Ostyak and Northern Vogul

	Ostyak	Vogul
Nom.	*xååp-Ø*	*ala-Ø*
Lat.	*xååp-a*	*ala-n*
Loc.	*xååp-na*	*ala-t*
Abl./Ela.	/	*ala-nəl*
Ins.	/	*ala-l*
Tra./Ess.	/	*ala-γ*

Korhonen (1992/6: 223) proposes to eliminate the Gen. *-n, arguing as follows:

> There are many reasons to assume that the *n*-Genitive and *n*-Lative historically belong together . . . The dative function is regularly taken by the Lative Case in the Uralic languages, and probably this was also the case in Proto-Uralic. It is possible that the Dative (or the Lative in the Dative function) started to be used also as an adnominal Case in the possessive function, if the Possessivity was emphasised, or if the reference of the possessive attribute was animate, human, definite or pronominal. Otherwise, the Case of the possessive attribute was the Nominative . . . From the typological point of view, the direction of the development Lative > Dative > Genitive is natural. As is known, the semantic development of morphological as well as lexical elements proceeds from the concrete to the abstract, rather than vice versa

For a similar interpretation see also E. Itkonen (1968b). Similarly, Künnap (1998a: 66–8) argues that there are no sufficient grounds to assume, for example, the existence of an originally P-U Accusative in Finnish. In other words, taking into account the topical nature of the Accusative (which is generally used only at the singular), the possible syncretism of Genitive and Lative, the lack of clarity with regard to the various, co-existent forms of Lative, only two Case endings can safely be reconstructed: Locative and Ablative/Separative. Besides this, one of the Locative endings, the second Locative -*t*, is not really distinguishable in sound-shape and function from the Ablative/Separative (see point 5 and 6a in Appendix III).

In addition to the Case endings reported in Table 8.1, there are within U local Case endings which are not mentioned in the traditionally reconstructed Case system because they are only present in a few languages. They are:

1. the Ostyak Lative -*a* ~ -*ä* (for which see below and point 10 in Appendix III);
2. the Lative/Illative -*s*, present in Cheremis, Mordvin and (possibly) in the Balto-Finnic interior local Cases (see Table 8.3 and point 9 in Appendix III);
3. the Ablative -*l*, present in Vogul, in Hungarian and (possibly) in the Finnic local Cases (see Tables 8.3 and 8.4; see point 5 and 6b in Appendix III).

Regarding the nature and distribution of these Case endings, the following is worth observing:

(i) Both the endings included in Table 8.1 and the three other endings not usually included in the P-U Case system are to be found in the Asiatic languages, as illustrated in Appendix III.

(ii) Hungarian, Vogul and Ostyak, once again, do not behave in a uniform way. For example, Honti states that (1998a: 344)

> The functions of the three primary spatial Cases – Dative/Lative, Locative, and Ablative – are performed, in Ostyak and Vogul, by morphemes which are not historically connected.

The Ostyak Dative/Lative ending is -*a* ~ -*ä* (not included in Table 8.1), whilst the Vogul Dative/Lative ending is -(*ə*)*n*, -*na* ~ -*nä* (see point 7 in Appendix III). The Ostyak Dative /Lative ending is considered 'obscure' by Honti[7] (1998a: 344).

Vogul and Ostyak do not share the same Locative ending: Vogul has -(*ə*)*t*, -*ta* ~ -*tä* (see points 5 and 6a in Appendix III), whilst Ostyak has -*nə*~ -*nə̂* /-(*ə*)*n*, the formant -*n* being present also in Hungarian (see point 4 in Appendix III).

The endings of Ablative/Elative are again codified by different morphemes. Vogul has the ending -*na-l*~ -*nä-l*~ -*nə-l*, probably a 'complex' ending (see next section), whose component -*l* (not included in Table 8.1) is shared with Hungarian, but not with Ostyak. Nevertheless, this ablatival component -*l* is generally considered as originating at least from Ugric times (Liimola 1963: 66). The component -*n* is usually assumed to be the P-U Dative/Lative *-*ń*. In contrast, in those dialects of Ostyak where the Ablative is codified by a Case ending, it is expressed by a range of morphemes, which, according to Honti (1998a: 344–5), 'probably all go back to a spatial noun of the shape * $V\gamma^w$' (see also Honti 1984: 61; Rédei 1977: 208–9).

These facts constitute further pieces of evidence against the validity of the Ugric node.

(iii) Some of the above-listed formants have the same function throughout the languages involved, as in the case of Genitive *-*n* and Topical/ Accusative *-*m*. However, apart from these, one can generally observe a certain confusion in the association between sound and function, particularly in the area of local Cases. That is, the specific function of a formant may change from language to language, or even within the same language; this is particularly evident in the Locative/Separative *-*t*(*V*), or the Locative/Lative *-*n*(*V*).

(iv) As evident from the data reported above and in Appendix III, the distribution of the primary Case endings does not respect the traditional subdivision in branches of P-U, although there are exceptions (for example, the Finnic interior and exterior local Cases are formed on a rather regular basis). In other words, the variety and randomness in distribution (and combination, see below) of the primary Case endings confirms the non-validity of the conventional family tree at the morphological level.

(v) A Gen. *-n, a Lative/Dative *-k are present also in the Dravidian languages; similarly, the so-called Accusative *-m may correspond to the sporadic Accusative *-n in Dravidian, according to Tyler (1968). For a possible connection between the formant *-s and the Indo-European ending *-s see Orr (1997).

One may conclude this section by drawing attention to the distance between the reconstructed P-U Case system and the P-Indo-European system. In P-Indo-European, each reconstructed form represents a composite set of possibilities, and no single form reflects them all (Szemerényi 1980). In contrast, most reconstructed P-U formants are actually present as such in the modern languages, whether on their own, or in combination with other formants.

8.3. THE FORMATION OF THE 'SECONDARY' CASE ENDINGS

The majority of the Case endings of the modern U languages, particularly in the languages with rich Case systems (like Finnish, Hungarian, Mordvin), are not inherited from a common source, a common ancestor. On the contrary, they are new, relatively recent, language-specific creations. Unlike the primary Cases, these secondary Case endings are complex, because they are formed through the re-utilisation and combination of existing, more 'archaic' elements. They are created through two basic, general processes of formation: the process of Grammaticalisation of postpositions, in turn derived from Grammaticalisation of (originally) ordinary, independent nouns and the process of more or less random combination, co-optation, that is, Exaptation of two existing, primary endings.

Both these types of complex, secondary endings are found throughout the U languages, but with different distribution. The secondary endings derived from Exaptation (let us call them 'exaptated' endings), are particularly productive, or at least still particularly transparent, in the Finnic branch whilst the secondary endings, originating from postpositions/nouns (let us call them 'grammaticalised' endings), are retrievable particularly in Hungarian, the Ob-Ugric and most Samoyed languages. This will be illustrated in the two following sections.

8.3.1. *Secondary endings formed through Exaptation*

The process of Exaptation[8] (Gould & Vrba 1982; Lass 1997: 320–1; Orr 1999) consists basically of two major steps: (a) splitting of the original, more general senses of some of the original Cases; and (b) building new subsystems, through the combinations of old Case endings, or derivational and other kinds of formants. As a result, new, complex (and often coherent) subsystems are formed of a type which is not attributable to the P-Language,

Table 8.3　Formation of new, 'exaptated' Case endings in Finnish

a. Old 'primary'/ simple Case endings

Nominative	kala-Ø	'fish'	
Essive	kala-na	'as a fish'	
Partitive/(Ablative)	kala-(t)a	'some fish'[9]	

b. New 'secondary'/complex Case endings
b.1 Interior local Cases

Inessive	kala-ssa	'in [inside] the fish'	-ssa < *-s-na
Elative	kala-sta	'out of [the inside of] the fish'	-sta < *-s-ta

b.2 Exterior local Cases

Adessive	kala-lla	'at /on the [surface of the] fish'	-lla < *-l-na
Ablative	kala-lta	'from [the surface of the] fish'	-lta < *-l-ta

and which is driven by quite new organisational principles. As to the types of endings re-utilised in the co-optation, in the Finnic languages they are typically, but not exclusively, the primary local endings (Korhonen 1979/ 96, 1981/96; Tauli 1966). Table 8.3 gives the declension (in the singular) of the Finnish word *kala* 'fish', and shows how some new, secondary Finnish Case endings have formed through Exaptation of some pre-existing, (presumed P-U) Case endings (adapted from Lass's (1997: 321) table). The components *-na (Locative), *-ta (Separative/Ablative), *-s (Lative) and *-l (Ablative) are all simple, primary Case endings. What this table shows, according to Lass (1997: 323–4), is that:

> two original Cases, Locative and Separative, which remain in restricted uses as Essive and Partitive respectively, have been built as well into productive new endings by co-opting other (largely derivational) material, and fusing it with the Case-endings in a systematic and novel way. The rest of the Cases, while not falling into this kind of system, none the less show similar conceptual novelty . . . The typical signature of exaptation is clearly visible: the combination of *bricolage* and conceptual innovation.

This process of (mostly random) combination of existing material to form new, complex Cases, is also illustrated by the Case system of Samoyed. According to Janhunen (1998: 469):

> Proto-Samoyedic nominal declension seems to have had a system of one unmarked and six suffixally marked Cases . . . this system is preserved as the core of the case systems of all the modern Samoyedic languages. Three of the cases express general grammatical relationships and have Proto-Samoyedic shapes deriving directly from proto-Uralic: the unmarked Nominative (Absolutive) in *-Ø, the Genitive in *-n, and the Accusative in *-m. The other four cases express local relationships and occur with two principal sets of endings, depending on whether they are attached to an

ordinary noun or to a spatial noun used as an adverb or postpositions. The declension of spatial nouns is structurally more simple and incorporates archaic endings deriving from proto-Uralic: $*$-ng for the Dative/Lative, $*$-na^2 for the Locative,[10] and $*$-$t(ø)$ [ø = reduced vowel] for the Ablative. The declension of ordinary nouns, on the other hand, was based on the coaffixal use of the elements $*$-$k(ø)$- and $*$-$ntø(-)$, which function basically as Dative/Lative endings with varying distribution in the modern languages. Nganasan [Samoyed Tawgi] is alone in using the Locative complex $*$-$ntø$-na^2 as opposed to $*$-$kø$-na^2 elsewhere, a situation which suggests that the local Case system was still being formed at the time when Nganasan broke off from the rest of Proto-Samoyedic. The ending of the remaining local Case, the Prosecutive/Prolative, may also have a coaffixal origin, in that it possibly contains a combination of the Accusative $*$-m- with the Locative $*$-na^2.

Table 8.4 Formation of new 'exaptated' Case endings in Finno-Permian (from Korhonen 1981/96: 202)

	Finnish	Cheremis	Zyrian	Proto-Finno-Permian		
Adessive	isä-llä	l	mort-lẹn			nA
Allative/Dative	isä-lle	kit-lan	mort-lị̈	l +		nl̥k
Ablative	isä-ltä	kit-leč	mort-lị̈ś			tA
	'father'	'hand'	'man'			

The fact that these complex Case endings are independent formations of the individual historical languages, and not shared innovation of a particular intermediate node, is proven by their random distribution even within closely related languages, such as the Finnic languages. Consider Table 8.4 from Korhonen (1981/96: 202–3), which shows the formation of new Case endings within the Finnic 'local-habitative' system, by combining the simple (Ablative) ending $*$-l with some other simple local endings (all of which are found in Table 8.1 above). The author comments on the situation as follows:

However, the lack of this Case type in the nominal declension of Lapp and Mordvin has given reason to presume that in Proto-Finno-Permian it was not yet part of the basic Case system, but rather that it formed a productive group of derivative particles. Nevertheless, it is thought to have begun by the addition of the primary Finno-Ugrian local Cases $*$-na/$*$-$nä$, $*$-ta/$*$-$tä$, $*$-n/$*$-k onto the particles formed from the local -l suffix.

Then Korhonen observes that in Finno-Permian there are other Cases, dating from different eras, which contain elements of the postulated common Case system. Similarly, Sinor (1961: 177) points out the absence of the expected Adessive Case in Cheremis, and the absence of the entire paradigm in Mordvin and Lapp. According to the author, this signifies that these Case endings are not common inheritance; they are instead instances of 'parallel, but independent evolution'.

The complex Case endings formed through Exaptation are found also in the Altaic languages and Yukaghir. Sinor (1961: 176f.) illustrates how the formation of some complex, exaptated Case endings in the U and Altaic languages 'montrent un parallélisme complet.' For example, in the parallel Finnish, Cheremis, Mongolian and Tungus Directive/Lative/Translative complex endings *-k-si*, *-g-si*, *-s-ki* one can see (according to Sinor ibid.) 'analogous but independent developments' which have brought about the formation of similar morphemes from the combination of elements phonetically and functionally similar, but combined in different orders: the Lative/Illative *-s* and the Lative *-k* (see points 8 and 9 in Appendix III); compare for example Finn. *tulla iloise-k-si* 'to=become happy'. Again according to the author, the parallelism is even more striking if one considers that these languages are geographically very far apart, so that influence through contact is unlikely. Quite striking too is the fact that the Translative *-k-si* etc. maintains the same function throughout the languages involved.

8.3.2. *Secondary Case endings formed through Grammaticalisation*

The Case endings (and/or related postpositions) formed through Grammaticalisation are present in almost all the U languages. They are present also in those Finnic languages, such as Cheremis (Kangasmaa-Minn 1998: 227; Driussi 1996; Hajdú 2000: 263), M. Mordvin (Zaicz 1998: 204;) and Lapp (Korhonen 1979/96: 169; see also Sebeok 1946), where, as we have seen, the process of Exaptation has been adopted as the favourite means of creating new Case endings. However, they are particularly well attested, transparent in structure and clearly observable in Vogul (Keresztes 1998: 416; Liimola 1963), some Samoyed languages, Old Hungarian, and Ostyak.

The chronology of the formation of postpositions and related Case endings in the U languages is quite 'late' (to use Korhonen's definition (1982/96: 208). In other words, these Case endings were not formed sometime in the unrecorded past. On the contrary, some of them have been created quite recently, in historical times, whilst some others are actually *in fieri* today. I believe that this is a relevant factor which demands an explanation, if one supports the thesis of the great antiquity of U. However, a proper scrutiny of this topic and possible implications for U studies is outside the scope of this book; therefore, here I shall limit myself to making only some speculations at the end of the chapter.

Grammaticalisation is a common phenomenon in languages and is accomplished through (apparently) regular, sequential, irreversible stages of development (Vincent 1980; Traugott & Heine (eds) 1991; Lass 1997: 267–

70; Hopper & Traugott 1993): 1) progressive reduction/simplification of the phonetic-shape of the original noun; 2) loss of its specific semantic content; and 3) cliticisation and (eventually) agglutination. These stages are retrievable in several U languages.

8.3.2.1. Examples of Grammaticalisation in Ostyak and some other Uralic languages

In Ostyak, the process of Grammaticalisation of nouns into postpositions is still clearly between the first and second stage along the path of development. In fact, as Abondolo (1998c: 367) says, postpositions:

> are nouns with defective paradigms and distributions. Some have only one form, with fossilised, synchronically opaque Morphology, e.g. the intrinsically Lative *močə* '(to)as far as', . . . Most, however, occur with at least one, and usually two or more synchronically segmentable local suffixes attached, e.g. Lative *piïr-aa* 'to behind' : Locative *piïr-nə* 'behind, after' . . . It is probably impossible to draw a sharp outer perimeter around the class of postpositions, since many nouns can enter into ad hoc postpositional constructions.

Similarly, according to Gulya (1966: 90–1):

> [Postpositions] are nouns that, by their more general range of meaning (e.g. 'interval', 'length', 'the interior of something' etc.) are suitable for expressing certain more general relations. . . . The postpositions form two large groups: a. one group contains the postpositions proper (old petrified inflected words used today in the function of postpositions only); b. the other group contains nouns that are used or can be used as postpositions (postpositions whose original substantival character has been preserved). It is impossible to draw a hard-and-fast line between the two groups.

The following sentence contains an example of postpositions proper[11] (text from Gulya 1966: 91):

(8.1) tom puɣəl močət   mənləm
      that village as=far=as I'll=go
      'I'll go as far as that village'

The following sentences illustrate the basic behaviour of the nouns used as postpositions (Gulya's Group (b)). The noun used in a postpositional function, like any normal noun, can occur without any ending, or can be inflected. In this last case, it may be inflected with a Possessive, as in (8.2), with a Case ending (normally a primary local Case ending), as in (8.3), or with both a Possessive and a Case ending, as in (8.4). As is evident from the examples, the context for the formation of postpositions is a Genitive/Possessive construction (texts from Gulya 1966: 92):

(8.2) nŏŋ möγl-än kojį jŏwǝl?
you side-your who comes
'who comes instead of you?'

(8.3) lŏγ kat   kas-nȝ̂   lal'wȝ̂l
he house space=behind-Loc. stands
'he stands behind the house'

(8.4) lŏγ möγl-ǝl-ä   ăt'į-l   jŏs
he side-his-Lat. elder=brother-his came
'instead of him his elder brother came'

These nouns/postpositions are also used in connection with participial verbs to form subordinate sentences. In the following sentence, the verb 'to go' is inflected with the Perfect Participle morpheme -mä- (for which see also below), and with the 3rd Possessive ending -l. The whole nominalised verbal phrase in turn co-occurs with a noun/postposition, which is inflected with a local Case: pįr-nȝ̂ 'space-Loc., after' (text from Gulya 1966: 93):

(8.5) lŏγ mǝn-mä-l   pįr-nȝ̂,   mä ăt'į-m   jŏs
he go-Perf.Part.-his space-Loc., I   elder=brother-my came
'after his having gone away /after he went away, my elder brother came'

Zyrian (/Komi) is another language which provides clear evidence for the process of formation of postpositions and Case endings (Wichmann & Uotila 1942; Baker 1985: 167; Hausenberg 1998). For example, according to Baker (1985: 167):

The postpositional series in din- derives from the substantive din which is still used in the language in its original meaning of 'butt-end of a tree'. The source, in turn, of this lexeme is Proto-Finno-Ugrian *tiŋe or *tüŋe, with the same signification; cf. Finnish tyvi 'base of a tree' . . . In Hungarian it has given rise to the Ablative (postpositional Case) -tól/-től . . ., and in Mordvin the Dative -ńd'i

Then the author states that (170–2):

there is no ready-made criterion by which an element can be judged definitively a Case suffix or a postposition. Often such an incisive touchstone is not required since, thanks to an abundance of general guidelines, the particular class membership of many forms is manifest. Thus, for instance, the Inessive -įn is obviously a Case ending, the form dorįn undisputably a postposition. However, borderline phenomena exist . . . the functional divide between Komi Cases and Postpositions is, in fact, not great.

Note that, according to UEW 523, the F-U root *tiŋe (*tüŋe), from which are derived Finn. tyvi /Hung. tő (Acc. töve-t)/Zyr. din, dįn etc. (and related postpositions/Case endings), has parallels in the Altaic and Palaeo-Siberian languages; compare for example Turkic *töŋ 'a tree-trunk', Kor. *tuŋk* 'base of a stick, tree' etc. (see also below).

In Finnish there seems to be no trace at all of Case endings formed through Grammaticalisation, although there are some postpositions just recently formed from former nouns, such as *taka-na* and *luo-ta*. Compare *koda-n taka-na* 'hut-Gen. back-in', that is 'behind the hut', *venee-n luo-ta* 'boat-Gen. presence-from', that is 'from the boat', etc. (Campbell 1990b). There are however instances of Grammaticalisation in Estonian, where the Grammaticalisation of the Comitative Case is well documented in texts since the 17th century.[12]

Regarding the formation of postpositions and related Case endings in the Samoyed languages, see for example Salminen (1998: 540) for Samoyed Yurak (/Nenets) and Simoncsics (1998: 590) for Samoyed Kamas (/Kamassian).

8.3.2.2. *Grammaticalisation in Hungarian*

In Modern Hungarian the process of transformation of nouns into postpositions and of postpositions into Case endings (suffixes) is basically fully accomplished. However, there is clear evidence that this process has taken place in recent historical times since it is beautifully recorded in the oldest Hungarian texts. As a consequence of this recent implementation, there are still in Modern Hungarian a few 'transparent' postpositions of the Ostyak type, although the original structure of most of them has now become 'opaque'.

The Hungarian postpositions are normally constructed with primary Case endings and Possessives (when required), as in other U languages (see the Ostyak examples in the previous section). The following examples are cases of 'opaque' postpositions, since the nouns out of which they have formed no longer have an independent status, that is, they do not exist as such in the Hungarian Lexicon, and can only be reconstructed:

(8.6) *ala-tt* 'under', *al-á* 'to, toward under', *aló-l* 'from under' (< P-U *ala* 'space under [something]'; see example (4.8)). Here *-t* ~ *-tt* is the Locative, *-á* is the Lative (see point 8 in Appendix III), and *-l* is the Ablative.

(8.7) *mögö-tt* 'behind', *mög-é* 'to, toward behind', *mögü-l* 'from behind'. Like in the previous example, the noun which has become postposition no longer exists as an independent noun, but its origin is considered retrievable: it is assumed to derive from F-U *miŋä* (*müŋä*) 'space behind [something]' (UEW 276).

Among the few postpositions whose original noun still exists also as an independent noun, consider the following:

(8.8) *közö-tt* 'between, among ', *köz-é* 'to, toward between, among', *közü-l* 'from between, among'. The corresponding noun is *köz* 'interval, intermediate space, interstice', which has been reconstructed as F-U **kitɜ* (**kütɜ*) by UEW 163.

(8.9) *melle-tt* 'beside, next to', *mell-é* 'to, toward beside, next to', *mellő-l* 'from beside, from next to'. The corresponding noun is *mell* 'chest, breast, bosom', which is assumed to go back to F-U **mälke* (**mälʏe*), according to UEW 267 (see discussion below[13]).

(8.10) *belé* 'toward in/into', etc. (for which see below); the corresponding noun is *bél* 'entrails, interior' (Hajdú 2000: 263).

The Hungarian Case system is fully formed, although a few Case endings are still in the process of being created at present.[14] As anticipated, the process of transition from noun/postposition into Case endings has taken place in recent historical times, and it is documented in the oldest Hungarian texts. The examples given in Table 8.5, derived from the text *Halotti beszéd* 'Funeral Oration', speak for themselves: the complex Case endings derive from a 'spatial-type of noun' provided with a simple Case ending and (possibly) a Possessive ending. This spatial noun is in turn inserted within a Genitive/Possessive construction (from the edition by Molnár & Simon (1977: 27); see also Imre (1972: 333–4) and (1988: 433); Sauvageot (1971: 66–8)). In examples (1)–(5) we have the ordinary noun *bél* 'entrails, interior' either in the function of postposition, in (3)–(5), or in the function of Case ending, in (1) and (2). As a postposition, and then as a Case ending, *bél* is regularly constructed with simple, local endings: Locative -*n* (< **-n*, with a superessive function); Lative -*é* (see point 8 in Appendix III[15]), and Ablative -*l*. In particular, the form -*bel-e* is to be interpreted as the word *bél* inflected with the Hungarian Lative[16] -*é*. These constructions containing the noun *bél* (examples (1)–(5)) clearly show the transition from noun/postposition into Case ending. In fact, in the first two examples we have already the Case ending in its current form (as shown by the comparison with

Table 8.5 Formation of Case endings from postpositions in Old Hungarian

Old Hungarian		Modern Hungarian	
1) *gimilʁ-be-n*	>	*gyümölcs-ben*	'inside, in the fruit'
2) *milott-be-n*	>	*malaszt-ban*	'inside, in grace'
3) *vilag-bel-e*	>	*világ-ba*	'[movement] into [inside]the world'
4) *uruzag-bel-e*	>	*ország-ba*	'[movement] into [inside] the kingdom'
5) *timnuce-bel-ev-l*	>	*tömlöc-ből*	'[movement] out of [the inside of] prison'
6) *gimilcíc-tu-l* (~ -*tv-l*)	>	*gyümölcs-től*	'[movement] from the [surface of] fruit'
7) *uro-m-chuz*	>	*ura-m-hoz*	'[movement] toward my Lord'

Modern Hungarian), meaning 'position inside something'. This is not yet the case in (3)–(5), where *bél* has not undergone any reduction or change in its phonetic shape, as happens later on in Modern Hungarian. In other words, we find attested in these examples the intermediate stage in the formation of modern *-ba* ~ *-be* < *-bel-e* (in (3) and (4)), and the intermediate stage in the formation of modern *-ból* ~ *-ből* < *-bel-ev-l* (in (5)[17]). But we do not find attested here the intermediate stage in the formation of modern *-ban* ~ *-ben*, which should be **-bele-n,* if it were attested (Korhonen 1981/96: 200).

It is evident that the postposition/suffix in *miloszt-ben, vilag-bele, uruzag-bele* does not obey the rules of vowel harmony. This in turn means that the element has not yet completely lost its autonomy, although the way it is written – attached to the preceding noun – seems to suggest that the process of cliticisation has somehow started. This fact becomes even more relevant when we consider that the morphological elements which are already fully formed in this period do obey vowel harmony, as shown by the following examples, again from *Halotti beszéd: ovod-ni-a* 'undo-Inf.-3rd Poss. Sing., his undoing, to undo' vs *ket-ni-e* 'bind-Inf.-3rd Poss. Sing., his binding, to bind'.

In example (6) the form *-tu-l* (> Modern Hun. *-tól* ~ *-től* [movement away] from the vicinity of something') is already fully a Case ending, whose original noun/postposition cannot be retrieved without the help of the etymological dictionary. It is assumed to derive from F-U **tiŋe* (**tüŋe*) 'root, base (of the tree), stem', which gives Finn. *tyvi* and Hun. *tő* (Acc. *töve-t*), and which has become a postposition/Case ending also in Zyrian and Mordvin (as discussed in the previous section).

In example (7) *-chuz,* equivalent to Modern Hungarian *-hoz* ~ *hëz* ~ *-höz* '[movement] toward the vicinity of something', has completely lost its original nominal and then postpositional function, to become solely a Case ending. The original noun has been reconstructed as P-Ug. **kućз* 'space beside, next to something' (UEW 857; see below).

The status of the postpositions/Case endings as depicted above is confirmed by two facts: (a) some interesting fluctuation in the written forms, found in the same (and other) old texts; and (b) the 'form' of the stem to which they are attached. Regarding point (a), in *Halotti beszéd* we find forms written as: *muga nec* 'himself-to, to himself' (Modern Hun. *magá-nak*), next to *halalnec* (*halal-nec*) 'death-to, to the death' (Modern Hun. *halál-nak*), again without vowel harmony. Similarly, in the 'Foundation Charter of the Abbey of Tihany' we find the postposition *rea* (Modern Hun. *-re* ~ *-ra*), written in most cases separated from, but occasionally also attached to the preceding element, as shown below (the examples in a. are Old Hungarian, the examples in b. are the corresponding modern forms; from the edition by Molnár & Simon (1977: 17–18)):

(8.11) a. Feheruuaru   rea   meneh   hodu   utu   rea
        Fehérvár   to   going   military road   on(-to)
        'on, along the military road which goes to, toward Fehérvár'

(8.11) b. Fehérvár-ra   menő   had(i)   út-ra
        Fehérvár-to   going   military road-on(-to)

(8.12) a. bukurea
        bush=on(-to)   [movement]toward [the surface of] the bush

(8.12) b. bokor-ra
        bush-on(-to)

Regarding point (b), Sauvageot (1971: 144) remarks that the Case endings derived from the agglutination of an original noun/postposition are attached to the consonantic, and not the vocalic stem of the word. For example, given the word *ház* 'house', its Plural is *háza-k*, its Accusative *háza-t*. If however local Cases are added, then the stem becomes consonantic: *ház-on* 'house-on, on top of the house', *ház-ban* 'house-inside, in the house', *ház-ba* 'house-[movement] into, into the house', *ház-ból* 'house-[movement] out of, out of the house', etc. What this indicates is that the agglutination of the local suffixes, but not that of the grammatical ones, has been accomplished after the loss of the final, thematic vowel. This process in turn is quite recent, the final vowels being still attested in the earliest documents, as shown by the sequence *utu rea* itself (see also Section 4.5.5).

In a text produced about a century after *Halotti beszéd*, *Ómagyar Mária-siralom* 'Old Hungarian lament of Mary'[18], vowel harmony seems to be fully in place, judging, for example, from *virag-nac* 'flower-to, to the flower' (Modern Hun. *virág-nak*). However, as shown below, we still find occurrences of the form *-beleul* first encountered in *Halotti beszéd* (original text in (8.13a), Modern Hungarian version in (8.13b); text from Imre (1972: 334)):

(8.13) a. bu-a-beleul   kyniuhhad

(8.13) b. bú-já-ból   kinyújtsad (= kihúzzad)
        sorrow-her-from   relieve [her]
        'relieve her [Mary] from her sorrow'

What these data tell us is that the process of Grammaticalisation and transformation of the nouns into postpositions and of postpositions into suffixes is still *in fieri* between the 12th and the 14th centuries. This is a 'late' chronology indeed, especially if one considers that the textbook estimate for the disintegration of the P-Ugric community into P-Ob-Ugric and P-Hungarian is around the beginning of the first millennium BC, if not earlier. Therefore, one should conclude that it took at least over two millennia, if not much longer, for postpositions and Case endings, and, ultimately, agglutination, to be formed in Hungarian.

To conclude this section I would like to draw the attention of the reader to the following two factors, which could be relevant for the purpose of assessing relations among languages (as discussed below).

As mentioned, the U postpositional constructions were originally Possessive/Genitive constructions. This is evident from the examples reported in (8.2)–(8.4) and in Table 8.5 above. To take another example, the modern Hungarian nominal phrase *ház-tól* 'house-from, from the house', derives from an original construction of the type **hazu tüwü-l* 'house stem[its]-from, from the house stem/from the stem of the house' (see example (6) in Table 8.5 and related discussion). Within this type of constructions the 'spatial noun' (in this case the term for 'stem') represents the 'head' of the nominal phrase.

Secondly, the process of Grammaticalisation of nouns into postpositions and of postpositions into suffixes is well documented and transparent also in Turkic. The syntactic construction within which Grammaticalisation is implemented is the same as in the U languages, that is, a Genitive /Possessive construction containing a 'spatial noun' as the 'head' of the construction. This noun, provided with a Possessive and a simple Case ending, becomes the postposition/complex Case ending (see some examples in Johanson (1998: 112–13)).

8.3.3. *The reciprocal order of Case endings and Possessive endings*

In this section I would like to discuss a topic which might be relevant to understand the origin and nature of Morphology in the U languages, although at first it might look a bit marginal: the question of the reciprocal order of Case and Possessive endings when they co-occur within the same nominal phrase.

The reciprocal order of these endings may vary from language to language, while both opposite orders may be found within the same language.[19] For example, in Finnish the order is invariably Case–Possessive: *ystävä-lle-ni* 'friend-to-my, to my friend'. This order is found in Balto-Finnic, Mordvin, most of Samoyed languages and Lapp, whereas in the Ugric languages the order is, basically, Possessive–Case, with interesting variations to be dealt with below.

Modern Hungarian has the order Possessive–Case within a nominal phrase: *barát-om-nak* 'friend-my-to', but the reverse order within a post-positional phrase: *köz-t-ük* (~ *közö-tt-ük*) 'interstice-Loc.-3rd Plu., between, among them' (see the corresponding postposition in (8.8) above). Compare also *melle-tt-em* 'chest-Loc.-my, beside me', etc. If the item *mell* is used not as a postposition, but as an ordinary noun, then the opposite order is used, the one regularly required with nouns, that is: *melle-m-ben* 'chest-my-Loc., in my chest'. In this last case the Locative ending is not the 'primary', simple

Locative -*t* (supposedly from P-U *-*t*), but the secondary, complex ending: -*ban* ~ -*ben*, whose formation was illustrated in Table 8.5 above.

In the Permian languages and Cheremis both orders are found, 'occasionally as alternatives' (Comrie 1980: 81; Hajdú 1983: 105).

In most Ostyak dialects, within a nominal and postpositional phrase the order is as in the Hungarian nominal constructions: Possessive–Case. Compare also the two Ostyak and Hungarian synonymous and isomorphic constructions containing the postposition derived from F-U *kit3 (*küt3), whose Hungarian parallel has already been encountered above (example (8.8)):

(8.14) Ost. *köt-iin-nə* 'interstice-2nd Dual-Loc., between the two of you' (Abondolo 1998c: 367) vs Hun. *köz-t(e)-tek* 'interstice-Loc.-2nd Plu., between the two of you'. The isomorphism is perfect, except for the opposite order of the possessive and Case endings.

On the other hand, in other Ostyak dialects there are a few postpositions, generally considered older, which present the reverse order with respect to the one observed in *köt-iin-nə* above, that is, the same order found in the Hungarian postpositional phrases (Abondolo[20] 1998c: 368):

(8.15) Synja Ostyak *naŋ χoś-aj-ən* 'you space=beside-Lat.-2nd Sing., towards beside you', which is isomorphic and synonymous with Hun. *hozz-á-d* 'space=beside-Lat.-2nd Sing., towards beside you'.

Several explanations have been proposed to account for this (apparently?) random fluctuation. For example Honti (1995b: 78; see also 1997) states that:

Die relative Abfolge der Kasus- und der Possessivsuffixe war höchstwahrscheinlich von der Natur der Kasussuffixe abhängig: die grammatischen Kasus traten hinter den Possessivsuffixen auf (PxCx), die nichtgrammatischen standen vor den Possessivsuffixen (CxPx).

See also Luutonen (1997) and Künnap (1998b). The basic idea here is that the original order is Possessive–Case in connection with grammatical Cases, such as Genitive and Accusative, but Case – Possessive in connection with the other Cases, such as local, adverbial Cases. However, the formation of new Case endings through Grammaticalisation, which usually had adverbial, local meanings, is supposed to have disrupted this original pattern. According to this view, these new secondary Case endings, when agglutinated to the word, naturally occupied the position at the end of the form; this process therefore yielded the order Possessive–Case, originally typical of the grammatical Cases only. This new order was later on generalised in certain languages to cover the whole paradigm, in this way giving rise to the variation observed.

Comrie (1980: 83f.) however, following a suggestion by Tauli (1966: 119), argues for the opposite scenario. He claims that the order Case–Possessive is

the older order and that the order Possessive–Case represents an innovation. He bases this on the following facts: 1) the Case suffixes in U are of
'very different historical ages', some going back to P-U and others deriving
from language-specific innovations, particularly the transformation of
nouns into postpositions and then into suffixes; and 2) since postpositions
differ from Case suffixes in being separate words, where a postposition
develops into a Case suffix, there is an earlier order Noun stem–Possessive–
Postposition; in this case the noun stem and possessive suffix are a single
word. In (most) Balto-Finnic languages, where the great majority of Case
endings have been formed through Exaptation, we find the order Case–
Possessive, whilst in languages like Hungarian, where the major source of
formation of Case endings has been Grammaticalisation of postpositions,
we find, as expected, the order Possessive–Case, which reflects an earlier
order Possessive–Postposition.

However, as Comrie himself points out (ibid.), there is counter-evidence to
his analysis. For example, in Cheremis, contrary to expectation, one finds
the order Possessive–Case in connection with the Accusative and Genitive,
which are primary Case endings. Similarly in Mordvin M. one finds the
order Possessive–Genitive. In Cheremis and Vogul there are combinations of
nouns, possessive endings and postpositions where the Possessive is attached
optionally to the postposition, rather than to the noun. Furthermore, in the
Permian languages and Cheremis both orders can be found, occasionally as
alternatives.

To this list of counter-evidence, one can also add the co-existence of both
orders, Case–Possessive and Possessive–Case, in Ostyak postpositional
phrases, as shown in examples (8.14) and (8.15) above.

As one can see, there appear to be no convincing explanations to account
for the various orders of occurrence of Possessive and Case endings, as
depicted above.

Indeed, the reality is that there is no consistency, no pattern of any sort in
the use of one order or another. In other words, the combination of these
endings is simply and purely random, in the same way as the distribution of
the other morphological elements examined in this book appears to be
random. This interpretation, apart from being simple and consistent with
the data, is supported by the behaviour of the postposition *köz-* 'interval,
interstice' in Old Hungarian, as illustrated by the following example from
the text *Halotti beszéd* (the Latin text is provided):

(8.16) a. w   ſzentíí   eſ   unuttei   cuzi-c-un

(8.16) b. suos sanctos   et   electos   inter
          inter sanctos et electos suos

Here the postposition *cuzi-c-un* (literally 'interstice-their-Loc., among
them'), in Modern Hungarian would sound *köz-ük-ön* (Sauvageot 1971:

146), if it did exist in this form, instead of the attested *köz-t-ük* (~ *közö-tt-ük*); see in this regard the examples (8.8) and (8.14) above. As a matter of fact, the nominal phrase *cuzi-c-un* presents two interesting phenomena:

- the Locative is not *-t* ~ *-tt*, the ending normally used in the postpositional phrases (recall *melle-tt-em* 'next to me', *mögö-tt-em* 'behind me', *elő-tt-em* 'in front of me' etc.; see also (8.8) and (8.9) above), but the other (supposedly P-U) Locative ending *-n*, the one found in the complex ending *-ba-n* ~ *-be-n* (see Table 8.5);
- the order of Case and Possessive endings is reversed with regard to that normally found in Hungarian postpositional phrases, that is: first comes the 3rd Plu. Poss. *-c-* (read *-(ü)k-*), and then comes the local Case ending *-ön*. Here we find again that unmotivated fluctuation encountered within the Ostyak dialects: recall the equivalent forms *köt-iin-nə* 'interstice-2nd Dual-Loc., between the two of you' vs *χoś-aj-ən* 'space=beside-Lat.-2nd Sing., towards beside you' (see examples (8.14) and (8.15) respectively).

These example shows that the random distribution may extend not only to the reciprocal order of the endings within the same type of phrases, but also to the choice of the actual Case endings.

To conclude this section, note that similar fluctuations in the reciprocal order of the various endings occur in Turkic. This is illustrated, for example, by the different orders of the sequence Plurality–Possession–Case endings, as found in Chuvash and other Turkic languages (for details see Clark (1998: 434)).

8.4. MORPHOLOGICAL CORRELATIONS BETWEEN SAMOYED AND YUKAGHIR

We have already mentioned in Chapter 6 that lexical and morphological correlations have been identified in the literature between Yukaghir and the U languages, particularly between Yukaghir and Samoyed, and we have examined the lexical correlations (Section 6.4). Here I shall discuss just one aspect of the identified morphological correlations, the Case system, a comprehensive analysis of this area being impossible in the context of this book (see, for example, Hegedűs 1988, Audova 1996 and Klesment 1996).

8.4.1. *The Case system*

The Case systems of (northern) Samoyed and Yukaghir appear to be very similar (Collinder 1940, 1955, 1965a; Harms 1977; Sauvageot 1969: 348; Rédei 1999a; Hajdú 1953). For example, Collinder (1965a: 30) says that:

all the Finno-Ugric languages deviate more from Samoyed in their Case inflection than Yukaghir does.

As already discussed in Section 8.3.1, Samoyed has two sets of local Cases, one simple, and one complex (formed through Exaptation), depending on which category they are attached to. The simple set of endings is used with adverbs and postpositions. The complex set is used with nouns, and is formed with a co-affixal use of two elements: -*kǝ-* and -*ntǝ-*. Yukaghir too has two different sets of endings, one simple and one complex, depending on which category they are attached to. The complex endings are formed through the process of Exaptation, as in Samoyed. The co-affixal element is *-ka-*, which has generally been connected with the P-U (Pro-)Lat. *-ka* (see point 8 in Appendix III). The major (reconstructed) Case endings Samoyed and Yukaghir (ignoring dialectal variants) have in common are shown in Table 8.6 below. For Samoyed, I have reported the simple primary endings only (adapted from Janhunen's (1998: 469) table), without the co-affixal elements, because the combination with these two elements takes place in a consistent, regular way. For Yukaghir, both the co-affixal and the simple endings have been reported, because they combine in a rather inconsistent and 'messy' way (adapted from Sauvageot (1969: 348); compare also Rédei (1999a: 10–11)). The endings of Locative, Ablative and Prolative (/ Prosecutive) correspond bit by bit in the two languages. The other strikingly similar feature is the use of what seems to be the same co-affixal element *-k(V)*, although its distribution is quite random. For example, in Samoyed the co-affixal element is only used for nouns, whilst in Yukaghir it is used occasionally for nouns and pronouns. In Yukaghir, occasionally, the co-affixal element -*γa* ~ -*qa* is used also as a 'simple' ending, as in the Locative. Only in the case of Prolative and Ablative do the Case endings of the two languages behave in a way which is consistent: the same endings -*m-n-(V)* and -*t-(V)*, respectively, are used as 'simple' endings for the same categories (postpositions and adverbs), whilst, in combination with *-ka,* they are used for nouns and pronouns. This basically random distribution can only mean that the process of formation of new, complex endings (through Exaptation) has been achieved in Yukaghir independently of Samoyed, although the lexical material utilised in the Exaptation appears to be the same. This is not

Table 8.6 Parallel Case endings in Samoyed and Yukaghir

	Proto-Samoyed	Yukaghir
Loc.	*-n(V)	-γa ~ -qa (nouns and pronouns)/-γa-ne ~ -qa-ne (nouns)
Pro.	*-m-n(V)	-n (adverbs, postpositions)/-γa-n ~ -qa-n (nouns, pronouns)
Abl.	*-t(V)	-t (adverbs, postpositions)/-γa-t ~ -qa-t (nouns, pronouns)
Dat./Lat.	*-ng	-ń (pronouns)/-ŋi-ń (nouns)/-de ~ -ŋu-de (adverbs)

any different from the way exaptated Case endings are formed within U, as illustrated in the previous sections.

8.4.2. *The conventional interpretations of the Uralo/Yukaghir correlations*

The Uralic (Samoyed)/Yukaghir morphological correlations have been traditionally interpreted either as the result of 'genetic relationship' or as the result of 'intense contacts'. Those who support the 'borrowing' interpretation claim that the thesis of the genetic relationship is contradicted by the irregular character of the U and Yukaghir morphological correlations. For example, Rédei (1999a: 11–14) states that there is no full correspondence in sound-shape and function in the various shared endings, particularly in the Case endings.

However, fluctuations of this sort are more than normal, since these endings (although formed through the same process and the utilisation of the same lexical material) have been created independently in the languages involved. Indeed, this is also the case within the U area, as amply illustrated above, and further illustrated below. Moreover, Rédei himself recognises that there are at least two instances where the endings of Samoyed and the endings of Yukaghir display full agreement in sound-shape and function (1999a: 13–14):

(8.17) a. Yukaghir Abl. *-gət ~ -γət* vs Samoyed Yurak Abl. *-χad ~ -kad*;
     b. Yukaghir Com. *-ńə(ŋ)*, which is a nominalised form of the
        Samoyek Yurak noun *ńā* 'comrade, brother'.

Whilst recognising the possibility of the 'belonging together' of these and other endings ('Ihre Zusammengehörigkeit ist durchaus möglich'), Rédei claims nevertheless that one cannot think in terms of 'Urverwandtschaft' (1999a: 14), but only in terms of intense borrowing from Samoyed into Yukaghir, although no specific evidence or justification for this claim is actually provided.

One might simply observe that, yet again, through the application of the Comparative Method, no conclusive results can be achieved in this linguistic area.

8.5. GRAMMATICAL ENDINGS

In the following sections I shall examine several grammatical and derivational endings present in the U (as well as the Altaic) languages. In reviewing the evidence, I shall concentrate on what are generally considered to be the main functional, grammatical and derivational morphemes reconstructable for P-U, without embarking on the difficult task of defining the difference between grammatical and derivational Morphology[21] (see for example Johanson 1999). As we shall see, the reconstruction of single endings, as well as the reconstruction of coherent grammatical paradigms, has proven difficult, if not impossible so far within U.

8.5.1. *Possessive and Personal endings*

Table 8.7 (from Sinor 1988: 725) shows the reconstructed Possessive endings for P-U, for P-Turkic and P-Tungus[22] (for the P-U series see also Hajdú 1966: 141–3). Some of the reconstructed endings display full agreement.[23] Despite the uniform picture presented in this table for each language and language group, and despite the obvious parallels, these reconstructions do not go without problems (if interpreted within the framework, the traditional P-Languages and Comparative Method) for the following reasons.

Table 8.7 Reconstructed Possessive/Personal endings (Sinor 1988: 725)

		Proto-Uralic	Proto-Turkic	Proto-Tungus
Sing.	1	* -*m*	* -*m*	* -*m*
	2	* -*t*	* -*ng*	* -*t*
	3	* -*s(V)*	* -*s(V)*	* -*n*
Plu.	1	* -*m* + Plural	* -*m* + Plural	* -*m* + Plural (exclusive)
	2	* -*t* + Plural	* -*ng* + Plural	* -*t*
	3	* -*s* + Plural	* -*ø*	* -*t*

Firstly, the major concern is the question of how complete and consistent the system of Possessive (and Personal) endings might have been originally in P-U (Raun 1988b: 560). In fact, the Possessive ending systems in the modern U languages are rather complex, and show many deviations from the reconstructed system. This is particularly evident when the Possessive endings co-occur with the endings of Plurality or Duality, in which case they enter into sophisticated, complex relations (some of which are illustrated below, in the discussion of Duality and Plurality). And, in fact, the way in which the Plural endings are supposed to have combined with the Possessive endings in the P-Language cannot be ascertained. Furthermore, Hungarian, once again, distances itself from the other U languages even more. For example, Kulonen (1993: 72) observes that the Possessive system of Hungarian does not derive directly from the reconstructed P-U system. Abondolo (1998b: 439) states that the Hungarian Possessive system might be 'the result of analogical levelling which favoured one or the other of two originally complementary sets of suffixes, one set marking singular, the other non-singular possessions'.

Secondly, the Possessive endings are generally claimed to have developed from the corresponding personal pronouns, through the process of Grammaticalisation, but, the reconstruction of the P-U pronouns themselves poses several difficulties, as discussed below.

Thirdly, the reconstruction of *-s(V) for the 3rd Singular of P-U is only partially justified. This morpheme appears for example in Finnish *kala-nsa* 'fish-his', and in most of the U languages. In Hungarian, however, the actual Possessive ending is *-a* ~ *-e* in the Singular (including Old Hungarian), as in *hal-a* 'fish-his', so that *-s- is generally supposed to have disappeared, merging with the preceding vowel. Similarly, the expected reflexes of the reconstructed P-U ending are not present in Vogul, Ostyak or Samoyed. Vogul has in the Singular *-(t)e* after vowel (for example *ula-te* 'bow-his'), and just *-e* in all the other cases (Keresztes 1998: 411). Ostyak has *-(ə)ł* if the Possessor and the Possession are in the Singular[24] (Abondolo (1998c: 365); see also Gulya (1966: 58) for Eastern Ostyak and the examples (8.4) and (8.5) above). To account for the actual endings of Vogul and Ostyak, an original P-Ob-Ugric morpheme *-(V)θ ~ *-θ(V) has been reconstructed by Honti (1988, 1998a: 342). However, nothing prevents us from assuming that these Vogul and Ostyak Possessive endings are not connected (as is the case for other endings, as discussed above), in which case the Vogul component *-t-* could be equivalent to the P-Samoyed formant *-t(V) (Janhunen 1998: 471). Compare also 3rd Sing. *-ta* ~ *-ty* of Yakut, according to Menges (1968/95: 114). Whatever the connections, this is yet another case of non-convergence between Ob-Ugric and Hungarian, and of a (possible), 'horizontal' convergence between Ob-Ugric, Samoyed and a Turkic language.

Fourthly, the Possessive endings of the 2nd Singular in Vogul and Ostyak differ, yet again, from those of Hungarian and other U languages; in fact, Vogul and Ostyak have the ending *-(V)n*, and not *-t*, as reconstructed for P-U. Compare Hun. *ház-a-d* vs Finn. *talo-si* 'house-your' vs Vog. *ula-n* 'bow-your' (Keresztes 1998: 411). Several connections have been proposed for *-(V)n* (compare for example Sinor 1988: 733; Hajdú 1966: 132–3). Among these connections, one may consider that of the formant *-n-* in P-Samoyed. As Janhunen puts it (1998: 471):

> From the Proto-Uralic point of view, one of the most interesting features is that the second-person singular predicative ending seems to have been *-n in proto-Samoyedic, as opposed to *-t in most sub-branches of Finno-Ugric.

According to Collinder (1965a: 134), there might have been two words to indicate 'you': *-t and *-n; this duplicity is found in the demonstrative pronouns of Finnic, Estonian, Mordvin, Cheremis and Permian, as shown by Finn. *tämä* 'this' vs *nämä* 'these'. According to the author this could be 'probably a case of expletivism'.

In summary, the U languages have very different Possessive systems, particularly in connection with Plurality and Duality, and it is difficult to trace back their origins to a single, common source. In addition, even those morphemes (and/or components of morphemes) that can be reconstructed pose some difficulties. In fact, there is no doubt that the major endings and/ or components in P-U, P-Turkic and P-Tungus are the same, namely: *-*m*, *-*t*, *-*n* and *-*s,* but their behaviour and distribution are inconsistent, not to say chaotic, and certainly cannot fit within the ordered, linear family tree model, whether U only, Altaic only, or Ural-Altaic. In contrast, their distribution gives a strong impression of 'messiness' and 'inter-changeability'. A better way to analyse the situation could be to consider these endings as forming a basic, common Eurasiatic stock, whose elements are chosen and utilised randomly by each language involved. Obviously, the possibility also exists that these morphemes are similar just by chance, given their simple, basic phonological nature. This will be discussed in detail below.

Finally, the Possessive endings also function as Personal endings for the verb both in the U and the Altaic languages (through the process of Grammaticalisation). It is also generally recognised that the formation of both the Possessive and Personal endings has been implemented independently and rather recently in historical times, in each language or language group (Collinder 1960: 308, 1965a: 107; Sinor 1988: 733; Aalto 1969/78: 329).

According to some researchers, the reconstructed Singular, Personal/and Possessive endings reported in Table 8.7 are to be connected to the reconstructed Indo-European endings *-*m*, *-*s*, *-*t*.[25]

8.5.2. *Personal pronouns*

The reconstruction of the paradigm of Personal pronouns again encounters several difficulties. As Abondolo ((ed.) 1998: 24) puts it:

> The reconstruction of the Uralic personal pronouns encounters difficulties specific to this word class. Like numerals or kinship terms, pronouns enter easily into analogical subpatterns which allow cross-infection. A further difficulty arises from the relatively small size of the Proto-Uralic pronominal root, which was canonically monosyllabic (C)V(C).

Janhunen (1981a: 232) whilst reconstructing P-U **mun*/P-Finno-Permian **mun* 'I' (item (50)), and P-U **tun*/P-Finno-Permian **tun* 'you' (item (51)), remarks that these forms have not been preserved in all the present-day U languages, but only in Lapp, in Mordvin and Samoyed. The other U languages, the Ugric, the Permian languages, Cheremis, the Balto-Finnic languages and even south Lapp point to a different type: **mӟ* and **tӟ,* which normally appear as double-syllable words because of the presence of derivative material, as in Finnish *minä* 'I', and *sinä* 'you'. In other words, these (Singular) pronouns divide the whole of the U language family into two big groups: from the point of view of reconstruction, the pronoun roots with front vowel cannot be traced back further than the F-U level.

Suppletive root forms are rare in this word class, being present only in a few U languages: Hungarian, Samoyed Yurak and Yenisei. However, there does not seem to be any correlation among them. For example, compare the Nominative and Accusative of the 1st and 2nd Person pronouns in Hungarian, respectively: *én* vs *en-ge-m* 'I' vs 'me', *te* vs *té-ge-d* 'you'. It has been argued that *-ge-* is probably related to the root **kit ~ *kät* 'face', from which the suppletive Accusative forms of Samoyed are probably derived, but there does not appear to be any justification for this (see Abondolo (ed.) 1998: 25 for details). These suppletive forms have been often connected to equivalent forms in Indo-European (Greenberg[26] 1996).

In Finnish and Ostyak the pronouns take in the Accusative the suffix *-t* (Finn. *minu-t* and Ost. *män-t* 'me'); the origin and possible connections of this ending have attracted several, different explanations within the field.

8.5.3. *Plurality and Duality in the Uralic languages*

The reconstruction of the endings of Plurality and Duality, as well as the reconstruction of a Plurality/Duality paradigm, have proven again rather difficult within the framework of the traditional methods of analysis. In fact, there are three major problems:

(a) the endings of Plurality that are in common between (some and/or many) U languages are several, so that at least four endings have to be reconstructed for the P-Language; these endings are not unique to the U languages;

(b) the distribution of the endings of Plurality and Duality is quite restricted and/or defective in several U languages;

(c) in some languages (Permian, Cheremis and, partially, Hungarian), there is hardly any trace of the reconstructed endings. In contrast, these languages have developed new, relatively recent endings.

8.5.3.1. *The endings of Plurality and Duality*

There is a variety of Plural endings in the U languages, a variety which is in contradiction with the assumption of their common origin from a single, well defined P-Language. Generally, at least four endings are reconstructed for Plurality: **-t, *-n, *-k, *-j ~ *-i* (Raun 1988b: 557; Honti 1995a, 1995b and 1997; Hajdú 2000: 266–7). The etymological connection among them is not easy to establish, despite some claims to the contrary. There are also other endings which could be candidates for the reconstruction, but they are not widely accepted because of their limited distribution (within U). For example, according to some scholars, in early U times there must have been up to ten endings to express 'collective Plurality', some of which must have changed their function later on (see, for example, Serebrennikov 1966 and 1973). Honti (1995b: 62) raises two insightful questions in relation to this (he will provide some answers in a subsequent paper; see below):

> (a) Galten die in mehreren uralischen Sprachen vorhandenen, etymologisch voneinander untrennbaren Pluralsuffixe bereits in der Grundsprache als Pluralsuffixe, oder sind sie nur für Produkte späterer konvergenter Entwicklungen zu halten? (b) Wenn sie uralt wären, wie erklärt sich dann der Umstand, daß es mehrere Pluralsuffixe in der Grundsprache gab?

What follows is an overview of the most common endings of Plurality and Duality to be found in the U languages (for more details see Honti 1997). This section will also illustrate the variety of functions the endings may have, the 'fuzziness' of their distribution, and their occurrence also in non-U languages. These endings apply both to nouns and verbs, whereby the co-occurrence with the noun or with the verb is generally not marked by any particular phonetic or morpho-phonetic signal. This factor reflects in turn a general property of several U endings, and has led to the view, held by most scholars, that in P-U there was no distinction between the category of verb and that of noun.

-*t*. Most U languages, like Finnish, Vogul, Ostyak, Samoyed, have an ending -*t*, as in Finn. *talo-t* 'houses'. This morpheme -*t* is also used in the verbal conjugation in several languages, for example in Vogul (Honti: 1988: 157–8; Keresztes 1998: 398–9).

A formant -*t* is also present in Mongolian, in Turkic (although here it is rare, to the point that it is often considered a borrowing from Mongolian) and in Tungus, although its use is limited to some pronouns and Personal endings (Poppe 1952, 1955; 1977a; Sinor 1952, 1988: 728–31).

-*n*. Another frequent morpheme of Plurality is -(*a*)*n*, which is found for example in Zyrian, Mordvin, Samoyed, Estonian (as a prefix in Personal pronouns), and Vogul. In this last language it is also used in connection with verbs, to express Plurality of the Definite Object in the Definite Conjugation. It is mainly used to form Plurality of nouns when the Possessive ending is present as well, and it indicates Plurality of the Possession (and/or Possessor). Compare Vog. *kol* 'house', *kol-um* 'house-my' vs *kol-an-um* 'house-Plu.-my, my houses' (recall that the Plural in Vogul is -*t*, if the Possessive is not present).

Note that in some Samoyed languages the ordinary Plural -*la* can also be used to indicate Plurality in connection with Possession (see below).

The formant -*n* is generally believed also to have existed in P-Finnish. For example, in modern Finnish the form *talo-ni* has two grammatical meanings: (1) 'my house' < **talo-mi* (where **-mi* is the 1st Possessive); (2) 'my houses' < **talo-n-mi*, where -*n*- indicates Plurality. Similarly, *talo-n-sa*, where -*sa* is the ending of 3rd Possessive, has four grammatical meanings, given that *-n-sa* indicates Singularity and Plurality of the Possessor as well as of the Possession: 'his house' vs 'their house'/'his houses' vs 'their houses' (in these cases the noun does not take the normal ending *-t*: *talo-t*). It is therefore assumed that there must have been a process of syncretism between the forms *talo-mi* and *talo-n-mi*, as well as between *talo-sa* and *talo-n-sa*, the second terms of the pair containing the ending of Plurality *-n-* (Abondolo 1998b: 440). Compare here the equivalent Mordvin constructions, where the syncretism has not taken place: *kudo-m* 'house-my' vs *kudo-n* 'houses-my', *kudo-zo* 'house-his' vs *kudo-n-zo* 'house-Plu.-his, his houses' (Zaicz 1998: 195).

A formant *-n-* is well attested in the Altaic languages with similar functions (Sinor 1988: 726; Menges 1968/95: 111).

-l. An ending of more restricted, although not of less complex distribution within U is *-l*, which in fact is not always reconstructed for P-U. It is present in Ostyak, in Cheremis and in Samoyed. In Samoyed Selkup it is present in the form *-la*, simply to mark Plurality, as in *loga* 'fox' vs *loga-la* 'fox-Plu.'. However, here it can also express Plurality in connection with Possession, as in *loga-la-m* alongside with *loga-ni-m*, which both mean 'fox-Plu.-my, my foxes' (Honti 1997: 38) – as discussed above, *-n(i)-* is the Plural ending mostly used in connection with Possession. In Eastern Ostyak *-l* is a marker of Plurality only in connection with Possession (*-t* otherwise), as in *weli-t* 'reindeer-Plu., reindeers' vs *weli-l-äm* 'reindeer-Plu.-my, my reindeers' (Gulya 1966: 58). This formant is also the marker of the Plurality of the Definite Object within the Definite Conjugation. Honti (1997: 85) considers this ending *-l* to be a new ending which developed separately in the languages in question.

An *-l* formant is also present in Tungusic (to indicate Plurality in nouns and verbs), in Old Mongolian and some present-day Mongolian dialects. It is also present in Turkic, where it is believed to be a constituent element of the Turkic plural *-la-r*, at least according to some interpretations (Sinor 1952: 214; 1988: 729: Poppe 1952, 1955).

Once again there is a connection between Plurality as such and Plurality of Possession, the morpheme *-l* being in most cases a simple morpheme of Plurality and, in some cases, a morpheme expressing Plurality in connection with Possession.

-j ~ -i. This ending is used in connection with oblique Case endings and/or Possession to express Plurality. Compare Hun. *háza-m* 'house-my' vs *háza-i-m* 'house-Plu.-my, my houses'; Finn. *talo* 'house'/*talo-t* 'house-Plu., houses' vs *talo-ssa* 'house-inside, in the house' vs *talo-i-ssa* 'house-Plu.-inside, in the houses'. This is also found in Lapp and in Samoyed, Kamassian excluded. A lot has been said about the origin of this morpheme, even if little consensus has been achieved so far (Raun 1988b: 558; Imre 1988: 434; Hajdú 1988; Mikola 1988; Honti 1997: 26; Sammallahti 1998: 47).

A formant *i* is found in Turkish and in other Turkic languages.[27] Notice also that in Estonian in oblique Cases both *-i* and *-t* (and other Plural endings) may occur.

-r. Finally, one should mention the ending *-r*, although its distribution is very restricted. It is present in the function of a collective suffix in Samoyed Yurak and in Cheremis. This formant is believed to be the same as the one present in Turkish, where it is a component of *-la-r*,[28] and in Tungus (Sinor 1952: 217).

The P-U ending of Duality has been generally reconstructed as $*-k(\partial)$ (Janhunen 1981b: 29; Collinder 1965a: 131; Honti 1997: 2), even though in the actual languages the category of Duality (like that of Plurality) is expressed by a wide range of endings, which is difficult to trace back to a common source[29] (see Künnap 2000: 31 for a critical review).

8.5.3.2. *'Plurality is a relatively new grammatical category'*

It is generally recognised in U studies that Plurality and Duality must have had a defective functioning in P-U. These categories did not have a full Case paradigm like the category of Singularity: there was neither Dual nor Plural except in the Nominative. In other words, in P-U there must have been a period of an undistinguished *numerus absolutus*. This claim is based on two facts: i) the defective distribution of the reconstructable endings of Plurality and Duality; ii) the absence of these (supposedly) P-U endings in several languages, where instead totally new endings are present (Ravila 1938, 1941; Fokos-Fuchs 1961; E. Itkonen 1962; Collinder 1965a: 128; Raun 1988b: 556; Rédei 1980, 1981, 1988b, 1999b; Luutonen 1999).

The thesis of the P-U *numerus absolutus* has recently been questioned by Honti (1995a, 1995b, 1997), who claims instead that in P-U there was probably an (almost) complete Case paradigm in all numbers.[30] To explain the mismatch between the assumed (almost) complete paradigm and the defective, restricted distribution of the endings of Plurality in the modern languages the author argues that:

a) in some present-day languages (Cheremis, Permian languages and (partially) Hungarian) the ancient number endings ($*-t$ and $*-j \sim *-i$) have disappeared, to be replaced by new endings;

b) in some other languages (Lapp and Samoyed) these endings have changed their function.

However, the author recognises that the changes listed above cannot be explained in terms of historical phonology. In particular:

c) there does not appear to be phonetic justification for the (assumed) loss of the endings of Plurality in Permian and Cheremis;

d) there is not (yet) any satisfactory explanation for the (assumed) functional changes in the Plural endings of Lapp and Samoyed, although an explanation should be sought within the development of the morpho-syntax of the individual languages.

Like Honti, Luutonen (1999: 83) argues that the Permian languages and Cheremis have lost the original P-U ending *-t, and that their actual endings are new, recent 'replacements' through the adoption of more analytic, secondary morphemes (in turn derived from ordinary words). Unlike Honti, Luutonen tries to argue that there is instead a phonetic justification for the loss of the original P-U endings in Permian: the word-final phonemes in these languages have undergone a 'strong reductive tendency'; this phenomenon in turn caused the loss (and consequent replacement) of the old endings of Plurality. However, the author (1999: 83) can only identify the loss of two word-final consonants (-k and -m) for 'apparently phonetic reasons'. Furthermore, as also remarked by the author himself (1999: 81), in Cheremis there are several traces of the ending *-t, which is in fact the ending of 3rd Person Plural for verbs and nouns; compare: ila-t 'they live' and kuðə-š-t 'house-his-Plu., their house(s)'. This seems to lend support to the thesis that no phonetic justification has so far been identified for the disappearing of -t, as argued for by Honti.

It is important to highlight at this point that the (presumed) 'replacement' endings of Plurality in Permian and Cheremis are widely considered to be either of uncertain origin or of Turkic origin. In particular, the endings of Zyrian and Votyak (-jas ~ -jez ~ -ez and -jos ~ -os respectively) are of uncertain origin according to most scholars (for example Luutonen (1999: 73) and Hajdú (2000: 266); but see Rédei[31] (1988b: 379–80) for a different opinion). The endings -ßlä of Hill Cheremis and -ßlak of Eastern Cheremis are believed to derive from Common Turkic, compare Tur. bölük 'group, body (of man)'. The ending -šaməč of Meadov Cheremis, according to Luutonen (1999: 73), 'much resembles the Chuvash plural suffix sem[32], probably originating in the Bulgar word *sām "number"'; Bereczki (1988: 341) and Hajdú (2000: 266) share the same opinion. Another ending of Plurality deriving from Turkic seems to be the ending -lar of Samoyed Kamas, which is only used in connection with ethnonyms: mator-lar 'the Mators' (Hajdú 2000: 267).

Whatever the interpretations, the fact remains that the distribution of the endings of Plurality and Duality within U may be quite restricted and/or defective, whilst some languages have developed new, 'secondary' plural endings. For example, Duality is only present in Ob-Ugric, Samoyed and Lapp. In most of the Samoyed languages, there is a Dual and a Plural only in the Nominative, although, according to Hajdú (1968), there are some Case endings other than the Nominative which can co-occur with the ending(s) of Plurality. In Lapp the Dual is restricted to verbal endings, to nouns inflected with Possessive endings and Personal pronouns. The opposition 'Singularity' vs 'Plurality' is neutralised in all Cases except the Nominative, for example, in Mordvin (Indefinite Declension): *kudo* 'house' vs *kudo-t* 'house-Plu.', but *kudo-sto* 'house-out=of, out of the house/houses' (Zaicz 1998: 191). The most frequent ending of Plurality (which is therefore considered to be one of the oldest), *-t*, is missing (partially, see above) in Cheremis, in the Permian languages and (partially) in Hungarian (see below), whilst in Samoyed Selkup it is only used for animate beings. Among the languages that have developed new endings one can also quote Samoyed. As Janhunen (1998: 469–70) says:

> proto-Samoyedic retained the proto-Uralic markers for the dual and plural numbers. These were originally not combinable with the normal Case endings; various types of plural paradigm were constructed secondarily out of the available elements.

Furthermore, in the present-day languages there are several kinds of nominal constructions which, yet again, suggest a restricted use of Plurality. Some of these constructions are listed below (from Fokos-Fuchs (1961: 266–90); for some more examples see Rédei (1999b)):

- use of Singular after a numeral: Finn. *kaksi talo-a* 'two-house-Partit., two houses' (in Finnish the noun preceded by a numeral requires the Partitive);
- use of Singular after twin body-parts: Hun. *a szem-e közé néz* 'the eye-his [toward]between he=looks, he looks between his eyes';
- to refer to one member only of the twin parts, the languages make recourse to expressions of the kind: Hun. *fél szem*, Finn. *silmä-puoli* 'one-eyed' (literally 'half eye');
- use of collective Singular to indicate a group of elements, as in Che. *pi jimä* 'tooth dull, the teeth are dull';
- use of Singular for each of the several owners, if they own only one item, as in Finn. *laki-t lensi-vät pää-stä* 'hat-Plu. flew-Plu. head-from, the hats flew from the heads'; etc.

These very same constructions, and many others indicative of the *numerus absolutus*, are present also in the Altaic languages (see again Fokos-Fuchs (1961: 266–90) for details; compare also Fokos-Fuchs (1937)).

In summary, in several U languages/language groups 'morphological Plurality is a relatively new grammatical category' ('suhteellisen nuori muotokategoria'), to use Ravila's (1938: 296) expression. Furthermore, some of the new endings which (supposedly) replaced the lost P-U endings appear to have a Turkic origin. This fact does not seem to have given rise to suspicion about the validity of the conventional interpretation. On the contrary, for example Luutonen[33] (1999) appears to consider more than natural the fact that Cheremis, for instance, has adopted 'new Turkic endings', rather than 'new U endings' – as one might reasonably expect. This is explained by stating that the new 'replacement' endings have been borrowed. However, evidence from other language groups does not support the (hidden) assumption that grammatical borrowing is a common, natural linguistic phenomenon. In fact, grammatical borrowing, including borrowing of grammatical Plurality, tends to be very rare. If it happens at all, it tends to take place only within a context of 'mixed languages' (see below) and/or within restricted, specific lexical and grammatical environments (see some examples in Hock (1986: 387)).

Finally, one might observe that the process of formation of relatively recent, new endings of Plurality has taken place also in the Altaic languages (see Poppe 1960c: 34–5; Menges 1968/95: 57–8; Doerfer 1964: 89, Luutonen 1999: 74).

8.5.3.3. *Plurality in Hungarian*

Unlike most U languages, Hungarian has a different Plural ending, used both for nouns (in 'non-oblique' Cases), and for verbs: the ending *-k*. A Plural *-k* is found also in Lapp, although this is generally considered as deriving from **-t* (Ravila 1935; Honti 1997: 32).

In nouns *-k* expresses simply Plurality, as in *ember* 'man' vs *ember-e-k* 'man-Ep.Vow.-Plu., men'. The ending *-k* is also a component of the Plural Possessive endings, as in *ház-unk* 'house-our', which derives from **háza-mï-k* (to use Abondolo's (1998b: 439) transcription), that is 'house-1st Poss.-Plu.' This reconstruction is clearly reflected in the forms found in the text *Halotti beszéd*: compare for example *uro-m-c* 'Lord-1st Poss.-Plu., Lord-our' (Modern Hun. *urunk*). The modern form *urunk* is perceived and reanalysed as *ur-unk* instead of *uru-n-k* (see for further details Imre (1988: 432–4)).

In its verbal function, *-k* it is a component of Plurality both in the Definite and the Indefinite Conjugation (Imre 1988: 436). For the Indefinite Conjugation compare the following forms: *lát-unk* 'we see', *ül-ünk* 'we seat', etc. The component *-unk* represents the modern development and re-analysis of the original components and segmentation, as recorded again in the text *Halotti beszéd*: *vog-mu-c* 'be-1st Poss.-Plu., we are', corresponding to Modern Hun. *vagy-unk*. For the Definite Conjugation compare the following forms: *lát-ju-k* 'we see [them/him/it etc.], *lát-já-to-k* 'you see', *lát-já-k* 'they see', where a clear segmentation of the various morphemes is still possible – although this is not always the case in the verbal paradigm of Hungarian.

The origin of *-k* is disputed. Some researchers believe that it derives from a derivational suffix **-kkV*, compare Finn. *puna-kka* 'rubicund' from *puna* 'red' (Abondolo 1988b: 439). This explanation looks a bit far fetched. Abondolo himself (ibid.) also considers the possibility that the verbal element -*k* is the same as the possessive element -*k* in *uru-n-k*. This is indeed the interpretation which is chosen here, but this interpretation still does not tell us where the component -*k* comes from. Aalto (1969/78: 326) considers the possibility of connecting *-*k* with the Samoyed co-affixal element *-*k*(ø)- discussed above (Section 8.4.1), as well as with the Tungus, Turkic and Mongolian collective ending -*g*. Menges (1968/95: 129) on the other hand remarks that in a number of Turkic languages the 1st Poss. Plu. -*ym* ~ -*yz* (normally used in connection with a verbal noun) is replaced by -*yq* ~ -*ik* (the two forms coexist in some languages), whose origin is considered unclear, but whose meaning and sound-shape could be connected with Hun. -*k*. A Plural -*k* exists also in Dravidian.

8.5.3.4. *Summary and conclusion on Plurality and Duality*

I would like to summarise the situation regarding the category of Plurality with the following comments by Sinor ((1952: 228–30); see Section 6.3 for the identified, lexical Uralo-Tungusic correlations):

> The Finno-Ugrian and Tunguz facts observed in connection with -*n* . . . are as closely parallel as if they belonged to the same language. This may also be said, although less emphatically, about the -*t* plural. Both these suffixes are well represented in Mongol, . . . The plural -*l*, common to Samoyede and Tunguz, with some traces in the other Ural-Altaic languages, is a new fact in this connexion. . . . The study of Ural-Altaic plural suffixes shows clearly that the crucial problem is that of the interrelation of these languages. . . . The adoption of a suffix by one language from another is perhaps the most interesting feature we have been able to ascertain in this study . . . This presupposes something more than contacts between the languages involved; we actually have to reckon with the fusion of different languages. . . . It appears that Ural-Altaic languages originally disposed of only two or perhaps three personal endings used indiscriminately for singular and plural. Plurality was expressed by specialised suffixes added to the singular personal endings. Chuvash *kil-əm-ər* 'our house' is . . . formed by *root + possessive suffix + plural suffix*. Even *ju-w-ur* 'our own house' is its exact counterpart, whereas, e.g. in Ostiak-Samoyede the same pattern is used with various plural suffixes: *loga-u* or *loga-m* 'my fox', *loga-u-t* or *loga-m-en* 'our fox'. -*m*, -*w*, -*u* are phonetic variants of the same possessive suffix, -*r*, -*t*, -*n* are various plural suffixes used in a similar rôle. The Samoyede forms are particularly interesting because they show the inter-changeability of the tools serving the same semantic purpose within the framework of one and the same language. . . . The question now arises whether different languages using the same constructions composed from the same elements developed the forms separately or continued forms which were already present in a primitive, let us say Ural-Altaic language. The answer is not easy

8.5.4. *Tense, Aspect, Mood and other derivational morphemes*

It is recognised within the field that the reconstruction of single verbal morphemes for P-U is practically impossible – let alone verbal paradigms.

The U languages do not share common verbal morphemes expressing temporal and/or aspectual notions. In particular, there is no clear shared Past Tense marker. It is generally accepted that the original tense system might have been similar to that found nowadays in Samoyed, where the verbs have an inherently stative, non-perfective meaning/connotation, or an inherently perfective, punctual one, on the basis of their lexical meaning only.

Similarly, the existence of various frequentative endings in the U languages can lead to the conclusion that the opposition Iterative vs non-Iterative, if it did exist in their ancestor/ancestors, did not develop into a common, formal, morphological distinction. The same holds true for the expression of Mood: P-U might have had an unmarked Indicative vs a marked Imperative, which however did not leave relevant traces in the daughter languages.

In other words, most U languages have enriched the basic Past vs non-Past opposition, as well as the basic Indicative vs Imperative distinction (assumed to have existed in P-U), in different, independent ways. It is therefore widely accepted that the original verb form in P-U must have been a kind of 'aorist', neutral with regard to time, to which the Personal endings (reported in Table 8.7 above), were attached directly (Abondolo (ed.) 1998: 28; Raun 1988b: 563; Janhunen 1981b: 36).

The following are the few verbal endings which could possibly be traced back to a common source:

- *-s ~ -š*: marker of Past Tense. It is present in most Samoyed languages, Ob-Ugric, probably Mordvin in 3rd Person and in negative sentences only (Mikola 1988: 248; E. Itkonen 1966b: 80; Künnap 2000: 29–30), Cheremis, Lapp (but also Swedish), South Estonian, Livonian. This morpheme is mainly used in negative and/or interrogative sentences, so that it might not be, consistently, a temporal marker. Note that there is a an aspectual *-š* ending in Chuvash, of disputed origin, probably borrowed from the Volga-Finnic languages, according to Menges (1968/95: 156). There is a temporal suffix in *-s* also in the Palaeo-Siberian languages, including Yukaghir (Audova 1996).
- *-j ~ -i*: marker of Past Tense. It is present in Finnish: *sa-i-n kirjeen* 'receive-Past.-1st Sing. letter, I received the/a letter', in East Cheremis and North Lapp. It has also been proposed that an original **-j ~ *-i* is at the basis of the morpheme of Past Tense of Old Hungarian *-á ~ -é*. An ending *-i* expressing Present/Continuative/Aorist is present in the Abaquan languages, although quite rare elsewhere (Menges 1968/95: 156), as well as in Dravidian (Tyler 1968).

• -*k*(*V*): marker of Present. The evidence for this ending is scarce. It has been reconstructed as being an ending of Present Tense, but, in this function, it is only present in the Ob-Ugric languages. It is used in Negative and Imperative/Optative sentences in the Permian and Volgaic languages (E. Itkonen 1966b: 80; Künnap 2000: 30). This morpheme is probably the same as the one present in Lapp and Samoyed Kamas (Collinder 1965a: 132). It has also been associated to the Optative -*gai* of the Altaic languages.

Compare also the widespread U and Altaic Gerundive ending -(*V*)*n,* and the widespread U and Altaic Perfective/Tense/Factitive -*t,* for which see the next section.

One could add to the list of reconstructed morphemes the following morphemes, which are traditionally classified as 'derivational': the endings for the ordinal numbers *mt-, mc-* which appear to have parallels in the Turkic languages (Räsänen 1959; Sinor 1959); the endings to express 'Reflexivity' in verbs (Finn. -*u-, -pu-*), which have been associated to Turkic and Mon. -*bu-*, Tun. -*wu-*; the Frequentative, which is -*ele-* in Finnish (*astele-* 'step along, walk', *kävele-* 'walk for a certain length'), and which has been associated to Turkic *älä ~ ala* (Räsänen 1963/4: 183–4).

8.6. ISOMORPHIC CONSTRUCTIONS

According to recent research Syntax (or at least certain aspects of it), like Morphology, also seems to occupy one of the lowest positions in the hierarchy of 'easiness of borrowability'. For example, Campbell (1993: 104) remarks that there are, if not 'absolute constraints', certainly well-documented general 'tendencies', on the basis of which the following 'hierarchy of borrowability' has been established and basically agreed upon, although minor variations exist (Thomason & Kaufman 1988: 64–76; E. Moravcsik 1978; Lass 1997: 184–90; Danchev 1988):

(8.18) Lexicon > Phonology > Morphology > Syntactic/Typological structures

Furthermore, within each linguistic level in this hierarchy, further tendencies have been identified, which are quite well documented:

(8.19) Noun > Verb > Function Words (adverb, conjunction etc.) > Preposition/Postposition

In contrast, when the phenomenon of intense, widespread structural borrowing is encountered, as in the case of the Cushitic language Ma'a, we are already dealing with what is technically defined a 'mixed language' (Thomason & Kaufman 1988: 65–109; McMahon 1994: 211–12). It has also been argued that syntactic constructions can be 'inherited', just like phonemes and morphemes; see the work by Campbell (1990b) on the reconstruction of some Balto-Finnic constructions. Similarly, regarding isomorphism, which is usually believed to be 'diagnostic' of areal convergence only, Bynon (1977: 244) remarks:

> Isomorphism of structure . . . is not of course necessarily diagnostic of convergence, for it is also a common feature of genealogically related languages whether these have become geographically separated or not.

Statements such as this tie in with the fact that in recent years typological criteria have come to be regarded as significant in the process of assessing relations, in the sense that they could give an indirect contribution to the more traditional methods of reconstructions. For example, Nichols (1992: 2–3) argues that:

> the comparative method does not apply at time depths much greater than about 8000 years . . . [but] . . . population typology gives us the heuristic method that standard comparative-historical method lacks for greater time-depth

Finally, with specific reference to the U and Asiatic linguistic area, Janhunen (1996: 229–33) argues that the homeland of the languages involved in the 'Altaic complex' can be located in the east (in the Manchurian region), and that (2000: 65) the U family can be conceived of as an early member of the same areal and typological complex. This member then expanded to the west, forming a new genetic unit (see also Austerlitz (1970) for similar ideas).

It is therefore appropriate to take into consideration some isomorphic constructions and, very briefly, some typological features, for the purpose of assessing relations in this linguistic area. In particular, the isomorphic constructions, in my opinion relevant to the task, to the best of my knowledge have not so far been paid adequate attention. In fact, several isomorphic constructions shared by the languages under investigation utilise what seems to be the same morpheme, and, occasionally, even up to three identical morphemes. I believe that such complex constructions are unlikely to arise by chance, independently of whether or not the lexical material contained in them can be proven to be etymologically connected.

8.6.1. *Negative verb*

Some U and Altaic languages, and Yukaghir, have a so-called negative conjugation. In other words, negation is expressed not through a negative particle co-occurring with the verb, but through a kind of auxiliary verb, which is conjugated regularly, whilst the actual verb takes a neutral, fixed form, as shown by the following Finnish paradigm (see Table 8.8).

Table 8.8 Negative conjugation in Finnish

lue-n	'I=read'	*e-n*	*lue*	'I=do=not read'
lue-t	'you=read'	*e-t*	*lue*	'you=do=not read'
luke-e	'he /she=reads'	*e-i*	*lue*	'he/she=does=not read'

A negative verbal form is used in Finnish also in the Imperative, as shown by the pair *lue* 'read' vs *älä lue* 'do=not read' (2nd Person Singular). The negative form *älä* is often compared with the equivalent Yukaghir *el ~ ele*. Equivalent negative verbs and related isomorphic constructions are found in the majority of the Tungusic language (*e- ~ ä-*), in Mongolian (*e-se*) (UEW 68; SSA 100) and in Dravidian.

8.6.2. *Aspect markers and verbal constructions*

In all the Turkic languages there is an Aspect/Tense marker *-t- ~ -d-*. It occurs, among others, in constructions traditionally called 'Perfectum Definitum', that is, constructions containing a nominalised verb, conjugated with a Possessive, as in *git-t-im* 'go-Asp.-1st Poss., my going/I went' (Menges 1968/95: 129–30). The Turkic constructions are isomorphic with the equivalent Hungarian constructions,[34] as shown in *men-t-em-ben* 'in my going, while I was going', where *-t-* is the Past Tense, *-m* is the Possessive (*-e-* the Epenthetic vowel), and *-ben* is the new, secondary Locative ending discussed above (see Table 8.5). It is clear that what is now the ordinary Hungarian Past Tense form (*men-t-e-m* 'I went') developed from a nominalised verbal phrase, whose original meaning was 'my-having-gone, my going' (their participial origin is indeed still retrievable in Old Hungarian; see Marcantonio & Nummenaho (1998)).

Within U the formant *-t* is present also in Zyrian, Ostyak, Finnish, Balto-Finnic, and some Samoyed languages. For example in Vakh Ostyak there is an Imperfect Participle *-t(ə) ~ -t(ə̂)*, which has two basic functions. It can be an ordinary Participle (with active and/or passive value), as in: *kul wel-tə ku* 'fish kill-Imp.Part. man, fish killing man/fisherman'. Or it can be a component of the subordinate sentences, in which case it is constructed together with a Possessive and/or a Case ending (like in Hungarian and Turkic; see also the Ostyak example (8.5) above). Similarly, in Finnish there is a Passive Past Participle *-tu ~ -ty*, which can also be used in subordinate sentences isomorphic to the Ostyak constructions. Compare the following sentences, which show two verbal phrases, the first in Ostyak and the second in Finnish. The Ostyak phrase is constructed with the Imperfect Participle *-t* and the Possessive *-ȫγ* 'our' (text from Gulya 1966: 127), the Finnish construction contains in addition a Case ending, the Partitive *-a* :

(8.20) məŋ sajâw   täl-t-ŏγ, . . .   /tul-tu-a-ni, ...
we fishing=net haul-Imp.Part.-our,   /come-Past.Part.-Partit.-my
'our fish-net hauling, when we were fishing,/after my coming, after I
came'

In Samoyed Selkup the morpheme *-t* can have the value of both Perfect
and Imperfect Participle, as in *kuubedi* 'a dead man', *minta-* 'the one who is
going' (Janhunen 1998: 473; Collinder 1965a: 115: Hajdú 1988). Finally, *-t*
can also express Causativity/Factitivity in both the U and the Altaic
languages. According to some scholars, it has to be connected to the
Indo-European dental Preterite.

8.6.3. *Infinitive, gerundive and verbal constructions*

Among the several isomorphic constructions shared by the U and Altaic
languages, particularly interesting are those verbal constructions of the type
seen in the previous paragraph. These constructions may contain up to three
identical morphemes, such as the following Turkish (8.21) and Ostyak (8.22)
Gerundive/Participial constructions:

(8.21) memleket-i   tanï-ma-ma-m-a, . . .   (text fromTrask 1996: 126)
country-Obj. know-not-Ger.-my-Loc./Dat.
'to ~ at my not knowing the country, . . .'

(8.22) mä lŏγə käs-m-äm-ä, . . .   (text from Gulya 1966: 129)
I   him   look-Perf.Part.-my-Lat.
'to ~ at my looking him, as I saw him, . . .'

In Turkish there is a morpheme *-ma- ~ -mä-* (Menges 1968/95: 162), which
has various infinitival functions, including Gerundive. In Ostyak there is a
morpheme *-m-* (*-əm- ~ – ə̂m-; -mə- ~ -mə̂* -), according to vowel harmony
and the nature of the verbal stem (Gulya 1966: 124–7)), with a Past
Participle, Perfect value.[35] These are the first identical morphemes. The
second identical morphemes are the Turkish Locative/Dative *-a* and the
Ostyak Lative *-ä* (see point 10 in Appendix III). The third identical
morphemes are the Possessive *-m*.

A morpheme *-ma ~ -mä* is present also in Finnish (and other Finnic
languages, see Kangasmaa-Minn 1969), where it has two functions: Infinitive and (passive) Participle, as shown below:

(8.23) menin kävele-mä-än / Peka-n   rakenta-ma talo
I=went walk-Inf.-Illa. / Pekka-Gen. build-Part. house
'I went to walk, walking, for a walk / the house build by Pekka'

In the first sentence, the Illative ending *-än* has been added to the Infinitive
-ma. In the second sentence the morpheme *-ma* is the (passive) Participle,
and the Agent takes the Genitive case (it is the so-called *agenttipartisiippi*).

The morpheme *-ma* in this function is present throughout the U, Altaic languages and Yukaghir (in this last language it also has different functions; Sauvageot (1969: 353)).

Within the field of infinitival verbal phrases, one may quote the following, striking isomorphic Gerundive/Participial endings and constructions: Old Turkic *-pa-n ~ -pä-n* vs Hun. *-vá-n ~ -vé-n* (this last one being the long form of the Gerundive/Participial *-va ~ -ve*). Compare Hun. *vár* 'to wait', *vár-va ~ vár-ván* 'waiting', etc. These Hungarian and Turkic constructions consist of the following components: Part. **p-* + Ep.Vow. + *-n*, this last morpheme being probably the Locative ending used as a modality adverb (see below). The Turkic morpheme *-p* regularly corresponds to *-v* in Hungarian and *-p* in other U languages (Sinor 1961: 177). These forms and constructions are found in the oldest documents, the Turkic 'Inscriptions' and the Hungarian text the 'Old Hungarian lament of Mary'. The morpheme *-p* is also found in Mongolian, although only in combination with other suffixes, and in Tungusic (Menges 1968/95: 135–6).

The Gerundive/Instrumental ending *-(V)n* is: 'un morphème particulièrement répandu dans les langues ouralo-altaïques,' to use Sinor's words (1943: 226). It is (probably) the original Locative ending, which can be used both for nouns and verbs. In connection with verbs the morpheme has assumed a modality adverb function, as illustrated above. In connection with nouns it has also assumed (as often happens) more abstract functions than the original local one, such as instrumental, modal and temporal functions. Compare the following examples within U: Finn. *alka-en* 'starting', *jala-n* 'by foot'; Hun. *tél-en* 'in winter; Finn. *tänä päivä-nä* '(during) this day', *tänä kesä-nä* '(during) this summer'; Hun. *gyors-an* 'quickly', etc. (but see E. Itkonen[36] 1966b: 72 for a different interpretation of this ending).

8.6.4. *Postpositional constructions*

The U and Altaic languages (and Yukaghir) share yet another important isomorphic construction, the postpositional constructions, some of which also contain similar or identical lexical material.

The postpositions can be constructed with Possessive and/or Case endings (depending on function and context), as shown by the Hungarian postposition *ala-tt* 'under': *asztal ala-tt* 'table under', *ala-tt-am* 'under me', *ala-tt-ad* 'under you', *ala-tt-a* 'under him/her' etc. In these constructions *ala-* is the original 'spatial' noun meaning 'space under'; *-t-* (*~ -tt-*) is the Locative, *-am*, *-ad*, *-a* are the 1st, 2nd and 3rd Person Possessive respectively (see the examples (8.6) – (8.10) above). The Finnish equivalent is the form *alla-ni*, where *-ni* is, again the 1st Person Possessive. In Turkish, the equivalent isomorphic construction is *alt-ïm-da*, where *alt-* means 'space under', *-ïm* is the 1st Person Possessive, and *-da* is the Locative. The only difference between the Hungarian and the Turkish constructions is the reverse order of the sequence of the Possessive and Case endings, a normal feature in this linguistic area (see Section 8.3.3).

There are other nouns which have been, or can be grammaticalised into postposition, and which are similar between U and Altaic, or U and Yukaghir, see for example the F-U root *tiŋe (*tüŋe) discussed in Section 8.3.2.1.

In light of the hierarchy of 'borrowability' reported in (8.18) and (8.19) above, it is possible that these postpositional constructions are particularly resistant to borrowing.

8.6.5. *The role of Typology*

I have argued above that Syntax and Typology may play a role in assessing relations in the linguistic area under investigation, particularly in view of the fact that the 'primary evidence' of relatedness in this area cannot rely either on Morphology or on Phonology. Therefore, I would like to conclude this paragraph by simply listing some typological and morpho-syntactic structures shared by the U languages and their eastern neighbouring languages. The reader should be warned however that this is just an overview of some 'superficial' typological properties, and that a proper, comprehensive analysis of this kind lies outside the scope of this book.

It is received wisdom that the U and Altaic languages 'simply share typological similarities' (for example Dixon 1997: 32). Apart from the fact that this is, really, not true, one might observe that not all of the typological features these languages have in common can be ascribed to the 'Universals of language', and their 'implications' (Greenberg 1963). Compare the following features, some of which are present in all, others in many U and Altaic languages:

(1) agglutination;
(2) absence of grammatical gender;
(3) absence of consonant clusters (CCV) in initial position;[37]
(4) absence of articles (with the exception of Modern Hungarian, and Mordvin, which has an enclitic article);
(5) *determinant* precedes the *determinatum;*
(6) Possession is expressed through constructions of the type *mihi est*, see Finn. *minu-lla on* and Hun. *nekem van* 'I have';
(7) use of Singular in connection with a noun preceded by numeral, as in Hun. *három asztal-Ø* 'three tables'; Finn. *kolme pöytä-ä-Ø* 'table-Partit.-Ø, three tables';[38]
(8) basic (S)OV word-order (there are several 'deviations', such as in Modern Hungarian and Modern Finnish);
(9) lack of the verb 'to be' in predicative sentences, as in Hun. *ez ablak* 'this

[is] a window'; *a virág szép* 'the flower [is] beautiful'; this is not the case in Finnish: *kukka on kaunis* '[the] flower is beautiful';

(10) use of the Possessive endings for the conjugation of nouns and verbs;

(11) use of a suffix to mark interrogative sentences (this is present for example in Finnish *tulee-ko hän*? 'does he/she come?', but not in Estonian);

(12) use of nominalisation to form subordinate sentences, instead of constructions of the type '*that* + finite verb' (this latter type however is present in languages like Modern Hungarian and Modern Finnish);

(13) use of a (so-called) Accusative marker to mark only the Definite/Topical Object (-∅ being used instead otherwise); this is present in all the Turkic languages (including Chuvash), in Finnish, in some dialects of Vogul, and probably, in Old Hungarian (see Marcantonio 1981, 1983, 1994).;

(14) presence of *nomenverba*, that is, stems which are inherently ambiguous. In more general terms, absence of word-classes distinction (for Uralic see Laakso (1997); for Altaic see Doerfer (1982) and Kara (1997)).

It is true that features (1), (5) and (12), for instance, are implicational, universal characteristics of all the OV languages, whilst most of the other features are quite often associated with them, so that they are not relevant for the purpose of assessing relations. It is also true that (S)OV is the most common word-order in the world and that a (S)OV word-order has been reconstructed also for P-Indo-European. However, this does not appear to be the case for all the features listed. As far as I am aware of, the use of a marker to codify the Definite/Referential/Topical Direct Object is not an implicational feature of the OV languages; nor is the absence of consonant clusters in initial position, or the *numerus absolutus*.

Other, less 'superficial' typological features can be added to the above list, if one accepts Nichols' (1986, 1992) analysis. According to the author, the following are major 'typological diagnostics', whose distribution may be of relevance in assessing relations among languages:

- 'head-marking' vs 'dependent marking';
- the degree of morphological complexity;
- the particular type of 'clause alignment', that is, Accusative, Ergative, Stative-Active, or other types of constructions (see point (13) in above list);
- the dominant word order.

In particular, Nichols (1986: 84) argues that the 'marking type' is a very stable parameter in languages, hence languages will retain their original type even when subject to foreign influence. This in turn means that this specific typological classification 'may offer historical linguistics a tool we so far lack: a criterion for NON-relatedness at any recoverable time' (ibid.).

As we have seen while discussing the formation of postpositions and Case endings (Sections 8.3.2.1. and 8.3.2.2 above), the U languages tend to be 'head-marking', contrary to what happens, for instance, in English. Compare the following Hungarian and English Genitive/Possessive constructions:

(8.24) az ember ház-*a*   /   the man-*s* house
      the man   house-his
      'the man's house'

In Hungarian the marking of Possession takes places at the 'head' of the nominal phrase, *ház-a*, whilst in the equivalent English construction the marking takes place on the 'dependent' noun, *man-s*. As mentioned at the end of Section 8.3.2.2, the Turkic languages share with Hungarian and other U languages this kind of 'head-marking' construction. Furthermore, both in some U languages and in the Turkic languages these constructions are the basic morpho-syntactic context within which postpositions and Case endings were formed.

It is possible that a comprehensive analysis of the 'typological diagnostics' of this linguistic area could yield some conclusive results.

8.7. DISTRIBUTION OF CONSONANTAL FORMANTS IN EURASIA

In this section I shall carry out a mathematical analysis of the most common U, Altaic and Yukaghir formants discussed in this chapter – the actual formants, and not their (possible) reconstructions – to verify whether their similarity and/or identity can be interpreted as genuine linguistic correlations. Indeed, the simple phonological shape, the messy distribution, the interchangeability in sound and function typical of these formants could well be interpreted as a symptom of mere chance resemblance. The calculation adopted is the same as the one adopted for the analysis of the U Lexicon, for which see Chapter 5.

I shall include in the calculation some formants of Dravidian, but not the formants of Indo-European, for the reasons discussed in Section 6.6.

8.7.1. *The formants*

The formants selected for mathematical analysis are those discussed in the text and listed in Appendix III with the exclusion of formants which are of rare occurrence, such as the plural -*r*- and the plural -*i*-, or whose common origin is considered uncertain, like the connection between the U Acc. -*n*/-*m* and the sporadic Dravidian Acc. -*n*. Similarly, I have not taken into consideration the Yukaghir co-affixal element -*ka*-, often connected to Mordvin Pro. -*ka* (~ -*ga*, ~ -*va*), and therefore to (P-U) Lat. *-*ka*, although in Yukaghir this ending also frequently has a Lative function. Neither have I considered the formant of the negative verb, generally *-e ~ -i*, because I have decided not to include vocalic formants, due to their instability. For the Lappic languages I have considered the plural *-t* as well as the plural *-k*, present in old orthographies. Sammallahti (1998: 69) observes that the Lapp plural marker was *-k*, which goes back either to P-U *-t* or *-k* (the same *-k* present in Hungarian), although the overall situation is not clear.

All in all, it is very difficult to be sure about the exact number of formants to identify and include in the calculation, given their interchangeability, their instability in sound-shape and function, their messy distribution (also as possible components of complex endings), etc. Besides, there are often several, even contradictory interpretations found in the literature for each formant. The situation becomes particularly difficult with Lapp, because syncretism and morphophonemic alternations have transformed a great part of its structure into a flectional system. Not counting the variety and complexity of the various Lapp languages and dialects (see in this regard also Korhonen 1988a, 1988b). Anyway, I hope that the selected formants, as reported in Tables 8.9 and 8.10 below, can represent a reasonable approximation of the number and distribution of the most common and clearly identifiable formants present in the Eurasiatic area.

To conclude this section, note that an analysis of this type, extended to U, Altaic and Yukaghir, has already been attempted by B. Collinder, in a paper dating back to 1947. The calculation is applied to 13 formants only: (a) the functional morphemes: Genitive, Accusative, Locative/Ablative *-t*, Locative *-n*, Lative *-k*, to which the author connects, although with reservation, Yukaghir *-ge* (that is, the co-affixal element *-γa ~ -qa*) and Lapp *-ge*; (b) the pronominal and demonstrative stems; (c) a few verbal morphemes (the Imperative/Optative *-k(V)* and the negative verb *-e*). Collinder concludes that (1947: 24)

> les concordances entre les langues altaïques et les langues ouraliennes ne peuvent pas être l'effet du hasard. Il nous reste à faire le choix entre la parenté, d'une part, et l'emprunt et l'affinité élémentaire, de l'autre. Voilà qui semble être inaccessible au calcul, du moins en l'état actuel de nos connaissances.

8.7.2. *Mathematical analysis*

This section displays the distribution of the functional and grammatical formants and carries out the related calculation. The formants analysed have been quoted only by consonants, because vowels normally represent a (contextual) variant, apart from being often unstable. The consonantal formants I have examined are listed in Table 8.9 below, where a formant is marked with an 'X' if it appears in at least one of the languages/language

Table 8.9 The principal consonantal formants in Eurasia

	k	l	m	n	s	t	Total
Ablative		X				X	2
Accusative			X				1
Aspect						X	1
Dual	X						1
Genitive				X			1
Gerundive			X				1
His				X	X	X	3
Lative	X			X	X		3
Locative				X		X	2
Mine			X				1
Partitive						X	1
Plural	X	X				X	3
Yours				X		X	2
Plural (Poss.)				X			1
Total	3	2	3	6	2	7	23

groups analysed (see Appendix III for the number and distribution of the Case endings, Section 8.5.1 for the number and distribution of the Possessive/Person endings, Section 8.5.3.1 for the number and distribution of the endings of Plurality and Duality, and Section 8.5.4 for the endings of Tense/Aspect).

Table 8.10 shows the languages/language groups in which these formants appear. The languages and language groups are the same as those identified for the mathematical analysis of the Lexicon (see Section 5.2). If a formant with a given meaning is present in at least one modern language of a language group, it is marked with an 'X'.

The distribution of these formants is shown in Figure 8.1. It has to be stressed that most of them are highly represented. For example, the formant -*m* 'mine' is present in 10 of the language groups. Three formants are present in 9 of the language groups: Inf./Ger. -$(V)m$- ~ -$m(V)$-, also used in nominalised verbal phrases (see above Section 8.6.3), Genitive and Locative -*n*. There are three formants that are present in 8 groups: Plural, Ablative and Aspect/Tense -*t*. Two formants are present in 7 groups: Plural/Possessive -*n* and Locative -*t*, and so on. The only scantily represented formant is -*n* meaning 'his', present in only 2 languages, supposing that this -*n* is a distinct morpheme from the -*n* expressing Plurality/Possession.

For the purpose of comparison, the graph in Figure 8.1 also shows the distribution we would expect if the data were completely random, and therefore the data represented completely 'false matches'. There are 6 sounds to choose from (*k*, *l*, *n*, *m*, *s*, and *t*) and, supposing a close correlation within the groups, there would be a 1/6 probability of a given sound being present

Table 8.10 Distribution of consonantal formants in Eurasia

Sound	Meaning	B-F	Perm.	Ob-U.	Hun.	Sam.	Lapp	Turkic	Mon.	Tungu.	Yuk.	Dra.	Score
m	Mine	X	X	X	X	X	X	X	X	X	X		10
n	Locative	X	X	X	X	X	X	X	X		X		9
m	Gerundive	X	X	X		X	X	X	X	X	X		9
n	Genitive	X	X			X	X	X	X	X	X	X	9
t	Plural	X	X	X		X	X	X	X	X			8
t	Aspect	X	X	X		X		X	X	X		X	8
t	Ablative	X	X			X	X	X	X	X	X		8
n	Plural (Poss.)		X	X		X	X	X	X	X			7
t	Locative			X	X	X	X	X		X	X		7
m	Accusative	X	X	X		X	X			X			6
l	Plural		X	X				X	X	X		X	6
k	Lative	X	X			X	X	X		X			6
n	Lative	X	X	X		X					X		5
t	Yours	X	X		X		X			X			5
s	His	X	X		X		X			X			5
s	Lative	X	X				X	X	X				5
k	Plural				X	X	X	X				X	5
k	Imperative	X				X	X	X	X				5
t	Partitive	X				X	X		X				4
k	Dual			X		X				X			3
t	His			X		X		X					3
n	Yours			X				X		X			3
l	Ablative			X	X					X			3
n	His							X		X			2

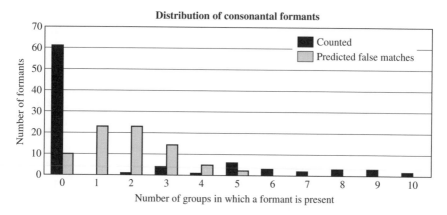

Figure 8.1 Distribution of consonantal formants

in each cell in Table 8.10. This would result in the binomial distribution as shown (the analysis is similar to that for the Lexicon, as discussed above).

The distribution observed is strikingly different from the random distribution. We are unable to get the two distributions to match, even approximately, even by assuming that there was no correlation between the languages within the groups. More precisely, the following observations can be made: -

- We do not find any formants that are present in only one group. We can conclude that if a formant is present in one group, then it is also present in at least one other group.
- If the distribution were totally random, then there would be far fewer empty slots in the table of formants. Over fifty of possible formants do not appear in any of the languages of the area. This is strong evidence for a correlation between the languages.
- The formants that are present in 7 or more groups appear to be statistically significant. These are the first nine formants in Table 8.10, some of which also exhibit a certain stability in the association of form and function, that is: 1st Pers. Poss. -*m*, Gen. -*n*, Ger./Inf. -*m*- and Loc. -*n*.

One may conclude that the distribution of these formants could not be the result of chance, since there are too many formants that are present too widely. Of course, the question whether these genuine correlations are the effect of borrowing (although Morphology is rather resistant to borrowing) or of inheritance, or, most probably, of both processes, is bound to remain for ever open, as already remarked by Collinder, because of the reasons expounded in Chapter 6.

8.8. SUMMARY AND CONCLUSION

8.8.1. *The status of Morphology in the Uralic languages*

The following picture is supported by the data discussed in this chapter:

- It is difficult, if not impossible, to trace back to a common source the variety of endings – functional, grammatical, derivational – which are encountered in the modern U languages. In fact, major, relevant areas of U Morphology are not reconstructable. They include: (a) the complex Case endings, which are innovations implemented in the life of the single languages; (b) the verbal endings, whose reconstruction is in fact considered unsafe even within the conventional paradigm; (c) several endings of Plurality, which, again, have been formed in the independent life of the single languages; (c) the endings of Duality, whose distribution is restricted; (d) even within the pronominal paradigm there is a major split, which divides the U languages into two groups.
- There is a handful of widely distributed morphological elements, that is: two or three simple local Cases, some Possessive and some Plural endings. However, these are generally also present in the Altaic languages and Yukaghir (and, according to some scholars, Dravidian and Indo-European as well).
- The Person, Possessive and Plural endings shared by the U (and the Altaic) languages can be used interchangeably for the noun and the verb. If there was a significant ancestor, this factor (together with others) would suggest that it made no distinction between the categories of noun and verb. For similar reasons, one can assume that in the ancestor language there was no categorial distinction between noun and adjective, noun and adverb, or noun and postposition. These claims are in fact held also within the conventional paradigm; see, for example, Ravila (1957); E. Itkonen (1966b: 226); Abondolo ((ed.) 1998: 18, 27) and Laakso (1997). The absence of a clear distinction between noun and postposition in some modern U languages has been amply illustrated in this chapter.

In the absence of nominal, verbal, pronominal (sub-sets of) paradigms, etc., it is hard to see how, using evidence from Morphology, the genetic status of the U languages can be illuminated effectively using the Comparative Method. If, however, one also adopts different methods of analysis, more suitable to this linguistic area, more significant results emerge. For example, the mathematical analysis reveals that the U, Altaic languages and Yukaghir share a stock of formants whose number becomes significant if they are taken into account and analysed together.

How to interpret this evidence? The distributional criteria show a scattered pattern that provides no evidence for a conventional, binary family tree, and there is an interchangeability between forms and functions for most of the shared morphological elements. These factors make it impossible to reconstruct P-morphemes.

An alternative interpretation, that appears to better account for this picture, is to regard the modern forms as stemming from a 'pull' of common material, spanning throughout a vast dialectal area, from which each language has picked up building material independently, although, probably, in parallel. This material in turn has been utilised and combined, to form complex endings, and/or sequences of endings, in a way which is specific for each language involved. To use Andronov's (1968: 32) words, these languages must have picked up 'pieces of roughly the right shape or with meaning of a reasonable kind, but with no particular system,' in order to build different structures or fulfil (not too) different functions.

Indeed, this interpretation fits better with the evidence from areas of language that are traditionally disregarded within the Comparative Method. For example, several isomorphic constructions, whose similarity in syntactic structure and lexical components is quite striking, form again an intersecting set of isoglosses spanning the whole area.

8.8.2. *Case endings and the antiquity of the Uralic languages: some speculations*

We have observed that the complex Case endings in the U languages appear to have formed individually, and relatively recently. For example, the recent creation of Case endings formed through Grammaticalisation is documented in Old Hungarian, and the bulk of the Case endings are *in fieri* at the present time in Ob-Ugric and (partially) Samoyed. The evidence clearly suggests that agglutination has formed in our era.

The suggestion that Grammaticalisation was a recent process is in agreement with evidence from other language groups, where it is also reported as being a fast and often sudden process, particularly with regard to Case endings (Dixon[39] 1997: 54–5). Grammaticalisation is usually quoted as becoming complete within three centuries, or four centuries at most, as demonstrated by the pidgin/Creole languages (Hopper & Traugott 1993: 208–20).

This picture, if accepted, is inconsistent with the conventional model that the U languages formed at least 2,000 years ago. One would have to conclude that the formation of the modern U languages does not date that far back in time, a conclusion which is not incompatible with the evidence (see Chapter 7 on the issue of the 'assumed' antiquity of P-U).

A younger age for the formation of the U languages would also be consistent with the stage of development of the Altaic languages, for which a relatively young age has been envisaged, at least by some scholars (see Chapter 6). Indeed, as we have seen, the U and Altaic languages, as well as Yukaghir, appear to be more or less at the same phase of development with regard to morphological structure: Grammaticalisation and Exaptation seem to be operating in all these languages more or less in parallel, and the elements grammaticalised or exaptated are basically the same. Of course, for this picture to be confirmed, a proper investigation encompassing the whole area would be required.

To counter the view that the U languages may be relatively young the existence of 'cyclicity' in Morphology could be advocated (Anttila 1989; Dixon 1994: 182–6), namely, that language development follows the well-defined typological cycle:

$\longrightarrow$ isolating $\longrightarrow$ agglutinating $\longrightarrow$ fusional $\longrightarrow$ isolating $\longrightarrow$

According to this model, although most of the U languages are at the agglutinating phase now, they might have gone through this morphological cycle several times before; therefore, they might still be very old languages indeed.

Whilst this is of course a possible interpretation, we have no evidence to distinguish it from the simpler assumption that the languages are relatively young. This being the case, I personally believe that the ancestor(s), or at least the 'immediate' ancestor(s) of the U languages, whatever their nature, were relatively young and had simple morphological structure. This personal interpretation is contrary to what is usually claimed within the field and generally perceived outside the field, see for example Janhunen[40] (1981b), Dixon[41] (1994: 184, 1997: 42) and the discussion in Chapter 7.

9

COMPLETING THE PICTURE: PROPER NAMES, ARCHAEOLOGY AND GENETICS

The Finns have a proportion of 90% European genes and 10% Uralic, with a standard error of ± 4.1%[1]
Luigi Luca Cavalli-Sforza et al.

No review of the U languages would be complete without a discussion of the extensive literature relating to the proper names, and of the evidence from the areas of archaeology and genetics. As we shall see, these fields of research have also been strongly influenced, and in some cases significantly distorted or misrepresented, by the belief that the U languages form a family.

We begin by examining proper names. As we shall see, hardly any evidence has been identified so far of proper names that can be traced back to a common node or sub-node of the Uralic family tree. In contrast, there are striking isoglosses of proper names spanning the boundaries of the U linguistic context. For example, there are isoglosses connecting Hungarian and Turkic (particularly Turkic Bashkir), and isoglosses connecting the Finnic area with central Asiatic areas. In this respect, the proper names are consistent with the other levels of language that we examined in previous chapters, in the sense that, again, they appear to be more consistent with a model of intersecting isoglosses than with a model based on a family tree. As we shall see, some of these correlations are unlikely to be the result of chance resemblance, in the statistical sense discussed in Chapter 5. For example, there are four matching consonants in a total of six phonemes between the Bashkir and Hungarian names *Jurmatï* and *Gyarmat* (respectively). Similarly, there are five matching phonemes between the Hungarian and Bashkir names *Jenej* ~ *Jeneγ*, whereas none of the Uralic Lexicon we examined has more than three matching phonemes. Furthermore, some Bashkir proper names are claimed to have also preserved the original quality in first syllable vowel of the corresponding Hungarian names; compare Bas. *Jurmatï* and Hun. *Gyurmot,* the Old Hungarian variant of *Gyarmat* (Németh 1966a: 16–17).

In the 'mainstream' Uralic interpretation, evidence from proper names is usually brushed aside as meaningless. It is assumed that proper names are unreliable – or, more accurately, it is assumed they are unreliable unless they support the Uralic theory. For example (as we have seen in Chapters 2 and 4), the supposed connections *hungarus/Yugria* and *magyar/Mansi* are assumed to be exceptions to this rule because they form almost the only 'evidence' in favour of the Ugric node. When we come to examine the assumed etymology of *magyar* in this chapter, we shall find that it is ad hoc and does not match the historically attested forms. Similarly, the Finnish self-denomination, *Suomi*, was originally connected with credible, straightforward parallels found in an area that is now regarded as Altaic; however, in order to fit in with the U paradigm when it later came into prominence, this origin had to be rejected, and one now reads of highly convoluted and undeniably implausible explanations for the origin of this term.

We shall then very briefly examine the evidence from genetic studies. It is frequently noted in textbooks that geneticists refer to a 'Uralic gene'. As we shall see, the original authors of this definition were at pains to point out that this was merely a linguistic definition, which was adopted in spite of the fact that it does not correspond to the much simpler picture that actually does emerge from genetic studies – a picture of a gradual gradation of genetic material across the area.

Finally, we shall see that in the field of archaeology, the little evidence there is suggests a movement of people and technology from the South-West to the North-East, in the opposite direction to the supposed migrations involved in the Uralic theory.

9.1. PROPER NAMES

This chapter begins with an examination of proper names. Outside Uralic studies, these are often regarded as particularly relevant forms of language, for example in Indo-European studies (Renfrew 1987: 21; see his quote reported in the Introduction) and in Anglo-Saxon studies (see for example Gelling[2] 1978). In general linguistics, there is a debate on the status of proper names: some authors argue they can be highly suggestive of the correct links (Kiviniemi 1980a), whereas others argue the opposite, because people and places may easily change their denomination in the course of time under the pressure of historical and social events (Trask 1996: 350).

As we saw in Chapter 2, the Uralic theory had its origins in a connection of proper names, and *magyar-Mansi* is still cited as evidence in favour of the Uralic theory today. As we shall see here, there are a large number of proper names that appear to clearly contradict the Uralic theory if taken at face value, because they span the supposed boundaries of the Uralic area. These have attracted a number of learned papers within the field. This large body of counter-evidence has led to its being generally assumed in Uralic studies that one can deduce nothing from proper names (with the exception, of course, of *magyar-Mansi*).

9.1.1. *The ethnonyms in the Uralic languages*

Hardly any evidence has been identified so far of ethnonyms – whether self-designation or external designation – that can be traced back to a common P-Language – let alone P-U. In most cases, the origin of the ethnonyms present in the U languages remains unknown. When etymologies have been reconstructed, often with uncertainty, they turn out to be of European, Asiatic, or just local origin. In most cases, the meaning of the ethnonyms is simply something like 'man, right man, land, people' etc., so that they are not useful for the purpose of identification. Furthermore, the degree of variation is as high within this semantic field as in any other semantic field examined so far, if not higher. Often, there are several variants, duplets, triplets, for the same name. Compare *Eesti, Viro, Igaunija* for the Estonians (Grünthal 1997); *Fenni ~ Finni, Screrefennae, Scrithiphinoi* (in Latin and Greek sources; see also Chapter 2) to indicate, probably, the Lapps, or no better identified people of north Europe, etc. (Sammallahti 1984). Often, it is also difficult to decide if it is the place which has given the name to the people or vice-versa, as in the place-names which contain the element *lappi*, the term itself being of uncertain origin (Häkkinen 1996: 173). It would take too long to discuss in detail the etymology of all the ethnonyms of the U languages, but one can find detailed information in Joki (1973) for the ethnonyms of (presumed) Indo-European origin, Gy. Décsy (1965: 231 f.), Gheno & Hajdú (1992), Häkkinen (1996: 167–80), Grünthal (1997) for the ethnonyms of the Balto-Finnic areas, and, of course, in the dictionaries, including UEW.

The etymologies of the self-denominations of the U peoples/languages are reported in Appendix IV.

9.1.2. *The 'etymologies' of* Suomi

Let us now discuss the term *Suomi* (~ *Suome-*), the self-denomination of the Finns, which is attested as *sum* in the historical records (see Section 2.1.1). Castrén reports to have found, during his extensive travelling in Asia, several toponyms which are very similar to some Finnish proper names, including the toponym *Sumi.* He found them in the area of the Sayan mountains, where some Samoyed languages are located (see family tree diagram in Figure 1.1). But, the name *Sumi* (and the other names reported) has been considered as an instance of chance resemblance by later researchers, and has not been taken into consideration as a possible candidate for the origin of *Suomi.* In contrast, a variety of etymologies (at times cumbersome) and derivations have been proposed, all of which are assumed to be of Indo-European origin (for an overview see Koivulehto 1993). Here I would like to mention only what seems to be nowadays the most commonly accepted interpretation (Koivulehto 1993; Grünthal 1997: 56; another common explanation is reported in Note 3), in which *Suomi* derives from P-Baltic *žemē* '(low-lying/flat) land', compare for example Latv. *zeme*. There is a clear sound mismatch between the modern *Suomi* and this proposed *žemē*, and this is accounted for by hypothesising that the name migrated forward and backward between the north and south coasts of the Baltic Sea, changing little by little on each step. Basically, the following sequence of events occurred (adapted from Koivulehto's (1993: 405–6) summary):

(a) The first step in the reconstruction is to assume that some early P-Finnish tribes were known and referred to by the Baltic/P-Baltic people by the name *žemē*, '(low-lying/flat) land'.

(b) The next assumption is that these Finnish tribes adopted this foreign name as their self-denomination, changing it into the sound-shape *šämä*.

(c) The next assumption in the chain is that the Lapps adopted this name *šämä* (of these Finnish tribes) as their own self-denomination, in their own sound-shape: *sāmā*, later > *sāmē* > *sabme* ~ *saame* (the self-denomination of the *Hämäläiset* people: *hämä-läinen*[4], also derives from *šämä*). Alternatively, if one believes that the Lapps and the Finns are descendent from the same ancestors (fact contradicted by the genetic evidence, see below), one should assume that *sāmā* is the normal development of *šämä*, which arose when the modern Lapps separated from the rest of the community.

(d) It is then assumed that some Baltic tribes, who were in close contact with the Lapps, started to call these Lapps with the name *sāmā*, but in their own, Baltic sound shape *sāmas* (compare Latv. *sāms*), between 800 and 600 BC.

(e) In the next assumed step, this name *sāmas* was extended by these same Baltic tribes to refer not only to the Lapps, but also to Balto-Finnic peoples, because the original name based on *žemē* '(low-lying/flat) land', was now considered inappropriate to refer to a population; they needed this name for other purposes.

(f) History now supposedly repeats itself: the most southern Balto-Finnic tribes adopted for themselves this 'new' Baltic name *sāmas*, in the sound-shape *sōme*, originally possibly *sōma*. From *sōme* has derived *Suomi*, and from *sōma* has derived *suoma-lainen* 'Finnish', *Suoma-laiset* 'the Finns'; this probably took place in the period of Middle-P-Finnish.

(g) Finally, in a later period, this last name *sōme* (with its modern reflexes) was used to indicate the south-western regions of Finland and their people (*Varsinais-Suomi* 'original Finland, Finland proper'), and not the Balto-Finnic tribes who originally adopted it. Researchers emphasise that in this last step of the story, the correspondence P-Baltic *ā* vs P-Finnish *ō* is a regular one. This is reported as if this regular sound-change added credibility to the entire picture. Researchers also mention that there are toponyms containing this *sōme element on the south coast of the Baltic Sea, such as Some-linde 'castle of Some' (from year 1211 in Estonia; SKES 1115). This would be a testimony that this name was first adopted by Balto-Finnic peoples, before being restricted to today's Finns.

In this chain of assumptions, no step is supported by any actual historical records. I leave it to the reader to judge this reconstruction[5] against simpler and more realistic assumptions, such as either accepting that the origin of Suomi is unknown, or starting to investigate also other directions, for example by reconsidering the toponym Sumi, reflected in the old form sum.

9.1.3. The Hungarians' self-denomination

As mentioned on several occasions, the Hungarians' self-denomination has been central in the emerging and establishment of the conventional paradigm. It is therefore important to examine closely the origin of this name, its conventional linguistic connection and the connections actually attested in the historical sources. I consider the whole issue of the historical and linguistic connections of magyar as one of those 'especially Gordian' aspects of the conventional paradigm, and the following is an attempt to separate out the 'evidence' from the chain of assumptions.

9.1.3.1. The chronological and linguistic development of magyar

As we have seen in Chapter 2 (Section 2.1.2.3), it is usually reported in textbooks and mainstream literature that one of the earliest occurrences of the Hungarians' self-denomination – magyar – is in the text De Administrando Imperio, by Constantine Porphyrogenitus.

However, this is not quite the true story, because Constantine never actually mentions the term magyar; he mentions instead the name Μεγέρη. The structure of the text suggests that he is referring to the name of a leader, but it is nevertheless widely interpreted that he was referring to the ancestors of the Hungarian magyars. A linguistic connection has been made between the terms Μεγέρη and magyar, even though it is often stated that this correspondence is irregular. The historically attested candidate words associated with magyar are shown in Figure 9.1a (see Section 2.1.2.4 for the term Mogerii/magyeri). The Greek term from circa 950 is apparently reflected in place-names present in modern Hungary, such as Puszta-megyer, Tót-megyer, Békás-megyer, Káposztás-megyer, etc.

It is acknowledged that these words are not in regular correspondence because of mismatches in the vowels. On a strict application of the Comparative Method one would have to conclude that these words are not related to one another, and that Μεγέρη is unrelated to the Modern Hungarian term magyar. However, in the literature it is assumed that all

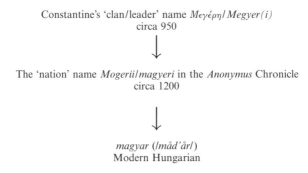

Constantine's 'clan/leader' name *Μεγέρη/Megyer(i)*
circa 950

↓

The 'nation' name *Mogerii/magyeri* in the *Anonymus* Chronicle
circa 1200

↓

magyar (/måd'år/)
Modern Hungarian

Figure 9.1a The chronological development of *magyar*

these words are nevertheless related. The main vowel mismatches are explained (for example Ligeti 1986: 400) by assuming that the original attested form of 950 was a mere 'secondary variant'[6], despite its being reflected in Modern Hungarian place-names. This secondary variant is supposed not to appear in the linguistic tree. The early form is instead supposed to be P-Hun. **mogyër(i) ~ *majǧër(i) ~ *majγir(i)* (Németh 1930/ 91: 246; Gheno & Hajdú 1992: 15; UEW 866–7; TESz II, 816–17; Ligeti 1986: 400), so that the various reflexes of these names appear to be more regular, as shown in Figure 9.1b. In this model the modern term *magyar* has developed from a reconstructed P-Hungarian form **mogyër* through progressive assimilation, whilst *Μεγέρη* has developed from the same reconstructed form through regressive assimilation, according to the principles of vowel harmony, a feature typical of modern Hungarian. The change **mogyër > magyar ~ megyer* supposedly took place in the late P-Hungarian period, before the time of the 'home conquest', that is before the time of the conquest of the present-day Hungarian territory (at least according to some scholars).

Although the processes of assimilation described above are totally normal, common phenomena in languages, there are two problems

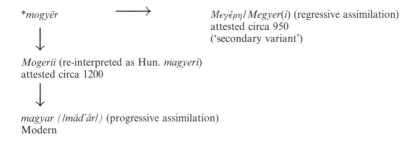

*mogyër   ⟶   *Μεγέρη/Megyer(i)* (regressive assimilation)
                                                     attested circa 950
↓   ('secondary variant')

Mogerii (re-interpreted as Hun. *magyeri*)
attested circa 1200

↓

magyar (/måd'år/) (progressive assimilation)
Modern

Figure 9.1b Ligeti's model for the linguistic development of *magyar* associated with this explanation. Firstly, the rejection of the early attested form *Μεγέρη*/*Megyer(i)* and its replacement by a reconstructed form that has, by design, fewer sound mismatches with the modern form, is clearly an ad hoc process that does not accord directly with the historical record and that is contradicted by the toponyms. Secondly, the explanation on the basis of the principles of vowel harmony is not satisfactory, because (as we have seen in Section 8.3.2.2) the first Hungarian text, written in about 1200, shows that vowel harmony is just about in the process of formation. It is not therefore a fully developed feature, as would have been required for these processes of assimilation to run to completion before the time of the home conquest (around 896 AD).

9.1.3.2. *The 'etymologies' of* magyar

Most textbooks report only the ad hoc connection *magyar-Mansi*. However, the specialist literature contains two competing accounts for the etymology of *magyar*: alongside *magyar-Mansi* (the 'Ugric' connection), there is *majǧir(i)* ~ *bajǧir* (the Turkic connection), the connection which is actually attested in the historical sources.

As discussed in Section 2.1.2.3, the term *magyar* is mentioned in 10th century Arabic sources where it occurs in the regular variant forms *majǧir(i)* ~ *bajǧir*. From the variant *magǰgir(i)* the term *magyar* has developed, whilst from the variant *bajǧir* the forms *bašǧir* ~ *bašjir* ~ *bašɣir* have developed, that is, the name of the Turkic Bashkirs. Indeed, by the designation *magǰgir(i)* ~ *bajǧir* the sources explicitly referred to a Turkic population. We have also seen in the same section and in the section above that the name *Μεγέρη* (*Megyeri*), mentioned by Constantine and universally associated with *magyar,* is a clan name which occurs within a list of other clan names of recognised Turkic origin.

Nevertheless, *magyar* is universally reported in textbooks and dictionaries as being connected to a totally different name – *Mansi.* No historical or linguistic evidence has been identified to support this connection, apart from the superficial similarity of the two names and the 'presumption' of the close connections between the Hungarians and the Voguls (which is in turn based on another apparent similarity between two proper names, *hungar-* and *Yugria*; see Section 2.1.2.5). Therefore, an etymology has been created in order to justify the connection. As we shall see, this etymology is highly ad hoc, and one is drawn to the conclusion that it does not in fact contribute towards 'building up' the scientific credibility of this superficial similarity. Textbooks often contain an apparently circular argument, where this etymology is then cited as 'evidence' in support of the F-U origin of the Hungarians and, of course, of the validity of the Ugric node. The 'standard' etymology of *magyar* is as follows (TESz II, 817; UEW 866; EWUng II, 923-4):

(9.1) *magy-ar* consists of two parts. The first part, *magy-* derives from Ug. *mańćɜ* 'man, human being', from which also the self-denominations of the Voguls, *Mansi*, and the self-denomination of one of the Ostyak clans, *mańt' ~ mońt' ~ maś*, is derived[7] (UEW 866). The sources usually point out that Hun. /-*d'*-/ is a regular development from *-*ńć*-. The second element of *magy-ar*, that is -*ar* (~ -*ér, -ër*) 'man', is claimed to be the same component found for example in Hun. *emb-ër* 'man'. This root in turn would be connected with Finn. *yrkä* 'bachelor', *yrkö* 'man' < F-U *irkä (*ürkä)* (UEW 84).

This etymology presents a major difficulty: the segmentation *magy-ar* does not have any independent justification, because neither of the two members (*magy-* and -*ar*) are ever found as stand-alone elements; the same holds true for *emb-(ër)*.

Even if the segmentation *magy-ar* were correct, the etymology would present further problems. Firstly, all the denominations recorded in the historical sources contain a final -*i* (Latin *mogerij ~ mogerii*, Arabic *m.ğ.γ.rīya* (see Chapter 2, Note 8) and Greek Μεγέρη/*Megyeri*), for which there is no corresponding vowel in the presumed Old Hungarian component -*ar ~ -ér, -ër*. Secondly, Hun. -*gy*- /-*d'*-/ may be the reflex not only of *-*ńć*-, but also of several other sounds within U, apart from being also a sound-change attested in Turkic and in the Turkic loan-words in Hungarian (compare *mańć- > *maǰ- > magy-* according to Ligeti 1986: 400). Therefore this sound-change on its own cannot constitute evidence in favour of the validity of the etymology. Finally, if the etymology were correct, it would be a redundant compound word, consisting of two elements which have exactly the same meaning (although this is not unusual in this linguistic area); it would literally mean 'man-man' (Róna-Tas 1988b: 131). And, in fact, the sources that support this etymology admit that there are difficulties (see Ligeti 1986: 400 and Németh 1972: 156). For example, UEW 84 and 866 says that compound nature of the noun is no longer retrievable, the compound has now become 'opaque, obscure'.

Stating that the denomination *magy-(ar)* is of Ugric, and therefore of U origin, does not *ipso facto* explain away why the Arabic sources link the Hungarian self-denomination to that of the Bashkirs: this link has to be accounted for. In order to square this datum with the U paradigm there has arisen an array of inconsistent interpretations and speculations, which can be summarised as follows (among the extended bibliography in this regard see for example Németh 1930/91 and 1966a, 1996b; Gombocz 1908, 1912; Munkácsi 1905; Györffy 1948; Fodor 1982; Ligeti 1986: 400 f.):

• The Hungarians are the ancestors of at least part of the Turkic Bashkir population, but are not related to any other Turkic tribes.

- The Bashkir assimilated the Volga Hungarians (those Hungarians left behind in their eastern homeland) in historical times and inherited their name at this time (Németh 1930/91: 345).
- The Arabic authors, who talk about the *majɣir - bajɣir* people, confused the Hungarians and the Bashkirs because the Hungarians lived for a period nearby the area that is now Bashkiria. This area was the traditional *Magna Hungaria* mentioned in the Chronicles.
- The oriental authors simply confused the two names by mistake. There was no connection between the Bashkirs and the Hungarians, who have never settled in the area nearby Bashkiria.
- The Bashkir moved into the area that was previously occupied by the Hungarians and adopted their self-denomination.

To give a flavour of the explanations, let us take the example of the last interpretation, which is due to Ligeti (1986: 400), and appears to be based on no more significant evidence than that already given above (a similar type of interpretation is to be found, among others, in Németh 1966a). According to this story, before the times of the *honfoglalás* (the occupation of the current territory of Hungary), the original Hungarians' self-denomination *magǰgir(i)* developed two variants: on the one hand the denomination *magyar ~ megyer* and, on the other hand, the denomination *bajɣir*. The latter arose as a Turkic variant within a Bulgar Turkic environment, at the time of the close Bulgar Turkic/Hungarian contacts. After the disintegration of the Khazar empire, the '*majɣir - bajɣir* people' ('a majɣir – bajɣir nép'), that is, the Hungarians, wandered about for a while in the former Khazar territory, before moving westward. Subsequently these territories remained basically empty, and the (Kipchak) Bashkir type of people moved into the vacated area. Therefore, they were thereafter called with the name of the previous inhabitants of the region. In other words, the Turkic Bashkirs inherited the original name of the Hungarians, in its Turkic variant form *bajɣir* (> *bašǧir ~ bašǰir ~ bašɣir*), due to their dwelling in the Hungarians' original land in the Khazar area.

9.1.4. The 'Bashkiro-Hungarian complex'

We have seen in the previous section that the standard etymology of the Hungarian self-denomination, *magyar*, is ad hoc and does not match the historical record. In contrast, the connection *majɣir ~ bajɣir* suggests, both on linguistic and historical grounds, that there is some sort of connection between Hungarian and Turkic Bashkir. This suggestion is further supported by the report by Friar Julianus, who, as we saw in Chapter 2, could communicate 'in Hungarian' in the year 1235 with a group of people living in an area near modern Bashkiria. According to Fodor (1982: 268–71) this connection is also supported by archaeological findings from the Bashkir cemetery of Sterlitamak, which (according to the author) suggest at a minimum widespread mixed marriages among these two populations.

In fact, there are further striking isoglosses of proper names (ethnonyms and toponyms/hydronyms) connecting the Hungarian and Bashkir areas. These connections, which appear to contradict the Uralic theory, are so well acknowledged that they have attracted a label in the specialist literature: the 'Bashkiro-Hungarian complex' (Vásáry 1985/7). There is an extensive literature on this subject, see the following sources: Pauler (1900: 126); Németh (1921a, 1930/91: 325–7, 1966a, 1966b, 1972); Györffy (1948: 184 f.); Fodor (1975a, 1975b: 158–71, 1982: 265 f.); Benkő (1972: 241); Ligeti (1963, 1964, 1978, 1986: 375, 378–9); Róna-Tas (1978a); Di Cave (1995: 34 f.); Vásáry (1975, 1977, 1985/7) and Golden (1990b: 245).

Here we have space to examine in detail only a small part of this literature. We shall choose as our sample the old clan names that supposedly were at the origin of the Hungarian nation, that is, the eight clan names listed by Constantine Porphyrogenitus (see Section 2.1.2.3). Six of these eight names are considered in the literature to have modern equivalents in both Hungarian and Bashkir, and these are the names we shall examine in detail. The remaining names are also considered to be of Turkic origin, but are not reported as having Bashkir equivalents.

(9.2) -*Germatos,* identified with Modern Hun. *Gyarmat,* is equivalent to the Bashkir clan name *Jurmatï ~ Yurmatï.* In Old Hungarian this name had also the variants *Gyurmot ~ Gyormot.* According to Németh (1966a: 16–17), the Bashkir forms have preserved the vowel quality (in first syllable) of the Old Hungarian forms.

(9.3) *Genach,* identified with Modern Hun. *Jenő*[8] < Old Hun. *Jeneγ,* has parallels in the Bashkir clan name *Jenej ~ Yänäy ~ Yeney*[9]

(9.4) *Nekis,* identified with Modern Hun. *Nyék,* has an equivalent in the Bashkir clan name *Neg-men ~ Näg-män*[10]

(9.5) *Kasi,* identified with Modern Hun. *Keszi* < Old Hun. *Keszeγ ~ Kesző,* has been identified with the 'identical' (Németh 1966a: 11) Bashkir clan name *Kese* < **Kesey* (recall that *sz* in Hungarian stands for /s/)[11]

(9.6) Μεγέρη / *Megyeri* has been connected to the Bashkir ethnic appellatives (and place-names; see Appendix V) *Mišer ~ Mišar ~ Mišär ~ Meščer ~ Mižer ~ Mižar ~ Mižär.* Similarly, *magyar* has been connected to the Bashkir ethnic appellatives *Možar ~ Možerjan ~ Možer ~ Močar* (these names were attested in the Bashkir region in the 15th and 16th centuries according to Russian sources[12]). These names are often recognised to be regular correspondences (for example by Németh 1966a and 1972: 298).

The denomination *Mišer* occurs as a family name in Hungary. In the 16th century there was a *Miser* family in Szeged (Sándor 1963); a renowned Hungarian philologist was called '*Pesti Mizser Gábor*'[13] (Szinnyei 1908: 49); *Mizser* ~ *Mizsér* remains a family name in Hungary today.

The Hungarian tribal name *Tarján* (*Tarianos* in Constantine's text) also has an equivalent in Bashkir, but there are equivalents in several other Turkic languages as well.

One could observe that also the nobility title *gyula* (now the proper name *Gyula*), reported in the Arabic sources, has been connected to a Bashkir proper name, *Jula-man* ~ *Yula-man*.

Finally, the other nobility name, *kündü* ~ *kende*, reported both in Constantine and the Arabic sources, has parallels in Turkic and Mongolian (see Section 2.1.2.3).

9.1.4.1. *Interpretation in the literature*

The interpretation of the above-reported data vary greatly. A few authors recognise their validity and relevance, and admit that they represent evidence counter to the conventional paradigm. For example, Ligeti (1963: 239; 1986) and Németh (1966a: 12; 1972: 298) consider the terms *mišer* and *možar* regular correspondences of *megyer* and *magyar* respectively. Similarly, Németh (1966a: 11) states that Bas. *Kese* (< *Kesey*) is 'identical' with Old Hun. *Keszey*. Taking these facts into consideration, Ligeti (1986: 375) states that the magyar/Bashkir connection 'belongs to the open questions of Hungarian prehistory'.[14]

However, most scholars attempt to square this evidence with the U paradigm by proposing various, (often) contradictory explanations or justifications. Etymological dictionaries tend to deny, or minimise, or even omit mentioning the existence of these correlations. It is also the case that the same authors (such as Németh or Vásáry), after acknowledging the commonality and regularity of some Hungarian/Bashkir proper names, deny that they are connected (for further interpretations see Vásáry 1975). Below I list some examples of how scholars attempt to square the data with the predictions of the conventional paradigm:

- According to TESz (II, 1123), the Hungarian name *Gyarmat* is of 'uncertain origin', even though it certainly comes from Turkic, probably from a form *jormati* 'tireless'. The connection with Bas. *Jurmati* is considered to be 'not totally convincing' (no explanation is provided as to why this is the case). In EWUng (I, 496), this Bashkir connection is not mentioned at all.
- TESz II, 1039; UEW 874 and EWUng II, 1038, following Németh's (1930/91: 242–4) proposal, claim that *Nyék* is a name of F-U origin, deriving from Old Hun. *nyék*, which has several meanings, including '(game) preserve/wattle enclosure', 'sheep-fold/pen', 'forest located nearby a

river'. The word *nyék* in turn is assumed to derive from a Ugric form
näkɜ-* (nekɜ-*) 'to tie'.[15] According to UEW, Hun. *nyék* at some point in
time 'must have changed its meaning' from the assumed original meaning
'preserve, fence' to the actual meanings '(game) preserve, etc.' The tribe
name *Nyék* is a formation from the expression: '*Nyék népe* "das Folk der
Nyék" (*Nyék* "eine Art Grenzbefestigung")'. UEW then mentions that
Bas. *Näg-* is 'probably' a borrowing from the tribe name *Nyék* .

- According to TESz (II, 1137–8) and EWUng (I, 501), the name *Gyula*,
  whilst certainly of Turkic origin, is not directly connected to the Bashkir
  clan name *Jula-man*, but it 'probably' entered Hungarian from a Turkic
  Khazars form *jula. The same interpretation is found in Ligeti (1986:
  485), who, however, remarks what follows: the presence of initial *j* is
  indication of a Bulgaro-Khazar origin, but the nobility name itself is not
  known from the Khazars, from whom we would expect it. Similarly,
  Németh (1966a: 16–17) observes that this ethnonym was pronounced
  *Džula in Hungarian and Bulgar Turkic languages, but *Jula* in non-
  Bulgar Turkic languages, whilst at the same time pointing out the two
  following facts: (a) in Old Hungarian also the variant *Jula* (reminiscent of
  the non-Bulgar Turkic variant) is attested; and (b) Bas. *Yula-man* has
  preserved the quality of the Hungarian vowel *-u-*.
- The name *Jenő* (and its variant *ïnaq*) 'could be' of Khazar origin,
  according to Ligeti (1986: 486), because this is a name of Chuvash type,
  although no specific explanation is provided. The same interpretation is
  found in Németh (1966a: 18).
- Vásáry (1975: 238, 272–4) denies the connection between Bas. *mišer* and
  Hun. *megyer*. The author argues that Bas. *mišer* is of unknown origin, and
  that further investigation into the dialects and ethnography of Russia is
  needed to clarify its origin. In contrast, the connection between Bas.
  možar and Hun. *magyar* is accepted. The author argues that the denomination *možar* has been preserved by the *Mišär* people (a Tatar-speaking
  population mentioned by the Russian medieval Chronicles). The author
  further argues that these *Mišär/Možar* people were the descendents of the
  Volga Hungarians, that is, of those 'eastern' Hungarians who remained in
  Magna Hungaria. These Volga Hungarians (who were under the supremacy of the Volga Bulgars) supposedly survived the Mongolian invasion
  which completely destroyed the Volga Bulgars' empire.
- The presence of many *Mišer*-toponyms (alongside the many *Mišer*-
  ethnonyms) in Hungarian territory (see Appendix V) is explained as
  follows by Németh (1972: 298–9): the name *Mišer* originated in Bashkiria.
  The *Mišer* population formed between 800 and 1000 AD on the eastern
  side of the Volga river, where we find today several 'Hungarian ethnonyms'. Part (?) of this *Mišer* population, who originally spoke both
  Hungarian and Kipchak, at some point, for some reason (probably
  escaping from the Mongols), moved westward, diffusing over a large

territory, including the present-day Hungarian territory.[16] At some later point, when most of the Kipchak population was assimilated by the Bashkirs, this *Mišer* population slowly forgot the Hungarian language.

The reader is left to form his own opinion with regard to these explanations.

9.1.5. The toponyms in the Uralic languages

The situation of the toponyms is similar to that of the ethnonyms: hardly any toponym has been identified which can be traced back to a U/F-U origin. Their origin is in most cases unknown, or at least highly controversial. When etymologies have been proposed, they tend to be of Indo-European or of local origin. For example, there are many toponyms interpreted as being of Germanic and/or Baltic origin present in the Finnic area (Grünthal 1997; Häkkinen 1996: 178–80). In Finland there are many toponyms interpreted as being of Lappic origin, as testified by the names containing the element *lappi*, although the origin of *lappi* itself is still controversial (Häkkinen 1996: 173). Compare also the Ob-Ugric toponyms (Kannisto 1923, 1927), on the basis of which it has been established that the Voguls in the past have also lived on the western side of the Urals. As Kannisto (1927: 75) correctly remarks, the crucial question here is for how long they also lived on the eastern side of the Urals, given that, according to the conventional model, they should have originated and lived for a while on the western side (see Section 3.1).

Basically, toponyms have been useless so far in the investigation of the supposedly oldest phases of U, although they have been very helpful in the investigation of single, historical languages, particularly in the Scandinavian and Balto-Finnic regions (Korhonen 1981: 40–1; Salo 1984; Kiviniemi 1984; Vahtola 1986).

9.1.5.1. Toponyms that span across the Uralic border

In Finland there are proper names of large water systems for which no Finnish, Lapp, or Germanic/Baltic origin can be retrieved. Similarly, there are in Finnish and other U languages toponyms built with the component -*ŋkV* (V = vowel) whose origin is considered unknown, such as *Ilva-nka, Kimi-nki, Säämi-nki* etc. (Kiviniemi 1980b: 334). The component -*ŋkV* is believed to be a very old element. Häkkinen (1996: 173), in acknowledging that there are in Finland old hydronyms for which no plausible origin has been found so far, such as *Imatra* and *Päijänne*, considers them probably as 'remnants from the language of an unknown population' ('jäänteitä jonkin tuntemattoman kansan kielestä'), which inhabited Finland before the arrival of the Finns' Uralic ancestors.

However, Räsänen (1963/4: 189) remarks that in the peninsula of Kola there is a lake whose name is *Imandra*, of Tungusic origin (Tun. *imandra* 'snow'), and he wonders whether this name bears any connection to the Finnish name *Imatra*.

Similarly, Castrén (1856: 476, 1858: 139–40; see also Räsänen 1963/4: 189), reports to have found in the area of the Sayan mountains (central Asia[17]) several hydronyms/toponyms which are very similar to some Finnish hydronyms/toponyms. For example, two of the Yenisei river tributaries are called, respectively, *Sim* ~ *Sym,* for which compare Finn. *Simo-joki* (*joki* = 'river'), and *Ija* ~ *Ijus*, for which compare Finn. *Ij-* ~ *Ii-joki.* The old, Turkic name of the Yenisei river is *Kem,* for which compare Finn. *Kemi* (a town in north Finland) as well as *Kemi-joki* and *Kymi,* the name of a large river. Another tributary of the Yenisei river is called *Oja,* for which compare Finn. *oja* 'ditch, trench, drain'. In the area of the Irtish river Castrén found a place called *Sumi* which he connected to the term *Suomi* (Castrén 1858: 139–40). On the basis of these findings (and other considerations) the author concluded that the Finnish people originated from the same area as the Samoyed and the Turks, that is the area of the Sayan mountains in central Asia. As mentioned above, *Sumi/Suomi,* and the other parallels in the Finnish and Asiatic proper names, have been subsequently dismissed as similar by chance. Although this is certainly a possibility, I personally cannot see on which grounds the currently accepted etymology of *Suomi,* from P-Baltic **žemē* (as discussed above), is considered to be a better match than *Sumi.*

There is a cluster of isoglosses intersecting the Hungarian and Turkic Bashkir area. In this sense, the distribution of the shared Hungarian and Bashkir toponyms appears to be consistent with that of the shared ethnonyms, as discussed in Section 9.1.4 above. The details of these correlations are reported in Appendix V.

To conclude this section, one may notice that in Balto-Finnic, and possibly in Lapp, there are terms referring to the semantic domain of 'land, terrain' for which again no etymology has been found, Uralic or borrowed. These terms include: *mäki* 'hill', *niemi* 'cape, headland, peninsula (*niemi-maa*)', *saari* 'island' (no origin is proposed in SKES 938), *salo* 'wilds, woodland' (uncertain origin, according to SKES 956), *suo* 'bog', swamp', *sammal* 'moss' (uncertain origin, according to SKES 961–2), etc. (Ariste 1971: 256; 1981a: 13–19). The above-mentioned Finn. *oja* 'ditch, trench' is also considered as being of unknown origin.

9.2. GENETICS

Genetic studies show a gradation from mainly Mongoloid character in the eastern U areas near the Ural mountains (Samoyed, Ob-Ugric), to mainly Europoid character in the western U areas and Finland. The Lapps are classified as mainly European, but they differ from the other populations (and also from the nearby Finns) by having an admixture of oriental and

Caucasoid alleles (Cavalli-Sforza, Menozzi & Piazza 1994: 510–12; Cavalli-Sforza 1996: 173–7; Sammallahti[18] 1995). This gradation across the whole Uralic area does not support the traditional interpretation of the existence of a U family. Instead it suggests that the area results from a mixture of eastern and European characteristics. Several authors explain this by observing, correctly, that genetic groups need not correspond to linguistic groups.

However, in spite of this, it has been reported in the literature that there is evidence for a 'Uralic gene', as shown by the quote by Cavalli-Sforza et al. reported at the beginning of the chapter. Cavalli-Sforza (1996: 176–7, 217) also talks about various U populations, together with the 'proportion' of 'Uralic genes' they contain. Probably, the authors do not really mean that there is a specific Uralic gene, but the reader might be misled by the way the results of this genetic research are reported. This way of reporting probably originates from a calculation first made by Guglielmino et al. (1990), and published in a paper with the misleading title: *Uralic genes in Europe*. The authors calculate a measure of genetic distance between sample populations. They take samples from Europe, Hungary, the Finnish area, and an area near the Ural mountains (Samoyed, Komi/Zyrians and Mari/Cheremis). They do not consider samples from the Turkic or Mongolian areas. They do not consider other evidence which suggests that the populations near the Ural mountains are mainly Mongoloid in character. Instead, based on linguistic studies, they merely define the populations near the Ural mountains as representing a 'Uralic' gene. Their results are broadly consistent with the general gradation reported above: there is a large genetic distance between the Hungarians, the Finns and what the authors call the 'Ural populations' (the above-mentioned Samoyed, Zyrian and Cheremis), and much smaller genetic distance between the Hungarians, the Finns and the European populations. They express this by saying that the Hungarians and the Finns contain a very low proportion of the 'Uralic gene'. In summary, the reader should be aware that this paper presents no evidence to support the existence of a 'Uralic gene': it is merely written using the terminology of linguistics.

For an up-to-date view on the status of genetic studies in the Finno-Ugric area see Rootsi et al. (2000).

9.3. ARCHAEOLOGY

On the archaeological side, as already mentioned, there are very few records. Even so, there appears to be no evidence of migrations from the area of the Ural mountains towards the west. On the contrary, it appears that populations moved the other way round, northwards, in concomitance with the receding ice sheets. For example, according to Indreko (1948a: 406–9, 1948b), the first post-Ice Age inhabitants in the area extending from the

Baltic Sea up to the Urals were 'Finno-Ugric' populations of the Europoid type, who moved there from southern and western Europe, in the wake of the receding ice sheet. Indreko (1948a) identifies these post-Ice Age inhabitants with the F-U people because, at the time, the existence of the F-U node, and therefore of the F-U people, was not questioned. Notice, however, that the author expresses reservations about the U node, that is, about the belonging together of the Samoyed peoples and the F-U peoples. In fact, he considers the Samoyeds as a distinct population, to be associated with other 'Arctic' populations (see Marcantonio 2001b).

This basic picture has generally been confirmed by later research; compare Nuñez (1987, 1997), Niskanen (1997, 2000), Lipták (1975a), Julku (2000: 130) and Carpelan (1999, 2000). For instance, Carpelan (1999) has suggested the alternative, 'non-migrationistic' thesis that the inhabitants of Finland came to adopt the language (and some other cultural traits) of successful F-U-speaking traders from central Russia. According to the author, these populations were active in the area in the late fifth millennium BC, and their F-U language was used as a lingua franca in that region.

Carpelan (2000: 13) summarises the basic thesis that there is no evidence of migrations from the East as follows:

I find it clear that the Uralic development and any spiritual elements thought to be associated with it did *not* originate in Siberia.

One might also observe that there is no trace of common, F-U, or U folklore, or oral tradition, despite the existence of publications whose title could be misleading[19] for an external reader, such as the book by Saarinen (1990): *Suomalais-ugrilaisten kansojen folklore*: 'the folklore of the Finno-Ugric people', or the paper by Siikala (2000): *What myths tell about past Finno-Ugric modes of thinking*. This fact is generally explained away as usual, when features which 'should be there' are not to be found: surely the U community must have had its own culture, beliefs, traditional poems etc. (Laakso 1999b: 48–9).

For further information about the status of archaeological, anthropological and genetic research see, for example, Carpelan (1996), Fodor (1975a, 1975b), Veres (1996), Künnap (1998a), J. Vilkuna (1996), Heapost (2000), Nuñez (2000), Dolukhanov (2000a, 2000b) and Alinei (2000: 138–79). See also the articles contained in the seventh volume of C8IFU: *Litteratura, Archaeologia & Anthropologia*, or in the volumes (already quoted in this book) edited by Julku & Äärelä (1997), Gallén (1984), Fogelberg (1999) and Künnap (2000). See also Voigt (1999, 2000: 83–101) for the 'conquest-time' Hungarian folklore.

9.4. Conclusion

It is remarkable that hardly any common 'Uralic' Onomastics has been identified so far within the U languages. In contrast, there are many proper names in common on a local level.

The most striking evidence contradicting the U theory is the common Onomastics between the Hungarian and Turkic (especially Bashkir) areas on the one hand, and the common Onomastics between the Finnish and the central-Asiatic areas on the other. This evidence is highly suggestive of strong local links that have no relation to the supposed Uralic areas.

The archaeological evidence is scanty. In what we do have, there is no trace of a migration towards the south-west from the areas of the Ural mountains as demanded by the Uralic paradigm. On the contrary, the evidence suggests that population movements were in a northerly direction, with the receding ice sheets, and there is evidence of a migration of technology from the south-west to the north-east.

The genetic evidence shows a simple gradient from Europoid character in the west, to Mongoloid character in the east. Despite the way in which genetic evidence is often reported, there is no evidence at all for a 'Uralic gene': this phrase is used (misleadingly) merely as a definition of the genetic mixture that is found in the region of the Ural mountains.

One may conclude this chapter by stating, following Häkkinen (1996: 9), that there is no self-evident link between the linguistic tradition, and the genetic and archaeological findings.[20]

10

SUMMARY AND CONCLUSION

Continuous interest in Opabina *has not been accompanied by critical study of the specimens, so that fancy has not been inhibited by facts . . . My conclusions on morphology have led to a reconstruction which differs in many important respects from all earlier ones*[1]

H. B. Whittington

In the preceding pages I have reviewed the evidence relating to the U languages. This review has included evidence from historical sources, Phonology, Lexicon, Morphology, Morpho-syntax, ethnonyms, toponyms, archaeology, and genetics. Regarding the linguistic models that have been adopted to account for the correlations between the U languages, this review has examined the origin and development of the mainstream interpretation as well as the many competing interpretations that are found in the literature. From the point of view of scientific evidence, this review has found that the Comparative Method, as it has been applied to these languages, is usually unable to decide whether a linguistic correlation is borrowed, inherited or an accidental look-alike, and so this book has also introduced statistical methods to quantify these correlations.

10.1. SUMMARY

In Chapter 1, I set out my programme for reviewing the U languages and the linguistic models that might account for their history and relationships. The central thrust of this programme was, wherever possible, to refer directly to primary evidence. If one is to illuminate the relationships between the languages, and to test the suitability of one linguistic model over another, it is only possible to do this convincingly by referring always to the actual data.

I rejected the approach, which is sometimes taken in the field, of basing the analysis on assumed reconstructions. We saw how these reconstructions usually incorporate hidden assumptions – and these assumptions in turn are often based on a particular linguistic model, perhaps the very model that is being tested! This can lead to a circularity of argument, and we touched on several examples of this.

In Chapter 2 we reviewed the historical sources and the historical foundation of the U theory. It was important to begin my treatise with these topics, because many linguists simply assume that the U paradigm was established scientifically and decisively in historical times. However, as we saw, this is not the case.

We saw that the origin of the U theory can be traced back to the emergence of a belief in a close relationship between Vogul, Ostyak and Hungarian (the 'Ugric' node). Between the 15th and 17th centuries, it came to be taken for granted that the Eastern origin of the Hungarians, which was indicated in the Chronicles, could be identified with an area near the Ural mountains called *Yugria* (hence the term 'Ugric'). This belief was originally based on nothing more than the apparent similarity between the toponym *Yugria* and the ethnonym *hungarus*. It is unclear whether this connection is still regarded as valid in the modern literature, since *hungarus* is now usually reported as connected with the *On-ogur* Turkic tribe. It was then discovered in the 19th century that the Voguls called themselves *Mansi*, which, according to Kálmán (1988: 395) 'to the lay ear slightly resembles the name *magyar*'. Today, the connection *magyar-Mansi* is widely regarded as important evidence in favour of the Ugric node, having been justified using an etymology that, as we saw in Chapter 9, is ad hoc and does not in fact accord with the historically attested forms. This ethnonym appears to form the only concrete evidence in favour of the Ugric node, since it is generally recognised that Hungarian is radically different in Phonology, Morphology, Lexicon and Syntax from the other Ugric languages and, as a consequence, the Ugric node has defied all attempts to reconstruct it from the primary evidence (see Chapter 4).

In the late 19th century, the belief in the Ugric connection was extended, and gained scientific respectability, mainly through the work of the founder of the field, Budenz. Budenz was the first author to attempt to apply the Comparative Method to 'prove' the relationship between Hungarian and the Ugric languages (which Budenz extended to cover Finnish and some other north-eastern languages). We saw that his comparative corpus is unsatisfactory in modern terms. Budenz did not define the sound-laws on which his 'correspondences' are supposed to have been based, and, in many cases, they are rather 'forced' in sound and meaning. This is reflected in the fact that 81% of a sample of these correspondences are no longer recognised in the modern literature. The reasons for this poor quality can be understood in historical terms, since the Comparative Method was in its infancy at the time, and a similar situation has been observed in the development of other language models such as Indo-European.

In Chapter 3 we examined the modern mainstream textbook interpretation of the relationships between the U languages, and compared it with the alternative interpretations that are published in the literature. The range of interpretations is very wide. They range from extensions to the family – to include, for example, Altaic or Yukaghir or both – to variations on the family tree, to rejection of the very genetic affinity on which the Uralic unity is supposed to be based.

These theories all have a remarkable common thread: all of these authors claim to use substantially the same evidence, and to apply the same method of analysis, namely the Comparative Method. How then is it possible that they arrive at radically different family trees? This appears to be the first concrete indication that there is something wrong with the way the Comparative Method is applied to this language family. Either most of these authors have made some key mistake, or the method itself is so flexible that it can be used to support many contradictory family trees, based on the same evidence.

In Chapter 4 we examined in detail the principal 'mainstream' attempts to reconstruct the U family tree using the Comparative Method. We saw that most modern reconstructions are based on the comparative corpus of Janhunen (1981a). This corpus is referred to as the 'P-Uralic' node, but this name might be misleading to an outside scholar because the corpus omits systematic consideration of the assumed key Ugric node.

At the heart of the Comparative Method is the requirement that, in a properly constituted reconstruction, each sound-rule must be obeyed by a significant number of regular etymologies. Provided this criterion is met (together with some others), it is statistically unlikely that the reconstruction could be the result of chance resemblances. This is sometimes called the 'cumulative effect' of the Comparative Method. However, we found that Janhunen's 'P-Uralic' corpus does not meet this criterion. It has a large number of sound-rules and a small number of etymologies – in fact, the sound-rules outnumber the etymologies if one counts only 'regular' etymologies. This means that it would be consistent with the evidence to interpret this comparative corpus as mostly the result of chance resemblances.

We then examined the attempts to reconstruct the key intermediate nodes, Ugric and Finno-Ugric. These nodes had hitherto defied all attempts to reconstruct them, mainly because, as mentioned, Hungarian is radically different from its assumed siblings in the Ugric node. Sammallahti (1988) nevertheless assumed that the conventional, historically established family tree is valid, and that it was necessary to find an alternative way to overcome the apparent contradiction between the evidence and the model. He 'bridged the gap' between the reconstructed P-Uralic node and the reconstructed P-Ob-Ugric node. In the main, this work compared reconstructions against other reconstructions, rather then referring directly to primary linguistic evidence. We identified some of the problems with this method – for example the fact that it is based on the 'P-Uralic' node which was discussed above – and concluded that it would be consistent with the evidence to interpret that this reconstruction, too, was mostly the result of chance resemblances.

In Chapter 5 we applied alternative statistical methods to the same linguistic evidence. The results of this method were in agreement with the conclusion of Chapter 4, namely that one cannot tell whether the Uralic corpus is the result of a true linguistic correlation or of chance resemblances. However, this analysis did identify a small number of etymologies that might have statistical significance because they are particularly widely represented in many languages. We found that all but two of these etymologies are also present in the nearby Asiatic languages, so that, if these words are significant, they suggest a wider relationship than just the Uralic area.

In Chapter 6 we examined the lexical correlations with languages that are not normally classified as part of the Uralic family, some of which appear to be genuine correlations, due to their wide distribution. We found there is evidence for strong isoglosses that intersect the supposed boundary of the Uralic area. In the North there are strong isoglosses encompassing Tungusic and some of the northern Uralic languages (the so-called 'arctic vocabulary'); in the South there are strong isoglosses encompassing Hungarian, Chuvash, Mongol and Common Turkic languages; and in the North-East there are strong isoglosses encompassing Samoyed and Yukaghir. The authors who study these correlations at times go so far as to express surprise that some of these parallels can be so 'flawless' in sound and meaning.

We reviewed the 'mainstream' interpretation of these isoglosses. When it comes to interpreting these 'flawless' correlations using the Comparative Method, they are not considered evidence of a linguistic relationship (since they contradict the assumed established families). Instead they are explained as the result of 'convergent development' or of regular 'direct borrowing'. These interpretations are in direct contradiction to the assumed Neo-grammarian view, which is at the heart of the conventional paradigm, that borrowed words can be identified because they are irregular. A similar contradiction with the Neo-grammarian view has been found in modern linguistic studies outside the Uralic sphere.

We concluded that the Comparative Method, at least as it is applied in the Uralic context, does not allow us to distinguish borrowed words from inherited words (and even, as we have already seen, from chance resemblances). In order to model the relationships with languages outside the Uralic area, one is inexorably drawn by the evidence into an approach that is based on the recognition of the identified, intersecting isoglosses that span the whole area.

In Chapter 7 we examined the evidence relating to the generally accepted explanation for the very poor quality of the Uralic comparative corpus, namely, its great antiquity. This evidence is supposed to be founded on two areas: palaeo-linguistic evidence, mainly in the form of reconstructed tree-names, and the borrowing of words from early Indo-European.

We saw that the palaeo-linguistic evidence amounts to five reconstructed words, and the evidence from early Indo-European borrowings amounts to between five and fifteen words, depending on the interpretation. There are problems with all these words. For example, most of them have questionable reconstructions, including the presence of laryngeals on the Indo-European side and the presence of an unspecified segment *x on the Uralic side. Most of them have parallels outside the U and Indo-European areas, some of them being considered as cases of *Wanderwörter*.

In Chapter 8 we examined the morphological evidence. Here, too, we found the evidence in support of the U theory to be rather poor. For example, only two or three Case endings are shared by most of the Uralic languages. These are very simple formants which are also shared by most of the Altaic languages. A similar picture holds true for the endings of Plurality, Possession, Tense and Aspect. Furthermore, one cannot reconstruct any morphological paradigms (or sub-sets of paradigms) of the type found within Indo-European, such as verbal, nominal or pronominal; and one cannot identify any shared cases of suppletism or syncretism.

Indeed, this lack of common endings should not be surprising because major areas of Morphology, including Case endings, verbal endings, endings for Plurality, etc., are independent innovations which have formed during the life of the individual languages. For example, we saw that the Case ending system in Hungarian was formed recently in historical times through the process of Grammaticalisation. This process is attested in the oldest Hungarian records dating from the 12th century.

In Chapter 9 we examined other areas of evidence relating to the Uralic theory. We began with proper names. We found striking isoglosses spanning the boundaries of the U linguistic context. For example, there are strong isoglosses connecting Hungarian and Turkic, and connecting the Finnic area with Central Asiatic areas. Some of these are statistically significant because they contain a large number of matching phonemes. The proper names are generally consistent with the other levels of language that we examined above.

In the 'mainstream' Uralic interpretation, this evidence is brushed aside. It is assumed that proper names are unreliable – that is, unless they support the Uralic theory, such as the alleged relationships *magyar–Mansi* and *hungarus–On-ogur* or *Yugria*.

We then turned our attention to the evidence from genetic and archaeological studies, and we saw that none of them lend support to the U theory. From genetics, there is no evidence for a 'Uralic gene' as anything more than a definition based on the linguistic model. From archaeology, there is evidence of movement of people and technology from the South-West to the North-East, in the opposite direction to the supposed migrations involved in the Uralic theory.

10.2. CONCLUSIONS

In this review I have examined the Uralic languages at all relevant levels of language. I have failed to uncover any evidence at all to support the notion that these languages form a unique genetic family. Most of the evidence that is usually put forward in the 'mainstream' interpretation fails tests of statistical confidence, or it is not tested against primary linguistic data, or it fails to qualify as 'scientific evidence' at all because it is not falsifiable. What is usually reported as 'evidence' is in fact the result of an interlocking set of assumptions; the reported proofs are usually a consequence of, not evidence for, the assumption that the Uralic languages form a family.

My first conclusion, therefore, is that there is no evidence to support the notion that the Uralic languages form a unique genetic family. One may speak of the principal language groupings, namely Finnic, Ob-Ugric, Hungarian, Samoyed and Lapp, and one may talk of the relationships among these groupings (as well as their relationships with the neighbours to the East), but there is no evidence that they all derive genetically from the same node, the P-U node, as traditionally conceived.

This review has identified a handful of statistically significant lexical and grammatical correlations that span a very wide Eurasiatic area (possibly with the exclusion of Indo-European). They include some local (primary) Cases, the Infinite/Gerundive -mA, and a handful of basic terms, phonological features and sound-matches. There are also further features that appear to be significant because of their wide distribution, but for which we have not undertaken any formal statistical tests. These include several isomorphic constructions containing the same lexical material, and a great many common morpho-syntactic and typological features.

My second conclusion, therefore, is that these correlations testify to some sort of communication across a very wide geographical area, spanning several thousand kilometres. There may be several models for the nature of this communication. Possible models include: genetic transmission; diffusion through contact and trade-related activities; and diffusion of population through marriage and local movement, which Renfrew (1987) calculates would spread at the rate of 1,000 kilometres in 1,000 years in a relatively sedentary agricultural economy, and which would undoubtedly be much faster in the more mobile economy of the area at the time. My personal speculation is that all of these types of communication are involved, and I do not believe the evidence permits us to tell them apart.

In addition, this review has identified correlations that appear to be clustered into isoglosses that often cross the traditional boundary of the Uralic area. These isoglosses are also supported by evidence from proper names. It appears that the strongest clusters of isoglosses crossing the Uralic boundary join Hungarian, Turkic and Mongolian; they join Samoyed and Yukaghir; they join Northern Tungusic and nearby Uralic languages; and they join Lapp with Finnic (lexically). It is remarked in the literature that these correlations are striking and numerous, some of them being described as 'flawless'. Although no formal statistical tests have been undertaken in this field, at least some of these correlations are statistically significant because they have many matching sounds within the same word, or because they have a wide distribution.

My third conclusion therefore is that the correlations among the U languages and between the Uralic languages and their neighbours are better described in terms of intersecting isoglosses. These languages form a dialectal continuum.

The position of Hungarian is of particular importance as a cornerstone of the conventional paradigm. The extremely poor correlations between Hungarian and the Ugric and Finnic languages, coupled with the strong isoglosses joining Hungarian, Turkic and Mongolian suggest that, if one insists on a simple classification, Hungarian should be classified as an 'Inner Asian' language.[2] This classification would be consistent with the testimony of the historical sources.

Finally, this review has highlighted a number of issues connected with the use of the Comparative Method to model the correlations in this linguistic area. We observed that the method is often not applied properly, for example, with reconstructions that have more sound-rules than regular etymologies and which therefore do not meet the prerequisites for the applicability of the method. Even if this were not the case, there is a deeper methodological problem: in the absence of historical records, it does not appear possible to distinguish borrowed words from inherited words, because the Neo-grammarian assumption that they can be identified by their regularity or irregularity simply does not apply.

My fourth conclusion therefore is that a re-examination of the linguistic method that is used to classify languages is required.

10.3. THE LINGUISTIC METHOD

The purpose of this book has been to focus on the classification of the U languages. It has not been its purpose to review the methods that have been adopted to classify other language families, in which perhaps different situations may apply. For example, in Indo-European the historical records are more numerous and there is a rich morphological system, at least for a subset of the Indo-European languages. Nevertheless, if my approach to the classification of the U languages were to be accepted as the correct one, then a similar approach might be considered also in the classification of other language 'families', and the validity of the Comparative Method as a whole might be called into question.

10.3.1. *The Comparative Method is not sufficient*

I believe it is a fundamental mistake to use primarily the method of comparative linguistics to classify languages. We have already seen in this book some of the inadequacies of this method, particularly as it is applied in this context where there are no old records and there is a high degree of variation. The central problem with the method is that it can introduce a strong bias – words that match the assumed reconstructions are cited as 'evidence' for a genetic relationship, whilst words that do not match the reconstructions are assumed to be in error, irrelevant, 'borrowed', due to 'convergent development', due to a supposed process of 'regular direct borrowing', or *Wanderwörter*. A further problem is that the practice has emerged – at least in the Uralic context and possibly elsewhere – of not applying the method properly. For example, the sound-rules on which the method is founded are usually not fully listed, or, where they are listed, they may actually outnumber the etymologies that obey them regularly.

In general, the family tree model makes certain predictions (such as the tenets described in the Introduction), but when it comes to testing them against the evidence, researchers should beware not to fall into the same trap that has crept into U studies, that is, of justifying data that are inconsistent with the predictions through statements which are not verifiable, and therefore, not falsifiable. This is not a scientific method. For example, within U studies, the absence of crucial features whose presence is predicted by the model, such as a shared Plural system or Case system, has been justified by postulating that these features 'have been lost'. Vice-versa, evidence which contradicts the predictions of the model has been justified by postulating the influence of an extinct (and therefore untestable) language. We have seen how in Hungarian many words are supposed to have been borrowed from an extinct language, which in turn is reconstructed, at least in part, using the (presumed) borrowed words.

At the very least, researchers should clearly identify deviations from the predictions, so that other researchers can form their own conclusions, rather than hiding these deviations under the carpet with these sorts of justifications.

In order to overcome these pitfalls, I believe that linguists in all language studies must now begin to do what all other scientists must do, namely, to go through the process of showing that their evidence is statistically significant. This must form the starting point for all interpretations. Demonstrating statistical significance may be achieved by showing that the Comparative Method has been applied properly, for example with many etymologies obeying each sound-rule systematically and fully, or alternatively by using statistical methods such as those introduced by Ringe, or both.

If this approach to U studies is accepted, it certainly demonstrates that Indo-European does not constitute a universal model for linguistic change and reconstruction, as already discussed in the literature, for example by Benveniste (1966: 103), Dixon[3] (1997: 13–14), Nichols (1992: 4–5). In fact, the validity of the family tree model has been questioned in several areas of linguistics, for example with regard to the Romance languages (Meillet 1954;

Hetzron 1976: 92) and the Semitic languages (Garbini 1984; Edzard 1998, 2000). In this respect, my book supports the work of these scholars.

It would be a challenging subject for further research to examine how far one could extend the lessons learned from U studies into the field of Indo-European studies. Any such research would have to be systematic and extensive, since conclusions based on anything less would correctly be classified as mere speculations. One might be encouraged to embark on research in this area by the observation that there are several parallels between the two fields. For example, Trubetzkoy (1939) argued over 60 years ago that there is no compelling evidence to support a 'unitary Indo-European P-language' but, as in Uralic studies, such ideas of course do not form the mainstream interpretation. I believe that the Indo-European paradigm would either be clarified and strengthened, or it would be significantly revised, through a systematic analysis of this sort.

10.3.2. *Where did the process go wrong?*

How is it possible that a community of scientists can base its work, for over 100 years, on a fundamental belief in the U node, which is simply not supported by the evidence, and indeed is contradicted by a good body of evidence?

There is a historical explanation. Early researchers were seduced by the Darwinian theory, and they shoe-horned what little evidence that they had into a Darwinian model of language development. For example, consider how Samoyed came to be classified as a Uralic language. At the end of the 19th century, the evidence was highly equivocal, with the correlations between Samoyed and other Altaic languages being approximately equivalent to the correlations with the Ugric and Finnic languages. However, in order to fit the Darwinian model, researchers were obliged to jump in one direction or the other. They had to make a simple and clear choice of one originating parent language. Accordingly, Samoyed was classified as a Uralic language on nothing more than the 'on-balance' opinion of one author (Donner). It is as though the scientific paradigm of the time would accept nothing less.

Linguistics was not alone in being seduced by the power of the Darwinian paradigm. A gross distortion of the evidence from palaeontology has been catalogued in a popular and highly readable book, *Wonderful Life* (Gould 1989). The author shows how the earliest fossil records were systematically distorted by shoe-horning the data into the assumption of a Darwinian tree that led to modern organisms. The actual data simply never fitted this classification, but it was as if, in later papers, researchers did not actually examine the records, but merely reproduced or extended classifications made by previous authors which were presented as immutable facts. As one of the researchers, Whittington (1975), remarks:

Continuous interest in *Opabina* has not been accompanied by critical study of the specimens, so that fancy has not been inhibited by facts

The evidence and interpretations of Whittington and his co-workers have led to a revolution in the models accepted in palaeontology.

There have been many forces holding back a re-examination of the Uralic paradigm. These include the emotional search by people for their origins, the process of peer-review in the context of a powerful paradigm, the strait-jacket of the adopted Darwinian model, and the belief that the use of the Comparative Method is sufficient to establish a relationship, whether or not it is actually demonstrated that the preconditions for the applicability of the method are met. I believe these forces have now all abated. The traditional Uralic model is now under assault on several fronts. I believe that a shift in the paradigm can no longer be delayed.

MAP   279

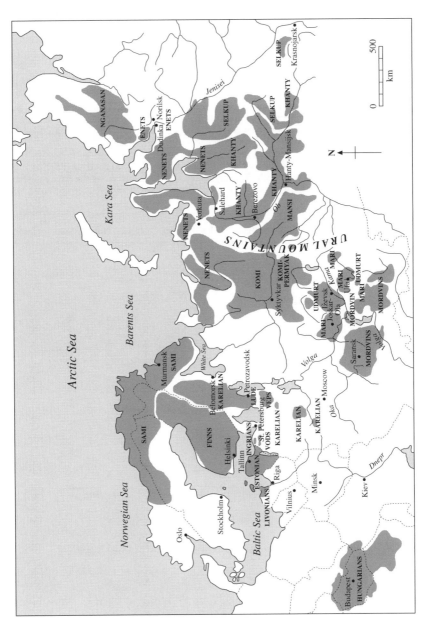

The Distribution of Uralic Languages

APPENDIX I

DISTRIBUTION OF
BODY-PART TERMS FROM UEW

This table shows the distribution of terms for body-parts listed in UEW, excluding etymologies that are marked as uncertain. Words that are identified as statistically significant are marked in bold; the words written in italics are the second-most significant ones. The interpretation of the words marked in bold is discussed in detail in the text of Chapter 5.

In the tables below the occurrence of the etymologies in the U languages examined is reported. If an etymology is reported as being present in one or more of the languages in a group, that group is marked with an X. The first column of the table shows the page reference in UEW.

Page	Meaning	Consonants	B-F	Perm.	Ob-U.	Hun.	Sam.	Lapp
644	*hair/stem*	*3*	*X*	*X*				*X*
801	lip/muzzle etc.	3	X	X				
645	shoulder	3	X	X				
380	navel	3		X	X			
355	shoulder/wing	3	X		X			
479	**eye**	**2**	**X**	**X**	**X**	**X**	**X**	**X**
285	**egg/testicle**	**2**	**X**	**X**	**X**	**X**	**X**	**X**
264	**liver**	**2**	**X**	**X**	**X**	**X**	**X**	**X**
210	**urine**	**2**	**X**	**X**	**X**	**X**	**X**	**X**
576	*blood*	*2*	*X*	*X*	*X*	*X*		*X*
444	*lap/bosom*	*2*	*X*	*X*	*X*	*X*		*X*
396	*diarrhoea*	*2*	*X*	*X*	*X*	*X*		*X*
159	*tear*	*2*	*X*	*X*		*X*	*X*	*X*
158	*elbow*	*2*	*X*	*X*	*X*	*X*		*X*
140	*hand*	*2*	*X*	*X*	*X*	*X*		*X*
36	*nipple/wart*	*2*	*X*	*X*		*X*	*X*	*X*
92	tendon/sinew	2	X	X	X	X		
479	saliva	2	X	X	X			X
402	hair	2	X	X	X	X		
393	knee	2	X	X			X	X
370	ear	2		X	X	X		X
322	saliva/mucus	2	X	X		X		X
313	tongue	2		X	X	X		X
303	nose/beak/etc.	2		X	X		X	X
267	breast	2		X	X	X		X
247	spirit/soul	2	X	X	X	X		
223	cough	2		X	X		X	X
178	armpit	2		X	X	X		X
157	nail	2	X	X	X			X
142	membrane/skin	2	X	X	X			X
121	membrane/scale	2	X	X	X	X		
88	foot	2	X	X		X		X
472	buttock	2		X	X	X		
449	finger	2				X	X	X
396	cheek	2	X		X		X	

383	lip	2			X		X	X
374	skin/bark	2			X	X	X	
225	back	2			X	X	X	
208	stomach/belly	2		X	X	X		
872	palm of hand	2			X	X		
854	hair	2			X	X		
754	lung/gill	2		X				X
670	stomach/womb	2	X	X				
625	side	2		X				X
472	kidney	2			X			X
384	palm of hand	2	X				X	
368	shoulder blade	2					X	X
353	tail	2		X	X			
341	chin	2		X	X			
338	(body) cavity	2			X			X
242	spleen	2		X		X		
137	palm of hand	2	X		X			
492	mouth/opening	1	X	X	X	X	X	X
477	heart	1	X	X	X	X	X	X
441	vein	1	X	X	X	X	X	X
365	head	1	X	X	X	X	X	
144	tongue/language	1	X	X	X		X	X
11	mouth/opening	1		X	X	X	X	X
473	neck	1	X	X	X			X
395	breast/bosom	1	X	X	X			X
382	tooth/stick	1	X	X	X	X		
254	bone	1	X	X	X		X	
636	skin/etc.	1	X	X				X
519	lungs	1	X	X			X	
25	chin/cheek	1		X	X		X	
25	voice/sound	1	X			X		X
14	hair	1		X	X		X	
542	head	1			X		X	
401	backside	1			X		X	

APPENDIX II

DISTRIBUTION OF TERMS FROM JANHUNEN'S (1981A) CORPUS

This table shows the distribution of the U etymologies which form Janhunen's corpus. The table excludes words that Janhunen himself identifies as unsafe. Words that are identified as statistically significant are marked in bold and in italics, in the same way as in the previous table. The interpretation of the words marked in bold is discussed in detail in the text of Chapter 5.

In the table below the occurrence of the etymologies examined in the U languages is reported. If an etymology is reported as being present in one or more of the language groups identified, that group is marked with an X. The first column of the table shows the page reference in UEW, the second shows the number item in Janhunen's list.

UEW page	Janhunen item number	Meaning	Consonants	B-F	Perm.	Ob-U.	Hun.	Lapp
560	25	**any metal/iron**	2	X	X	X	X	X
479	30	**eye**	2	X	X	X	X	X
444	60	**lap/bosom**	2	X	X	X	X	X
405	36	**drill**	2	X	X	X	X	X
375	28	**nest**	2	X	X	X	X	X
370	56	**(to) fear**	2	X	X	X	X	X
362	24	**half/relative/side**	2	X	X	X	X	X
305	58	**name**	2	X	X	X	X	X
285	19	**egg/testicle**	2	X	X	X	X	X
272	55	**to go**	2	X	X	X	X	X
264	41	**liver**	2	X	X	X	X	X
210	65	**urine**	2	X	X	X	X	X
203	12	**wave/hillock/etc.**	2	X	X	X	X	X
119	8	**fish**	2	X	X	X	X	X
115	2	**drop, let go**	2	X	X	X	X	X
536	67	to feel/know	2	X	X		X	X
534	37	crossbar	2		X	X	X	X
477	76	coal	2	X	X	X		X
430	10	to steal/secret	2	X	X	X		X
350	9	swallow	2	X	X	X	X	
304	59	stalk/stem	2	X	X	X		X
222	80	spruce	2	X	X	X		X
201	33	fall	2	X	X	X		X
144	81	tongue/language	2	X	X	X		X
124	3	to carry	2	X	X	X		X
92	72	tendon/sinew	2	X	X	X	X	
65	82	(bird)cherry	2	X	X	X		X
34	26	uncle	2	X	X	X		X
577	14	fence/fortress	2		X	X		X
531	32	fight	2	X	X			X
454	64	lizard	2	X	X			X
451	48	summer	2	X		X		X
450	68	ski	2	X	X	X		

397	66	stem/cane	2	X	X			X
377	78/79	height/length	2	X		X	X	
377	29	tall/long	2	X		X	X	
353	54	to put	2	X	X	X		
336	11	good/head	2	X	X			X
322	88	hare	2		X		X	X
289	62	to wash	2	X	X		X	
287	20	cloudberry	2	X	X	X		
223	44	(to) cough	2		X	X		X
214	17	to put out	2	X	X			X
208	34	to close (eyes)	2		X	X	X	
66	31	glue	2	X	X			X
22	22	needle	2	X	X			X
642	1	sun/brightness	2		X			X
449	21	finger	2			X	X	
445	70	*pinus cembra*	2		X	X		
396	63	cheek	2	X		X		
381	73, 74	dark	2	X	X			
261	16	dew	2		X			X
253	45	(to) snow	2	X	X			
223	61	(to be)dry	2		X			X
218	35	knife	2	X				X
9	39, 40	mother-in-law	2	X				X
548	6	root	2		X			
189	13	grandmother	2					X
111	43	present/sacrifice	2		X			
317	*83*	*arrow*	*1*	*X*	*X*	*X*	*X*	*X*
99	*15*	*river*	*1*	*X*	*X*	*X*	*X*	*X*
73	*27*	*to live*	*1*	*X*	*X*	*X*	*X*	*X*
14	*71*	*father-in-law*	*1*	*X*	*X*	*X*	*X*	*X*
6	*38*	*[space]under*	*1*	*X*	*X*	*X*	*X*	*X*
535	85	feather/wing	1		X	X	X	X
434	87	pus	1		X	X	X	X
294	50	I	1	X	X		X	X
570	57	water	1	X	X		X	
535	52	fire	1	X	X			X
14	69	hair	1		X	X		X
539	51	you	1	X	X			
535	47	to come	1	X	X			
169	84	birch	1	X	X			
340	75	tame, domestic	1					X
309	49	to scratch	1			X		

APPENDIX III

THE PRIMARY CASE ENDINGS AND THEIR DISTRIBUTION WITHIN AND OUTSIDE THE URALIC AREA

1. The Nominative/Absolutive is always – Ø

2. The Genitive -*n* within U is present in Finnish, Cheremis, Lapp, Mordvin, and Samoyed Selkup. There is a Genitive -*n* in some Turkic languages, in Mongolian, in some Tungusic languages and in Dravidian (Aalto 1969/78: 323; Ramstedt 1952: 25–7; Poppe 1955: 187–91; Hajdú 1981: 136–7; Sinor 1988: 715; Tyler 1968).

3. The Accusative -*m* is present in a few U languages: Cheremis, some dialects of Lapp, some dialects of Vogul and Samoyed. Ostyak has -Ø. Perhaps reflexes of *-*m* can be found in the Finnish Accusative -*n*, in Permian and Mordvin (Hajdú 1981: 136). If present, this ending applies only to known, referential, Definite Objects, so that it might be the reflex of an original Topical marker, rather than of a proper Accusative marker. This is still the case in Vogul and this function is still transparent in the behaviour of Acc. -*n* in Finnish (see Marcantonio 1988 and 1994).

There is an Accusative -*m* also in some Tungusic languages (alongside with other endings). There is no such ending in Turkic and Mongolian (Menges 1968/95; Ramstedt 1952: 28–31; Sinor 1988: 714–15).

In Hungarian the Accusative is -*t*. It can be analysed as being an original marker of Topic (Marcantonio 1981). The ending itself is considered by some researchers as the original Locative and by others as the 2nd Person Possessive (see Driussi (1995) for a review of the debate).

To conclude one may also notice that the distribution of the Partitive and Accusative endings for the marking of the Direct Object in Old Finnish is considerably different from Modern Finnish (Nummenaho 1989).

4. The locative I -*n*(*V*) is found in the majority of the U languages (but not in Vogul), in more or less productive functions. It is present in all the U language groups established for the purpose of the mathematical analysis (see Table 8.10).

A Locative -*n*(*V*) is present also in Old Turkic and in all the modern Turkic languages, with several functions. It is attested, although with restricted distribution, in Classical Mongolian and in most modern languages. It does not appear to be present in Tungusic (Sinor 1988: 718–19). It is present in Yukaghir (see Table 8.6).

5. and 6a. The Locative II -*t* and the Ablative -*t*(*V*) are considered here as two distinct entities for the purpose of the mathematical analysis (see Tables 8.9 and 8.10), according to the view of several scholars. However, they could well be the same morpheme, because they have identical and/or similar sound-shape and functions.

The ending -*t*(*V*) is fully functional as Locative in Vogul (but not in Ostyak); it is present in Hungarian and Samoyed Yurak in fossilised forms. The ending -*t*(*V*) is also present in Balto-Finnic, Permian, Samoyed, Lapp. In Finnish it has the function of Partitive.

There is a Locative/Dative -*t*(*V*) in Mongolian, Locative/Ablative -*t*(*V*) in Turkic, and there is an ending -*ti* in some Tungusic languages, with Ablative/Illative/Allative/Instrumental functions. A -*t*(*V*) ending is also found in Yukaghir (see Table 8.6).

To summarise, -*t*(*V*) is present in U, in Altaic and Yukaghir, but not always with the same function.

In Turkic there is a 'complex' Ablative -*da-n* ~ -*dä-n*, which, according to Menges (1968/95: 110), is formed with Loc. -*da* and the ending -*n*, the latter being 'an ancient Ural-Altaic Lative Suffix' (see also Aalto 1969/78: 226; Poppe 1955: 196; Németh 1928; Sinor 1988: 716–17).

5. and 6b. The Ablative -*t*(*V*) is absent in the Ob-Ugric languages. In Hungarian, in addition to -*t*, there is an Ablative -*l*, which is also used to form complex endings, such as -*t*V-*l* (see Table 8.5). This morpheme is found also in Vogul, where it is used to express Instrumental/Comitative functions. In its Ablative function it co-occurs with the Vogul Dative/Lative *-*n*V* (see point 7 below), to form the complex ending -*n*V-*l*. The ending -*l* is not present in Ostyak. It has also been suggested that -*l* is a component of the Finnish complex endings Adessive -*lla* and Ablative -*lta* (see Tables 8.3 and 8.4). As a component of the Finnish complex Cases, this ending -*l* has not been included in the mathematical analysis, because for this purpose only simple Case endings have been taken into consideration. An -*l* ending, with a Locative function is present in all the Tungusic languages, but not in Mongolian and Turkic.

7. The existence of P-U Lative/Dative I *-*ń* ~ *-*n,* or perhaps *-*ŋ* (see Section 8.2), is not widely accepted, because its reflexes are to be found only in the Vogul Lative -*n*(*V*) and in Mordvin, where it has a Dative/Allative function (Zaicz 1998: 192). Possible reflexes are to be found in adverbial forms such as Finn. *kohde-n* 'towards' and in Samoyed, for which compare the reconstructed Samoyed Dative *-*ng* in Table 8.6. It is present in Yukaghir; see again Table 8.6.

8. The Lative II *-k(V)* is supposed to have developed in most languages into spirants (-γ, -χ, -w) or into vowels, as in Hun. *fel-é* 'towards', *id-e* 'toward here', according to the traditional, but not widely accepted, analysis (Raun 1988b: 560; Hajdú 1981: 142). It is preserved as such in a few languages, such as Ingrian *ala-k* '[towards] under'. Traces of this ending can be found in Lapp (Korhonen 1988a: 280). There is in Mordvin a Prolative *-ka* (Raun 1988a: 101), which could be the reflex of Lative II *-k(V)*.

Common Turkic has a Dative *-qa ~ -ke ~ -γa ~ -ge ~ -kä* (reconstructed as *-k(V)*), which has concrete, local as well an abstract, grammatical functions. A 'Directive' morpheme *-ki ~ -χi* occurs in Tungusic. There appear to be no traces of this morpheme in Mongolian (Menges 1968/95: 110).

Sinor (1988: 719–720) says that: 'The data on *-k ~ -*kV* is difficult to interpret but I would be tempted to think that it is an archaic, strongly eroded morpheme. In the U languages it has rarely maintained its original form . . . In Turkic *-k* appears only in conjunction with another local suffix (thus as *-kV*), in Tunguz it does occur alone though most of the time in compounds'.

9. The Lative/Illative *-s* is active in Cheremis and Mordvin (Raun 1988a: 100) and exists also in Lapp. It is present in Finnish in fossilised adverbs, such as *ala-s* 'downwards'. It is (probably) the morpheme forming some Finnish complex endings (see Table 8.3).

This ending is not attested in Turkic, but is well represented in Mongolian and in Tungusic (Szinnyei 1922; Sinor 1961: 169–77; Aalto 1969/78: 328).

10. The ending *-a ~ -ä* is found in Ostyak in a Lative/Dative function; compare also the Zyrian and Votjak Illative *-e* (with an *-a* variant in certain contexts). There seems to be an Old Turkic local suffix *-a ~ -e*, and a similar Dative/Locative in pre-Classical Mongolian (Sinor 1988: 722; Menges 1968/95: 110; Poppe 1955: 198).

APPENDIX IV

THE SELF-DENOMINATIONS IN THE URALIC LANGUAGES

The self-denomination of the Ostyaks, *Khanty*, is of uncertain origin (UWE 206). *Komi*, the self-denomination of the Komi-Zyrians and Komi-Permiaks, has been connected, although with uncertainty, to U *koj(e)-mɜ* 'man, human being'; compare Hun. *hím*, Vog. *kom, kum* etc. (UEW 168); notice also Tur. *kün* 'people' and Mon. *kümün* 'man' (Németh 1934/90: 161). *Ud-murt*, the self-denomination of the Votjaks, consists of two parts: *-murt* (~ *-mort*) 'man, human being', considered to be of Indo-European origin, despite some sound-difficulties; and *ud-*, of unknown origin (Gheno & Hajdú 1992: 67; Décsy 1965: 239; Joki 1973: 281–2, item (75); UEW 702). *Mari* 'man, male', the self-denomination of the Cheremis, is of uncertain origin, although some scholars consider possible an Indo-European origin (Joki 1973: 280, item (74); Gheno & Hajdú 1992: 71; Décsy 1965: 23). *Mordvin* 'man, husband', the external denomination of the Mordvins (Erzya and Moksha), is believed to have been in the past also their self-denomination. The terms *Mordvin* and *Mordva*, as well as the Erzya term *miŕd'e* and the Moksha term *miŕd'ä* 'man, husband', have all been connected to the second element of the Votjaks self-denomination (*ud*)-*murt*; compare also Zyr. *mort* (Décsy 1965: 236; Rédei 1986: 53; Joki 1973: 281–2, item (75); UEW 702; Zaicz 1998: 185). The Mordvins call themselves exclusively by the tribal names *Eŕza* and *Mokšă*, both etymologies generally considered to be of uncertain origin. The term *mokšă* is connected by UEW 289 to Hun. *mos* 'to wash' which in turn is believed to derive from I-E *mozge- ~ *mezge-* 'sink'. Notice however that this term is used as an ethnonym also in Chuvash, Tatar and Russian (Gheno & Hajdú 1992: 78). *Karjala* (attested as *kiriali*, see Chapter 2), the self-denomination of the Karelians, is found as a toponym in Finland and in Estonian. It has been connected to the Finnish words *karja* '(live)-stock, cattle', *karjakko* 'milker', *karjalainen* 'shepherd'; however the term itself is of uncertain origin, probably Baltic or Germanic (Gheno & Hajdú 1992: 104; SSA I, 313–14; Grünthal 1997: 96; Viitso 1998: 100). Similarly, *Viro ~ Viru*, the self-denomination of the Estonians, is of unknown origin, although it has been connected with a Baltic root meaning 'man' (SKES 1115; Grünthal 1997: 204). The denominations of the other Balto-Finnic languages/peoples, such as *Livonian, Veps, Ingrian, Votic*, etc., are of uncertain or controversial origin (see a detailed discussion in Grünthal 1997: 250 f., 108 f., 178 f., 129 f. respectively). The denomination *Samoyed* is a comprehensive name, of Russian origin, for the following people: Samoyed Yurak/Nenet, Samoyed-Yenisei/Enet, Samoyed Tawgi/Nganasan, Samoyed Selkup/Ostyak-Samoyed, and the now extinct Samoyed Kamas/ Kamassian and Samoyed Mator/Motor. The self-denominations *Nenet*, *Enes* and *Nganasan* 'man, human being' are considered to be etymologically connected (Hajdú 1950: 43 f.; UEW 627–8; Gheno & Hajdú 1992: 148), and appear to be local, Samoyedic names (note that the Samoyed Tawgi people call themselves *Nya* 'mate'; Helimski 1998a: 480). For the self-denomination *Kamassian*, several etymologies have been proposed, none of which is however of U origin. Conversely, there seems to be agreement on the fact that this name contains the Siberian ethnonym *-as* or *-kaš* as a component (Hajdú 1950: 95–6; Simoncsics 1998: 581). The self-denomination S*el-kup*, which has many variants in the various dialects, consists of two components. The component *sel-* is considered by Hajdú (1950: 82) as a derivation from Sam. Se. *syy*, *söö* 'clay' (< P-U **šojwa* 'clay'); this derivation is considered wrong by UEW 483, which instead connects *sel-* to a different Selkup word: *šöt*, *süt* 'taiga, forest', a local name. The second component *-kup* is analysed as the Selkup equivalent of Hun. *hím*, Vog. *kom, kum* mentioned above, in connection with the self-denomination *Komi*.

To complete the picture briefly depicted above, the following data may be worthy of attention.

The denomination 'Ural' of the Ural mountains, the core area of the traditional P-U *Urheimat*, is of Russian origin (*Urál*). This denomination has been extended recently (in 1775) also to what is now the homonymous river, which flows from the southern Urals up to the Caspian Sea. The older denomination of the Ural river is the Russian name *Jaík* ~ *Yayik* (still used by Puškin), probably of Asiatic origin: compare Tur. *yayïk* 'large, big' and Classical Mon. *jayig* (Manzelli 1993: 430).

APPENDIX V

COMMON HUNGARIAN/BASHKIR
TOPONYMS

The following is a list of common Hungarian/Bashkir toponyms; the data reported derive from the sources quoted in Section 9.1.4.

(a) The Bashkir ethnonym *Mišer* ~ *Meščer* etc. (mentioned in Section 9.1.4), occurs frequently as a toponym both in Russian territory and in the present-day Hungarian territory. In Hungary it occurs (as old toponyms) in the following variants and compound names: *Mizsér, Mezserő, Miser, Nag-myser* (*Nag* = *nagy* 'big, large'), *Puztha-myser* (equivalent to *Puszta-megyer, Békás-megyer* etc., see Section 9.1.3.1), *Mizsere-puszta, Mizsér-fa, Mizsér-fa-puszta* (Hun. *fa* < *falva* 'his village'), and many others. For more detail see Németh (1972: 295–7), who also provides a little map showing the distribution of these names. Németh (1972: 297) remarks that the toponyms formed with the Hungarian and Bashkir corresponding elements are to be found in the same Hungarian regions, not far from each other. Regarding the distribution of these toponyms in Russian territory, see a detailed list in Vásáry (1975: 261–3).

(b) The Bashkir ethnonym *Možar* occurs frequently in Russian territory also as a toponym and as a hydronym. Vásáry (1975: 246–8) provides a long, detailed list.

(c) The followings are further examples of common Hungarian/Bashkir toponyms, some of which are actually hydronyms or oronyms in Bashkir (from Vásáry 1985/7: 217–18; see also Németh 1972: 294 and 1975):

- Bas. *Kondoroš* vs Hun. *Kondoros*, meaning something like 'a place where there are many beavers', compare Bas. *qondoδ* 'beaver'.
- Bas. *Bekaš* vs Hun. *Békás* 'a place where there are many frogs', compare Hun. *béka* 'frog'.
- Bas. *Magaš* (hydronym and oronym) vs Hun. *Magas* (recall *s* in Hungarian stands for /š/); compare Hun. *magas* 'high, tall'.
- In the Bashkir territory there are hydronyms constructed with the following Hungarian words: *veres* 'red', *vasas* 'ferrous' (*vas* 'iron') etc. (Erdélyi 1972: 307);

Hun. *Béká-s* is an adjectival formation from *béka*, a noun in turn considered to be a loan-word from Turkic (Munkácsi 1902; Erdélyi 1972: 307). Hun.

Kondoros is probably a similar kind of derivational formation. In Modern Hungarian 'beaver' is indicated by the term *hód*, which, according to UEW 858, derives from P-Ug. **kumtɜ* (**kuntɜ*), in turn to be compared with Turkic, see for example Cha. *qunduz* (< Ancient Turkic *qumtu*(*z*/*r*) according to Róna-Tas (1988a: 750)).

.

NOTES

Notes to Prelims

1 Some authors, such as U. Sutrop (personal communication) believe that the designation Balto-Finnic is not a good one for several reasons, including the fact that it could create confusion with the Baltic languages. Although I agree with this remark, I maintain this term here, because this is the term used in most of the literature I refer to, and to change it would create even more confusion.

2 *Viru* (*Viro* in Finnish) or *Viru-maa* (*maa* 'land') is a county in north Estonia. The people living there are called *virulased* (Sing.: *virulane*); U. Sutrop, personal communication.

3 The word Permian is quite controversial (Riese 1998: 249); here it indicates, traditionally, the sub-group consisting of Komi/Zyrian and Votyak/Udmurt, both spoken in the north-eastern part of European Russia. I have not reported either in the language list or in the family tree the language/dialect (Komi-)Permyak, often reported in Uralic family trees, because it is considered here as a dialect of Zyrian, after UEW. Notice that the name 'Komi' is often applied to the Zyrians only, a fact which may create further confusion (Hausenberg 1998: 305).

4 I have chosen to use the full names 'Turkic' and 'Tungusic', in order to avoid a possible confusion between 'Turkic languages' and 'Turkish' and between 'Tungusic languages' and 'Tungus' respectively.

5 I have included in this list also SKS and WSOY, which are abbreviations of Finnish publishing companies which occur frequently in the bibliography.

1 Introduction

1 1999/2000: 76.

2 There are other languages/dialects classified as U, such as the other Sayan Samoyed dialects (not reported in Austerlitz'(1987) diagram): Koibal, Karagas, Taigi (see Helimski 1987), or the other Balto-Finnic languages: Lüdian, Veps, Votic, Ingrian. They have not been reported in the language list and family tree because they have not been mentioned in the text. Notice that I have not added the symbol '*' before the designations 'SAMOYED' and 'BALTO-FINNIC' because these represent actual language groups, and not simply reconstructed nodes, as in the case of the other designations, such as 'URALIC', 'PERMIAN' etc. Notice that Lapp is not connected to any of the reconstructed nodes, to indicate that it is an isolated branch within the family, as discussed in the text. In this, I have followed Austerlitz' (1987) classification and diagram.

3 Samoyed Kamas was moribund at the time of the First World War; the other Sayan Samoyed languages are known from records predating the 19th century.

4 This expression is found several times in Janhunen 1981a; see below in Chapter 4, where this expression is reported in connection with the appropriate examples.

5 The dictionary UEW uses the expression 'affective character' quite often, to justify the irregularity of kinship and other basic terms. As an example, see the reconstructed item *wäŋe* 'son-in-law', p. 565.

6 The author states that the Hungarians spent about two hundred years in the Khazar Kingdom (600–800 AD), without mentioning that this is an interpretation of the text by the emperor Constantine.

7 The full title is: *Karhunkieli. Pyyhkäisyjä suomalais-ugrilaisten kielten tutkimukseen*, literally: 'The language of the bear. Glance at the research of the Finno-Ugric languages'.

The author, whilst accepting the traditional model, points out some of its shortcomings, such as the question of the Ugric node.

8　Rédei (1998) considers this and other similar books, as 'dilettante' (see also, Chapter 2). Here I do not want to enter into the merits of these books; I just want to highlight that in the last ten years or so the publications which challenge the textbook origin of the Hungarians have multiplied.

9　The author says that since the times of Donner (see below), the Finnish researchers have not given much thought to the foundation of the family tree, which has basically been 'accepted as self-evident' ('hyväksytty lähes itsestään selvänä').

2　The historical foundation of the Uralic paradigm

1　1998: 395.

2　*Nestor's Chronicle* is another name for the oldest version of the '*Russian Annales*', at one time believed to have been written by a monk from Kiev, called Nestor. Whoever the original author may have been, it was first copied by a monk from Kiev in the year 1116.

3　Here I report the major, traditional sources, that is the Latin, Greek and Arabic sources, whose importance has been recently re-affirmed in a congress held in Budapest in 1993. I shall not deal, therefore, with sources of more recent acquisition, such as Turkic and Tibetan or Chinese sources, etc. (see Di Cave 1995: 343).

4　Notice that for the designation of the Bashkirs I am using the English term, and not their own designation, because this is not relevant for the discussion. In contrast, *magyar* is the actual Hungarian self-designation.

5　The Scythians were nomads, of Caucasoid type (according to Cavalli-Sforza, Menozzi & Piazza 1994: 377–8), who wandered in a vast territory which extended between the Black Sea and the Altai mountains. The term 'Scythia' is taken from Herodotus, and did not have any real connotation at the time, indicating any non-better specified, eastern population. It was also used in the 19th century to indicate the Ural-Altaic languages, and other Asiatic languages.

6　The Huns were people of Asiatic origin, probably the first Mongolian nomadic tribes. They dominated the western Eurasiatic steppes between 300 BC and 500 AD. A group of Huns, the 'European Huns', to use Golden's (1998: 17) definition, under the chief Attila, posed a serious threat to Europe, including Rome, through their terrifying raids. They were based in Pannonia, an area which is now part of the present-day Hungarian territory. The European Huns were defeated in 451 AD, and their 'state' crumbled after the death of Attila in 453. Since this time, the Huns 'faded into the background, becoming part of the various Turkic tribal unions that were entering the steppe' (Golden 1998: 18). See also Golden (1990b).

7　The phrase 'Avari, qui dicuntur Ungari' is found also in the *Annales* of year 896 and 900 AD.

8　Ligeti (1986: 376–7) remarks that in the ending -*īya* (a typical Arabic ending) the long *ī* may be due to a final vowel -*i* present in the original (non-Arabic) word, therefore the transcription '*majǧiri*' is also possible, if not more appropriate. I shall come back to the question of this final -*i* in Chapter 9.

9　Bashkir is spoken principally in the Russian Republic of Bashkortostan, which lies between the Volga and the southern slopes of the Ural mountains. It is a language of the Kipchak type, a north-western group. More precisely, Bashkir belongs to the 'north Kipchak or Volga-Ural' group, which comprises also (Kazan) Tatar and the Mishar dialect (Johanson 1998: 82; Berta 1998: 283). According to Vásáry (1985/7: 215) Bashkir, in its present form, is a typical Kipchak Turkic language, and the Bashkirs, like most Turkic peoples, are a very mixed ethnic group.

10　Constantine also reports several famous proper names present in Hungarian, such as *Álmos, Árpád, Tas,* the place names *Etelköz* and *Levedia,* and the nobility name *kündü,* already indicated by the Arabic sources.

11　This is a compound name: *Kourtou-germatos.*

12　Németh claims that the names *Νέκη* and *Μεγέρη*/*megyer(i)*/*magyar* are of F-U origin, whilst all the others are of Turkic origin. The explanation is as follows: in Νέκη, that is *Nyék*, the F-U origin is evident from the initial *ny-*, that is, palatal nasal. Notice, however, that palatal nasals exist also in the Altaic languages (see Chapter 4). In Μεγέρη/*magyar* the F-U origin is evident from the fact that the first member of the name, *magy-* is connected to an Ob-Ugric word, whilst the second member is of Turkic origin (see Chapter 9).

13 These '*Gesta*' constitute the first historical narration about the Hungarians. It tells us about the origin of the 'Árpád House', the migration of the Hungarians from their Scythian homeland towards the Carphathians, the foundation of the first Christian Hungarian Kingdom etc. The author does not reveal either his name, or the name of the person who commissioned the narration. He describes himself as '*P. dictus magister*', and reveals that he was the clerk of the king of Hungary, to be identified probably with King Béla II (1131–41), or III (1173–96). This is why the text is normally called '*Anonymus*'.

14 This sentence is found several times in the text; here it is quoted from the *Prologus*. The variant *Scithica* is used here, although in other places *Scythica* is used.

15 *Hetu-moger* occurs several times in the text; for example at p. 39. *Hetu-* corresponds to Modern Hungarian *hét* '7'.

16 The expression '*Huni sive Hungari*' occurs several times in the text; see for example at p. 147: 'inter Hunos sive Hungaros'.

17 I am not going to deal here with sources later than the ones presented so far, because they are not relevant for the current discussion.

18 Notice that I shall not go into the details of attributing the various versions to their respective authors. This would take too long and would go beyond the scope of this book. For more details, and also for reference to some specific scholars, see Chapter 9.

19 According to Czeglédy (1983), the Avars were the 'Uar-Huns', or 'Juan-Juans'. They first appeared on the European scene in 568 AD. They established a Turkic empire in the Carpathian Basin (a territory much coveted by the nomadic tribes because of its fertile lands), and were defeated by Charles the Great, after a five-year long struggle, between 791 and 796 AD (Halasi-Kun 1986/8: 34–5).

20 According to the author, the leading layer of the 'Conquest-time' Hungarians was undoubtedly of Turkic character, as testified by the anthropological material found in a cemetery of the 8th/9th century Volga Bulgars.

21 In examining the data relating to this battle, I shall not consider the contribution of other scholars who took part in it, such as J. Szinnyei, P. Hunfalvy, B. Munkácsy.

22 In 1882 Vámbéry published the work: *A magyarok eredete. Ethnologiai tanulmány* 'The Origins of the Hungarians. Ethnological Study', where he strongly claimed that the Hungarian language and people are of Turkic origin, basing his claim also on the fact that the Hungarians are consistently called 'Turks' in the historical sources.

23 Here is Pusztay's (1977: 107) original text followed by my translation: '[Budenz] A korabeli nyelvészet színvonalán dolgozott, annak hibáival és erényeivel együtt. Néha talán túlontúl is akarta igazolni a magyar nyelv finnugor voltát, . . . Annak ellenére, hogy a mai finnugor összehasonlító nyelvtudomány az általa összeállított etimológiáknak csak egy részét fogadja el, érdemei a magyar nyelv finnugor voltának bizonyításában elévülhetetlenek'. 'Budenz worked according to the methods of the time, with its mistakes and virtues. Sometimes perhaps he wanted to prove the Finno-Ugric nature of the Hungarian language far too much, . . . Despite the fact that modern Finno-Ugric comparative linguistics accepts only one part of the etymologies collected by him, his merits in the establishment of the Finno-Ugric nature of the Hungarian language are imperishable'.

24 Notice that the author uses the term 'Turkish', which is in fact the correct English translation of Hun. *török*; however, given that the 'battle' is about the relationship between Hungarian and the various Turkic languages (in Hungarian '*türk*'), and not just Turkish, it is better to use the term 'Turkic', as I do here.

25 The author recognises that 'the great majority', not all, of Vámbéry's Hungarian/Turkic parallels are regarded as late loan-words.

26 Budenz (1871–3: 75) says: 'a szóegyezéseket négy csoportra osztva sorolom elé: I. Olyanokat, melyek helyeseknek fogadhatók el, vagy mint a törökből való magyar kölcsönvételek, vagy mint az "ugor-török ősrokonság" tárgyalásához tartozó adatok'. The following is my translation: 'I will list the word correspondences dividing them into four groups: group I: those which are to be considered correct, either as loan-words from

Turkic, or as data pertaining to the discussion of the "Ugric-Turkic original genetic relationship"'.

27 The authors have examined all the core-Lexicon Hungarian/Turkic parallels contained in Vámbéry's paper of 1869, and subsequently analysed by Budenz first in his paper of 1871–3 and then in his dictionary. In other words, the authors have analysed all the core-lexicon etymologies listed in the Classes I, II & III as established by Budenz. The etymologies of Class IV have not been taken into consideration, being indeed irrelevant.

28 kŏdök = kődök. For more details see Salvagni (1999).

29 This U etymology has parallels in the Altaic languages. The Finnish dictionary SSA I, 353 mentions the similarity between the U and the Altaic forms, without taking position about the status of the similarity.

30 I think it is worth reporting here the relevant passage in full: '[The proponents of] the Ural-Altaic theory did not treat the three Altaic families as being more closely related to each other than to Finno-Ugric or Samoyedic, nor did they conceive of the latter two as forming a grouping of their own. In fact the Ural-Altaic theory was proposed, under the label "Scythian", in a posthumous and unfinished work by Rask (1834), who also saw a connection to several more distant language groups . . . As for the term "Ural-Altaic", it was introduced (perhaps by Kellgren), in place of "Scythian" or "Tatar", and referred to the Ural and Altai mountains rather than to any linguistic division into "Uralic" and "Altaic". As for the term "Altaic", when first introduced, around 1845 by Castrén (see Castrén 1847 [. . .]), it was yet another synonym for "Ural-Altaic". The history of the term "Altaic" in its modern sense (excluding Uralic), is somewhat obscure. The earliest quotable instance seems to be by Kellgren (1847: 194), from whom it must have been picked up by Schleicher (1850: 63) . . . At any rate, we do not find this term in many much later works, such as Müller (1876: 70), and Munkácsi (1884), though it does appear in Müller (1882: 258 . . .). Moreover, it is not clear that Kellgren or Schleicher had any clear conception of Altaic (in the sense of Turkic, Mongolic, and Tungusic) as a linguistic unit, nor can we be sure who first formulated this idea'.

31 'Chazar', instead of 'Khazar', is the actual spelling by the editors of the text.

32 In his paper of 1937, p. 636, footnote 1, Grégoire says that the original information provided by Constantine (three years) is 'ridiculous'.

33 The author says that, given the extensive influence of the Khazars on the social and military organisation of the Hungarians, one should postulate a period of co-habitation of 200 to 300 years.

34 At p. 25 the author comments: 'But the De Administrando does not conceal the ambiguousness of the Hungarians' relations with the Khazars: the period of full-blown military alliance is implausibly allocated only three years, perhaps as a symbolic way of indicating that it was quite brief'.

35 The lecture was given in 1980, and the title was: Uralilaisten kielten kulttuurisanasto.

36 Compare the following quote (1986: 53): 'A VII-XIII században a magyar nyelv a török, ezen belül az ócsuvas nyelvvel számos esetben konvergens hangtani fejlődést mutat'. The following is my translation: 'In the 7th–13th centuries the Hungarian language shows in numerous cases convergent sound-developments with Turkic, in particular with Old Chuvash'. The author accurately reports many examples of parallel sound-developments within words shared by Turkic and Hungarian (see Note 38 below).

37 Compare the following quote (1975a: 282): 'j'ai remarqué que certaines séries de la phonétique historique sont parallèles dans le turc et dans le hongrois'.

38 In what follows I shall list just a few examples of 'convergent Turkic/Hungarian sound-developments' as listed in Ligeti (1986). The following examples show the development of initial č: Hun. sereg 'army'/Chu. śară / Turkic čärig; Hun. sátor 'tent'/Chu. čatăr / Tat. čatïr (1986: 57). The following examples show the development of internal Turkic -g- and -γ- respectively, which (if the vowels are of the same quality) disappear in the Hungarian equivalent forms yielding a long vowel: Hun. bű /Turkic bügü 'weise, zauberkundig'; Hun. bátor 'courageous'/Turkic (and Mongolian) bayatur (1986: 66).

39 The following is the original text: 'Az urál-altaji alap-nyelv helyett, melynek létezését eddig nem sikerült bebizonyítani, az említett keleteurópai-középázsiai összefüggő nyelvlánc elméletét kell elfogadnunk . . . E nyelvlánc tagjainak ősi kapcsolata egyes pontokon valószínűleg nem ősrokonságon, hanem intenzív érintkezésen alapszik'.

40 The original text reads as follows: 'Ősi nyelvi egyezések a törökséget kétségtelenül az uráli népekhez kapcsolják'.

41 I am grateful to Miklós Lojkó for having helped me to outline this sketch of Hungarian history.

42 His real name was Paul Hundsdorfer.

43 A list of Hungarian/Bashkir parallels is found in Vásáry (1985/7: 212–14).

44 It would go beyond the scope of this book to discuss or even mention these recent publications that challenge the textbook thesis of the F-U origin of the Hungarians. One can find a list and description of the content in Rédei (1998: 57 f.), who classifies all of them as 'dilettante'.

45 Literally 'picture magazine of Finland'. The issue quoted was published on 28th February 1997.

46 The original text reads as follows: 'Ajatus Volgan mutkasta sopi hyvin kansallisiin tieteisiin, jossa ugrilaisuus korostui omaleimaisuutena ja erilaisuutena muista skandinaaveista. Irtiotto tehtiin myös slaaveihin, tulihan todistettua, että "olimme täällä ennen teitä"'.

47 The original text reads as follows: 'Ensimmäisiä suomalaisia kodanpaikkoja etsiskeltiin alunperin Uralin tienoilta ja Keski-Aasiasta. Venäläinen **Köppen** pelasti kuitenkin suomalaiset, jotka olivat yliherkistymässä puheille mongolidisesta perimästä'.

48 For these words see Chapter 7.

49 This sentence, and instances when Räsänen said it, are reported in the article: *Ihmisen alkukielen lähteillä*, literally 'At the Roots of Person's Proto-language', written by H. Broms, which appeared in the newspaper '*Helsingin Sanomat*' (the biggest national newspaper) of 2nd February 1995.

3   Modern interpretations of the Uralic paradigm

1 1997: 17–18. The text is from the English summary provided at the end of the paper.

2 With reference to the Swadesh list of 100 basic words, it has been calculated that Ostyak and Vogul have 45 words in common whereas Hungarian shares 34 words with Vogul and 28 with Ostyak.

3 According to Sutrop (2000a), one can divide family trees into two types: phenetical (metrical), and cladistic. Häkkinen's tree in neither phenetic nor cladistic, it is instead 'intuitional, naïve', like most U trees. This means that, whichever time scale is associated with them, this time scale is not metrical, but simply intuitive.

4 For example, according to the statistical analysis carried out by Honti (1993) on the etymologies listed in UEW, it turns out that the Finnic lexical sub-stock – and not the most eastern lexical sub-stock – shares the greatest number of words with other U sub-stocks. One could argue that this is a distortion of the method of analysis, due to the fact that many reconstructions are rather Finno-centric, as demonstrated in the next chapter. However, this is not the case for the etymologies listed in UEW.

5 Compare the following quote (Hajdú, P. & Domokos, P. 1978: 67): 'Megjegyezzük azonban, hogy ez az ábrázolásmód nagyon leegyszerűsített képet ad **bonyolult** nyelvtörténeti folyamatokról és a mai rokon nyelvek rendszereinek egybevetésére semmikképpen nem alkalmas'. The following is my translation: 'We remark however that this kind of representation [of the traditional family tree] gives a very simplified picture of the **intricate** historical processes and it is by no means suitable for the comparison of the systems of the current, related languages'(translation and bold are mine).

6 I have utilised Sinor's diagram because it provides the English translation.

7 Here, like in other diagrams, I have used my own way of referring to the U languages, for the sake of consistency, according to the policy stated in 'Abbreviations'. Note that in the original diagram, the author says 'Finnic', and not 'Balto-Finnic', as reported here. This was changed because by 'Finnic' I mean all the non-Ugric languages, as stated in 'Abbreviations' and illustrated in the family tree diagram.

4   Reconstructing the sound-structure and Lexicon of the Uralic family tree

1   This quote is from D. Abondolo ((ed.) 1998: 8). The families the author refers to are: Uralic, Semitic, Tibeto-Burman, Japanese-Ryuku, Eskimo-Aleut.

2   The original text reads as follows: 'Zwischen die heutigen Sprachen . . . und die uralische Grundsprache sind hypothetische, sekundäre Grundsprachen eingeschoben. Die reale Existenz und Glaubwürdigkeit dieser sekundären Grundsprachen wird von der neueren Forschung – mit wenigen Ausnahmen – stark in Zweifel gezogen.'

3   The original text reads as follows: 'The reconstruction of the proto-languages of the north-western Finno-Ugric languages down to Proto-Finno-Permic (PFP) can be regarded as settled . . ., however, there are no generally accepted reconstructions of Proto-Ob-Ugric, Proto-Ugric, or Proto-Finno-Ugric sound-structure so far, although the questions of reconstruction have been touched upon by many scholars'.

4   The original text reads as follows: 'On huomattava, että kaikki esitetyt oletukset *x:n itsenäisestä fonemaattisesta statuksesta ja distribuutiosta ovat todella tentatiivisia. Muitakin selitysmahdollisuuksia epäilemättä on. Erityisen ongelmallista on *x:n erottaminen etymologisessa aineistossa klusiilista *k, nasaalista *ŋ sekä puolivokaaleista *w ja *j, joilla kaikilla on ollut taipumusta monilla tahoilla . . . kadota,'.

5   The original text reads as follows: 'Vaikka monet fonologiset yksityiskohdat antavatkin mahdollisuuksia vaihtoehtoisiin tulkintoihin, voitaneen olla jokseenkin varmoja siitä, että kaikki edellä luetellut, vokaalisuhteittain luokitellut sanarinnastukset (n:ot 1–94) ovat kantauralin ja sitä lähinnä seuranneiden kantakielten kannalta äänteellisesti säännöllisiä ja semanttisesti luontevia, siis etymologisesti moitteettomia. . . . Korpus ei ole iso, mutta se riittää antamaan ainakin yleiskuvan kantakielen äännerakenteesta'. Notice that the pronouns are the last items in the list of etymologies.

6   *ü* is written as 'y' in Finnish.

7   Notice that some long vowels in initial position, as in *kuusi* 'spruce', are considered to be the result of contraction after loss of a consonantal segment, as discussed later in the text.

8   Notice that in the word *ämp* ~ *imp*, which reproduce Gulya's transcription, the vowel is not long, as it is in the transcription by Honti reported soon after in the text.

9   Notice that I reproduce the author's transcription, where the length is rendered by doubled letters.

10   Here the author argues in favour of a common, U origin of this phenomenon.

11   The author argues in favour of the separation of the Samoyed CG from that present in Finnic and Lapp.

12   The author argues that even the CG in Finnic and Lapp are due to parallel, but independent, developments, because of certain relevant differences present in the two systems.

13   Hajdú states as follows: 'a phenomenon reminding of gradation occurs in Nganassan [Samoyed Tawgi]: however, the researches have indicated that the changes of some consonants in the mora of the word structure cause gradation. These cases of gradation differ from those of Finnic-Lapp. Both phenomena belong to separate characteristic features of the languages mentioned'.

14   This is a slightly suspect fact, if these forms are really 8,000/6,000 years old!

15   Here is the original text of some of the most significant claims, from Korhonen (1974: 243–4): 'Varhaiskantasuomalaisia äänteenmuutoksia on todettu vain muutamia. Suomalais-volgalaiseen kantakieleen sijoittuu enää enintään pari äänteenmuutosta. Suomalais-permiläiseen kantakieleen ja sitä vanhempiin kantakieliin ei voida rekonstruoida luotettavasti yhtään äänteenmuutosta. Käytännössä tämä ilmenee siten, että kirjallisuudessa esiintyvät suomalais-permiläiset, suomalais-ugrilaiset ja kantauralilaiset rekonstruktiot eivät eroa äänteellisesti toisistaan lainkaan ja myös suomalais-volgalaiset ja varhaiskantasuomalaiset rekonstruktiot tulevat lähelle tätä samaa tyyppiä'.

16   Here is the relevant part of the original text: 'Nyt voidaan kysyä, eivätkö sisäisten rekonstruktioiden ja vertailevan menetelmän tuloksena saatu kantakieli ja sen rekonstruoidut muodot kuulu pikemmin synkronisen kuin diakronisen lingvistiikan käsitteistöön. Kantakieli on nähtävissä puhtaasti synkronisena metakielenä, johon sukulaiskielten ominaisuudet projisioidaan'.

17 Compare the following examples in Finnish: *tyttö-Ø* 'girl-Nom.' ~ *tytö-n* 'girl-Gen.' ~ *tyttö-j-ä* 'girl-Plu.-Partit.' ~ *tyttö-nä* 'girl-Ess.', etc.

18 The *a* ~ *e* alternation is evident in the intermediate stage: **kote-i-δä;* see also **pes-i-δä.*

19 The original text reads as follows: 'Vaikka perinnäinen uralilainen sukupuu perustunee pikemminkin jonkinlaiseen karkeaan sormituntumaan kuin aineiston eksaktiin analyysiin,'. The author continues by saying that, nevertheless, the family tree appears to reflect at least the basic path of differentiation of the U languages.

20 According to Janhunen (1998: 463), among the modern languages, consistent traces of the vowel sequences are preserved only in Nganasan (Samoyed Tawgi) and Enets (Samoyed Yenisei).

21 Note that in these cases one must also consider the structure of a minimal phonological word. In Finnic, a monosyllabic word must have long vowel or diphthong. Therefore, there could be no need to reconstruct the words under discussion as bisyllabic. The same holds for the Finnish words *luu, puu, suu* etc. discussed in the text.

22 This form is found in the text *Halotti beszéd*, which will be introduced and discussed later in the text.

23 The illabial **i* (and its long variant), which is supposed to have developed toward the end of the P-Hungarian period and then to have disappeared, has reflexes in present-day *u* and *i/í.* Other words containing the reflex of this sound are: *híd* 'bridge' and *ír-ni* 'to write' (Imre 1988: 426).

24 Note that also in Turkic there is a velar illabial *ï*, often alternating with *a* – one of the several 'phonological convergent sound developments' between Hungarian and Turkic, between the 7th and the 13th centuries (Ligeti 1986). This alternation is reflected in the Turkic loans in Hungarian, where sometimes the illabial sound is maintained, as in: Hun. *szirt* 'rock' vs Turkic *sïrt* 'spine, backbone' (TESz III, 765), Hun. *kín* 'pain, torture' vs Turkic *kïn* (TESz II, 491); whilst other times it is substituted with a back vowel, as in Hun. *karvaly* 'sparrow-hawk' vs Tur. *kïrği* (TESz 395), etc. (see also Sauvageot 1971: 54).

25 Janhunen uses the symbol 'η' instead of 'ŋ' here and in other similar reconstructions. I have changed all 'η' into 'ŋ', the latter being also the symbol present in the actual examples, according to UEW transcription.

26 This etymology, like the previous one, has been associated to Dravidian by Tyler (1968, item (90)). According to Tyler, the reconstructed U etymology should contain intervocalic -γ-, and not -w-, in order to match the Samoyed Yurak form.

27 Here is the original text (1981a: 259): 'Vihdoin on joukko kantauralilaisia sanavartaloita, joiden rekonstruointiin liittyy vielä ratkaisemattomia äänteellisiä ongelmia tai muita epävarmuustekijöitä. Tähän joukkoon voitaisiin oikeastaan sisällyttää valtaosa niistä "uralilaisista" sanarinnastuksista, joita etymologinen kirjallisuus on tulvillaan'.

28 Janhunen's (1981a: 259) text reads as follows: 'Siksi on syytä rajoittaa tarkastelu niihin tapauksiin, jotka täyttävät etymologisen analyysin sormituntumaehdot: riittävän äänteellisen ja semanttisen samankaltaisuuden'.

29 In the modern Hungarian writing the word is actually written as *szem.* In fact, *ë* is never used. However, given that the UEW's transcription has been adopted here for all the U languages, for the sake of consistency, I have to adopt this way of writing.

30 In the original text the meaning of *sajog-*, that is 'to hurt acutely', is missing.

31 Voiced plosives are present also in the Permian languages and in Cheremis. In the other U languages they do not occur, or they occur as allophones of the voiceless equivalents.

32 The situation of the Turkic loan-words in Hungarian is not clear (as discussed in Chapter 6). For example, whilst a Turkic influence is certainly plausible, the examples (4.31)–(4.32) show that the introduction of a voiced occlusive may take place also in words for which there is no Turkic parallel, or where the Turkic parallel has a voiceless plosive. Similarly, alongside etymologies where an initial Turkic *b-* has been rendered as *b-* in Hungarian, there are etymologies where a Turkic *t-* has been rendered sometimes as *d-*, as in *dél* 'south, midday' (compare Kir. *tüš;* TESz I, 606), and sometimes as *t-*, as in *tenger* 'sea' (compare Cha. *tängiz;* TESz III, 888). Also, there are Mongolian parallels with initial *b-*, as shown in example (6.7).

33 *A halotti beszéd és könyörgés* (HB) 'The Funeral Oration and Prayer'– the first Hungarian text – is a short but revealing text of only 32 lines. As the title says, the HB is a brief funeral

sermon and a prayer (probably delivered at the grave), whose author is unknown. The prayer codex in which this document is preserved also contains a Latin version, from which the text is more or less freely derived. Such a text provides the first reliable data for the examination of several phonological and morpho-syntactic phenomena of Hungarian, including the postpositions (discussed in the text) and the question of the article, which is still missing.

34 This word is interesting also in other respects: one can capture the formation of the category of noun by adding an ending -*t* (which typically expresses Perfective/Tense/ Aspect), a Possessive, and, if necessary, a Case ending (see below Chapter 8). The U term for 'to die' is usually derived from P-U **kola-*: Vog. *kōl-*, *χōl-* /Ost. *kāla-*, *χăt-*/Sam.Yu. *χā-*/Sam.Ye. *kā-* (UEW 173).

35 Note that the element meaning 'time' is different between Old and Modern Hungarian, respectively -(*u*)*l* and -*szor*.

36 The ending -*hoz* (~ *hez* ~ *höz*) is usually derived from P-Ug. **kuća*, compare Ost. *χŏśa*; (UEW 857). See Chapter 8 for more details.

37 The Old Hungarian text *A tihanyi apátság alapítólevele* 'Foundation Charter of Tihany Abbey', was issued in 1055 by order of King Endre 1st. It is a text written in Latin, but contains 58 Hungarian words, mainly proper names and place-names, plus 33 suffixes, together with some phrases and fragments of sentences.

38 According to Tekin (1994), in P-Altaic there were the following consonants: stops (*p*, *b*, *t*, *d*, *k*, *g*), affricates (*č*, *ǰ*), spirants (*s*, *y*), nasals (*m*, *n*, *ń*, *ŋ*), and liquids (*l*^{1}, *l*^{2}, *r*^{1}, *r*^{2}). The liquids and the nasal *ŋ* did not occur in initial position. In Middle Mongolian (12th–14th century) initial **p-* developed into *h-* in all Mongolian languages, to disappear later on, except in Monguor, where it is represented by *f-* and *χ-*. The development **p-* > *f-* occurred in Manchu; the change **p-* > *h-* occurred in Tungus and P-Turkic, to disappear later on in most Turkic languages.

39 The Hungarian term for 'fox' is actually *róka*; however, *ravasz róka* has become a fixed collocation.

40 According to SSA the other U correspondences are uncertain.

41 The reason why these shared Hungarian and Permian changes are generally believed to have taken place independently is basically as follows. The Permian languages have evolved a correlation of voice for the plosive (and the fricative) series, in the same way as Hungarian. Rédei (1988b: 357) observes that the number '10', which has been borrowed from an Iranian language (see for example Ossete *das*), has been rendered as *das* in Zyrian, but as *tíz* in Hungarian, therefore the correlation of voice, as well as the other changes in question, must have taken place independently in the two languages. This is certainly a plausible scenario, although it appears strange that the voiced consonant of the borrowed Iranian word has been maintained in Permian, where the correlation of voice is not yet well established today (see Section 4.5.5), whereas it has been rendered as *t-* in Hungarian, where instead the correlation of voice is well established. We have observed a similar oscillation between voiced and voiceless consonants in the words borrowed into Hungarian from Turkic (see Note 32 above). What this tells us is that nothing safe can be concluded from these sound-substitutions and oscillations (see discussion in Section 6.1). Similarly, Rédei (1988b: 356–7) and Bereczky (1980a: 50–1) have tried to explain why the cluster simplification in Permian should be considered totally independent from the same phenomenon in Hungarian. Judging from the loan-words of Bulgar Turkic origin present in Permian, the denasalisation must have been completed between the 6th and 9th centuries in this language group. At this time, the Hungarian and the Permian languages are 'not supposed' to be still in contact. In contrast, in the Bulgar Turkic loan-words in Hungarian the consonant cluster is preserved, as shown in *tenger* 'sea'. Since the Hungarian/Bulgar Turkic contacts are generally 'believed' to have started around 700–750 AD, it follows that this change was already accomplished before that time in Hungarian, whilst it was 'probably' just starting in Permian.

42 Here is the translation of the Hungarian words, not provided in the original text: *csap* 'to strike, hit', *csegely* 'wedge-shaped ornament', . . ., *csomó* 'knot', *csupor* 'jar, pot'. See example (4.27) for the parallels of Hun. *csomó*.

43 According to Honti (1998a: 332), from P-Ugr.*ɵ̆-* a (secondary) voiceless lateral fricative **ł* developed in P-Ostyak.

44   This type of change is testified in other, non-related languages, such Old Greek and it is *in fieri* in some Tungusic dialects.

45   Honti (1998b: 352–5) lists several other presumed shared innovations to prove the existence of the Ugric node. For example, he reports the change of internal *-l-* into *-r-* in the term for '3': Hun. *három*/Vog. *kōrəm*; however, this change does not occur in Ostyak, where we find *χoləm*. The author also claims that the Ugric languages present the dichotomy Definite vs Indefinite Conjugation; however other U languages have it too, such as Mordvin. Furthermore, the morphemes which express 'Definiteness', as well as the overall structure of the two Conjugations, are quite different in the three Ugric languages. Compare on this issue Perrot (1984a, 1984b). Another shared innovation is supposed to be the Ablative *-l*, which, however, is absent in Ostyak (see Appendix (III), point 5, 6b). See Chapter 8 for details.

46   Note that here UEW uses the symbol *-η-* even though this is not used in the list of the reconstructed consonants at p. IX of vol. I.

47   The author claims that vowel harmony was an original P-U feature, which has disappeared in some languages ('Vokaaliharmonia pyrkii häviämään').

48   Abondolo states that many U language and most Ob-Ugrian dialects have 'lost' vowel harmony.

49   Vowel harmony is claimed to be very much subject to foreign influence, and can change quite rapidly. For example, some Anatolian dialects of modern Greek have developed vowel harmony under the influence of Turkish.

50   The original text reads as follows: 'Näin ollen omaperäisen sanaston porrastaminen eri ikäkerrostumiksi ei äänteellisten tuntomerkkien avulla ole mahdollista. Samasta syystä levikin osuus on vanhastaan ollut ratkaiseva yksityisten sanojen ikää arvioitaessa: se on ollut ainoa mahdollinen kriteeri'.

51   This is particularly true for the etymologies which belong to the U layer proper. For example, this number varies from a minimum of 140 (actually much less) in Janhunen (1981a), to a maximum of 472 in Décsy (1990) and UEW. The accepted etymologies are again about 400 in Paasonen (1912/13; 1916/17: 13–17) and Collinder (1977a), going down to about 200 in Sammallahti (1979). The same holds for the etymologies which belong to the F-U layer and other intermediate layers. On this topic see also Nummenaho (1988).

52   The author suggests that if we have 'contradictory' correspondences, we have to reconstruct the different prototypes, that is as many P-Phonemes as there are 'contradictions'. And, in fact, at one point, he suggests about 30 vowel phonemes for P-Turkic.

5   False matches or genuine linguistic correlations?

1   1999: 213.

2   Probabilistic reasoning is also required by the 'flat' classification proposed by some scholars (see Chapter 3).

3   Embleton (1991) reviews the attempts that have been made in the literature to develop mathematical models of genetic classifications.

4   Actually, the probability is slightly higher than 1/9 because the consonants do not have all the same frequency of occurrence. This effect is relatively small (see Ringe 1999 for a discussion) and in neglecting it we bias the die slightly in favour of the validity of reconstructed Lexicon and slightly against the likelihood of a false match.

5   For the number '2' Janhunen (1981a: 258) reconstructs **kektä ~*käktä* (see example (4.6)); UEW 118–19 reconstructs **kakta ~ *käktä*; Sammallahti (1988: 537) reconstructs **kektä.* For the number '5/10' Janhunen (1981a: 261) reconstructs **wixti ~ *witti ~* ?**witi* (and remarks how unstable the numerals can be); UEW 577 reconstructs **witte;* Sammallahti (1988: 541) reconstructs **witi ~ witti.*

6   In Sammallahti's list of Hungarian reflexes of P-F-U consonant clusters the cluster *-kt-* is missing.

7   The alternative choice that would have remained consistent and testable, would have been to completely disregard all forms that include a Ø. However this choice would have substantially reduced the sample size.

8 The author reports the variety and quantity of meanings ascribed to the majority of the etymologies listed in UEW. Among the examples he reports compare the following (quoting from Finnish): the word *ilma*, whose meanings are: 'sky, weather, wind, world, air, heavy snowfall, snowstorm' (UEW 81); the word *poika*, whose meanings are: 'son, boy, grandchild, man, young man, young of animals' (UEW 390).

9 If the groups are all of the same size, the actual formula is $p' = 1 - (1 - p)^n$, p' is the probability of a false match in n languages and p is the probability of a false match in one language. In practice the groups are not of equal size and so this figure is approximate.

10 The infinitive form of the verb is *porata* (SSA II, 397).

11 SSA confirms the analysis that two words have been confused here: *pieli*, which also means 'side', and the word in question, today meaning 'half (side)', that is *puoli*.

6 Borrowed or inherited?

1 1968: 43.

2 Personal communication.

3 Halasi-Kun (1975) examines the Turkic loan-words in Hungarian in the light of new Kipchak Turkic philological evidence and concludes that there is much more loaning of Kipchak nature than it has hitherto been envisaged. Consider, as an example, the Hungarian word for 'child': *gyerek ~ gyermek*, which (also according to EWUng I, 495–6) could be compared with the Bashkir and Tatar proper name *Jermäk*. However, the dictionary considers the derivation of this word from a Chuvash type of language as more 'probable', compare Chu. *Šarmǝk*.

4 For example, Ligeti (1986: 487–9) and Rédei (1998: 57) classify Khazar as 'western Turkic', in the same way as Chuvash and Bulgar Turkic, but other scholars believe instead that Khazar was a 'Common Turkic' type of language. Czeglédy (1983: 104–6) supposes that the Khazar empire consisted of three basic groups: the real Khazars, who were of Sabir origin, a Turkic people of undetermined type (Johanson 1998: 18); the Western Turks, who organised the tribal union; and the Caucasian Huns, who were remnants of the Avars (see Zimonyi 1990: 58–9 for a review of the debate). Whatever the case, the reality is that the Khazar kingdom was a multi-ethnic, multi-lingual society, which also included several other ethnic groups than just Turkic.

5 Chuvash is the national language of the Chuvash people who live in the Volga river region. According to Clark (1998: 434), the development of this language from P-Turkic 'is complicated by a series of sound changes and replacements'. Still according to the author these changes, and those associated with the 'assimilation of Cheremis', tend to obscure its Turkic character.

6 Word-final *-r* has been preserved both in Chuvash and Common Turkic; compare Common Turkic *är* vs Chu. *ar* 'man'.

7 Some scholars, such as Benzing & Menges (1959: 1–2) observe that 'Turkologists have not yet succeeded in reaching agreement on the classification of the Turkic languages and dialects'. This state of affairs has been recently confirmed by Johanson (1998: 82 f.), who states that it is difficult 'to set up a classification of modern Turkic languages that combines geographic and genetic criteria'. Whatever the case, in the absence of records and any other items of independent information, it is impossible to ascertain through which route the isoglosses under discussion spread in Hungarian.

8 Note that Janhunen (1996: 237) considers these parallels and related reconstruction as 'phantom reconstructions'.

9 According to EWUng, *nyár* with the meaning 'summer' is a L-W from Chu. *šúr*, whilst *nyár* with the meaning 'marsh' has a parallel in Yukaghir.

10 In EWUng no parallels from non-U languages are mentioned.

11 According to EWUng a derivation from Turkic is unlikely.

12 The verb in question is *le-*; it is the equivalent of Finn. *lie-*/Hun. *lë-* (*lëv-, lësz-,*)/Zyr. *lo-*/ Vot. *lu-* < F-U **le-*. This verb in Finnish is used to express Possibility, Potentiality of the verb 'to be' (*ole-, olla*), compare: *lienen, lienet, lienee*, 'I might be' etc. (SSA, II, 68). For the

parallels of Finn. *ole-* compare: Hun. *vol-, val-, vagy-*/Mor. E. & M. *ule-*/Ost. *wăl-* etc. < F-U **wole-* (UEW 580). Similar words are present in Altaic.

13 To the best of my knowledge, Ringe's and Oswalt's analyses are the only analyses of this type carried out between U and non-U lexical parallels.

7 The antiquity of Proto-Uralic

1 2000: 64. Janhunen (1981a: 252) also remarks that it would be far too much to expect perfect sound regularity from all the correspondences accepted as U in such a highly differentiated language family.

2 Notice that Tauli (1955: 16–17) expresses doubts about the great antiquity of P-U, although only on a speculative basis. Similarly, Pusztay (1995: 120f.) argues that P-U was not a starting-point language, but only a very recent phase in the development of the U languages, which formed out of the different types of languages present throughout Siberia.

3 Campbell supports this estimate through an 'argument from negative evidence': the Finno-Permian languages share a term for 'oak': Finn. *tammi*/Est. *tamm*/Mor. E. *tumo*/Zyr. *tu-pu* (*pu* 'tree') < F-P **toma* (UEW 798). In Hungarian this tree is indicated by a non-related word: *tölgy*. This should be interpreted in the sense that by the time the oak had arrived to the Petchora region, about 3000–2000 BC, the Finno-Permian branch had already separated from the Ugric one. This interpretation is generally accepted, despite the fact that the term *tölgy* does not seem to have cognates in the Ob-Ugric languages (it is not listed in UEW), whilst *tammi* is a Finno-Volgaic, and not a Finno-Permian term.

4 Consider also the difficulty of deriving *i* of Hun. *szil* from **a* of **śala*, if the proposed development **a* > velar illabial ** į* > *i* is not accepted; see discussion in Section 4.4.5.2.

5 According to some scholars, such as Ramstedt, Common Turkic evolved between 400 and 600 AD. Some other scholars, like Vovin, suggest that Altaic as a whole is quite old, and this accounts for much of the controversy in comparing its branches.

6 This is a passage from a journalistic interview with A. Csillaghy in the Italian newspaper 'Il sole 24 ore' of 15th February 1998.

7 The author believes, nevertheless, that the U homeland must have been a 'narrow' one.

8 There are several other hypotheses about the original P-U homeland. Since they are all based on the methods of Palaeo-linguistics, however, I shall not discuss them here. Compare for a review Campbell (1997: 835–41), Suhonen (1999) and Rédei (2000).

9 The quote is from the English summary provided at the end of the paper.

10 Here are the original passages: (1973: 363) 'dass sich die ältesten Kontakte zu den Finnougriern erst seit der uriranischen Periode feststellen liessen'; (1973: 373) 'Die arischen Elemente des Samojedischen stammen durchweg erst aus iranischen Sprachformen (frühestens aus dem sog. Altiranischen)'.

11 *Vaski* is usually interpreted as a *Wanderwort* which entered the U languages after their separation (Joki 1973: 339–40; UEW 560–1). Janhunen (1983) explains the Samoyed parallels as borrowed directly into P-Samoyed from P-Tocharian.

12 The Indo-European palatal *k'* has changed into occlusive in the *kentum* languages, (Latin, Greek, Germanic), and into sibilants in the *satəm* languages (Slavic, Baltic etc.). Notice also the irregularity of the Votyak vowel *-a-*.

13 According to Korenchy (1972: 42f.), there are only two other sound-changes relevant for classifying the Indo-European L-Ws into several layers: Iranian *r* > F-U *l*; Iranian *a* > Ob-Ugric *ä.*

14 Note that the word *vasara* in itself means 'hammer'.

15 Note that there are semantic difficulties involved here: the Baltic word from which Finn. *lahti* (Gen. *lahde-n* > **lakte*) could have been borrowed, Lit. *lañktis*, means: 'Henkel, Bügel; Garnwinde, Haspel'. Problematic, one way or the other, are also the other lexical items mentioned in Posti's article.

16 SKES tentatively proposes a connection with the etymology meaning 'to melt': Finn. *sulaa*, Hun *olvad*.

17 The other four etymologies are, according to Koivulehto's reconstruction: P-U **näxi:* Finn. *nainen* 'woman' (item (9): 52); P-U **pexi-:* Hun. *fő-* 'to cook' (item (10): 55); P-U**suxį-:*

Lapp *sukkâ-* 'to row' (item (12): 59); P-U **toxi-*: Finn. *tuo-* 'to bring' (item (13): 63). Most of these items have been mentioned in this book in connection with their irregularities.

18 Recall that Janhunen reconstructs P-U ? **pɜxi̯*, whereby ɜ indicates non-well specified vowel, because in this word it seems impossible to reconstruct even approximately the quality of the vowel of first syllable; see example (4.17).

19 **DʰuH-li* is the nominal formation; however, here I have also listed the meanings of the verbal forms.

20 The author says that one should not deny the existence of 'a laryngeal' in P-Indo-European, as long as, by 'laryngeal' one does not refer to the phonetic nature of this phoneme, which is difficult to define.

21 If this were a later, Indo-Iranian L-W the substitution in F-U would be with -*ś*- or -*ć*-, according to the author.

22 Note that these 13 items do not include the 6 items listed in Koivulehto (1991), and which contain the P-U segment *x* as a reflex of I-E laryngeals.

23 Note that, according to some researchers (for example by Wiik 1999: 46), the negative Genitive in Russian is characteristic of Common Slavic, although most of the other Slavic languages 'have lost' it more recently. This construction is characteristic also of Lithuanian (Michalove, personal communication). Whatever the case, this phenomenon reflects an influence from Finnic, rather than from U, given that the negative constructions are not widespread in the U languages.

24 See also the journalistic interview in the Finnish magazine: *Suomen Kuvalehti* **9**, 28th February 1997.

26 Examples of these terms are: *sea, strand, east, north, sword, ship, carp, eel, lamb, calf, drink, leap, bone, wife.*

8 Morphology

1 1992: 313.

2 Compare the following example from north-western Cheremis (Ivanov & Tužarov 1970): *pi* 'dog'; *pi-em* 'dog-my'; *pi-βlä* 'dog-Plu., dogs'; *pi-em-βlä* 'dog-my-Plu., my dogs'; *pi-län* 'dog-Dat., to (the) dog'; *pi-em-län* 'dog-my-Dat., to my dog'; *pi-län-βlä* 'dog-Dat.-Plu., to the dogs'; *pi-em-län-βlä* 'dog-my-Dat.-Plu., to my dogs'.

3 For example, in the Finnish pair: Acc. Sing. *talo-n* vs Acc. Plu. *talo-t*, the absence of a coherent agglutinative form **talo-n-t* or **talo-t-n* for Plurality may not be due to syncretism, as normally assumed, but to a different reason. The Finnish Accusative -*n* was originally a Topical element. Therefore, it was used in the Singular only, since it is the elements which are singular (concrete and referential), which are typically chosen for the purpose of Topicalisation.

4 The Sherkal and Nizyam dialects are transitional between North and South; Obdorsk is in the far North.

5 Note that Abondolo uses the spelling 'Nizyam' at p. 361, but the spelling 'Nizjam' in the list of Abbreviations. For the examples reported in the table I have used the transcriptions of the two authors respectively.

6 Note that the superscript *j* indicates 'palatal(isation) in Abondolo's transcription.

7 Note that according to Honti (1998a: 344), the vowels of the Vogul and Ostyak endings are long.

8 The term 'Exaptation' was coined by Gould & Vrba (1982) to indicate the process of co-optation during the evolution of structures originally developed for other purposes.

9 The actual endings of Partitive in Finnish are -*a* ~ -*ta*, according to the type of stem they are added to. In this case it is actually *kala-a*. Note also that what has now become in some languages a Partitive has a basic Separative function.

10 The superscript symbols indicate variations resulting from vowel harmony.

11 Note that I shall not provide the segmentations of the words which are not relevant for the current analysis.

12 Urmas Sutrop, personal communication.

13 Note that Hun. -*ll*- represents a difficulty, deriving perhaps through the stages *-*lk*- > *-*ly*. Note also the equivalent Yuk. *melut.*

14 More than ten Case endings developed in Hungarian relatively late from postpositional structures, and others are still forming, such as the temporal suffix -*kor*, as is demonstrated by the lack of vowel harmony: *hat-kor* 'at six o'clock', *öt-kor* 'at five o'clock', etc.

15 Compare modern Hungarian *belé* '[movement toward] inside him/her', *belé-m* '[movement toward] inside me', *belé-d* '[movement toward] inside you', etc. Notice also that *bele* can be used as a co-verb to give the idea of 'movement, penetration into something', as in *bele=esett a kút-ba* 'into=fell the well=into, he fell into the well', whereby the notion 'movement into' is actually expressed twice, once by the *bele* component of the verb, and once by the suffix -*ba* derived from it.

16 Compare modern Hun. *belőle-m, belőle-d, belől-e* '[movement] out of inside me, you, her/him, etc.

17 Notice the presence of the long vowel -*ev*- in this postposition, indicating possibly the presence of a Possessive ending.

18 *Ómagyar Mária-siralom* is the oldest Hungarian poem, dated about 1300. It is preserved in a codex originating from northern Italy, and it is a more or less free translation of a poem belonging to the hymn literature of the Middle Ages, known as *Planctus Sanctae Mariae*. The author and/or copyist might have been a Hungarian monk attending the University of Bologna.

19 The same fluctuation is observed also in the Altaic languages: the Turkic languages have Possessive–Case, but Mongolian and Tungusic have Case–Possessive.

20 The Ostyak example is from Abondolo, but I have not followed here the author's trancsription of palatal sounds.

21 Derivational morphemes are claimed by some scholars to be closer to the root than the inflectional morphemes; therefore, they might be more resistant to the process of borrowing.

22 Old and Classical Mongolian and Manchu have no Possessive suffixes; the same is true for Estonian.

23 Notice that at the 3rd Person I have added '(V)' to Sinor's Table, to indicate vowel.

24 This is in reality a simplification: there are several endings, according to the various combinations of Possessor and Possession; see also below.

25 The formation of Possessive/Person suffixes as a result of Grammaticalisation of (at least) 1st and 2nd Person pronouns is quite a common phenomenon across languages. It appears also (to quote just languages geographically close to ours) in Kartvelian, Chukchi-Kamchatkan and Eskimo-Aleut, not to mention Indo-European.

26 Greenberg (1996) refers to the (presumed) case of suppletion just described to support the existence of the Eurasiatic family. He claims that the suppletion found in U is reminiscent, and probably genetically related to, the 'Eurasiatic ancestry' of the Indo-European 1st Person Nominative *$e\hat{g}(h)om$, which alternates with suppletive forms beginning with *m*- in other Cases. Of supposed special importance is the Genitive, usually reconstructed as *$mene$, whose stem *men- has been extended to other Nominative Cases in some languages. This kind of suppletion is supposed to have survived in almost all Indo-European languages (English *I/me*, French *je/moi* etc.), as well as other branches of the Eurasiatic family, including U, where these forms are to be found in Hungarian, as just described. However, the suppletion found in the U languages cannot really be traced back to P-U, not only because it is present only in a few languages, but also because the presumed etymological connection is rather weak.

27 The -*i* formant is attested also in Germanic and Slavic. It might well be possible that there is no connection at all among all these -*i* formants, and in fact it has not been taken into consideration in the mathematical analysis carried out below.

28 The analysis of the non-Chuvash Turkic plural in -*lar* as reflecting a combination of *-*l* + *-*r* is usually accepted, but there are also different interpretations. For example, according to Georg (1989/91: 144–8), -*lar* is a re-analysis of Old Turkic -*ol* (3rd Singular pronoun) vs -*olar* (3rd Plural pronoun). Here, the Plural is supposed to be simply *-*ar*/*-*er*, but, according to the rules of Turkic syllabification (a final syllable of the shape VC preceded by a C takes the preceding C into the last syllable: VC-VC > V-CVC), the -*l* of the pronoun was taken by analogy to be part of the Plural ending.

29 A Plural -*t* and a Dual -*k* are attested also in Chukchi-Kamchatkan, Eskimo-Aleut and Gilyak; there is a Plural -*k* in Dravidian. The distribution of these two elements seems to suggest that -*k* is used as a marker of Plurality in those languages that do not have Duality, such as Dravidian and some Chukchi-Kamchatkan languages. Hungarian *-*k* could be included here if it is considered connected with the Dual *-*k*(*ə*). Furthermore *-*t* and *-*k* function as nominal and verbal endings in these non-U languages too, exactly as in the U languages.

30 Compare the conclusion by Honti (1997: 103): 'Ich postuliere ein Numerussystem – auch in dem Kasusparadigma– für die Grundsprache, worin die eizelnen Numeri und deren Suffixe ihre bestimmten Funktionen gehabt haben; . . . Die funktionelle Ausbreitung einiger Numerus- und Kollektivsuffixe sowie die Entstehung neuerer Kollektivsuffixe haben die morphologischen und funktionellen Änderungen in den verschiedenen Sprachgruppen und Sprachen ausgelöst'.

31 According to the author, the Permian endings can be understood as deriving from a Permian root *jos* 'people'. However, there are recognised difficulties in the process of formation of the endings of Plurality in these languages; furthermore, the meaning 'people' is not present in Votyak.

32 This ending -*sem* is used in Chuvash instead of the Common Turkic ending -*lar*.

33 Luutonen appears to believe that the borrowing of the grammatical morphemes of Plurality from totally different, unrelated languages is a common, natural phenomenon. In fact, the author argues that a similar situation is to be observed in the field of some Indo-Aryan morphemes of Plurality.

34 Constructions containing a Participle/Gerundive are the most common way of expressing subordinate objective sentences in U and Altaic languages, equivalent to the Indo-European type '*that* + finite verb'. However, the latter type of construction has recently become widespread in some western languages, such as Modern Hungarian, Finnish and Lapp.

35 This -*m*- is the other Participle present in this language, alongside the Imperfect Participle -*t* discussed in the previous section (see (8.5)).

36 According to Itkonen (1966b: 72) the Case ending in question, the Essive, derives from an original Locative, as in *koto-na* 'at home'.

37 Also liquids are rare in initial position in the U and Altaic languages.

38 In Finnish the noun preceded by a numeral takes the Partitive.

39 Here is the relevant passage: 'When postpositions develop into a Case system, the whole system is likely to evolve more or less at the same time, rather than one postposition becoming one Case . . . then a hundred years later a second postposition developing into a second Case and so on, so that a system of seven Cases develop in seven separate stages . . . I am not suggesting that an established grammatical category cannot be added. Once a language has a system of, say, five Cases, others may well be added; or a new noun class; or further nouns may become open to incorporation. My point is that, when a new category develops, it will do so in a decisive manner. There will be no Cases at all and then, – within perhaps a couple of generations – a system of half-a-dozen or so Cases, rather than one, then two, then three . . . But then, as a further increment, a seventh Case could well develop at some later stage. Similar remarks apply to the development of bound pronouns. At one stage of language's development Subject and Object are shown by free pronouns outside the verb. Then these develop into obligatory clitic pronouns that every verb must include, . . . a fairly full set of bound pronouns would develop more or less simultaneously'.

40 Janhunen does not explicitly states that P-U is rich in morphology, but this is what appears to be implied in the paper.

41 Dixon (1997: 42) states that P-U/P-F-U 'may have been' agglutinative, at around nine o'clock in the morphological cycle, with the modern languages moving toward the fusional type.

9 Completing the picture: proper names, archaeology and genetics

1 1994: 273.

2 The author says that the aim of her book is to 'set out the place names evidence in such a way that archaeologists and local historians will understand its strengths and weaknesses'.

The author also stresses the following: 'if it be accepted that place-name etymologies and identifications must be of specialist origin or have specialist agreement, then the study may be whole-heartedly recommended to the specialist in other fields'.

3 The other commonly reported etymology (reported also in SKES 1114–15, although with uncertainty) is from a presumed person name, in turn from the verb *suo-da* 'give, grant, accord [permission]'.

4 These people, together with the *Suomalaiset*, and others, form the modern Finnish nation.

5 Koivulehto himself (1993), at the end of his summary, wonders whether this is a plausible scenario, and asks for feedback from the reader.

6 Ligeti (1986: 400) explicitly says that *magyar* is the 'original version' of the name and that Μεγέρη is the 'secondary pair' of *magyeri*. The author also states that the change *majǵir(i)* > *magyar* ~ *megyer* took place in the late P-Hungarian period, before the time of the 'home conquest'.

7 The self-denomination of the Voguls has several variants; compare also Vogul (Lozva dialect) *måńś*, the common denomination of Voguls and Ostyaks.

8 This name is not listed in TESz and in EWUng.

9 This tribe is currently resident in the Bashkir territory (Di Cave 1995: 409). See too the map provided by Németh (1966a: 9) for the distribution of the Bashkir ethnonyms.

10 *-man* ~ *-men* is a well-known Turkic suffix, the same found in *türk-men*.

11 This word is not listed in TESz and in EWUng.

12 In one of these Russian documents, a '*diploma*' of the Šack Archives, dated 9th July 1539, the *Možerjanov* people are reported to be living together with the Bashkirs and other Turkic populations in a locality west of the Volga (Vásáry 1975: 242–4).

13 *Pest-i* is an adjectival formation from the name *Pest* (one of the components of the Hungarian capital name: *Buda-Pest*). *Pest-i* means 'from Pest, of Pest', so that the phrase *Pesti Mizser Gábor* means: 'Mizser Gábor from/living in Pest'. The philologist Mizser Gábor writes in the front page of his translation of the New Testament that, regarding his ethnic nationality, he comes from the '*Mysser*' clan.

14 The original text reads as follows: '[The Bashkirs] a magyar őstörténet nyitott kérdései közé tartozik'.

15 The semantic development from 'to tie' to 'preserve, fence' is justified with a similar development; compare Hun. *sző-* 'to weave' vs Hun. *sövény* 'fence'.

16 According to Németh, these *Mišer* people probably had been in Hungary since the beginning of the 13th century, given that a toponym '*Mišer*' seems to be attested in 1216.

17 These mountains are located in the area between the Yenisei river and the Baikal lake, at the border between central and northern Asia.

18 In this paper the author also points out the contradictions between the genetic evidence and some of the tenets of the U paradigm, proposing interesting ways forward.

19 Notice that also the title of the paper by Lipták (1975a) can be equally misleading.

20 The original text reads as follows: 'Kielen ja geneettisen perimän tai arkeologisten muinaisjäänteiden välillä ei kuitenkaan vallitse mitään itsestään selvää sidosta'.

10 Summary and Conclusion

1 Whittington (1975), quoted in Gould (1989: 132).

2 My thanks to Juha Janhunen for suggesting this phrase.

3 For example, Dixon (1997: 5) says: 'Unfortunately, there has been a tendency to see family trees as the only model of language development; the model has been overapplied, producing "results" that are not scientifically valid'.

REFERENCES

Aalto, P. 1969/78. Uralisch und Altaisch. UAJb **41**: 323–34. [Reprinted in: *Studies in Altaic and Comparative Philology. A Collection of Prof. P. Aalto's Essays in Honour of his 70th Birthday.* SO **59**. Helsinki 1987].

Aalto, P. 1975. G. J. Ramstedt and Altaic linguistics. *Central Asiatic Journal* **19/3**: 161–3.

Abondolo, D. 1987. Hungarian. In B. Comrie (ed. 1987a), *The Major Languages of Eastern Europe.* 185–200.

Abondolo, D. 1994. Uralic languages. In R. E. Asher (ed.), 4855–8.

Abondolo, D. 1995. Proto-Uralic vocalism revisited: evidence from centre and circumference. C8IFU **III**: 5–12.

Abondolo, D. 1996. *Vowel Rotation in Uralic: Obug[r]ocentric Evidence*, School of Slavonic and East European Studies Occasional Papers **31**. London: University of London.

Abondolo, D. (ed.) 1998. *The Uralic Languages.* Routledge Language Family Descriptions. London: Routledge.

Abondolo, D. 1998a. Finnish. In D. Abondolo (ed.), 149–83.

Abondolo, D. 1998b. Hungarian. In D. Abondolo (ed.), 428–56.

Abondolo, D. 1998c. Khanty. In D. Abondolo (ed.), 359–86.

Alinei, M. 2000. *Origini delle Lingue d'Europa, II. Continuità dal Mesolitico all'Età del Ferro nelle Principali Aree Etnolinguistiche.* Bologna: Il Mulino.

Andronov, M. 1968. *Two Lectures on the Historicity of Language Families.* Annamalainagar: Annamalai University Press.

Annales Fuldenses 1937–43. In F. A. Gombos (ed.), *Catalogus fontium historiae Hungaricae aevo ducum et regum ex stirpe Arpad descendentium ab anno Christi DCCC usque ad annum MCCCI,* I–IV. Budapest: Szent István Akadémia.

Anonymus Gesta Hungarorum 1937–38. = *P. MAGISTRI, qui Anonymus dicitur, Gesta Hungarorum.* In I. Szentpétery et al. (eds), I, 13–119.

Anttila, R. 1989. *Historical and Comparative Linguistics.* Amsterdam: J. Benjamins [2nd edition].

Anttila, R. 1999/2000. The Indo-European and the Baltic Finnic interface: time against the ice. In C. Renfrew, A. McMahon & L. Trask (eds), *Time Depth in Historical Linguistics,* **II**. Cambridge: The McDonald Institute for Archaelogical Research. 481–528.

Ariste, P. 1971. Die ältesten Substrate in den ostseefinnischen Sprachen. LU **4**: 251–8.

Ariste, P. 1981a. *Keelekontaktid. Eesti keele kontakte teiste keeltega.* Emakeele Seltsi Toimetised **14**. Tallinn: Valgus.

Ariste, P. 1981b. Saksa laensõnadest vadja keeles. In G. Bereczki & J. Molnár (eds), *Lakó-emlékkönyv. Nyelvészeti tanulmányok.* Budapest: ELTE. 7–19.

Asher R. A. (ed.) 1994. *The Encyclopedia of Language and Linguistics,* I. Oxford: Pergamon Press.

Audova, I. 1996. On the *ś*-preterite of Uralic languages and the verbal *s*-suffixes in the Siberian non-Uralic languages. In A. Künnap (ed.). F-U **20**: 23–8.

Austerlitz, R. 1968. L'ouralien. In A. Martinet (ed.), *Le Langage. Encyclopédie de la Pléiade.* Paris: Gallimard. 1331–87.

Austerlitz, R. 1970. Agglutination in northern Eurasia in perspective. In R. Jakobson & K. Kawamoto (eds), *Studies in General and Oriental Linguistics Presented to Shiro Hattori on the Occasion of his Sixtieth Birthday.* Tokyo: TEC Corporation for Language and Educational Research. 1–5.

Austerlitz, R. 1987. Uralic languages. In B. Comrie (ed. 1987a), 177–84.

Baker, R. 1985. The development of the Komi case system. MSFOu **189**: 1–266.

Bakró-Nagy, M. 1988. Phonotaktische Regeln in der uralischen Grundsprache. SpS **1**: 9–15.

Bakró-Nagy, M. 1990a. PU/PFU Dx *-rV*. NyK **91**: 9–14.

Bakró-Nagy, M. 1990b. PU/PFU *č/ć* (phonotaktische Erläuterungen zu Affrikaten der Grundsprache). SpS **3**: 13–32.

Bakró-Nagy, M. 1992. *Proto-Phonotactics.* Phonotactic Investigation of the PU and PFU Consonant System. Wiesbaden: O. Harrassovitz.

Bammesberger, A. 1988 (ed.). *Die Laryngaltheorie und die Rekonstruktion des indogermanischen Laut- und Formensystems.* Heidelberg: Winter.

Bárczi, G. 1958a. *Magyar hangtörténet.* Budapest: Tankönyvkiadó [2nd edition].

Bárczi, G. 1958b. *A magyar szókincs eredete.* Egyetemi magyar nyelvészeti füzetek. Budapest: Tankönyvkiadó [2nd edition].

Bárczi, G. 1965. À propos des vieux mots d'emprunt turcs en hongrois. AOH **18**: 47–54.

Bárczi, G. 1966. *A magyar nyelv életrajza.* Budapest: Gondolat.

Bárczi, G., Benkő, L. & Berrár, J. (eds), 1967. *A magyar nyelv története.* Budapest: Tankönyvkiadó.

Bartha, A. 1988. *A magyar nép őstörténete.* Budapest: Akadémiai Kiadó.

Bartha, A., Czeglédy, K. & Róna-Tas, A. (eds), 1977. *Magyar őstörténeti tanulmányok.* Budapest: Akadémiai Kiadó.

Baskakov, N. A. 1969. *Vvedenie v izučenie tjurkskikh jazykov.* Moskva/Leningrad: Vysšaja škola [2nd edition].

Bátori, I. 1980. Die maschinelle Kontrolle der hypothetischen uralischen Formen. C4IFU **III**: 124–54.

Baxter, W. H. & Manaster Ramer, A. 1996. Review article of the book by D. Ringe. *On Calculating the Factor of Chance in Language Comparison.* The American Philosophical Society. *Diachronica* **13/2**: 371–84.

Baxter, W. H. & Manaster Ramer, A. 1999. Beyond lumping and splitting: probabilistic issues in historical linguistics. Paper presented at the conference: *Time Depth in Historical Linguistics.* Cambridge: McDonald Institute for Archaelogical Research.

Bednarczuk, L. 1991. Balto-Slavic and Finno-Ugric linguistic convergences in typological and areal aspects. *The 6th International Congress of Baltists.* Vilniaus Universiteto Leidykla. 13–24.

Belardi, W. 1958. Recensione a Heinz Kronasser (*Vergleichende Laut- und Formenlehre des Hethitischen*). *Ricerche Linguistiche* **4**: 185–92. Roma.

Belardi, W. 1990. Genealogia, tipologia, ricostruzione e leggi fonetiche. In W. Belardi (ed.), *Linguistica Generale, Filologia e Critica dell'Espressione.* Roma: Bonacci. 154–216.

Bendefy, L. (ed.) 1937. *Fontes authentici itinera (1235–1238) Fr. Iuliani illustrantes.* Budapest: Sarkany-nyomda.

Benkő, L. 1967. A magyar szókészlet eredete. In G. Bárczi, L. Benkő & J. Berrár (eds), 329–50.

Benkő, L. 1972. Hungarian proper names. Personal name (anthroponyms) terms during the earliest periods. In L. Benkő & S. Imre (eds), 227–53.

Benkő, L. 1984. A magyarság honfoglalás előtti történetéhez *Lëved* és *Etëlköz* kapcsán. MNy **80**: 389–419.

Benkő, L. and Imre, S. (eds) 1972. *The Hungarian Language.* Janua linguarum. Series practica **134**. Budapest: Akadémiai Kiadó [The Hague: Mouton].

Benveniste, E. 1966. *Problèmes de Linguistique Générale.* **I**. Paris: Gallimard.

Benzing, J. 1956. *Die tungusischen Sprachen: Versuch einer vergleichende Grammatik.* Akademie der Wissenschaften und der Literatur in Mainz. Abhandlungen der geistes- und sozialwissenschaftlichen Klasse **11**: 1–159. Wiesbaden: F. Steiner.

Benzing, J. 1959. Das Tschuwaschische. In J. Deny, K. Grønbech, H. Scheel, Z. V. Togan (eds), *Philologiae Turcicae Fundamenta,* **I**. Wiesbaden: F. Steiner. 695–752.

Benzing, J. & Menges, K. 1959. Classification of the Turkic languages. In J. Deny, K. Grønbech, H. Scheel, Z. V. Togan (eds), *Philologiae Turcicae Fundamenta,* **I**. Wiesbaden: F. Steiner. 1–5.

Bereczki, G. 1968. W. Steinitz és E. Itkonen a finnugor vokalizmus elmélete és a cseremisz nyelv. NyK **70**: 23–34.

Bereczki, G. 1969. Die finnisch-ugrische Vokalismustheorie von W. Steinitz und E. Itkonen und das Tscheremissische. ALH **19**: 305–19.

Bereczki, G. 1980a. *A magyar nyelv finnugor alapjai.* Budapest: Tankönyvkiadó.

Bereczki, G. 1980b. L'unité finnoise de la Volga a-t-elle jamais existé? ÉFOu **15**: 81–90.

Bereczki, G. 1988. Geschichte der wolgafinnischen Sprachen. In D. Sinor (ed.), 314–50.

Bereczki, G. 1998. *Fondamenti di Linguistica Ugro Finnica.* Udine: Forum.

Berta, Á. 1989/91. Historische Zeugnisse der ungarischen Stammesnamen. In B. Brendemoen (ed.), 23–38.
Berta, Á. 1998. Tatar & Bashkir. In L. Johanson & É. Á. Csató (eds), 283–300.
Bloomfield, L. 1933. *Language*. New-York: H. Holt.
Bouda, K. 1940. Die finnisch-ugrisch-samojedische Schicht des Jukagirischen. UAJb **20**: 71–93.
Bouda, K. 1953. Dravidisch und Uralaltaisch. UAJb **25**: 161–73.
Brendemoen, B. (ed.) 1989/91. *Altaica Osloensia. Proceedings from the 32nd Meeting from the Permanent International Altaistic Conference*. Oslo: Universitetsforlaget.
Bright, W. (ed.) 1992. *International Encyclopedia of Linguistics*. Oxford: OUP.
Budenz. J. 1869 and 1870. A magyar és finn-ugor nyelvekbeli szóegyezések. NyK **6**: 374–478 and **7**: 1–62.
Budenz, J. 1871–3. Jelentés Vámbéry Á. magyar-török szóegyezéseiről. NyK **10**: 67–135.
Budenz, J. 1878/9. Ueber die Verzweigung der ugrischen Sprachen. In L. Meyer et al. (eds), *Festschrift zur Feier seines fünfzigjährigen Doctorjubiläums am 24. October 1878 Herrn Professor Theodor Benfey gewidmet*. Beiträge zur Kunde der indogermanischen Sprachen **4**. Göttingen: Robert Peppermüller.192–258.
Burrow, T. & Emeneau, M. B. 1961. *A Dravidian Etymological Dictionary*. Oxford: Clarendon.
Bynon, T. 1977. *Historical Linguistics*. Cambridge: CUP.
Campbell, L. 1990a. Indo-European and Uralic tree names. *Diachronica* **7/2**: 149–80.
Campbell, L. 1990b. Syntactic reconstruction and Finno-Ugric. In H. Andersen and E. F. K. Koerner (eds), *Historical Linguistics 1987: Papers from the Eighth International Conference on Historical Linguistics* [8ICHL] Amsterdam: J. Benjamins. 51–94.
Campbell, L. 1993. On proposed universals of grammatical borrowing. In H. Aertsen & R. J. Jeffers (eds), *Historical Linguistics 1989: Papers from the Ninth International Conference on Historical Linguistics* [9ICHL]. Amsterdam: J. Benjamins. 91–110.
Campbell, L. 1996. On sound change and challenges to regularity. In M. Durie & M. Ross (eds), 72–89.
Campbell, L. 1997. On the linguistic prehistory of Finno-Ugric. In R. Hickey & S. Puppel (eds), *A Festschrift for Jacek Fisiak on his 60th Birthday*, I. Berlin: Mouton De Gruyter. 829–61.
Cardona, G. R. 1976. *Introduzione all'Etnolinguistica*. Bologna: Il Mulino.
Cardona, G. R. 1985. *I sei Lati del Mondo. Linguaggio ed Esperienza*. Roma/Bari: Laterza.
Carlson, C. 1990. Semantic parallels in Uralic and Altaic. C7IFU **III**: 229–38.
Carpelan, C. 1996. Mikä on alkuperämme? *Hiidenkivi* **4/96**: 10–14.
Carpelan, C. 1999. Käännekohtia Suomen esihistoriassa aikavälillä 5100–1000 eKr. In P. Fogelberg (ed.), 249–80.
Carpelan, C. 2000. Essay on archaeology and languages in the western end of the Uralic zone. C9IFU **I**: 7–38.
Castrén, M. A. 1847. Lettre de M. le Dr. Castrén à M. l'Académicien Sjoegren. Lue le 30 jan. 1846. *Bulletin de la Classe Historico-philologique de l'Académie Impériale des Sciences de St.-Pétersbourg.* **3**: 225–44. St. Pétersbourg.
Castrén, M. A. 1854. *Grammatik der samojedischen Sprachen*. In A. Schiefner (ed.), *Castrén's Nordische Reisen und Forschungen* 7. St. Petersburg: Buchdruckerei der Kaiserlichen Akademie der Wissenschaften. [Reprinted in 1966 as vol. **53** of the Indiana University Uralic and Altaic Series. Bloomington: Indiana University.]
Castrén, M. A. 1856. Reiseberichte und Briefe aus den Jahren 1845–1849. In A. Schiefner (ed.), *Castrén's Nordische Reisen und Forschungen 2*. St. Petersburg: Buchdruckerei der Kaiserlichen Akademie der Wissenschaften.
Castrén, M. A. 1858. Hvar låg det finska folkets vagga? *Nordiska resor och forskningar 5. M. A. Castréns smärre afhandlingar och akademiska dissertationer*. Helsingfors: Finska Litteratur-Sällskapets Tryckeri. 126–42.
Castrén, M. A. 1967. *Tutkimusmatkoilla Pohjolassa*. Porvoo: WSOY.
Cavalli-Sforza, L. 1996.*Gènes, Peuples et Langues*. Paris: Jacob.
Cavalli-Sforza, L., Menozzi, P, & Piazza, A. 1994. *The History and Geography of Human Genes*. Princeton: Princeton University Press.
Chambers, J. K. & Trudgill, P. 1980. *Dialectology*. Cambridge: CUP.
Chen, M. 1972. The time dimension: contribution toward a theory of sound change. *Foundation of Language* **8**: 457–98.

Cipriano, P. 1988. Implicazioni metodologiche e fattuali della teoria di W. Belardi sull'indoeuropeo. *Studi e Saggi Linguistici* **28**: 101–26. Roma.

Clark, L. 1998. Chuvash. In L. Johanson and É. Á. Csató (eds), 434–52.

Clauson, Sir G. 1956. The case against the Altaic theory. *Central Asiatic Journal* **2**: 181–7.

Clauson, Sir G. 1962. *Turkish and Mongolian Studies.* The Royal Asiatic Society of Great Britain and Ireland. London: Luzac.

Clauson, Sir G. 1969. A lexicostatistical appraisal of the Altaic theory. *Central Asiatic Journal* **13**: 1–23.

Clauson, Sir G. 1972. *An Etymological Dictionary of Pre-Thirteenth Century Turkish.* Oxford: Clarendon Press.

Collinder, B. 1940. Jukagirisch und Uralisch. *Uppsala Universitets Årsskrift.* Recueil de travaux publié par l'université d'Uppsala **8**.

Collinder, B. 1941. *Die urgermanischen Lehnwörter im Finnischen. II, Supplement und Wortindex.* Skrifter utgivna av. K. Humanistiska Vetenskaps-Samfundet i Uppsala. Stockholm: Almqvist & Wiksell [Leipzig: O. Harrassowitz].

Collinder, B. 1947. La parenté linguistique et le calcul des probabilités. *Språkvetenskapliga Sällskapets i Uppsala Förhandligar 1946–1948.* 1–24.

Collinder, B. 1952. Ural-altaisch. UAJb **24**: 1–26.

Collinder, B. 1955. *Fenno-Ugric Vocabulary. An Etymological Dictionary of the Uralic Languages.* Stockholm: Almqvist & Wiksell.

Collinder, B. 1957. *Survey of the Uralic Languages.* Stockholm: Almqvist & Wiksell [2nd edition 1969].

Collinder, B. 1960. *Comparative Grammar of the Uralic Languages.* Stockholm: Almqvist & Wiksell.

Collinder, B. 1965a. *An Introduction to the Uralic Languages.* Berkeley: University of California Press.

Collinder, B. 1965b. Hat das Uralische Verwandte? Eine sprachvergleichende Untersuchung. *Acta Universitatis Upsaliensis* **1/4**: 109–80.

Collinder, B. 1970. Der Sprachforscher 'behind the looking glass'. *Filologiskt Arkiv* **16**: 1–28. Stockholm.

Collinder, B. 1977a. *Fenno-Ugric Vocabulary,* Stockholm: Almqvist & Wiksell [2nd revised edition].

Collinder, B. 1977b. Pro hypothesi Uralo-Altaica. MSFOu **158**: 67–73.

Comrie, B. 1978/9. On the morphological typology of Balto-Finnic: a reassessment. ÉFOu **15**: 91–9.

Comrie, B. 1980. The order of case and possessive suffixes in Uralic languages: an approach to the comparative-historical problem. *Lingua Posnaniensis* **23**: 81–6.

Comrie, B. 1981. *The Languages of Soviet Union.* Cambridge Language Survey. Cambridge: CUP.

Comrie, B. (ed.) 1987a. *The Major Languages of Eastern Europe.* London: Croom Helm.

Comrie, B. (ed.) 1987b. *The Major Languages of Western Europe.* London: Croom Helm.

Comrie, B. 1988. General features of the Uralic languages. In D. Sinor (ed.), 451–77.

Csepregi, M. (ed.) 1998. *Finnugor kalauz.* Budapest: Panoráma.

Csepregi, M. 1998. Kérdések a nyelvrokonságról. In M. Csepregi (ed.), 9–18.

Csillaghy, A. 1977–81. Alessandro Kőrösi-Csoma e la provenienza asiatica dei Magiari come motivo di fondo dell'orientalistica ungherese. In A. Csillaghy (ed.), *Studi Miscellanei Uralici e Altaici. Dedicati ad Alessandro Kőrösi-Csoma nel Secondo Centenario della Nascita (1784–1984).* Quaderni dell'Istituto di Iranistica, Uralo-Altaistica e Caucasologia dell'Università degli Sudi di Venezia **20**: 297–340. Venezia: Cafoscarina.

Czeglédy, K. 1945. A IX századi magyar történelem főbb kérdései. MNy **41**: 33–45.

Czeglédy, K. 1983. From east to west. In P. B. Golden, T. Halasi-Kun, Th. S. Noonan (eds), AEMAe **3**: 27–125.

Czeglédy, K. 2000. The name of Hungarian people *hungar.* *Uralica* **12**: 47–59. Tokyo.

Danchev, A. 1988. Language contact and language change. *Folia Linguistica* **22**: 37–53.

Décsy, Gy. 1965. *Einführung in die finnisch-ugrische Sprachwissenschaft.* Wiesbaden: O. Harrassowitz.

Décsy, Gy. 1967. Is there a Finnic substratum in Russian? *Orbis* **16**: 150–60.

Décsy, Gy. 1969a. Finno-ugrische Lautforschung. UAJb **41**: 33–75.

Décsy, Gy. 1969b. Die Streitfragen der finnisch-ugrischen Lautforschung. UAJb **41**: 183–211.

Décsy, Gy. 1988. Slawischer Einfluß auf die uralischen Sprachen. In D. Sinor (ed.), 616–637.

Décsy, Gy. 1990. *The Uralic Protolanguage. A Comprehensive Reconstruction.* Eurolingua. Bloomington: Indiana University.

Deér, J. 1952. Le problème du chapitre 38 du De Administrando Imperio. *Annuaire de l'Institut de Philologie et d'Histoire Orientales et Slaves* **12**: 93–121. Bruxelles.

Deguignes, J. 1756–8. *Histoire Générale des Huns, des Turcs, des Mogols, et des autres Tartares Occidentaux.* Paris: Desaint & Saillant.

Di Cave, C. 1995. *L'Arrivo degli Ungheresi in Europa e la Conquista della Patria: Fonti e Letteratura Critica.* Spoleto: Centro Italiano di Studi sull'Alto Medioevo.

Di Giovine, P. 1997. Gli studi sul sistema verbale indoeuropeo ricostruito: problemi di metodo e prospettive di ricerca. *Incontri Linguistici* **20**: 11–27. Roma.

Dienes, I. 1972. *A honfoglaló magyarok.* Hereditas. Budapest: Corvina [French translation by É. R. Szilágyi: *Les Hongrois Conquérants*].

Dixon, R. M. W. 1994. *Ergativity.* Cambridge: CUP.

Dixon, R. M. W. 1997. *The Rise and Fall of Languages*, Cambridge: CUP.

Doerfer, G. 1963–75. *Türkische und mongolische Elemente im Neupersichen, unter besonderer Berücksichtigung älterer neupersischer Geschichtsquellen, vor allem der Mongolen- und Timuridenzeit*, I–IV. Akademie der Wissenschaften und der Literatur. Wiesbaden: F. Steiner.

Doerfer, G. 1964. Die mongolische Schriftsprache. In B. Spuler (ed.), *Mongolistik. Handbuch der Orientalistik.* Erste Abteilung, Fünfter Band, Zweiter Abschnitt. Leiden: E. J. Brill. 81–95.

Doerfer, G. 1968. Zwei wichtige Probleme der Altaistik. JSFOu **69**: 3–21.

Doerfer, G. 1971. *Khalaj Materials.* Indiana University Uralic and Altaic Series **115**. Bloomington: Indiana.

Doerfer, G. 1982. Nomenverba im Türkischen. *Studia Turcologica Memoriae Alexii Bombaci Dicata.* Istituto Universitario Orientale, Seminario di Studi Asiatici, Series Minor **19**: 101–14. Napoli.

Doerfer, G. 1985. *Mongolo-Tungusica.* Wiesbaden: O. Harrasowitz.

Dolgopolsky, A. 1998a. *The Nostratic Macrofamily and Linguistic Palaeontology.* Cambridge: The McDonald Institute for Archaeological Research.

Dolgopolsky, A. 1998b. The nostratic macro-family: a short introduction. Paper presented at the conference: *Symposium on the Nostratic Macrofamily.* Cambridge: The McDonald Institute for Archaeological Research.

Dolukhanov, P. M. 2000a. Archaeology and language in prehistoric Europe. In A. Künnap (ed.), F-U **23**: 11–22.

Dolukhanov, P. M. 2000b. 'Prehistoric Revolutions' and languages in Europe. In A. Künnap (ed.), F-U **23**: 71–84.

Donner, K. 1924. Zu den ältesten Berührungen zwischen Samojeden und Türken. JSFOu **40**: 3–42.

Donner, O. 1872. *Öfversikt af den Finsk Ugriska Språkforskningens historia.* Helsingfors: J. C. Frenckell.

Donner, O. 1874–88. *Vergleichendes Wörterbuch der finnisch-ugrischen Sprachen*, I–III. Helsingfors: Frenckell & Son.

Donner, O. 1879 /80. Die gegenseitige Verwandtschaft der finnisch-ugrischen Sprachen. *Acta Societatis Scientiarum Fennicae* **11**: 406–567. Helsinki.

Donner, O. 1881. Die samojedischen Sprachen und die finnisch-ugrischen. *Atti del IV Congresso Internazionale degli Orientalisti* **2**: 231–51. Florence [First presented in 1878.]

Donner, O. 1901. Die uralaltaischen Sprachen. FUF **1**, S: 128–46.

Driussi, P. 1995. The Hungarian accusative *-t*. Udine. [Manuscript].

Driussi, P. 1996. Due sviluppi grammaticali mari. In A. Marcantonio (ed.), *Rivista di Studi Ungheresi* **11**: 143–60. Roma: Sovera.

Durie, M. & Ross, M. (eds) 1996. *The Comparative Method Reviewed.* Oxford: OUP.

Edzard, L. 1998. *Polygenesis, Convergence and Enthropy: an Alternative Model of Linguistic Evolution Applied to Semitic Linguistics.* Wiesbaden: O. Harrassowitz.

Edzard, L. 2000. Monogenesis and polygenesis in comparative Semitics and Arabic: implication for linguistic change. In A. Künnap (ed.), F-U **23**: 85–93.

Embleton, S. 1991. Mathematical methods of genetic classification. In S. M. Lamb & E. D. Mitchell (eds), 365–88.

Embleton, S. 1999/2000. Lexicostatistics/glottochronology: from Swadesh to Sankoff to

Starostin to future horizons. In C. Renfrew, A. McMahon & L. Trask (eds), *Time Depth in Historical Linguistics*, **I**. Cambridge: The McDonald Institute for Archaeological Research. 143–66.

Erdélyi, I. F. 1972. Fouilles archéologiques en Bachkirie et la préhistoire hongroise. AOH **25**: 301–12.

Fodor, I. 1975a. Suomalais-ugrilaisen arkeologian pääongelmia. In P. Hajdú (ed.), *Suomalais-ugrilaiset*. Pieksämäki: Suomentanut Outi Karanko-Pap. 45–74.

Fodor, I. 1975b. A finnugor régészet fő kérdései. In P. Hajdú (ed.), 47–76.

Fodor, I. 1975c. *Verecke híres útján . . . a magyar nép őstörténete és a honfoglalás*. Budapest: Gondolat.

Fodor, I. 1977. *Bolgár-török jövevényszavaink és a régészet*. In A. Bartha, K. Czeglédy & A. Róna-Tas (eds), 79–14.

Fodor, I. 1982. *In Search of a New Homeland. The Prehistory of the Hungarian People and the Conquest*. Budapest: Corvina.

Fogelberg, P. (ed.) 1999. *Pohjan poluilla: Suomalaisten juuret nykytutkimuksen mukaan*. Bidrag till kännedom av Finlands natur och folk **153**. Helsinki: Finnish Society of Science and Letters.

Fokos-Fuchs, D. R. 1933. Übereinstimmende Lativkonstruktionen in den finnisch-ugrischen und türkischen Sprachen. MSFOu **67**: 105–114.

Fokos-Fuchs, D. R. 1937. Übereinstimmungen in der Syntax der finnisch-ugrischen und türkischen Sprachen. FUF **24**: 292–322.

Fokos-Fuchs, D. R. 1960. Aus der Syntax der ural-altaischen Sprache. ALH **10**: 423–454.

Fokos-Fuchs, D. R. 1961. Uráli és altaji összehasonlító szintaktikai tanulmányok, VI A; numerus absolutus v. indefinitus ('egyesszám') használata. NyK **63**: 263–91.

Fokos-Fuchs, D. R. 1962. *Rolle der Syntax in der Frage nach Sprachverwandtschaft, mit besonderer Rücksicht auf das Problem der ural-altaischen Sprachverwandtschaft*. Ural-altaische Bibliothek **11**. Wiesbaden: O. Harrassowitz.

Fox, A. 1995. *Linguistic Reconstruction: an Introduction to the Theory and Method*. Oxford: OUP.

Franklin, S. & Shepard, J. 1996. *The Emergence of Rus; 750–1200*. London: Longman.

Friedrich, P. 1970. *Proto-Indo-European Trees: the Arboreal System of the Prehistoric People*. Chicago: University of Chicago Press.

Fromm, H. 1957/8. Die ältesten germanischen Lehnwörter im Finnischen. *Zeitschrift für deutsches Altertum und deutsche Literatur* **88**. 211–40. Wiesbaden.

Gallén, J. (ed.) 1984. *Suomen väestön esihistorialliset juuret*. Helsinki: Bidrag till kännedom av Finlands natur och folk **131**. Helsinki: Finnish Society of Science and Letters.

Gallén, J. 1984. Länsieurooppalaiset ja skandinaaviset Suomen esihistoriaa koskevat lähteet. In J. Gallén (ed.), 249–63.

Gamillscheg, E. 1911. Über Lautsubstitution. *Zeitschrift für romanische Philologie* **27**: 162–91.

Garbini, G. 1984. *Le Lingue Semitiche. Studi di Linguistica Storica*. Intercontinentalia, Series Minor/IUO. Studi Asiatici. Naples: IUO [2nd edition].

Gelling, M. 1978. *Signposts to the Past. Place-Names and the History of England*. London: J. M. Dent.

Georg, S. 1989/91. Some thoughts on the etymology of the Turkic plural suffix *-lar/-ler*. In B. Brendemoen (ed.), 141–52.

Georg, S., Michalove, P. A., Manaster Ramer, A. & Sidwell, P. J. 1999. Telling general linguists about Altaic. *Journal of Linguistics* **35**: 65–98.

Gheno, D. & Hajdú, P. 1992. *Introduzione alle Lingue Uraliche*. Torino: Rosemberg & Sellier.

Golden, P. B. 1990a. The peoples of the South Russian steppes. In D. Sinor (ed.), 256–77.

Golden, P. B. 1990b. The peoples of the Russian forest belt. In D. Sinor (ed), 229–53.

Golden, P. B. 1998. The Turkic people: a historical sketch. In L. Johanson & É. Á. Csató (eds), 16–29.

Gombocz, Z. 1902. Adalékok az obi-ugor nyelvek szókészletének eredetéhez. NyK **32**: 182–215.

Gombocz, Z. 1908. *Honfoglaláselőtti török jövevényszavaink*. Budapest: A Magyar Nyelvtudományi Társaság Kiadványai **7**.

Gombocz, Z. 1912. *Die bulgarisch-türkischen Lehnwörter in der ungarischen Sprache*. MSFOu **30**: 1–252.

Gombocz, Z. 1914. Az Árpádkori török személyneveink. MNy **10**: 241–438.

Gombocz, Z. 1921. A bolgár kérdés és a magyar hunmonda. MNy 17: 15–21.
Gombocz, Z. 1923. A magyar őshaza és a nemzeti hagyomány. NyK 46: 1–193.
Gombocz, Z. 1960. Honfoglalás előtti bolgár-török jövevényszavaink. NyÉrt 24: 1–32.
Gould, S. J. 1989. Wonderful Life, The Burgess Shale and the Nature of History. New York: Norton.
Gould, S. J. & Vrba, E. S. 1982. Exaptation – a missing term in the science of form. Paleobiology 8: 4–15.
Greenberg, J. H. 1963. Some universals of grammar with particular reference to the order of meaningful elements. In J. H. Greenberg (ed.), Universals of Language. Cambridge (Mass.): MIT Press. 73–113.
Greenberg, J. H. 1991. Some problems of Indo-European in historical perspective. In S. M. Lamb & E. D. Mitchell (eds), 125–41.
Greenberg, J. H. 1996. The Indo-European first and second person pronouns in the perspective of Eurasiatic, especially Chukotan. Anthropological Linguistics 39: 187–95.
Greenberg, J. H. 1997. Does Altaic exist? Journal of Indo-European Studies. Monograph Series 22: 88–93.
Greenberg, J. H. 2000. Indo-European and its Closest Relatives: the Eurasiatic Language Family, I. Stanford: Stanford University Press.
Grégoire, H. 1937. Le nom et l'origine des hongrois. Zeitschrift der Deutschen Morgenländischen Gesellschaft B. 91: 630–42.
Grégoire, H. 1952. Le nom grec de Novgorod. La Nouvelle Clio 4: 279–80.
Grünthal, R. 1997. Livvistä liiviin. Itämerensuomalaiset etnonyymit. Castrenianumin toimitteita 51. Helsinki.
Grünthal, R. & Laakso, J. (eds) 1998. Oekeeta asijoo. Commentationes Fenno-Ugricae in honorem Seppo Suhonen sexagenarii 16. V. 1998. MSFOu 228. Helsinki.
Guglielmino, C. R., Piazza, A. , Menozzi, P. & Cavalli-Sforza, L. L. 1990. Uralic genes in Europe. American Journal of Physical Anthropology 83: 57–68.
Gulya, J. 1966. Eastern Ostyak Chrestomathy. Indiana University Uralic and Altaic Series 51. Bloomington: Indiana University.
Gulya, J. 1974. Some eighteenth century antecedents of nineteenth century linguistics: the discovery of Finno-Ugrian. In D. Hymes (ed.), Studies in the History of Linguistics. Traditions and Paradigms. Bloomington: Indiana University. 258–76.
Gusmani, R. 1981. Saggi sull'Interferenza Linguistica. Firenze: Le Lettere.
Györffy, Gy. 1948. Krónikáink és a magyar őstörténet. Budapest: Néptudományi Intézet.
Györffy, Gy. 1959. Tanulmányok a magyar állam eredetéről. A nemzetségtől a vármegyéig, a törzstől az országig. A Magyar Néprajzi Társaság Könyvtára. Budapest: Akadémiai Kiadó.
Györffy, Gy. 1975a. Autour de l'État de Semi-nomades, le Cas de la Hongrie. Studia Historica Academiae Scientiarum Hungaricae 95. Budapest: Akadémiai Kiadó.
Györffy, Gy. 1975b. The original landtaking of the Hungarians. New Hungarian Quarterly 16: 3–27.
Györffy, Gy. (ed.) 1986. A magyarok elődeiről és a honfoglalásról. Kortársak és krónikások híradásai. Nemzeti Könyvtár –Történelem. Budapest: Gondolat [3rd edition].
Györffy, Gy. 1990. A magyarság keleti elemei, Budapest. Gondolat.
Györffy, Gy. 1993. Krónikáink és a magyar őstörténet. Régi kérdések – új válaszok. Budapest: Balassi Kiadó.
Hajdú, P. 1950. Die Benennungen der Samoyeden. JSFOu 54: 1–112.
Hajdú, P. 1953. A paleoszibériai népek és nyelvek. Nyr 77: 71–8.
Hajdú, P. 1954. Die sekundären anlautenden Nasale (η-, ń-) im Samojedischem. ALH 4: 17–67.
Hajdú, P. 1963. The Samoyedic Peoples and Languages. Indiana University Uralic and Altaic Series 14. Bloomington: Indiana University [The Hague: Mouton].
Hajdú, P. 1964. Über die alten Siedlungsräume der uralischen Sprachfamilie. ALH 14: 48–83.
Hajdú, P. 1966. Bevezetés az uráli nyelvtudományba. A magyar nyelv finnugor alapja. Budapest: Tankönyvkiadó.
Hajdú, P. 1968. Chrestomathia Samoiedica. Budapest: Tankönyvkiadó.
Hajdú, P. 1969a. A szamojéd konnektív-reciprok képző genetikai és areális-tipológiai össze-függései. NyK 71: 63–79.
Hajdú, P. 1969b. Finno-Ugrische Urheimatforschung. UAJb 41: 252–64.
Hajdú, P. 1969c. Zu den Kernfragen der finnisch-ugrischen Vokalforschung. UAJb 41: 179–182.

Hajdú, P. 1972. The origins of Hungarian. In L. Benkő & S. Imre (eds), 15–48.
Hajdú, P. (ed.) 1975. *Uráli népek. Nyelvrokonaink kultúrája és hagyományai.* Budapest: Corvina.
Hajdú, P. 1975a. A rokonság nyelvi háttere. In P. Hajdú (ed.), 11–43.
Hajdú, P. 1975b. Sukulaisuuden kielellistä taustaa. In P. Hajdú (ed.): *Suomalais-ugrilaiset.* Pieksämäki: Suomentanut Outi Karanko-Pap. 11–51. Helsinki: SKS.
Hajdú, P. 1975c. *Finno-Ugric Languages and People.* London: A. Deutsch. [Translated and adapted by G. F. Cushing.]
Hajdú, P. 1976. Linguistic background of genetic relationships. In P. Hajdú (ed.), *Ancient Cultures of the Uralian Peoples.* Budapest: Corvina. 11–46.
Hajdú, P. 1981. *Az uráli nyelvészet alapkérdései.* Budapest: Tankönyvkiadó.
Hajdú, P. 1983. The main characteristic features of the Uralic languages. ALH **33**: 98–120.
Hajdú, P. 1987. Die uralischen Sprachen. In P. Hajdú & P. Domokos 1987. *Die uralischen Sprachen und Literaturen.* Hamburg: H. Buske. 21–450 [Budapest: Akadémiai Kiadó].
Hajdú, P. 1988. Die samojedischen Sprachen. In D. Sinor (ed.), 3–40.
Hajdú, P. 2000. Innovations in Uralic languages. In A. Künnap (ed.), F-U **23**: 257–72.
Hajdú, P. & Domokos, P. 1978. *Uráli nyelvrokonaink.* Budapest: Tankönyvkiadó.
Häkkinen, K. 1983. *Suomen kielen vanhimmasta sanastosta ja sen tutkimisesta: Suomalais-ugrilaisten kielten etymologisen tutkimuksen perusteita ja metodiikkaa.* Publications of the Department of Finnish and General Linguistics **17**. Turku: University of Turku.
Häkkinen, K. 1984a. Lainasanat suomen ja sen sukukielten historian tutkimuksen apuvälineinä. Vir **88**: 287–306.
Häkkinen, K. 1984b. Wäre es schon an der Zeit, den Stammbaum zu fällen? UAJb, *Neue Folge* **4**: 1–24.
Häkkinen, K. 1990. *Mistä sanat tulevat. Suomalaista etymologiaa.* Tietolipas **117**. Helsinki: SKS.
Häkkinen, K. 1996. *Suomalaisten esihistoria kielitieteen valossa.* Tietolipas **147**. Helsinki: SKS.
Häkkinen, K. 1998. Uralilainen muinaiskulttuuri sanahistorian valossa. In R. Grünthal & J. Laakso (eds), 188–94.
Häkkinen, K. 1999. Esisuomalainen pyyntikulttuuri ja maanviljely sanastohistorian kannalta. In P. Fogelberg (ed.), 159–73.
Hakulinen, L. 1979. *Suomen kielen rakenne ja kehitys.* Helsinki: SKS [4th edition].
Halasi-Kun, T. 1975. Kipchak philology and the Turkic loanwords in Hungarian, I. In P. B. Golden and T. Halasi-Kun (eds), AEMAe **1**: 155–210.
Halasi-Kun, T. 1986/8. Some thoughts on Hungaro-Turkic affinity. In Th. Allsen, P. B. Golden, T. Halasi-Kun, A. P. Martinez, Th. S. Noonam & U. Schamiloglu (eds), AEMAe **6**: 31–9.
Halasi-Kun, T. 1990. A magyar-török rokonságról. *História* **2**: 1–15.
Hanzeli, V. A. 1983. *Grammatical Proof of the Affinity of the Hungarian Language with the Languages of Finnic Origin. By Sámuel Gyarmathi.* Translated, annotated and introduced by V. A. Hanzeli. Amsterdam Studies in the Theory and History of Linguistic Science. Series I. Amsterdam: J. Benjamins.
Harms, R. 1974. Uralic Languages. In *Encyclopaedia Britannica* **18**: 1022–32 [15th edition].
Harms, R. 1977. The Uralo-Yukagir focus system: a problem in remote genetic realtionship. In P. J. Hopper (ed.), *Studies in Descriptive and Historical Linguistics: Festschrift for Winfred P. Lehmann.* Amsterdam: J. Benjamins. 21–43.
Haugen, E. 1950. The analysis of linguistic borrowing. *Language* **26**: 210–34.
Hausenberg, A.- R. 1998. Komi. In D. Abondolo (ed.), 305–26.
Hawkins, J. A. 1987. Germanic languages. In B. Comrie (ed. 1987b), 58–66.
Heapost, L. 2000. On the anthropology and genetics of Estonians. In A. Künnap (ed.), F-U **23**. 93–114.
Hegedűs, I. 1988. Morphologische Übereinstimmungen in den uralischen, altaischen und einigen paläosibirischen Sprachen. SpS **1**: 71–86.
Hegedűs, I., Michalove, P. A. & Manaster Ramer, A. (eds) 1997. *Indo-European, Nostratic and Beyond: Festschrift for Vitalij V. Shevoroshkin.* Washington DC: Institute for the Study of Man.
Helimski, E. 1984a. Phonological and morphonological properties of quantity in Samoyed. In P. Hajdú & L. Honti (eds), *Studien zur phonologischen Beschreibung uralischer Sprachen.* Bibliotheca Uralica **7**. Budapest: Akadémiai Kiadó. 13–17.

Helimski, E. 1984b. Problems of phonological reconstruction in modern Uralic linguistics. LU 4: 241–57.

Helimski, E. 1987. Two Mator-Taigi-Karagas vocabularies from the 18th century. JSFOu 81: 49–132.

Helimski, E. 1995. Proto-Uralic gradation: continuation and traces. CI8FU I: 7–51.

Helimski, E. 1998a. Nganasan. In D. Abondolo (ed.), 481–515.

Helimski, E. 1998b. Selkup. In D. Abondolo (ed.), 548–79.

Helimski, E. 1999. Umlaut in Diachronie – Ablaut in Synchronie: Urostjakischer Umlaut und ostjakischer Ablaut. In E. Helimski (ed.), Diachronie in der synchronen Sprachbeschreibung. Mitteilungen der Societas Uralo-Altaica 21: 39–44. Hamburg.

Hetzron, R. 1976. Two principles of genetic classification. Lingua 38: 89–101.

Hint, M. 1997. The Estonian quantity degrees in prosody and morphophonology. In I. Lehiste & J. Ross (eds), Estonian Prosody: Papers from a Symposium. Tallinn: Institute of Estonian Language. 125–33.

Hock, H. H. 1986. Principles of Historical Linguistics. Berlin: Mouton de Gruyter.

Honti, L. 1972. Észrevételek a finnugor alapnyelvi szibilánsok és affrikáták képviseleteiről. NyK 74: 3–26.

Honti, L. 1975. On the question of proto-language reconstruction. NyK 77: 125–35.

Honti, L. 1979. Characteristic features of the Ugric languages (observations on the question of of the Ugric unity). ALH 29: 1–26.

Honti, L. 1981. A finnugor alapnyelvi affrikáták kvantitásáról. NyK 83: 361–9.

Honti, L. 1982a. Geschichte des obugrischen Vokalismus der ersten Silbe. In P. Hajdú (ed.), Bibliotheca Uralica 6. Budapest: Akadémiai Kiadó.

Honti, L. 1982b. Nordostjakisches Wörterverzeichnis. SUA 16: 1–211.

Honti, L. 1983. Ablautartige Vokalwechsel in den obugrischen Sprachen. FUF 45: 25–45.

Honti, L. 1984. Chrestomathia Ostiacica. Budapest: Tankönyvkiadó.

Honti, L. 1985. Ősmagyar hangtörténetei talányok (ugor hangtörténeti és etimológiai jegyzetek). MNy 81: 140–155.

Honti, L. 1987. Uralilaisten kardinaalilukusanojen rakenteista. JSFOu 81: 133–49.

Honti, L. 1988. Die Ob-ugrischen Sprachen. In D. Sinor (ed.), 147–96.

Honti, L. 1993. Statistisches zum Uralischen Etymologischen Wörterbuch. LU 29: 241–58.

Honti, L. 1995a. Der uralische Numerus Absolutus: Was ist er eigentlich? LU 31: 161–8.

Honti, L. 1995b. Zur Morphotaktik und Morphosyntax der uralischen/finnisch-ugrischen Grundsprache. C8IFU I: 53–82.

Honti, L. 1997. Numerusprobleme (Ein Erkundungszug durch den Dschungel der uralischen Numeri). FUF 54: 1–126.

Honti, L. 1998a. ObUgrian. In D. Abonbolo (ed.), 327–57.

Honti, L. 1998b. Ugrilainen kantakieli: erheellinen vai reaalinen hypoteesi? In R. Grünthal & J. Laakso (eds), 176–87.

Hopper, P. J. & Traugott, E. C. 1993. Grammaticalization. Cambridge: CUP.

Hymes, D. 1973. Lexicostatistics and glottochronology in the nineteenth century. (With notes toward a general history.) In I. Dyen (ed.), Lexicostatistics in Genetic Linguistics. Proceedings of the Yale Conference, April 1971. Janua Linguarum. Series Maior. The Hague: Mouton. 122–76.

Illič-Svityč, V. M. 1971–84. Opyt sravnenija nostratičeskikh jazykov (semitokhamitskij, kartvel'skij, indoevropejskij, ural'skij, dravidskij, altajskij), I–III. Moskva: Nauka.

Imre, S. 1972. Early Hungarian texts. In Benkő L. & Imre, S. (eds), 327–47.

Imre, S. 1988. Die Geschichte der ungarischen Sprache. In D. Sinor (ed.), 413–47.

Indreko, R. 1948a. Origin and area of settlement of the Fenno-Ugrian peoples. Science in Exile. Publications of the Scientific Quarterly 'Scholar' 2: 3–24. Heidelberg.

Indreko, R. 1948b. Die mittlere Steinzeit in Estland. Mit einer Übersicht über die Geologie des Kunda-Sees von K. Orviku. Kungl. Vitterhets Historie och Antikvitets Akademiens Handlingar 66. Stockholm.

Itkonen, E. 1939. Der ostlappische Vokalismus vom qualitativen Standpunkt aus, mit besonderer Berücksichtigung des Inari- und Skoltlappischen. MSFOu 79: 1–386.

Itkonen, E. 1946. Zur Frage nach der Entwicklung des Vokalismus des ersten Silbe in den finnisch-ugrischen Sprachen, insbesondere im Mordwinischen. FUF 29: 222–37.

Itkonen, E. 1954. Zur Geschichte des Vokalismus der ersten Silbe im Tscheremissischen und in den permischen Sprachen. FUF **31**: 149–345.

Itkonen, E. 1955. Die Herkunft und Vorgeschichte der Lappen im Lichte der Sprachwissenschaft. UAJb **27**: 123–50.

Itkonen, E. 1960. Die Vorgeschichte der Finnen aus der Perspective eines Linguisten. UAJb **32**: 2–24.

Itkonen, E. 1962. Die Laut- und Formenstruktur der finnisch-ugrischen Grundsprache. UAJb **34**: 178–210.

Itkonen, E. 1966a. Suomalais-ugrilaisen kielen- ja historiantutkimuksen alalta. Tietolipas **20**. Helsinki: SKS.

Itkonen, E. 1966b. Kieli ja sen tutkimus. Helsinki: WSOY.

Itkonen, E. 1968a. Suomen suvun esihistoria. In O. Ikola (ed.), Suomen kielen käsikirja. Helsinki: Weilin + Göös. 11–34.

Itkonen, E. 1968b. Zur Frühgeschichte der lappischen und finnischen Lokalkasus. C2IFU I: 202–11.

Itkonen, E. 1969. Zur Wertung der finnisch-ugrischen Lautforschung. Thesen und Antithesen in der finnisch-ugrischen Vokalforschung. UAJb **41**: 76–111.

Itkonen, E. 1988. Vokaaliston kysymyksiä. Vir **92**: 325–30.

Itkonen, Esa. 1998. Sukupuu ja kontakti. Vir **102**: 96–103.

Itkonen, Esa. 1999. There is nothing wrong with the comparative method: Part two. In A. Künnap (ed.), Indo-European-Uralic-Siberian Linguistic and Cultural Contacts. F-U **22**: 85–90.

Itkonen, T. 1984. Suomessa puhutun suomen kantasuomalaiset juuret. In J. Gallén (ed.), 347–63.

Itkonen, T. 1997. Reflections on Pre-Uralic and the 'Saami-Finnic protolanguage'. FUF **54**: 229–66.

Ivanov, I. G. & Tužarov, G. M. 1970. Severo-zapadnoe narečie marijskogo jazyka. Dialekty marijskogo jazyka. Vypusk 1. Joškar-Ola: Marijskoe knižnoe izdatel'stvo.

Jakobson, R. 1972. On the theory of phonological associations in languages. In A. R. Keiler (ed.), A Reader in Historical and Comparative Linguistics. New-York: H. Holt. 241–52.

Janhunen, J. 1977. Samojedischer Wortschatz. Gemeinsamojedische Etymologien. Castrenianumin toimitteita **17**. Helsinki.

Janhunen, J. 1981a. Uralilaisen kantakielen sanastosta. JSFOu **77**: 219–74.

Janhunen, J. 1981b. On the structure of Proto-Uralic. FUF **44**: 23–42.

Janhunen, J. 1983. On early Indo-European-Samoyed contacts. Symposium Saeculare Societatis Fenno-Ugricae. MSFOu **85**: 115–28.

Janhunen, J. 1984a. Altailaisen hypoteesin nykytila. Vir. **88**: 202–6.

Janhunen, J. 1984b. Problems of Nenets phonology. In P Hajdú & L. Honti (eds), 19–28.

Janhunen, J. 1986. Glottal Stop in Nenets. MFFOu **196**: 1–202.

Janhunen, J. 1996. Manchuria: an Ethnic History. MSFOu **222**: 1–311.

Janhunen, J. 1998. Samoyedic. In D. Abondolo (ed.), 457–79.

Janhunen, J. 1999. Euraasian alkukodit. In P. Fogelberg (ed.), 27–36.

Janhunen, J. 2000. Reconstructing Pre-Proto-Uralic typology spanning the millennia of linguistic evolution. C9IFU I: 59–76.

Jenkins, R. J. H. (ed.) 1962. Constantine Porphyrogenitus. De Administrando Imperio, II. Commentary. London: The Athlone Press.

Johanson, L. 1998. The history of Turkic. In L. Johanson & É. Á. Csató (eds), 81–115.

Johanson, L. 1999. Cognates and copies in Altaic verb derivation. In K. H. Menges & N. Naumann (eds), Language and Literature – Japanese and other Altaic Languages. Studies in Honour of Roy Andrew Miller on his 75th Birthday. Wiesbaden: O. Harrassowitz. 1–14.

Johanson, L. & Csató, É. Á. 1998 (eds). The Turkic Languages. London and New York: Routledge.

Joki, A. J. 1944. Kai Donners kamassisches Wörterbuch nebst Sprachproben und Hauptzügen der Grammatik. Lexica Societatis Fenno-Ugricae **8**. Helsinki: SKS.

Joki, A. J. 1952. Die Lehnwörter des Sajansamojedischen. MSFOu **103**: 1–393.

Joki, A. J. 1965. Kielisukulaisuuskysymyksiä. Vir **4**: 352–8.

Joki, A. J. 1973. Uralier und Indogermanen. Die älteren Berührungen zwischen den uralischen und indogermanischen Sprachen. MSFOu **151**. Helsinki.

Joki, A. J. 1975. Affinität und Interferenz in den Sprachen des nordeurasischen Areals. C4IFU III: 71–86.

Joki, A. J. 1988. Zur Geschichte der uralischen Sprachgemeinschaft unter besonderer Berücksichtigung des Ostseefinnischen. In D. Sinor (ed.), 575–9.

Julku, K. 2000. Die ältesten Wurzeln der finno-ugrischen Völker im Lichte der heutigen Forschung. In A Künnap (ed.), F-U 23: 125–30.

Julku, K. & Äärelä, M. (eds) 1997. Itämerensuomi–eurooppalainen maa. Studia Historica Fenno-Ugrica II. Jyväskylä: Atena.

Kalima, J. 1936. Itämerensuomalaisten kielten balttilaiset lainat. Helsinki: SKS.

Kallio, P. 1998. Vanhojen balttilaisten lainasanojen ajoittamisesta. In R. Grünthal & J. Laakso (eds), 209–17.

Kallio, P. 1999. Varhaiset indoeurooppalaiskontaktit. In P. Fogelberg (ed.), 237–9.

Kálmán, B. 1965. A magyar mássalhangzó-rendszer kialakulása. MNy 61: 358–98.

Kálmán, B. 1972. Hungarian historical phonology. In L. Benkő & S. Imre (eds), 49–83.

Kálmán, B. 1988. The history of the Ob-Ugric languages. In D. Sinor (ed.), 394–412.

Kangasmaa-Minn, E. 1969. Agenttirakenteen syntaktista taustaa. Sananjalka 11: 53–61. Turku.

Kangasmaa-Minn, E. 1998. Mari. In D. Abondolo (ed.), 219–48.

Kannisto, A. 1923. Vogulien aikaisemmista asuma-aloista paikannimitutkimuksen valossa. Suomi 5/2: 441–7.

Kannisto, A. 1927. Über die früheren Wohngebiete der Wogulen im Lichte der Ortsnamenforschung. FUF 18: 57–89.

Kara, G. 1997. Nomina-verba mongolica. AOH 50: 155–62.

Katz, H. 1972. Zur Entwicklung der finnisch-ugrischen Affrikaten und Sibilanten im Ugrischen. ALH 22: 141–53.

Katzner, K 1995. The Languages of the World. London: Guernsey (1st edition in 1977).

Kellgren, H. 1847. Das finnische Volk und der ural-altaische Völkerstamm. Jahresbericht der Deutschen Morgenländischen Gesellschaft 1846: 180–97.

Keresztes, L. 1998. Mansi. In D. Abondolo (ed.), 387–427.

Kézai, S. 1937–8. = Simonis de Keza Gesta Hungarorum. In E. Szentpétery et al. (eds), I, 129–94.

Kiparsky, V. 1969. Gibt es ein finno-ugrischer Substrat im Slavischen? Helsinki: Suomalainen Tiedeakatemia.

Kiparsky, V. 1970. Finnougrier und Slaven zu Anfang der historischen Zeit. UAJb 42: 1–8.

Kiszely, I. 1979. A föld népei. Budapest: Gondolat.

Kiszely, I. 1992. Honnan jöttünk? Budapest: Hatodik Síp Alapítvány-Új Mandátum Kiadó.

Kiviniemi, E. 1980a. Paikannimistön maailmankuva ja todellisuus. Vir 1: 1–6.

Kiviniemi, E. 1980b. Nimistö Suomen esihistorian tutkimuksen aineistona. Vir 4: 319–38.

Kiviniemi, E. 1984. Nimistö Suomen esihistorian tutkimuksen aineistona. In J. Gallén (ed), 123–45.

Klaas, B. 1996. Similarities in case marking of syntactic relations in Estonian and Lithuanian. In M. Erelt (ed.), Estonian. Typological Studies, I. Tartu. 37–67.

Klajn, I. 1972. Influssi Inglesi nella Lingua Italiana. Firenze: Olschki.

Klesment, P. 1996. Verbal l-affixes in Samoyed and Siberian non-Uralic languages. In A. Künnap (ed.), F-U 20: 39–41.

Klose, A. 1987. Sprachen der Welt. München: Saur.

Koivulehto, J. 1980. Die Datierung der ältesten germanischen Lehnwörter im Finnischen. C5IFU VII: 73–8.

Koivulehto, J. 1981. Reflexe des germ./ē¹/] im Finnischen und die Datierung der germanisch-finnischen Lehnbeziehungen. Beiträge zur Geschichte der deutschen Sprache und Literatur 103: 167–203.

Koivulehto, J. 1983a. Seit wann leben die Urfinnen im Ostseeraum? Zur relativen und absoluten Chronologie der alten idg. Lehnwortschichten im Ostseefinnischen. Symposium Saeculare Societatis Fenno-Ugricae. MSFOu 185: 135–57.

Koivulehto, J. 1983b. Suomalaisten maahanmuutto indoeurooppalaisten lainasanojen valossa. JSFOu 78: 107–32.

Koivulehto, J. 1984. Itämerensuomalais-germaaniset kosketukset. In J. Gallén (ed.), 191–205.

Koivulehto, J. 1987. Zu den frühen Kontakten zwischen Indogermanisch und Finnisch-ugrisch. In E. Lang & G. Sauer (eds), Parallelismus und Etymologie, Studien zu Ehren von Wolfgang Steinitz anlässlich seines 80. Geburtstags. Linguistische Studien, Reihe A. Arbeitsberichte 161/

II. Berlin: Akademie der Wissenschaften der DDR, Zentralinstitut für Sprachwissenschaft. 195–218.

Koivulehto, J. 1991 *Uralische Evidenz für die Laryngaltheorie.* Sitzungsberichte der Österreichischen Akademie der Wissenschaften, Philosophisch-historische Klasse **566**. Wien.

Koivulehto, J. 1992/3. *Suomen kielen indo-eurooppalaiset lainasanat ja indo-eurooppalais-uralilainen alkusukuongelma.* Academia Scientiarum Fennica, Vuosikirja 1992–1993. Helsinki.

Koivulehto, J. 1993. Suomi. Vir **3**: 400–6.

Koivulehto, J. 1994. Indogermanisch-Uralisch: Lehnbeziehungen oder (auch) Urverwandtschaft. In R. Sternemann (ed.), *Bopp-Symposium 1992 der Humboldt-Universität zu Berlin.* Heidelberg: C. Winter. 133–48.

Koivulehto, J. 1999. Varhaiset indoeurooppalaiskontaktit: aika ja paikka lainasanojen valossa. In P. Fogelberg (ed.), 207–36.

Koivulehto, J. & Vennemann, T. 1996. Der finnische Stufenwechsel und das Vernersche Gesetz. *Beiträge zur Geschichte der deutschen Sprache und Literatur* **118**: 163–82.

Korenchy, É. 1972. *Iranische Lehnwörter in den obugrischen Sprachen.* Budapest: Akadémiai Kiadó.

Korenchy, É. 1988. Iranischer Einfluss in den finnisch-ugrischen Sprachen. In Sinor (ed), 665–81.

Korhonen, M. 1974. Oliko suomalais-ugrilainen kantakieli agglutinoiva? Eli mitä kielihistoriallisista rekonstruktioista voidaan lukea ja mitä ei. Vir **78**: 243–56.

Korhonen, M. 1976. Suomen kantakielten kronologiaa. Vir **80**: 3–15.

Korhonen, M. 1979/96. Entwicklungstendenzen des finnisch-ugrischen Kasussystems. FUF **43**: 1–21. [Reprinted in M. Korhonen 1996. 165–78.]

Korhonen, M. 1981. *Johdatus lapin kielen historiaan.* Helsinki: SKS.

Korhonen, M. 1981/96. Typological drift in the Finno-Ugrian languages with special reference to the case system. *The Second International Conference of Linguists: Seoul 1981.* The Corean Language Society, I. Hangeul. 678–710. [Reprinted in M. Korhonen 1996. 195–206.]

Korhonen, M. 1982/96. Reductive phonetic developments as the trigger to typological change: two examples from the Finno-Ugrian languages. In A. Ahlqvist (ed.), *Papers from the 5th International Conference on Historical Linguistics* [5ICHL] Current Issues in Linguistic Theory **21**. Amsterdam: J. Benjamins. 190–5. [Reprinted in M. Korhonen 1996. 207–12.]

Korhonen, M. 1984a. Suomalaisten suomalais-ugrilainen tausta historiallis-vertailevan kielitieteen valossa. In J. Gallén (ed.), 55–71.

Korhonen, M. 1984b. Suomen kantakielten kronologiaa. In H. Paunonen & P. Rintala (eds), *Nykysuomen rakenne ja kehitys,* II. Tietolipas **95**. Helsinki: SKS. 85–100.

Korhonen, M. 1984c. Etymologian tila. Review of Häkkinen (1983). Vir **88**: 356–60.

Korhonen, M. 1986/96. History of the Uralic languages and the principle of lateral areas. FUF **47**: 156–62. [Reprinted in M. Korhonen 1996. 213–218.]

Korhonen, M. 1986. On the reconstruction of Proto-Uralic and Proto-Finno-Ugrian consonant clusters. JSFOu **80**: 153–67.

Korhonen, M. 1988a. The Lapp language. In D. Sinor (ed.), 41–57.

Korhonen, M. 1988b. The history of the Lapp language, in D. Sinor (ed.), 264–87.

Korhonen, M. 1988c. Uralilaisten kielten jälkitavujen vokaaliston historiaa. Vir **92**: 8–25.

Korhonen, M. 1989. Lehvät lännessä, juuret idässä. In S. Aalto, A Hakulinen, K. Laalo, P. Leino, A. Lieko (eds), *Kielestä kiinni.* Tietolipas **113**. Helsinki: SKS. 37–46.

Korhonen, M. 1992/6. Remarks on the structure and history of the Uralic case-system. JSFOu **82**: 163–80. [Reprinted in M. Korhonen 1996. 219–234.]

Korhonen, M. 1993. *Kielen synty.* Edited by U.-M. Kulonen. Porvoo: WSOY.

Korhonen, M. 1996. *Typological and Historical Studies in Language. A Memorial Volume Published on the 60th Anniversary of his Birth.* Edited by T. Salminen. MSFOu **223**. Helsinki.

Kristó, Gy. 1996. *Hungarian History in the Ninth Century.* Szeged: Szegedi Középkorász Műhely.

Kroeber, A. 1958. Romance history and glottochronology. *Language* **34**: 454–7.

Kuhn, T. 1970. *The Structure of Scientific Revolutions.* Chicago: Chicago University Press [2nd edition].

Kulonen, U.-M. 1993. Johdatus unkarin kielen historiaan. *Suomi* **170**: 1–137. Helsinki: SKS.

Kulonen, U.-M. 1995. Uralilaisten kielten sukupuu. *Hiidenkivi* **4**: 50. Helsinki.

Kulonen, U.-M. 1996. *Sanojen alkuperä ja sen selittäminen. Etymologista leksikografiaa.* Suomi **181**. Helsinki: SKS.

Kulonen, U.-M. 1999. Kulttuurisanat ja esihistoria. In P. Fogelberg (ed.), 240–4.

Künnap, A. 1995. What does a 'Uralic language' mean? C8IFU **IV**: 209–12.

Künnap, A. (ed.) 1996. *Uralic Languages in European and Siberian Linguistic Context,* F-U **20**.

Künnap, A. 1996. A map in disguise, encyclopaedic spirit and black eve. The newest views in Uralistics. In A. Künnap (ed.), F-U **20**: 42–60.

Künnap, A. 1997a. On the origin of the Uralic languages. In A. Künnap (ed.), *Western and Eastern Contact Areas of Uralic Languages.* F-U **21**: 65–8.

Künnap, A. 1997b. Uralilaisten kielten läntinen kontaktikenttä. In K. Julku and M. Äärelä (eds), 63–72.

Künnap, A. 1997c. Uralilaisten kielten jäljistä indoeurooppalaisissa kielissä. Vir: **101**: 79–83.

Künnap, A. 1998a. *Breakthrough in Present-day Uralistics.* Tartu: University of Tartu.

Künnap, A. 1998b. On the original order of case and possessive suffixes in Uralic. In R. Grünthal and J. Laakso (eds), 265–67.

Künnap, A. 1998c. Über uralisches Substrat in indoeuropäischen Sprachen. LU **34**: 1–7.

Künnap, A. (ed.) 2000. *The Roots of Peoples and Languages of Northern Eurasia* II and III. F-U **23**.

Künnap, A. 2000. About some morphological features of Proto-Uralic. In A. Künnap (ed.), F-U **23**: 27–34.

Kylstra, A. D. et al. 1991–6. *Lexikon der älteren germanischen Lehnwörter in den ostseefinnischen Sprachen,* I–II. Amsterdam: Rodopi.

Laakso, J. 1997. On verbalizing nouns in Uralic. FUF **54**: 267–304.

Laakso, J. 1999a. Pohjois-Euroopan väestön alkukysymyksiä kontaktilingvistiikan kannalta. In P. Fogelberg (ed.), 52–7.

Laakso, J. 1999b. *Karhunkieli. Pyyhkäisyjä suomalais-ugrilaisten kielten tutkimukseen.* Helsinki: SKS.

Labov, W. 1963. The social motivation of a sound change. *Word* **19**: 273–309.

Labov, W. 1972. *Sociolinguistic Patterns.* Philadelphia: University of Pennsylvania Press.

Labov, W. 1980. The social origin of sound change. In W. Labov (ed.), *Locating Language in Time and Space. (Quantitative Analyses of Linguistic Structures,* I) New York: Academic Press. 251–66.

Labov, W. 1981. Resolving the Neogrammarian controversy. *Language* **57**: 267–309.

Labov, W. 1994. *Principle of Historical Linguistics: Internal Factors.* Oxford: Blackwell.

Lamb, S. M. & Mitchell, E. D. (eds) 1991. *Sprung from some Common Source. Investigaton into the Prehistory of Languages.* Stanford (California): Standford University Press.

Larsson, L.-G. 1982. Some remarks on the hypothesis of an Uralo-Dravidian genetic linguistic relationship. *Fenno-Ugrica Suecana* **5**: 169–84. Uppsala.

Lass, R. 1984. *Phonology.* Cambridge: CUP.

Lass, R. 1993. How real(ist) are reconstructions? In C. Jones (ed.), *Historical Linguistics. Problems and Perspectives.* New York: Longman. 156–89.

Lass, R. 1997. *Historical Linguistics and Language Change.* Cambridge: CUP.

László, Gy. 1970. A 'kettős honfoglalás'-ról. *Archaeológiai Értesítő* **97**: 161–90.

László, Gy. 1978. *A kettős honfoglalás.* Gyorsuló Idő. Budapest: Magvető.

László, Gy. 1988. *Árpád népe.* Budapest: Helikon.

László, Gy. 1990. *Őseinkről. Tanulmányok.* Budapest: Gondolat.

László, K. 1998. Magyarságtudatunk és a finnugor rokonság. In M. Csepregi (ed.), 19–26.

Lees, R. B. 1953. The basis of glottochronology. *Language* **29**: 113–25.

Lehmann, W. P. 1993. *Theoretical Bases of Indo-European Linguistics.* London: Routledge.

Lehtinen, M. 1967. On the origin of the Balto-Finnic long vowels. UAJ **39**: 147–52.

Lehtiranta, J. 1982. Eine Beobachtung über die Gründe der raschen Veränderung des Grundwortschatzes im Lappischen. FUF **44**: 114–18.

Lehtiranta, J. 1989. Yhteissaamelainen sanasto. MSFOu **200**: 5–178.

Lehtisalo, T. 1936. Über die primären ururalischen Ableitungssuffixe. MSFOu **72**: 1–393.

Ligeti, L. 1935. Mongolos jövevényszavaink kérdése. NyK **48**: 190–271.

Ligeti, L. 1938. Les voyelles longues en turc. *Journal Asiatique* **230**: 177–204.

Ligeti, L. (ed.) 1943. *A magyarság őstörténete.* Budapest: Institute of Hungarology.

Ligeti, L. 1960. Néhány megjegyzés úgynevezett altáji jövevényszavainkról. MNy **56**: 289–303.

Ligeti, L. 1961. À propos des éléments 'altaïques' de la langue hongroise. ALH **11**: 15–42.
Ligeti, L. 1963. Gyarmat és Jenő. In L. Benkő (ed.), *Tanulmányok a magyar nyelv életrajza köréből*. NyÉrt **40**: 230–39.
Ligeti, L. 1964. A magyar nép mongol kori nevei (magyar, baskír, király). MNy **60**: 385–404.
Ligeti, L. 1975a. Quelques problèmes étymologiques des anciens mots d'emprunt turcs de la langue hongroise. AOH **29**: 279–88.
Ligeti, L. 1975b. La théorie altaïque et la lexico-statistique. In L. Ligeti (ed.). *Researches in Altaic Languages*. Bibliotheca Orientalis Hungarica **20**. Budapest: Akadémiai Kiadó. 99–115.
Ligeti, L. 1976. Régi török jövevényszavaink etimológiai problémái. NyÉrt **89**: 193–9.
Ligeti, L. 1977–9. *A magyar nyelv török kapcsolatai és ami körülöttük van*, I–II. In E. Schütz and É. Apor (eds), Oriental Reprints, Series A 1–2. Budapest: Kőrösi Csoma Társaság.
Ligeti, L. 1978. Régi török eredetű neveink. MNy **74**: 257–74.
Ligeti, L. 1986. *A magyar nyelv török kapcsolatai a honfoglalás előtt és az Árpád-korban*. Budapest: Akadémiai Kiadó.
Liimola, M. 1963. *Zur historischen Formenlehre des Wogulischen*, I: *Flexion der Nomina*. MSFOu **127**.
Lipták, P. 1975a. A finnugor népek antropológiája. In P. Hajdú (ed.), 129–40.
Lipták, P. 1975b. Origin and development of the Hungarian people on the basis of anthropological remains. *AA.VV., Magyar Múlt. Hungarian Past*. Sidney: Hungarian Historical Society. 79–94.
Lipták, P. 1977. A magyar őstörténet kérdései az antropologiai kutatások alapján. In A. Bartha, K. Czeglédy, and A. Róna-Tas (eds), 231–42.
Luutonen, J. 1997. The variation of morpheme order in Mari declension. MSFOu **226**: 1–201.
Luutonen, J. 1999. The history of Permian, Mari and Chuvash plural suffixes in the light of Indo-Aryan parallels. JSFOu **88**: 73–101.
Macartney, C. A. 1930/68. *The Magyars in the Ninth Century*. Cambridge: CUP.
Makkay, J. 1997. Erään unkarilaisen amatöörin käsitys suomalais-ugrilaisten alkuperästä. In K. Julku and M. Äärelä (eds), 23–44.
Malherbe, M. (ed.) 1995. *Les Langages de l'Humanité. Une Encyclopédie des 3000 Langues Parlées dans le Monde*. Paris: Laffont.
Manaster Ramer, A. & Hitchock, C. 1996. Glasshouses: Greenberg, Ringe, and the mathematics of comparative linguistics. *Anthropological Linguistics* **38/4**: 601–19.
Manzelli, G. 1993. Aspetti generali delle lingue non indo-europee d'Europa. In E. Banfi (ed.), *La Formazione dell'Europa Linguistica. Le Lingue d'Europa tra la Fine del I e del II Millennio*. Firenze: La Nuova Italia. 427–79.
Marcantonio, A. 1981. Topic-Focus and some typological consideration in Hungarian. ALH **31**: 219–35.
Marcantonio, A. 1983. La structure de la phrase simple en Finnois. ÉFOu **21**: 32–42.
Marcantonio, A. 1988. On the case of the Object in Finnish: a typological, diachronic and comparative analysis. FUF **48**: 130–70.
Marcantonio, A. 1994. Double conjugation vs double marking for the Object in some dialects of Vogul. ÉFOu **25**: 19–42.
Marcantonio, A. 1996. La 'questione' uralica. In A. Marcantonio (ed.), *Rivista di Studi Ungheresi* **11**: 5–44. Roma: Sovera.
Marcantonio, A. 1997. The classification of language families. *Proceedings of the 16th International Congress of Linguists* [CD-Rom]. Oxford: Pergamon. Paper No. 0420.
Marcantonio, A. 2001a. The current status of the Uralic theory; a critical review. In A.-M. Loffler-Laurian (ed.), *Études de Linguistique Générale et Contrastive – Hommage à Jean Perrot en l'Honneur de son 75e Anniversaire*. Paris: CRELS-Editions. 309–19.
Marcantonio, A. 2001b. Review of *The origin and area of settlement of the Finno-Ugrian peoples by Richard Indreko*, Heidelberg, 1948. In U. Sutrop (ed.), *TRAMES* **5**: 92–6. Tartu.
Marcantonio, A. & Nummenaho, P. 1998. On some participial forms in Hanti and Finnish. In R. Grünthal and J. Laakso (eds), 316–26.
Marcantonio, A., Nummenaho, P. & Salvagni, M. 2001. The 'Ugric-Turkic battle': a critical review. LU **37/2**: 81–102.
Martinet, A. 1959. Affinité linguistique. *Bollettino dell'Atlante Linguistico Mediterraneo* **1**: 144–52. Venezia/Roma.
Mathiassen, T. 1985. A discussion of the notion 'Sprachbund' and its application in the case of

the languages in the Eastern Baltic area (Slavic, Baltic and West Finnish). *International Journal of Slavic Linguistics and Poetics* **31/32**: 273–81.

Matthews, P. H. 1972. *Inflectional Morphology. A Theoretical Study Based on Aspects of Latin Verb Conjugation.* Cambridge: CUP.

McMahon, A. M. S. 1994. *Understanding Language Change.* Cambridge: CUP.

McMahon, A. M. S., Lohr, M. & McMahon, R. 1998. Family trees and favourite daughters. Paper presented at the conference: *Symposium on the Nostratic Macrofamily.* Cambridge: The McDonald Institute for Archaeological Research.

Meillet, A. 1908. *Les Dialectes Indo-européens.* Paris: Champion.

Meillet, A. 1954. *Introduction à l'Étude Comparative des Langues Indo-européennes.* Paris: Librairie Hachette (2nd edition).

Meillet, A. 1967. The Comparative Method in historical Linguistics. Paris: Champion. [Translation by G. B. Ford.]

Menges, K. H. 1964. Altajisch und Dravidisch. *Orbis* **13**: 66–103.

Menges, K. H. 1968/95. *The Turkic Languages and People. An Introduction to Turkic Studies.* Veröffentlichungen der Societas Uralo-Altaica **42**. Wiesbaden: O. Harrassowitz [1st edition of 1968 as volume **15** of the Ural-Altaische Bibliothek].

Menges, K. H. 1968. Die tungusischen Sprachen. In B. Spuler (ed.), *Tungusologie. Handbuch der Orientalistik.* Erste Abteilung, Fünfter Band, Dritter Abschnitt. Leiden: E. J. Brill. 21–41.

Mikola, T. 1976. Hangtan és jelentéstan az etimológiában. In L. Benkő and É. K. Sal (eds), *Az etimológia elmélete és módszere.* NyÉrt **89**: 209–12.

Mikola, T. 1988. Geschichte der samojedischen Sprachen. In D. Sinor (ed.), 219–63.

Miller, R. A. 1989/91. How dead is the Altaic hypothesis? In B. Brendemoen (ed.), 223–37.

Miller, R. A. 1991. Genetic connections among the Altaic languages. In S. M. Lamb & E. D. Mitchell (eds), 293–327.

Molnár, J. & Simon, Gy. 1977. *Magyar nyelvemlékek.* Budapest: Tankönyvkiadó.

Moora, H. 1956. Eesti rahva ja naaberrahvaste kujunemine arheoloogia andmeil. In H. Moora (ed.), *Eesti rahva etnilisest ajaloost.* Tallinn: Artiklite Kogumik. 41–119.

Moravcsik, E. 1978. Language contact. In J. H. Greenberg, C. A. Ferguson & E. Moravcsik (eds), *Universals of Human Languages,* I. Stanford: Stanford University Press. 93–123.

Moravcsik, Gy. 1930: Az onogurok történetéhez. MNy **26**: 4–18 and 89–109.

Moravcsik, Gy. 1958. *Byzantinoturcica, II: Sprachreste der Türkvölker in den byzantinischen Quellen.* Berliner Byzantinische Arbeiten **10-11**. Berlin: Deutsche Akademie der Wissenschaften zu Berlin [2nd edition].

Moravcsik, Gy. 1984/8. *Az Árpád-kori magyar történet bizánci forrásai. Fontes Byzantini historiae Hungaricae aevo ducum et regum ex stirpe Árpád descendentium.* Budapest: Akadémiai Kiadó.

Moravcsik, Gy. & Jenkins, R. J. H. 1949. *Constantine Porphyrogenitus. De Administrando Imperio.* Greek text edited by Moravcsik, English translation by Jenkins. Budapest: Pázmány Péter Tudományegyetemi Görök Filológiai Intézet.

Müller, F. 1876. *Einleitung in die Sprachwissenschaft.* Grundriß der Sprachwissenschaft **1**. **1**. Wien: A. Hölder.

Müller, F. 1882. *Die Sprachen der schlichthaarigen Rassen,* II. Grundriß der Sprachwissenschaft **2**. **2**. Wien: A. Hölder.

Munkácsi, B. 1884. Az altaji nyelvek számképzése. *Budenz –Album.* Budapest: Knoll Károly. 234–314.

Munkácsi, B. 1902. Baskir helynevek. *Ethnographia* **13**: 156–70. Budapest.

Munkácsi, B. 1905. Die Urheimat der Ungarn. KSz **6**: 185–222.

Németh, Gy. 1921a. Régi török jövevényszavaink és a turfáni emlékek. *Kőrösi Csoma Archivum* **1**: 71–6. Budapest.

Németh, Gy. 1921b. Török jövevényszavaink középső rétege. MNy **17**: 22–6.

Németh, Gy. 1928. Az uráli és altaji nyelvek ősi kapcsolata. NyK **47**: 81–8.

Németh, Gy. 1930/91. *A honfoglaló magyarság kialakulása.* Budapest: Magyar Tudományos Akadémia.

Németh, Gy. 1934/90. A törökség őskora. *Emlékkönyv Berzeviczy Albert úrnak, harmincadik évfordulója alkalmából.* Budapest. 158–74 [Reprinted in E. Schütz and É. Apor (eds) 1990. *Németh, Gyula. Törökök és magyarok,* I. Oriental Reprints, Series A **4**. Budapest: Kőrösi Csoma Társaság.]

Németh, Gy. 1966a. Ungarische Stammesnamen bei den Baschkiren. ALH **16**: 1–21.
Németh, Gy. 1966b. A baskir földi magyar őshazáról. *Élet és Tudomány* 13: 596–9. Budapest.
Németh, Gy. 1972. *Magyar und Mišer*. AOH **25**: 293–9.
Németh, Gy. 1975. Türkische und ungarische Ethnonyme. UAJb **47**: 154–60.
Nichols, J. 1986. Head-marking and dependent-marking Grammar. *Language* **62**: 56–119.
Nichols, J. 1992. *Linguistic Diversity in Space and Time*. Chicago: University of Chicago Press.
Nichols, J. 1996. The comparative method as heuristic. In M. Durie & M. Ross (eds), 40–71.
Nielsen, K. 1932–62. *Lappisk ordbok – Lapp Dictionary*, I–IV. Oslo: Instituttet for sammenlignende kulturforskning.
Niskanen, M. 1997. Itämerensuomalaisten alkuperä fyysisen antropologian näkökulmasta. In K. Julku and M. Äärelä (eds), 104–18.
Niskanen, M. 2000. The origins of Europeans: population movements, genetic relationships and linguistic distribution. In A. Künnap (ed.), F-U **23**: 33–59.
Nummenaho, P. 1988. Oskar Blomstedt etymologina. *Annali del Dipartimento di Studi dell'Europa Orientale* **6/7**: 237–350. Napoli.
Nummenaho, P. 1989. Observations on the object cases in southern Ostrobothnia dialects and in Old Finnish law translations. AION V-VI: 7–16. Napoli.
Nuñez, M. 1987. A model for the early settlement of Finland. *Fennoscandia Archaeologica* **4**: 3–18. Helsinki.
Nuñez, M. 1997. Uusi katsaus Suomen asuttamismalliin. In K. Julku & M. Äärelä (eds), 47–63.
Nuñez, M. 2000. Problems with the search for the ancestral Finns. In A. Künnap (ed.), F-U **23**. 60–8.
Orr, R. A. 1989. A Russo-Goidelic syntactic parallel: u nego svoja izba postavlena/tá sé déanta agam. *General Linguistics* **29**: 1–21.
Orr, R. A. 1992. Slavo-Celtica. *Canadian Slavonic Papers* **34**: 245–67.
Orr, R. A. 1994/5. A Slavic-Baltic-Finnic-hebridean Sprachbund? *Slavonica* **22**: 53–64.
Orr, R. A. 1997. But the chimera was made up of real beasts . . . Partially salvaging Indo-European ergativity. *Proceedings of the 16th International Congress of Linguists* [CD-Rom]. Oxford: Pergamon. Paper No. 0411.
Orr, R. A. 1999. Evolutionary biology and historical linguistics. *Diachronica* **16**: 123–57.
Östman, J. O. & Raukko J. 1995. The 'pragmareal' challenge to genetic language tree models. In S. Suhonen (ed.), *Itämerensuomalainen kulttuurialue. The Fenno-Baltic Cultural Area*. Castrenianumin toimitteita **49**. Helsinki. 31–69.
Oswalt, J. 1970. The detection of remote linguistic relationships. *Computer Studies* **3**: 117–29.
Paasonen, H. 1907. Zur Frage von der Urverwandtschaft der finnisch-ugrischen und indoeuropäischen Sprachen. FUF **7**: 13–31.
Paasonen, H. 1912/13–1916/17. Beiträge zur finnischugrisch-samojedischen Lautgeschichte. KSz **13–17**: 1–224.
Paasonen, H. 1918. Die finnisch-ugrischen s-Laute. MSFOu **41**: 3–20.
Paul, H. 1960. *Prinzipien der Sprachgeschichte*. Darmstadt: Wissenschaftliche Buchgesellschaft [6th edition].
Pauler, Gy. 1900. *A magyar nemzet története Szent Istvánig*. Budapest: Magyar Tudományos Akadémia.
Pedersen, H. 1931. *Linguistic Science in the Nineteenth Century*. Cambridge (Mass.): MIT Press.
Pedersen, H. 1933. Zur Frage nach der Urverwandtschaft des Indoeuropäischen mit dem Ugrofinnischen. MSFOu **67**: 308–25.
Pekkanen, T. 1984. Suomi ja sen asukkaat latinan- ja kreikankielisessä kirjallisuudessa 1000-luvulle asti. In J. Gallén (ed.), 227–47.
Perrot, J. 1984a. La double conjugaison (subjective et objective) dans les langues finno-ougriennes: aperçu des problèmes. *Lalies* **3**: 25–32. Paris.
Perrot, J. 1984b. Nom et verbe dans les langues ougriennes: le hongrois et le vogoul. *Modèles Linguistiques* **6**: 161–80.
Pokorny, J. 1968. Substrattheorie und Urheimat der Indogermanen. In A. Scherer (ed.), *Die Urheimat der Indogermanen*. Darmstadt: Wissenschaftliche Buchgesellschaft. 176–213.
Polomé, E. C. 1986. The non-Indo-European component of the Germanic lexicon. In A. Etter (ed.), *o-o-pe-ro-si: Festschrift für Ernst Risch zum 75. Geburtstag*. Berlin: Mouton de Gruyter. 661–72.
Poppe, N. 1927. Altaisch und Urtürkisch. UngJb **6**: 94–121.

Poppe, N. 1952. Plural Suffixes in the Altaic Languages. UAJb **24**: 65–83.
Poppe, N. 1955. *Introduction to Mongolian Comparative Studies.* MSFOu **110**: 1–300.
Poppe, N. 1960a. On some Altaic loanwords in Hungarian. The Indiana University Committee on Uralic Studies (ed.), *American Studies in Uralic Linguistics.* Uralic and Altaic Series I. Bloomington: Indiana University. 139–47.
Poppe, N. 1960b. *Vergleichende Grammatik der altaischen Sprachen. Teil I: Vergleichende Lautlehre.* Porta Linguarum Orientalium, n.s., **4**. Wiesbaden: O. Harrassowitz.
Poppe, N. 1960c. *Buriat Grammar.* Indiana University Publications. Uralic and Altaic Series **2**. Bloomington: Indiana.
Poppe, N. 1965. *Introduction to Altaic Linguistics.* Ural-Altaische Bibliothek **14**. Wiesbaden: O. Harrassowitz.
Poppe, N. 1977a. The Altaic plural suffix *-t.* SO **47**: 165–74.
Poppe, N. 1977b. The problem of Uralic and Altaic affinity. MSFOu **158**: 221–34;.
Poppe, N. 1983. The Ural-Altaic affinity. Symposium Saeculare Societatis Fenno-Ugricae. MSFOu **185**: 189–200.
Posti, L. 1953. From Pre-Finnic to Late Proto-Finnic. FUF **31**: 1–91.
Posti, L. 1977. Some new contributions to the stock of Baltic loanwords in Finnic languages. *Baltistica* **13**: 263–70. Vilnius.
Pusztay, J. 1977. *Az 'ugor-török háború' után. Fejezetek a magyar nyelvhasonlítás történetéből,* Budapest: Magvető Kiadó.
Pusztay, J. 1980. *Az uráli-paleoszibériai kapcsolatok kérdéséhez.* Budapest: A Magyar Nyelvtudományi Társaság Kiadványai **158**.
Pusztay, J. 1991. Zur Analyse des protouralischen Wortschatzes aufgrund des uralischen etymologischen Wörterbuchs. LU **27**: 157–77.
Pusztay, J. 1995. *Diskussionsbeiträge zur Grundsprachenforschung (Beispiel: das Protouralische).*Veröffentlichungen der Societas Uralo-Altaica **43**. Wiesbaden: O. Harrassowitz.
Pusztay, J. 1997. Ajatus uralilaisten kansojen ketjumaisesta alkukodista. In K. Julku and M. Äärelä (eds), 9–19.
Ramstedt, G. J. 1909. Olemmeko mongoleja? *Kansanvalistus-Seuran Kalenteri.* Helsinki: Kansanvalistusseuran Kustantamo. 180–5.
Ramstedt, G. J. 1935. Über die Entstehung der Verbalflexion mit Personalendung. *Sitzungsberichte der Finnischen Akademie der Wissenschaften 1933.* Helsinki. 144–8.
Ramstedt, G. J. 1946–7. The relation of the Altaic languages to other language groups. JSFOu **53**: 15–26.
Ramstedt, G. J. 1952. In P. Aalto (ed.), *Einführung in die altaische Sprachwissenschaft. II. Formenlehre.* MSFOu **104** (2): 1–262.
Ramstedt, G. J. 1957. In P. Aalto (ed.), *Einführung in die altaische Sprachwissenschaft. I. Lautlehre.* MSFOu **104** (1): 1–192.
Räsänen, M. 1920. *Die tschuwassischen Lehnwörter im Tscheremissischen.* MSFOu **48**: 1–274.
Räsänen, M. 1939. Spuren vom altaischen anl. *ń* in den türkischen Lehnwörtern im Ungarischen. UngJb **19**: 99–101.
Räsänen, M. 1947a. Uralilais-altailaisia sanavertailuja. Vir **51**: 162–73.
Räsänen, M. 1947b. Etymologisia lisiä. Vir **51**: 354–7.
Räsänen, M. 1949. Materialien zur Lautgeschichte der türkischen Sprachen. SO **15**: 10–28.
Räsänen, M. 1953. Uralaltaische Forschungen. UAJb **25**: 19–27.
Räsänen, M. 1955. Uralaltaische Wortforschungen. SO **18**: 1–59.
Räsänen, M. 1957. Materialien zur Morphologie der türkischen Sprachen. SO **21**: 1–256.
Räsänen, M. 1959. Ural-altailaisia ordinaaleja? In P. Virtaranta, T. Itkonen & P. Pulkkinen (eds), *Verba Docent. Juhlakirja Lauri Hakulisen 60-vuotispäiväksi 6. 10. 1959.* Helsinki: SKS. 87–8.
Räsänen, M. 1961. Gibt es im Baskirischen etwas Ugrisches? AOH **12**: 73–8.
Räsänen, M. 1963/4. Uralaltailaisesta kielisukulaisuudesta. In E. Öhmann (ed.), *Esitelmät ja Pöytäkirjat.* Helsinki: Suomalainen Tiedeakatemia. 180–9.
Räsänen, M. 1963/5. Über die ural-altaische Sprachverwandtschaft. *Sitzungsberichte der Finnischen Akademie der Wissenschaften.* Helsinki. 161–72.
Räsänen, M. 1969–71. *Versuch eines etymologischen Wörterbuchs der Türksprachen,* I–II. Lexica Societatis Fenno-Ugricae **17**. Helsinki: SKS.

Rask, R. K. 1834. Afhandling om den finniske Sprogklasse. In R. K. Rask (ed.), *Samlede tildels forhen utrykte afhandlinger af R. K. Rask* 1. Copenhagen: Det Poppske Bogtrykkeri. 1–46.

Raun, A. 1956. Über die sogenannte lexikostatistische Methode oder Glottochronologie und ihre Anwendung auf das Finnisch-Ugrische und Türkische. UAJb 28: 184–202.

Raun, A. 1958. Über die ältesten germanischen Lehnwörter im Ostseefinnischen. UAJb 30: 30–4.

Raun, A. 1971. *Essays in Finno-Ugric and Finnic Linguistics*. Ural-Altaic Series 107. Bloomington: Indiana.

Raun, A. 1988a. The Mordvin language. In D. Sinor (ed.), 96–110.

Raun, A. 1988b. Proto-Uralic comparative-historical morphosyntax, in D. Sinor (ed.), 555–74.

Ravila, P. 1935. Die Stellung des Lappischen innerhalb der finnisch-ugrischen Sprachfamilie. FUF 23: 20–65.

Ravila, P. 1938. Numerusprobleemeja. Vir 42: 286–97.

Ravila, P. 1941. Über die Verwendung der Numeruszeichen in den uralischen Sprachen. FUF 27: 1–36.

Ravila, P. 1951. Astevaihtelun arvoitus. Vir 55: 292–300.

Ravila, P. 1957. Die Wortklassen, mit besonderer Berücksichtigung der uralischen Sprachen. JSFOu: 59: 1–13.

Rédei, K. 1968. A permi nyelvek első szótagi magánhangzóinak a történetéhez. NyK 70: 35–45.

Rédei, K. 1977. Szófejtések. NyK 79: 201–16.

Rédei, K. 1980. Monikon tunnukset uralilaisessa ja suomalais-ugrilaisessa kantakielessä. C5IFU VI: 210–19.

Rédei, K. 1981. Többesjelek a PU-PFU alapnyelvben. NyK 83: 97–105.

Rédei, K. 1986. *Zu den indogermanisch-uralischen Sprachkontakten*. Sitzungsberichte der Österreichischen Akademie der Wissenschaften, Philosophisch-historische Klasse 468. Wien.

Rédei, K. 1988a. Die ältesten indogermanischen Lehnwörter der uralischen Sprachen. In D. Sinor (ed.), 638–64.

Rédei, K. 1988b. Geschichte der permischen Sprachen. In D. Sinor (ed.), 351–94.

Rédei, K. 1998. *Őstörténetünk kérdései. A nyelvészeti dilettantizmus kritikája*. Budapest: Balassi Kiadó.

Rédei, K. 1999a. Zu den uralisch-jukagirischen Sprachkontakten. FUF 55: 1–58.

Rédei, K. 1999b. The origin of the Proto-Uralic suffix *-t. LU 35: 1–6.

Rédei, K. 2000. Urheimat und Grundsprache (Wissenschaftliche Hypothesen und unwissenschaftliche Fehlgriffe). C9IFU I: 109–26.

Rees, M. 1999/2000. *Just Six Numbers*. London: Phoenix.

Relatio fratris Ricardi. «De facto Ungarie Magne a fratre Ricardo invento tempore domini Gregorii pape noni» 1937–8. In E. Szentpétery et al. (eds), II, 536–9.

Renfrew, C. 1987. *Archaeology and Language. The Puzzle of Indo-European Origins* London: J. Cape.

Riese, T. 1998. Permian. In D. Abondolo (ed.), 249–57.

Ringe, D. 1992. *On Calculating the Factor of Chance in Language Comparison*. Transactions of the American Philosophical Society 82: 1–110. Philadelphia: The American Philosophical Society.

Ringe, D. 1995. 'Nostratic' and the factor of chance. *Diachronica* 12/1: 55–74.

Ringe, D. 1998. A probabilistic evaluation of Indo-Uralic. In J. C. Salmons & B. D. Joseph (eds), *Nostratic: Sifting the Evidence*. Amsterdam Studies in the Theory and History of Linguistic Science. Series IV. Current Issues in Linguistic Theory. Amsterdam: J. Benjamins. 153–98.

Ringe, D. 1999. How hard is it to match CVC-roots? *Transactions of the Philological Society* 97: 213–44.

Robins, R. H. 1967. *A Short History of Linguistics*. Bloomington: Indiana University.

Róna-Tas, A. 1976. On the meaning of 'Altaic'. In W. Heissig et al. (eds), *Tractata altaica Denis Sinor sexagenario optime de rebus altaicis merito dedicata*. Wiesbaden: O. Harrassowitz. 549–56.

Róna-Tas, A. 1978a. Julius Németh: life and work. AOH 32: 236–61.

Róna-Tas, A. 1978b. *A nyelvrokonság*. Budapest: Gondolat.

Róna-Tas, A. 1980. On the earliest Samoyed-Turkic contacts. C5IFU III: 377–85.

Róna-Tas, A. 1981. The character of the Hungarian-Bulgaro-Turkic relations. In J. Káldy-Nagy (ed.), *Studia Turco-Hungarica* 5: 119–28. Budapest.

Róna-Tas, A. 1983. De hypothesi Uralo-Altaica. Symposium Saeculare Societatis Fenno-Ougricae, MSFOu **185**: 235–52.

Róna-Tas, A. 1988a. Turkic influence on the Uralic languages. In D. Sinor (ed.), 742–80.

Róna-Tas, A. 1988b. Ethnogenese und Staatsgründung. Die türkische Komponente in der Ethnogenese des Ungartums. *Studien zur Ethnogenese* **2**: 120–38. Rheinisch-Westfälische Akademie der Wissenschaften. Abh. **78**. Westdeutscher Verlag.

Róna-Tas, A. 1991. *An Introduction to Turkology.* SUA **33**: 1–167.

Róna-Tas, A. 1998. The reconstruction of Proto-Turkic and the genetic question. In L. Johanson & É. Á. Csató (eds), 67–81.

Rootsi, T. et al. 2000. On the phylogeographic context of sex-specific genetic markers of Finno-Ugric populations. In A. Künnap (ed.), F-U **23**. 148–64.

Ross, M. 1996. Contact-induced change and the comparative method. In M. Durie & M. Ross (eds), 58–64.

Rot, S. 1988. Germanic influences on the Uralic languages. In D. Sinor (ed.), 683–705.

Ruhlen, M. 1987. *A Guide to the World's Languages, I: Classification.* London/Melbourne: E. Arnold.

Saarinen, S. 1990. *Suomalais-ugrilaisten kansojen folklore.* Turku: Turun Yliopiston Suomalaisen ja Yleisen Kielitieteen Laitoksen julkaisuja **36**.

Salminen, T. 1993. Uralilaiset kielet maailman kielten joukossa. In T. Salminen (ed.), *Uralilaiset kielet tänään.* Kuopio: Kuopion Snellman-instituutin julkaisuja, A **13**: 24–30.

Salminen, T. 1997a. Tundra Nenets Inflection. MSFOu **227**: 1–154.

Salminen, T. 1997b. Facts and myths about Uralic studies. A review article of *Jazyki mira: Ural'skie jazyki.* Otvetstvennye redaktory: Ju. S. Eliseev, K. E. Majtinskaja [Languages of the World: Uralic Languages]. *Sprachtypologie und Universalienforschung* **50**: 85–95.

Salminen, T. 1998. Nenets. In D. Abondolo (ed.), 516–47.

Salminen. T. 1999. Euroopan kielet muinoin ja nykyisin. In P. Fogelberg (ed.), 14–26.

Salo, U. 1984. Esihistoriallisen asutuksen jatkuvuudesta Suomen rannikolla. In J. Gallén (ed.), 27–42.

Salvagni, M. 1999. *La 'Guerra Ugro-turca' e l'Affermarsi della Teoria Ugro-finnica.* Tesi di Laurea. Roma: Università di Roma 'La Sapienza'.

Sammallahti, P. 1977. Suomalaisten esihistorian kysymyksiä. Vir **81**: 119–37.

Sammallahti, P. 1979. Über die Laut- und Morphemstruktur der uralischen Grundsprache. FUF **43**: 22–66.

Sammallahti, P. 1984. Saamelaisten esihistoriallinen tausta kielitieteen valossa. In J. Gallén (ed.), 137–56.

Sammallahti, P. 1988. Historical phonology of the Uralic languages (with special reference to Samoyed, Ugric and Permic). In D. Sinor (ed.), 478–554.

Sammallahti, P. 1995. Language and roots. C8IFU I: 143–53.

Sammallahti, P. 1998. Saamic. In D. Abondolo (ed.), 43–95.

Sammallahti, P. 1999. Saamen kielen ja saamelaisten alkuperästä. In P. Fogelberg (ed.), 70–90.

Sándor, B. 1963. *Az 1522. évi tizedlajstrom szegedi vezetéknevei.* Budapest: A Magyar Nyelvtudományi Társaság Kiadványai **105**.

Sankoff, D. 1973. Mathematical developments in lexicostatistic theory. In T. A. Sebeok (ed.), *Diachronic, Areal and Typological Linguistics.* Current Trends in Linguistics **11**. The Hague: Mouton.

Sauvageot, A. 1964. L'appartenance du youkaguir. UAJb **35**: 109–17.

Sauvageot, A. 1969. La position du youkaguir. UAJb **41**: 345–58.

Sauvageot, A. 1971. *L' Édification de la Langue Hongroise.* Paris: Klincksieck.

Sauvageot, A. 1976. Le problème de la parenté ougrienne. ÉFOu **13**: 128–42.

Sauvageot, A. & Menges, K. H. 1973. Ural-Altaic languages. In *Encyclopaedia Britannica* **22**: 775–7 [15th edition].

Schleicher, A. 1850. *Die Sprachen Europas in systematischer Übersicht.* Bonn: König.

Schmidt, J. 1872. *Die Verwandtschaftsverhältnisse der indogermanischen Sprachen.* Weimar: H. Böhlau.

Schrodt, R. 1976. *Die germanische Lautverschiebung und ihre Stellung im Kreise der indogermanischen Sprachen. 2. Korrigierte und durch einen Nachtrag erweiterte Auflage.* Wien: Wiener Arbeiten zur germanischen Altertumskunde und Philologie.

Schuchardt, H. 1885 H. *Über die Lautgesetze; gegen die Junggrammatiker.* Berlin:

R. Oppenheim. [Reprinted in T. Venneman & T. H. Wilbur 1972 (eds), *Schuchardt, the Neogrammarians and the Transformational Theory of Phonological Change*. Frankfurt: Athenäum.]

Schuchardt, H. 1925. Das Baskische und die Sprachwissenschaft. *Sitzungsberichte der Akademie der Wissenschaften in Wien* **202/204**: 23–42. Wien.

Sebeok, T. A. 1946. *Finnish and Hungarian Case System. Their Form and Function*. Acta Instituti Hungarici Universitatis Holmiensis, Series B. Linguistica **3**. Stockholm.

Serebrennikov, B. A. 1966. K probleme proiskhoždenija suffiksov mnogokratnogo dejstvija v finno-ugorskikh jazykakh. LU **2**: 157–63.

Serebrennikov, B. A. 1973. *Strukturmerkmale der frühuralischen Grundsprache*. UAJb **45**: 65–79.

Setälä, E. N. 1896. Über Quantitätswechsel im Finnisch-ugrischen. Vorläufige Mitteilung. JSFOu **14**: 3–53.

Setälä, E. N. 1912/14. Über Art, Umfang und Alter des Stufenwechsels im finnisch-ugrischen und samojedischen. FUF **12**: 1–128.

Setälä, E. N. 1913–18. Zur Frage nach der Verwandtschaft der finnisch-ugrischen und samojedischen Sprachen. JSFOu **30**: 3–104.

Setälä, E. N. 1926. *Suomensukuisten kansojen esihistoria*. Suomen Suku **I**. Helsinki: Otava. 120–89.

Shepard, J. 1998. The Khazars formal adoption of Judaism and Byzantiums' northern policy. *Oxford Slavonic Papers*. Oxford: Clarendon. 11–34.

Sherwood, P. 1996. A nation may be said to live in its language: Some socio-historical perspectives on attitudes to Hungarian. In: R. B. Pynsent (ed.), *The Literature of Nationalism: Essays on East European Identity*. School of Slavonic and East European Studies. London: University of London. 27–39.

Shevoroshkin, V. (ed.) 1971. *Explorations in Language Macrofamilies: Materials from the First International Interdisciplinary Symposium on Language and Prehistory*. Bochum: Universitätsverlag, Dr. N. Brockmeyer.

Siikala, A.-L. 2000. What myths tell us about past Finno-Ugric modes of thinking. C9IFU **I**: 127–40.

Simoncsics, P. 1998. Kamassian. In D. Abondolo (ed.), 580–601.

Sinor, D. 1943. D'un morphème particulièrement répandu dans les langues ouralo-altaïques. *T'oung Pao* **37**: 226–44.

Sinor, D. 1952. On some Ural-Altaic plural suffixes. *Asia Major New Series* **2**: 203–30.

Sinor, D. 1958. The outlines of Hungarian prehistory. *Journal of World History* **4**: 513–40.

Sinor, D. 1959. A Ural-Altaic ordinal suffix. UAJb **31**: 417–25.

Sinor, D. 1961. Un suffixe de lieu ouralo-altaïque. AOH **12**: 169–77.

Sinor, D. 1963. Observations on a new comparative Altaic phonology. *Bulletin of the School of Oriental and African Studies* **26**: 133–44. University of London.

Sinor, D. 1965. Notes on the equine terminology of the Altaic peoples. *Central Asiatic Journal* **10**: 310–15.

Sinor, D. 1969. Geschichtliche Hypothesen und Sprachwissenschaft in der ungarischen, finnisch-ugrischen und uralischen Urgeschichtsforschung. UAJb **41**: 273–81.

Sinor, D. 1970. Two Altaic etymologies. In R. Jakobson & S. Kawamoto (eds), *Studies in General and Oriental Linguistics. Presented to Shirô Hattori on the Occasion of his Sixtieth Birthday*. Tokyo: TEC Corporation for Language & Educational Research. 540–4.

Sinor, D. 1973. 'Urine' ~ 'star' ~ 'nail'. JSFOu **72**: 393–7.

Sinor, D. 1975. Uralo-Tunguz lexical correspondences. In L. Ligeti (ed.), *Researches in Altaic Languages*. Bibliotheca Orientalia Hungarica **20**. Budapest: Akadémiai Kiadó. 245–56.

Sinor, D. 1976. The *-t ~ *-d local suffix in Uralic and Altaic. In Gy. Káldy-Nagy (ed.), *Hungaro-Turcica. Studies in Honour of Julius Németh*. Budapest: ELTE 119–24.

Sinor, D. 1978. The nature of possessive suffixes in Uralic and Altaic. In M. A. Jazayeri et al. (eds), *Linguistic and Literary Studies in Honour of Archibald A. Hill*. The Hague: Mouton. 257–66.

Sinor, D. 1988 (ed.). *The Uralic Languages. Description, History and Foreign Influences*. Handbook of Uralic Studies **I**. Leiden: E. J. Brill.

Sinor, D. 1988. The problem of the Ural-Altaic relationship. In D. Sinor (ed.), 706–41.

Sinor, D. (ed.) 1990. *The Cambridge History of Early Inner Asia*. Cambridge: CUP.

Sinor, D. 1990. *Essays in Comparative Altaic Linguistics.* Indiana University Research Institute for Inner Asia. Bloomington: Indiana University.

Steinitz, W. 1944. Geschichte des finnisch-ugrischen Vokalismus. In J. Lotz (ed.), *Acta Instituti Hungarici Universitatis Holmiensis.* Series B. Linguistica, II, Stockholm. 15–39.

Steinitz, W. 1950. *Geschichte des ostjakischen Vokalismus.* Berlin: Akademie Verlag.

Steinitz, W. 1955. *Geschichte des wogulischen Vokalismus.* Berlin: Akademie Verlag.

Suhonen, S. 1984. Lainasanat balttilais-itämerensuomalaisten kontaktien kuvastajana. In J. Gallén (ed.), 207–25.

Suhonen, S. 1988. Die baltischen Lehnwörter der finnisch-ugrischen Sprachen. In D. Sinor (ed.), 596–615.

Suhonen, S. 1989. Baltische und slavische Etymologien. In JSFOu **82**: 211–21.

Suhonen, S. 1999. Uralilainen alkukoti. In P. Fogelberg (ed.), 245–8.

Sutrop, U. 1999. Diskussionsbeiträge zur Stammbaumtheorie. In A. Künnap (ed.), *Indo-European-Uralic-Siberian Linguistic and Cultural Contacts.* F-U **22**: 223–51.

Sutrop, U. 2000a. The forest of Finno-Ugric languages. In A. Künnap (ed.), F-U **23**. 165–97.

Sutrop, U. 2000b. From the 'Language Family Tree' to the 'Tangled Web of Languages'. C9IFU I: 197–291.

Swadesh, M. 1971. *The Origin and Diversification of Language.* London: Routledge.

Sweet, H. 1900. *The History of Languages.* London: J. M. Dent.

Székely, Gy. (ed.) 1984. *Magyarország története. Előzmények és magyar történet 1242-ig.* I/ I. Budapest: Akadémiai Kiadó.

Szemerényi, O. 1980. *Einführung in die vergleichende Sprachwissenschaft.* Darmstadt: Wissenschaftliche Buchgesellschaft.

Szentpétery, I. et al. (eds) 1937–8. *Scriptores rerum Hungaricarum tempore ducum regumque stirpis Arpadianae gestarum,* I–II. Budapest: Academia Litterarum Hungarica.

Szinnyei, J. 1908. Pesthy Gábor származása. MNy **2**: 49–53.

Szinnyei, J. 1922. *Finnisch-ugrische Sprachwissenschaft.* Berlin: Mouton De Gruyter [2nd edition].

Szinnyei, J. 1927. *Magyar nyelv hasonlítás.* Budapest: L. Kókai [7th edition].

Taagepera, R. 1994. The linguistic distances between Uralic languages. LU **30**: 161–7.

Taagepera, R. 1997. *The Roots and Branches of the Finno-Ugric Language Tree.* (Manuscript.)

Taagepera, R. 2000. Uralic as a *Lingua Franca* with roots. In A. Künnap (ed.), F-U **23**: 381–95.

Tálos, E. 1987. On the vowels of Proto-Uralic. In. K Rédei (ed.), *Studien zur Phonologie und Morphologie der uralischen Sprachen.* Akten der dritten Tagung für uralische Phonologie. *Studia Uralica* **4**: 70–80. Wien.

Tauli, V. 1955. On foreign contacts of the Uralic languages. UAJb **27**: 7–31.

Tauli, V. 1956. The origin of affixes. FUF **32**: 170–225.

Tauli, V. 1966. *Structural Tendencies in Uralic Languages.* Indiana University Publications. Ural and Altaic Series **17**. The Hague: Mouton.

Tekin, T. 1986. Zetacism and sigmatism: main pillars of the Altaic theory. *Central Asiatic Journal* **30**: 141–60.

Tekin, T. 1994. Altaic languages. In R. E. Asher (ed.), 82–5.

Tereškin, N.I. 1961. *Očerki dialektov khantyjskogo jazyka. Čast' pervaja: Vakhovskij dialekt.* Moskva-Leningrad: Izdatel'stvo Akademii Nauk SSSR.

The 'Gallen-Kallela Museum & Authors & Artists'(eds) 2000. *Ugriculture 2000. Contemporary Art of the Fenno-Ugrian Peoples.* Helsinki.

Thomason, S. G. & Kaufman, T. 1988. *Language Contact, Creolization, and Genetic Linguistics.* Berkeley: University of California Press.

Toivonen, Y. H. 1949/50. Protolapin ongelmasta. In E. Öhmann (ed.), *Esitelmät ja Pöytäkirjat.* Helsinki: Suomalainen Tiedeakatemia. 159–83.

Trask, L. 1996. *Historical Linguistics.* London: Arnold.

Traugott, E. C. & Heine, B. (eds) 1991. *Approaches to Grammaticalization* I–II. Typological Studies in Language **191**. Amsterdam: J. Benjamins.

Trubetzkoy, N. S. 1939. Gedanken über das Indogermanenproblem. *Acta Linguistica* **1**: 81–9.

Trudgill, P. 1996. Dual-source pidgins and reverse creoloids: Northern perspectives on language contact. In Jahr E. & Broch I. (eds), *Language Contact in the Arctic. Northern Pidgins and Contact Languages.* Trends in Linguistics. Studies and Monographs **88**. Berlin: Mouton de Gruyter.

Tyler, S. A. 1968. Dravidian and Uralian: the lexical evidence. *Language* **44**: 798–812.
Uesson, A.-M. 1970. *On Linguistic Affinity: The Indo-Uralic Problem*. Malmö: Förlags AB Eesti Post.
Unger, J. M. 1990. Summary report of the Altaic panel. In P. Baldi (ed.), *Linguistic Change and Reconstruction Methodology*. Trends in Linguistics. Studies and Monographs **45**. Berlin: Mouton de Gruyter.
Vahtola, J. 1986. *Onomastinen metodi Suomen varhaishistorian tutkimisessa*. Turun Historiallinen Arkisto **41**. Tammisaari.
Vámbéry, Á. 1869. Magyar és török-tatár szóegyezések. NyK **8**: 109–89.
Vámbéry, Á. 1882. *A magyarok eredete; ethnologiai tanulmány*. Budapest: A Magyar Tudományos Akadémia Könyvkiadó-hivatala.
Van den Wyngaert, A. 1929 (ed.). *Sinica Franciscana*, I. Firenze: Quaracchi.
Vásáry, I. 1975. The Hungarians or Možars and the Meščers/Mišers of the Middle Volga region. In P. B. Golden & T. Halasi-Kun (eds), AEMAe **1**: 237–75.
Vásáry, I. 1977. A Volga-vidéki magyar töredékek a mongol kor után. In A. Bartha, K. Czeglédy and A. Róna-Tas (eds), 283–90.
Vásáry, I. 1985/7. The linguistic aspect of the 'Bashkiro-Hungarian complex'. In P. B. Golden, T. Halasi-Kun, A. P. Martinez, Th. S. Noonam (eds), AEMAe **5**: 205–32.
Veenker, W. 1967. *Die Frage des finnougrischen Substrats in der russischen Sprache*. Uralic and Altaic Series **82**. Bloomington: Indiana University.
Vennemann, T. (ed.) 1989. *The new Sound of Indo-European: Essays in Phonological Reconstruction*. Trends in Linguistics. Studies and Monographs **41**. Berlin: Mouton de Gruyter.
Veres, P. 1972. An outline of the ethnic history of the Hungarian people. *Néprajzi Értesítő* **54**: 155–82. Budapest.
Veres, P. 1996. The ethnogenesis of the Hungarian people. Problems of ecological adaptation and cultural change. *Occasional Papers in Anthropology* **5**: . 12–61. Budapest: Ethnographial Institute of the Hungarian Academy of Sciences. [Hungarian version: Veres, P. 1984. A magyar nép kialakulása és korai etnikus története. *Népi kultúra és népi társadalom* **14**: 49–101. Budapest.]
Vértes, E. 1994. Wie weit konnten die Finnougrier zählen? FUF **52**: 1–97.
Viitso, T.-R. 1992. Proto-Indo-European laryngeals in Uralic. LU **28**: 161–72.
Viitso, T.-R. 1995. On classifying the Finno-Ugric languages. C81FU **IV**: 261–6.
Viitso, T.-R. 1997a. Keelesugulus ja soome-ugri keelepuu. *Akadeemia* **9**: 899–929. Tartu.
Viitso, T.-R. 1997b. The prosodic system of Estonian in the Finnic space. In I. Lehiste & J. Ross (eds), *Estonian Prosody: Papers from a Symposium*. Tallinn: Institute of Estonian language. 222–34.
Viitso, T.-R. 1998. Estonian. In D. Abondolo (ed.), 115–48.
Vikár, L. 1975. A finnugor népek zenéje. In P. Hajdú (ed.), 305–19.
Vilkuna, J. 1996. Siperiasta vai? In H. Roiko-Jokela (ed.), *Siperiasta siirtoväkeen. Murrosaikoja ja käännekohtia Suomen historiassa*. Jyväskylä: Kopi-Jyvä Oy.
Vilkuna, K. 1950. Über die obugrischen und samojedischen Pfeile und Köcher. MSFOu **98**: 343–8.
Vincent, N. 1980. Iconic and symbolic aspects of syntax: prospects for reconstruction. In P. Ramat (ed.), *Linguistic Reconstruction and Indo-European Syntax*. Current Issues in Linguistic Theory **19**. Amsterdam: Benjamins. 47–68.
Voegelin, C. F. & Voegelin, F. M. 1977. *Classification and Index of the Worlds' Languages*, New York: Elsevier.
Voigt, V. 1975. A finnugor népek epikája. In P. Hajdú (ed.), 293–304.
Voigt, V. 1999. *Suggestions towards a Theory of Folklore*. Budapest: Mundus.
Voigt, V. 2000. *Világnak kezdetétől fogva*. Budapest: Universitas Könyvkiadó.
Vovin, A. 1994. Long-distance relationships, reconstruction methodology and the origins of Japanese. *Diachronica* **11**: 95–114.
Vovin, A. 1998. Altaic evidence for Nostratic. Paper presented at the conference: *Symposium on the Nostratic Macrofamily*. Cambridge: The McDonald Institute for Archaeological Research.
Wang, W. S.-Y. 1969. Competing sound change as a cause of residue. *Language* **45**: 9–25.
Wang, W. S.-Y. 1979. Language change: a lexical perspective. *Annual Review of Anthropology* **8**: 353–71.

Watkins, C. 1985. *The American Heritage Dictionary of Indo-European Plants.* Boston: Houghton Mifflin.

Weinreich, U. 1953. *Languages in Contact: Findings and Problems.* New York: Linguistic Circle of New York [2nd edition by The Hague: Mouton 1968].

Weinreich, U., Labov, W. & Herzog, M. 1968. Empirical foundations for a theory of language change. In W. P. Lehmann and Y. Malkiel (eds), *Directions for Historical Linguistics. A Symposium.* Austin: University of Texas Press. 95–196.

Whittington, H. B. 1975: The enigmatic animal Opabina regalis. Middle Cambrian, Burgess Shale, British Columbia. *Philosophical Transactions of the Royal Society.* London B **271**: 1–43.

Wichmann, Y. & Uotila, T. E. 1942. *Syriänjscher Wortschatz nebst Hauptzügen der Formenlehre.* Lexica Societatis Fenno-Ugricae **7**: 1–486. Helsinki: SKS.

Wiik, K 1995. *Itämerensuomalaisten kansojen ja kielten syntykysymyksiä B. Uusia kontaktiteoriaan perustuvia ratkaisuja.* Turku: University of Turku.

Wiik, K. 1997a. The Uralic and Finno-Ugric phonetic substratum in Proto-Germanic. LU **33**: 258–80.

Wiik, K. 1997b. Suomalaistyyppistä ääntämistä germaanisissa kielissä. In K. Julku and M. Äärelä (eds), 75–101.

Wiik, K. 1999. Pohjois-Euroopan indoeurooppalaisten kielten suomalais-ugrilainen substraatti. In P. Fogelberg (ed.), 37–52.

Wiik, K. 2000. European *Lingua Francas.* In A. Künnap (ed.), F-U **23**: 202–36.

Zaicz, G. 1998. Mordva. In D. Abondolo (ed.), 184–218.

Zichy, I. 1939. *Magyar őstörténet.* Kincsestár **5**. Budapest: Magyar Szemle Társulat.

Zimonyi, I. 1990. *The Origins of the Volga Bulgars.* SUA **32**: 1–212.

Zsirai, M. 1937. *Finnugor rokonságunk.* Budapest: Magyar Tudomáyos Akadémia [2nd edition 1994 by Trezor Kiadó].

Zsirai, M. 1951. Sámuel Gyarmathi, Hungarian pioneer of comparative linguistics. ALH **1**: 5–17.

GENERAL INDEX

INDEX OF LANGUAGES

INDEX OF AUTHORS